D0936883

ECONOMIC ORGANIZATIONS AND CORPORATE
GOVERNANCE IN JAPAN

HD
2907
M55
2004
web

Economic Organizations and Corporate Governance in Japan:
The Impact of Formal and Informal Rules

CURTIS J. MILHAUPT
and
MARK D. WEST

OXFORD
UNIVERSITY PRESS

OXFORD

UNIVERSITY PRESS

Great Clarendon Street, Oxford OX2 6DP

Oxford University Press is a department of the University of Oxford.
It furthers the University's objective of excellence in research, scholarship,
and education by publishing worldwide in

Oxford NewYork

Auckland Bangkok Buenos Aires Cape Town Chennai
Dar es Salaam Delhi Hong Kong Istanbul Karachi Kolkata
Kuala Lumpur Madrid Melbourne Mexico City Mumbai Nairobi
São Paulo Shanghai Taipei Tokyo Toronto

Oxford is a registered trade mark of Oxford University Press
in the UK and in certain other countries

Published in the United States
by Oxford University Press Inc., New York

© C. Milhaupt and M. West 2004

The moral rights of the authors have been asserted
Database right Oxford University Press (maker)

First published 2004

All rights reserved. No part of this publication may be reproduced,
stored in a retrieval system, or transmitted, in any form or by any means,
without the prior permission in writing of Oxford University Press,
or as expressly permitted by law, or under terms agreed with the appropriate
reprographics rights organization. Enquiries concerning reproduction
outside the scope of the above should be sent to the Rights Department,
Oxford University Press, at the address above

You must not circulate this book in any other binding or cover
and you must impose this same condition on any acquirer

British Library Cataloguing in Publication Data

Data available

Library of Congress Cataloging in Publication Data

Data available

ISBN 0-19-927211-5

1 3 5 7 9 10 8 6 4 2

Typeset by Newgen Imaging Systems (P) Ltd., Chennai, India
Printed in Great Britain
on acid-free paper by
Biddles Ltd., King's Lynn, Norfolk

For Terry

C. J. M.

For Mieko, Davis, and Eila

M. D. W.

Contents

Acknowledgments   ix
List of Figures   xi
List of Tables   xii

1. Introduction   1

2. Corporate Law and Governance: Shareholder
   Derivative Suits   9

3. Venture Capital   45

4. The "*Jusen* Problem"   73

5. Sokaiya   109

6. Organized Crime   145

7. Mergers and Acquisitions   179

8. Lawyers and Bureaucrats   207

9. Looking Ahead   241

Index   245

Acknowledgments

This book grew out of several projects we pursued over the past five years. Some of these projects we did together, others separately. Collectively, we received an enormous amount of help on this book. We received particularly insightful comments on substantial portions of the book from Ronald Gilson, Hideki Kanda, Atsushi Kinami, Rick Lempert, Ronald Mann, Hugh Patrick, Adam Pritchard, Mark Ramseyer, Roberto Romano, Robert Thompson, Frank Upham, and Michael Young. The research making up the individual chapters of this book was presented at over two dozen academic conferences and workshops, at which we received invaluable comments and criticism from participants too numerous to mention by name. This input from such a wide range of talented scholars (who, it should be noted, did not always concur in our conclusions) improved the final product immensely, and we are very grateful for their contributions. Any remaining shortcomings in the work persist despite such able assistance.

We thank Geoffrey Miller, who co-authored with Milhaupt the article on which Chapter 4 is based, for his gracious permission to publish a version of that work here.

In the course of pursuing the separate projects that make up this book, we were fortunate to receive substantial financial support from a variety of sources. The Center for International Political Economy funded our joint research on the mergers and acquisitions market, which appears in Chapter 7. The Abe Fellowship Program of the Social Science Research Council and the American Council of Learned Societies separately funded West's research on sokaiya (Chapter 5) and Milhaupt's research on the market for legal talent (Chapter 8). Milhaupt received financial support from the Marc and Eva Stern Faculty Research Fund at Columbia Law School in connection with the research on organized crime (Chapter 6). West's work is supported by the Nippon Life Insurance Company's endowment at the University of Michigan Law School.

We also benefited on a number of occasions from the collegiality and hospitality provided by the Faculties of Law at the University of Tokyo and Kyoto University. Our respective deans during the project, David Leebron and Jeff Lehman, supported the project in ways both tangible and intangible. Members of each of our faculties offered suggestions and assistance, ranging from water-cooler chats about relevant morning headlines to lengthy discussions of knotty problems.

Some of the work on which this book is based appeared in an earlier form in the following publications: "The Pricing of Derivative Actions in Japan and the United States," 88 *Northwestern University Law Review* 1436 (1994), Used with permission of Northwestern University School of Law, *Law Review*; "Why Shareholders Sue: The Evidence from Japan," 30 *Journal of Legal Studies* 351

(2001), © 2001 The University of Chicago; "The Market for Innovation in the United States and Japan: Venture Capital and the Comparative Corporate Governance Debate," 91 *Northwestern University Law Review* 865 (1997), © Northwestern University; "Cooperation, Conflict, and Convergence in Japanese Finance: Evidence from the 'Jusen' Problem," 29 *Law & Policy in International Business* (1997), reprinted with permission of the publisher, Law and Policy in International Business © 1997; "Information, Institutions, and Extortion in Japan and the United States: Making Sense of Sokaiya Racketeers," 93 *Northwestern University Law Review* 767 (1999), used with permission of Northwestern University, School of Law, *Law Review* "The Dark Side of Private Ordering: An Institutional and Empirical Analysis of Organized Crime," 67 *University of Chicago Law Review* 41 (2000), © The University of Chicago; Institutional Change and M & A in Japan: Diversity through Deals. in *Global Markets, Domestic Institutions: Corporate Law and Governance in a New Era of Cross-Border Deals* 295 (Columbia University Press 2003); and "Law's Dominion and the Market for Legal Elites in Japan," 34 *Law & Policy in International Business* 451 (2003), reprinted with permission of the publisher, Law and Policy in International Business © 2003.

Finally, we are especially grateful to our families (and in particular, our spouses), who supported us throughout, and bore many of the intangible costs of producing this research with patience and understanding. This book is for them.

List of Figures

3.1. Businesses in which Japanese venture capital firms own more
than 10% of the outstanding stock   52

6.1. Members of organized crime firms and membership
rates, 1972–2001   163
6.2. Numbers of firms, 1957–92   165

7.1. Mergers and asset sales reported, 1968–89   183
7.2. Ratio of bust-up value to market capitalization, 2000   190
7.3. Number of deals involving Japanese targets, 1993–2000   193

8.1. Bar exam takers and passers, 1960–2002   212
8.2. Law civil service exam takers and passers, 1978–2002   213
8.3. Comparative exam pass rates, 1990–2002   213
8.4. Amakudari waivers by NPA, 1988–2001   223
8.5. Lawyers, bar takers, and GDP growth, 1960–2000   232

List of Tables

2.1. Japanese derivative suits   23
2.2. Average abnormal returns on lawsuit filings (51 firms)   24
2.3. Settlement amounts per share   27
2.4. Attorneys' fees pursuant to Fee Rules   29

3.1. Relative size of the U.S. and Japanese venture
     capital markets (early 1990s)   49

4.1. Possible loss allocation methods and their impact
     on lenders to the *jusen* companies   91

6.1. Institutional gaps and illicit private ordering entrepreneurs   160
6.2. Percentage of arrested persons affiliated with organized
     criminal firms, 2001   162
6.3. Correlates of MEMBERS of organized criminal firms   166
6.4. Bivariate linear regressions of MEMBERS on law
     enforcement variables   169

7.1. Time from announcement to closing, U.S. and Japan   190
7.2. Corporate governance characteristics   196

8.1. Law hires by elite bureaucracy by exam year   214
8.2. Bar exam passers, by university   215
8.3. Law civil service exam passers, by university   216
8.4. Career choices of Todai legal elites, 1991–2000   217
8.5. Law civil service hiring from Todai and Waseda   218
8.6. Career choices of graduating Kyoto University legal elites   218

1

Introduction

This is a book about how Japan is governed, at least in the realm of economic organizations. "Why another book on this topic?," readers may ask. Is the Japanese economy not hopelessly mired in recession? Have the economists not debated the causes and fixes for years? More saliently, perhaps, has the question not already been resolved? Do we not know that, for better or worse, bureaucrats rule Japan? After all, the bureaucrats were widely credited with Japan's miraculous economic success in the postwar period, and they are widely condemned today for the "lost decade" of recession and financial turmoil that began in the early 1990s and continues to this day.

Those are fair questions, and we have several distinctive answers to them. At one stage in the writing process, the manuscript for this book bore the subtitle "Institutions and Empirics." It is gone, but the approach is prevalent throughout the book. We believe that many important insights into the economic and social structures of a society can be generated with an institutional and empirical approach. By an institutional approach, we mean an analytical framework–generally referred to as "new institutional economic (NIE) analysis"–that has proved extremely useful in conducting cross-national social science research. The NIE approach is to take the institution as the basic unit of analysis, and to examine how institutions are formed, interact, and evolve. An institution is any formal or informal constraint on human behavior. Law is one type of institution. But law interacts with other, less formal institutions, such as markets, codes of best practice, social norms, and shared beliefs about how the world works. So defined, institutions serve as an excellent unit of analysis and cross-national comparison.

Our principal focus is on the formal rules (law and regulations) and informal rules (norms, practices, and shared beliefs) that shape such economically integral factors as Japanese corporate governance, financial regulation, and markets for everything from venture capital to legal talent. In each chapter, we explain behavior in the Japanese economy as a function of the rules of the game. Where applicable, we describe how those rules are changing and why. Formal rule changes are coming fast and furious these days in the form of new laws, new regulatory structures, and repeated amendments to the Commercial Code. Informal rule changes are coming too–much more slowly and incrementally–as widely shared practices and mind sets are eroded and replaced.

The empirical part of our approach involves collecting and analyzing data to determine what impact these rules actually have on actors in the Japanese economy. Where possible and meaningful, we have performed statistical tests on the data to confirm or disprove a prediction from theory. At other times, we examine data simply to deepen our understanding beyond that available from casual observation. We believe that one contribution of the book is simply the unearthing of vast tracts of previously unexplored facts about Japanese corporate governance, economic organizations, and the actors who animate them.

Thus, our approach, which is novel in studies of Japan, is to look at the "big picture" rules of the game (the institutions) as well as the fine detail of how those rules are actually impacting incentives, information, and bargaining in the Japanese economy (the empirics). There is some tension between these two methods, to be sure. At times, we lack the empirical evidence that would ideally be available to test big picture theory of how the institutions are functioning. At other times, our discussion of the "big" picture is an attempt to understand, as best we can, an extensive body of previously unexplored facts. There are also considerable synergies between these two methods: We use data to inform institutional theory, and institutional theory to interpret the data. The approach is by no means foolproof, but we believe that it offers compelling answers to heretofore-unanswered questions, and provides new perspectives on debates that scholars may have thought to be settled. For example, why does Japan, universally considered to be a highly ordered, low crime society, have a thriving network of organized crime syndicates? What do employment patterns over the past decade tell us about the conventional wisdom that bureaucrats run the Japanese economy? How do Japanese corporate governance practices affect the market for entrepreneurial finance, and for takeovers?

This approach obviously can be applied to countries other than Japan, and one motivation for writing this book was to encourage similar analyses of other countries. Yet, there are several reasons why we believe it is uniquely helpful to examine Japan and its legal system through the twin lenses of institutions and empirics. Principally, this is so because Japan has a fascinating and distinctive set of institutions and a wealth of previously unexplored data on the impact of those institutions on private behavior. Indeed, in some areas, such as organized crime (Chapter 6), we are confident that the Japanese data are superior in both quality and quantity to any similar data in the world.

While this overall approach to the Japanese economy is new, we happily acknowledge the intellectual debt we owe to scholars who pioneered the NIE analysis. Many scholars could be discussed in this connection, but two in particular deserve mention. Nobel Laureate Douglass North is most closely associated with the NIE approach, and his work has influenced ours. North showed that throughout economic history and throughout the world, institutions like property rights protections have made the difference between economic prosperity and poverty.[1] It is commonplace today to think of institutions as providing the rules of the game for economic activity. It is commonplace, in large part, due to North's pioneering work.

Masahiko Aoki, a Stanford economist currently running a think tank in Tokyo, has applied institutional analysis, in combination with game theory, to

Japanese economic organizations both elegantly and powerfully, and we readily note the influence of his work on ours. One of Aoki's principal contributions was the construction of an integrated and robust theory of Japanese organizational structure linking the "main bank" system to other facets of firm structure, right down to the shop floor. As with North, much of what is now taken for granted in Aoki's field is the result of his influential thinking. This book differs from Aokian analysis in several ways. First, we are not principally engaged in the construction of an integrated and robust theory. Rather, we are interested in providing a thick and theoretically informed description of Japanese corporate governance and economic regulation in the broadest sense, including the entire range of constraints operating on Japanese managers and other stakeholders, including governmental actors. At the same time, our empirical approach allows us to penetrate many puzzling features of Japanese economic organization without resort to an overly determined theory of how things work in that country. We believe our empirical analysis is informed by, but not a captive to, any particular economic theory.

Perhaps a more important distinction between our work and that of Professor Aoki (and North, for that matter) is that our principal focus is unabashedly on *legal* institutions and their impact. As academic lawyers with similar backgrounds in corporate law practice, and indeed similar academic training and Japan backgrounds, we both tend to focus on how the legal rules of the game affect power relations in Japan. In practice at large New York law firms, we saw how our clients—U.S., Japanese, and otherwise—adapted their behavior and organization to the rules of the game (with a little help from their friends, the attorneys). As academics, we examine the same patterns from a broader perspective, by following how individuals—corporate managers, shareholders, bankers, bureaucrats, lawyers, university students, and even gangsters—organize themselves to exploit the rules of the Japanese economy. Indeed, the similarities in our approach convinced us that we should put some of our work together, and hopefully reap synergies from the merger.

So our first answer to the question, "Why another book on how the Japanese economy is governed?," is that we think we have a new approach to the question, some new answers, and a wealth of previously unexplored data bearing on the issue.

This leads to our second answer. In most analyses of Japan, law is conspicuous by its absence. There are exceptions to be sure, including most prominently the work of Mark Ramseyer and John Haley, both of whom have helped shape our perspectives on Japanese law.[2] Yet, despite the deserved attention of this work, perhaps no perception about Japan is more persistent than the notion that law is largely irrelevant to social and economic organization in that country. Indeed, we could refer readers to a veritable mountain of scholarly literature and journalistic writing in support of that claim. Since this is such a widely held view, however, we will spare readers the tedium of repetition here. By focusing on the rules of the game (many, though certainly not all of which are legal rules), and by reinforcing and enriching that focus with great attention to detail on how these rules actually affect behavior, we believe we have found a new and powerful way to show that law is both relevant and increasingly central to Japanese economic and social governance. Lo and behold, law occupies an important place in the Japanese economy.

We want to pause here to emphasize and elaborate upon several points that have already been made and that follow from our institutional and empirical approach. First, institutions determine power relations. That is, the rules of the game determine who has information and the quality of that information; they allocate bargaining endowments among the parties; they determine what types of deals are possible in the economy, who makes those deals, and whether those deals are subject to review or undoing by other actors in the system. The rules of the game determine whether economic regulation takes place informally or formally— in effect, whether law (promulgated and enforced by the state) or relationships (private ordering among the players themselves) govern deals, duties, and other facts of economic life. To put it colloquially, rules *rule*.

Second, as noted above, institutions include not only formal rules such as laws and regulations, but also informal rules, such as social norms. To paraphrase a definition by Richard Posner that we find particularly useful, a norm is simply a rule that is not promulgated by an official source nor enforced through legal sanction, yet is regularly complied with.[3] There is now a substantial literature on the central role of social norms in the governance of everything from diamond merchants to cattle ranchers and sumo wrestlers.[4] Here, we will confine ourselves to the more prosaic but salient role of norms in channeling behavior in Japanese firms, banks, and financial bureaucracies. The basic insights from this literature, applicable to a diverse range of specific groups, can be summarized as follows: Norms are extraordinarily important constraints on human behavior—in many circumstances, more important than laws and regulations. Exactly why most people abide by norms most of the time is not well understood, but several theories exist. One is that norm compliance signals cooperative behavior, which is beneficial to the complier. Another is that norm (non)compliance is (punished) rewarded in ways that people find meaningful. It is widely accepted that, all else being equal, norms are more prevalent and powerful in small, tight-knit communities than in larger, more atomized populations. Norms, like other institutions, can evolve over time. Norm evolution, like institutional evolution, is a relatively new field, and scholars have much work to do before the processes by which institutions change is fully understood. For our purposes, it is sufficient to illuminate the roles that both laws and norms play in Japanese economic life, and to understand the basic contours of institutional change currently underway.

Perhaps most importantly, our study shows that Japanese actors *respond* to institutional change. This is a crucial point, because the Japanese are often portrayed as captives of their culture, incapable of adaptation due to deeply rooted, shared understandings of how their world is supposed to work. To put it differently, Japanese social norms are commonly viewed simultaneously as all encompassing (leaving no room for law) and immutable (rooted, as they supposedly are, in centuries of tradition). We do not dispute that Japan has a relatively distinctive "culture," if that means a set of mutually reinforcing formal and informal institutions that affect behavior and people's understanding of their behavior.[5] But this hardly sets Japan apart from the United States, Germany, Kenya, Chile, or any other society, each of which has a distinctive institutional structure that channels behavior and through which behavior is filtered. Our approach allows us to unpack the ubiquitous references to Japanese "culture" by examining the formation and evolution of formal and informal rules, as well as their impact on important actors in the economy.

We believe that analyzing Japan in this way provides important new insights into the structure and governance of the world's second largest economy, including the possibility and likely avenues of change. Yes, as we write this, Japan is mired in recession, beset by a series of financial crises, and seemingly paralyzed by bureaucratic ineptitude and political factionalism. Largely over-looked in Japan's lost decade, however, is the reality of significant institutional change. Evidence of change is apparent in many of the chapters that follow, and is highlighted in Chapter 8 dealing with the allocation of elite legal talent in society. Quite simply, due to institutional change, the most elite talent in Japanese society is forsaking the bureaucracy for law, with potentially profound implications for the governance of the economy. Japan is not stagnant; it is a hotbed of change. Perhaps these are changes only a lawyer could love, but observers of Japan ignore them at considerable peril to their understanding of contemporary Japanese society, politics and economy.

The remainder of the book is organized as follows: We begin in Chapter 2 with a paradigmatic case of law's role in facilitating change in the Japanese economy—shareholder derivative suits. After discussing the structure of corporate gover-nance in Japan, we show how a seemingly technical and innocuous legal change in 1993 led to large-scale changes in the scope and mechanics of shareholder monitoring in that country.

Chapters 3 and 4 examine the role of law and informal rules in the financial sector. Chapter 3 examines entrepreneurial finance in Japan, focusing on how the institutional environment associated with Japanese corporate governance in its postwar heyday created problems for start-up firms by handicapping the development of an active venture capital market. Bubbles notwithstanding, the maturation and dynamism of the venture capital market in the 1990s was one of the signal economic successes of the United States in recent years. Not surpris-ingly, Japan has looked enviously at Silicon Valley. The search for an institu-tional structure supportive of entrepreneurial finance in Japan has motivated substantial corporate law reform over the past five years. Chapter 4 examines financial regulation and the resolution of financial institution failure in Japan, by analyzing how informal rules contributed to the collapse of Japan's home mortgage lending (*jusen*) industry and its resolution. We focus on this event, in part, because the "jusen problem" was the first of a series of crises in the Japanese financial sector, and it represents the paradigmatic case of financial regulatory failure that sadly still manifests itself in Japan today. As Robert Higgs has noted, "There is no way to substitute pure theory for a knowledge of history."[6] By getting to the bottom of the recent *jusen* history, one can understand much of what ails Japan today. Just as importantly, we present this case because it is an elaborate illustration of the dynamics between law and private ordering at work in a crucial industry.

Chapters 5 and 6 examine the dark side of Japanese economic institutions. Chapter 5 discusses the unusual and problematic form that shareholder activism has traditionally taken in Japan—professional disturbers of shareholders meetings, or "*sokaiya.*" Again we see the impact of institutions on behavior, as the workings of the *sokaiya* are directly linked to the quality of corporate information disclosure in Japan, a function of the institutional environment in which Japanese firms operate. Chapter 6 examines the problem of organized crime. This chapter shows how Japan's institutional environment for economic activity—specifically gaps between legal rights "on the books" and the state's ability to enforce those rights in practice—has provided incentives for entrepreneurship on the dark side of society. Japanese organized crime syndicates, like other actors in the economy, respond to the rules of the game.

Chapters 7 and 8 show how institutional changes can lead to positive results. Chapter 7 explains why there are so few changes of corporate control in Japan, and examines how legal and other reforms relating to mergers and acquisitions are bringing about potentially far-reaching changes in the way Japanese firms are governed. In Chapter 8, we examine the allocation of talent in Japan between the bureaucracy and the legal profession. This chapter both reflects and highlights the general transformation we see taking place in Japan, away from informal rules and toward more formal, law-based institutions. If Japan is moving toward a firmer "rule of law" (putting aside the very thorny question of precisely what that means), one likely consequence is a greater role for lawyers in the economy, and a diminished role for bureaucrats operating by fiat. Examining career choices of elites in Japanese society thus provides a novel way of testing whether the institutional changes we observe in the rest of the book are having a real impact on society. We present dramatic evidence that indeed they are: The cream of the crop in Japan is forsaking the bureaucracy for law. Chapter 9 provides our concluding observations.

NOTES

1. Douglass C. North, Structure and Change in Economic History (1981); id. Institutions, Institutional Change, and Economic Performance (1990).
2. See, for example, J. Mark Ramseyer and Minoru Nakazato, Japanese Law: An Economic Approach (1999); John Owen Haley, Authority without Power: Law and the Japanese Paradox (1990).
3. Richard A. Posner, Social Norms and the Law: An Economic Approach, 87 Am. Econ. Rev. 365 (1997).

4. Analysis of extra-legal social norms has become a matter of intense interest to American legal scholars. See, for example, Robert Ellickson, Order without Law (1991); Lawrence Lessig, The Regulation of Social Meaning, 62 U. Chi. L. Rev. 943 (1996); Symposium: Law, Economics, and Norms, 144 U. Pa. L. Rev. 1643 (1996); Mark D. West, Legal Rules and Social Norms in Japan's Secret World of Sumo, 26 J. Legal Stud. 165 (1997).
5. A few scholars *do* dispute the distinctiveness of virtually all "Japanese" economic organizations and institutions. See, for example, Yoshiro Miwa and J. Mark Ramseyer, The Myth of the Main Bank: Japan and Comparative Corporate Governance, 27 Law & Soc. Inq. 401 (2002). We are comfortable deflecting the direct engagement of that debate to other forums. See Curtis J. Milhaupt, On the (Fleeting) Existence of the Main Bank System and Other Japanese Economic Institutions, 27 Law & Soc. Inq. 425 (2002). Readers can make up their own minds about the distinctiveness of Japanese institutions at the end of the book.
6. Robert Higgs, Crisis and Leviathan 259 (1987).

2

Corporate Law and Governance: Shareholder Derivative Suits

INTRODUCTION

We begin our study of institutional incentives in Japan with a case study that introduces in microcosm corporate law, corporate governance, and the environment for corporate decisionmaking: The shareholder derivative suit. A derivative suit is an action brought by one or more shareholders on behalf of the corporation to redress a wrong that affects the corporation itself.[1] The right to sue "derives" from the corporation, and thus any damages awarded accrue to the corporation. Shareholders in Japan filed fewer than twenty derivative suits against directors from 1950 to 1990, while nearly one-fifth of a random sample of publicly traded U.S. corporations were involved in such suits during a similar period.[2] But by the end of 1993, eighty-four suits were pending in Japanese courts. By 1996, that number rose to 174, and by the end of 1999, there were 286 such suits, including ninety-five filed in 1999 alone.[3] The huge increase in suits—over 10,000 percent—has prompted calls by business for legislative reform, led to new corporate governance innovations, and sparked a general public debate of the proper role of shareholders and directors in Japanese corporate governance.

The loudest calls for reform followed a September 2000 judgment by the Osaka District Court against eleven directors of Daiwa Bank. In September 1995, it was revealed that a trader in Daiwa's New York branch had lost $1.1 billion through eleven years of illegal trading of U.S. Treasury bonds. A shareholder and former Bank employee subsequently filed suit. The Osaka court, citing the directors' failure to establish a monitoring system, found violations of the directors' duties of care and loyalty and ordered them to pay a whopping U.S. $775 million to the company.[4] The amount of damages (sixty-six times higher than the previous record award) and the basing of liability on "mere" failure to monitor jolted the Japanese business and legal community. The directors' insurance policy did not cover the period in which the violations occurred, and even if it had, it would not have covered the full amount of damages. Much like the Delaware reaction to the decision in the *Smith* v. *Van Gorkom* case (which found that directors violated their duty of care in evaluating a buyout offer),[5] a flurry of activity followed, as both sides appealed, legislators searched for legal fixes, insurance companies sold large new policies, editorials criticized, and companies sought legal advice.

In this chapter, in addition to the basic goal of exploring the legal framework for corporate governance in Japan, we attempt to explain why Japanese shareholders, who did not sue from 1950 to 1990, now sue with much greater frequency. We base our findings on our review of a data set of 140 cases filed between 1993 and 1999 and subsequent developments in these cases through the end of 2000.

A 1993 lowering of filing fees from a percentage of requested damages to a flat ¥8,200 (about $80) explains much of the increase in cases filed. Lower the cost of suing, and more people will sue: Japanese corporate actors respond to changes in the transaction cost environment. The post-bubble decline in the Japanese economy may also influence some cases, as plaintiffs may find it easier to prove damages against failing firms.

But the dramatic increase in the number or suits filed is, nevertheless, intriguing given the continuing lack of shareholder incentives to sue. Attorneys' fees, which drive U.S. derivative litigation,[6] have changed little in Japan. Because damages in derivative suits in Japan, as in the United States, are paid to the corporation, the most a plaintiff can hope for is a pro rata increase in the value of the plaintiff's individual stake. In Japan, as this chapter will show, plaintiff-shareholders usually lose. And filing fees, though reduced, are still nonzero. Shareholder–plaintiffs in Japan are undertaking costly activity–lawsuits–despite minimal evident benefits, in apparent contradiction with economic theory.

Japan presents a particularly appropriate comparative model from which to explore these issues. The derivative suit mechanism was transplanted directly from the U.S. model in 1950. Moreover, the simplicity of the Japanese legal environment in this area eliminates some variables that drive litigation in the United States. Because Japan has no class action mechanism, derivative suits account for almost all shareholder litigation. Because derivative suits may be brought only against directors and similar actors, there are no confounding variables of suits brought against outside third parties. The Japanese system also comes with relatively little historical baggage. Due to a scarcity of derivative litigation before 1993, Japan lacks consistent and thorough legal doctrine in many of the areas affected by such litigation.

In this chapter, we make two claims about derivative litigation in large, public Japanese corporations. First, derivative litigation does not appear to increase shareholder wealth directly. Japanese shareholders rarely win, and, unlike their counterparts in the United States, they only occasionally obtain settlement. Nor do they receive stock price gains. Importantly, we test for these gains to shareholders using the same event study methodology used in other studies to test gains from derivative actions in the United States. One advantage of this approach is that it allows for an examination of whether those studies—and ours— are biased by peculiarly national institutions, culture, or other nation-specific factors. The similarity of results suggests that such biases are minimal at best.

Second, while popular and academic critics sometimes blame U.S. derivative litigation on a peculiarly American excess of overpaid attorneys and litigious norms,[7] we find the same basic jumbled set of attorney and plaintiff incentives at work in Japan. Multiple causation and multiple motivations are of course at work on both attorneys and plaintiffs in both countries, and most players have some combination of monetary and non-monetary incentives. But in general, even with lower attorneys' fees, attorneys are the driving force behind Japanese derivative litigation. A residuum of suits can be explained by an amalgam of (*a*) non-monetary factors such as altruism, anger, and social concerns both among attorneys and plaintiffs, (*b*) corporate troublemakers, (*c*) insurance, and (*d*) "piggyback" enforcement. The Japanese experience suggests that the difficult issues of attorney incentives are endemic not only to the United States in particular, but also to the derivative suit mechanism in general.

The chapter proceeds as follows. Section I is an introduction to the contours of Japanese corporate governance; readers who are already familiar with those contours may choose to skim it. Section II places derivative suits in the corporate governance setting. In Section III, we examine derivative suit success rates. Using simple econometric tests, we examine whether shareholders in Japan benefit directly from derivative litigation. Section IV discusses attorney incentives and a residuum of non-monetary factors, corporate troublemakers, insurance, and public enforcement.

I. CONTEXT: JAPANESE CORPORATE GOVERNANCE

Before exploring derivative suits directly, we set forth a few basics of Japanese corporate governance structure and the legal environment in which it functions.

A. The Legal Framework for Corporate Governance in Japan

1. History   Only fifteen years after the first published description of the corporate form appeared in Japanese, the Japanese government in 1881 commissioned German legal scholar Hermann Roesler to attempt a first draft of a commercial code. The code that resulted from Roesler's efforts, which was promulgated in 1899, was based largely on the German code and is said to have drastically altered customary business practices.

The 1899 legal structure remained basically intact until its revision by the officials (known as "SCAP" for Supreme Commander for the Allied Powers or "GHQ" for General Headquarters) of the U.S. occupation of Japan following the Second World War (the "Occupation"). SCAP officials saw a need for great change in Japan's commercial and financial structure. They believed that shareholding should be widely dispersed, corporate governance should be democratic, and the wartime *zaibatsu* conglomerates should be dissolved and their executives purged. Although a number of tactics could have been used to accomplish these goals, the Occupation reformers had a New-Deal-nuanced vision of democracy that "relied on law as a vehicle to effect social and political change."[8]

Commercial Code revisions began in 1949. The task fell specifically to SCAP lawyers Lester Salwin and Irving Eisenstein. Both, coincidentally, were sons of German–Jewish immigrants, 1931 graduates of the University of Illinois, and trial lawyers from Chicago. In fact, of the five members of the Division who worked on the Commercial Code, three (Salwin, Eisenstein, and First Lieutenant Robert W. Hudson) were Illinois lawyers.

It is difficult to say what the Commercial Code might have looked like without the Illinois attorneys, who relied heavily on Illinois law in the reform process. As a "helpful guide," Salwin, the leader, began by furnishing the Japanese representatives with "citations to the Illinois Business Corporation Act of 1947" on each of the main points of corporate law reform.[9] Salwin's subsequent drafts–and the final product–relied heavily on Illinois law.[10] Thus, following the war, with one major exception,[11] the constituent organs of the Japanese corporation and the basic rules for its organization and governance took on a highly American cast.[12]

2. Analysis   Japanese corporate laws dictate that Japanese corporations are organized in part by mandatory structural and fiduciary rules that guide the internal processes of corporate decisionmaking and the external conduct of corporate actors. In part because of U.S. influence, the rules provide for a board of directors elected by shareholders for a limited term of office to serve as the basic governing organ.[13] Liability rules govern the relationship between the directors and the corporation.[14] Aggrieved shareholders have access to the courts to enforce these rules. Other rules give shareholders a voice in corporate affairs, require periodic disclosure of reliable financial data, regulate transactions that raise potential conflicts of interest between managers and the corporation, and protect the integrity of shareholder voting.[15]

The Securities and Exchange Law (SEL) also subjects the Japanese corporation to extensive rules concerning conflicts of interest and mandatory disclosure designed to protect investors. For example, under the SEL, a corporation's officers, agents, and employees may not trade in the corporation's securities on the basis of material undisclosed information. Officers and shareholders owning at least 10 percent of the outstanding shares must give up any profits from short-swing trades, even if the trades were not based on inside information. The corporation must file reports containing financial data audited by an independent accountant. Tender offers and disclosures by shareholders owning more than 5 percent of the shares of public companies are regulated in a manner very similar to the dictates of the U.S. Williams Act.[16]

This imported legal framework reflects not only the substance, but also the intellectual moorings of U.S. corporate and securities laws as articulated in Berle and Means' influential book *The Modern Corporation and Private Property*, which shaped U.S. corporate theory for nearly half a century.[17] Berle and Means started from the assumption of shareholder primacy implicit in U.S. corporate law, incorporated property rights and democracy theory into their analysis, and concluded that the modern corporation's need for huge inputs of capital and specialized management leads to the separation of shareholder ownership from management control. The separation gives rise to an inevitable divergence of interests between shareholders and managers because the latter do not bear a major share of the wealth effects of their decisions.

The separation of ownership and control is one of the principal notions animating U.S. corporate and securities laws. Mitigating the agency costs resulting from the separation framed the organizational imperative of corporate governance in the United States. As a result, the American template upon which Japan's corporate and securities laws are based is a discrete, shareholder-oriented, agency model of the corporation. It is a model that calls out for *legal* enforcement of the corporate contract.

B. The Japanese Corporate Contract

The shareholder-oriented agency model historically has shown little resemblance, however, to the Japanese corporation as it is actually has been organized and monitored. The Japanese firm traditionally has opted out of many of the shareholder-centered statutory provisions of the corporate and securities laws. Instead, as a supplement to the law, and sometimes as a substitute, the actions of key actors historically have been monitored by informal social and economic institutions, as described below. We hasten to point out that each of the institutions discussed here is undergoing significant transformation. Still, they continue to be the building blocks of Japanese corporate governance theory, and are useful for understanding the changes that have taken place in Japanese corporate governance in recent years.

1. Main bank relations   A central institution of Japanese corporate governance in its postwar heyday was the main bank system. In stylized form, the main bank was the largest single lender to a corporate client as well as one of its principal shareholders. As a central repository of information on the borrower, the main bank played an important role in monitoring the firm's management and rendering assistance in case of managerial crisis or financial failure. There was a strong presumption on the part of the main bank, the client, and of all relevant business and governmental actors that the main bank will restructure or merge a failing company rather than liquidate it.[18] Because management was often replaced by bank personnel in such situations, the main bank system was said to substitute for the missing takeover market in Japan.[19] We discuss this in much greater detail in Chapter 7.

Three key functions are supported by the relationship between a borrower and its main bank: Financing, monitoring, and information and management support. Each function is multidimensional, and the importance of any given function varies across relationships and with the financial state of the firm at a given time. As a leading commentary indicates, the "central ideal of main bank relations" is that they are "multi-faceted and . . . implicitly define a wealth-contingent corporate governance system."[20]

The main bank provides financing by serving as both lender and shareholder. This dual status lessens the conflicts of interest typically present between providers of debt and equity.[21] The main bank also supports public finance by playing an important role in domestic and international bond issues. It serves as the collateral trustee for domestic bond issues, and frequently serves as co-manager of foreign bond issues through wholly owned foreign subsidiaries. These services often entail de facto status as guarantor of the bonds. Though not strictly a financing function, the main bank typically also manages the payment settlement account of client firms, through which firms handle routine cash flow transactions.

As the largest lender to the borrowing firm as well as manager of its payment settlement account, the main bank accumulates a substantial base of information on the borrower's business and financial health. The monitoring function of the main bank–borrower relationship is highly state dependent. If the borrower is experiencing no financial difficulty, the main bank engages only in *ex ante* and interim monitoring, by assessing proposed and ongoing projects. If the firm becomes financially distressed, however, the main bank may engage in *ex post* monitoring by displacing management, arranging an acquisition of the firm, or acting as an informal chair of the creditor's committee. This activity is commonly referred to as a firm "rescue," although it is actually closer to a restructuring, often involving substantial reconfiguration of the business, including replacement of management and significant concessions by labor and suppliers.[22]

2. Inter-corporate relations   A second prominent feature of postwar corporate finance and organization in Japan is the practice of mutual shareholding among firms and financial institutions. Although cross-shareholdings are declining, with implications we discuss in Chapter 7, in the early 1990s approximately two-thirds of all corporate shares were held long term by "stable" shareholders friendly toward management.[23] This practice reaches its apex in the form of the *keiretsu*. The *keiretsu* are historically derived clusters of affiliated firms held together by stable cross-share ownership, interlocking directorates, extensive product market exchanges, and other linkages that enhance group identity and facilitate information exchange. Again, in the heyday of postwar Japanese corporate governance, a main bank was at the center of each of the six principal *keiretsu* corporate groups. Today, mergers among the main banks at the center of several *keiretsu* have weakened the identities of the corporate groups.

The *keiretsu* system and other, less cohesive corporate groupings are (or were?) a means of encouraging asset-specific investments and product-market competition, thus constraining both opportunism and shirking. Although cross-shareholding raised the cost of acquiring a controlling block of shares, thus virtually disabling the market for corporate control, the long-term relationships embedded in Japanese corporate shareholding, which were traditionally based on ongoing financial and product-market transactions, encouraged non-capital market forms of monitoring. These relationships, in effect, provided an alternative to the disciplining and risk-bearing functions played by the capital markets in some other economies. From its origin as an anti-takeover device, cross-shareholding in Japan evolved into a distinctive private monitoring and bonding mechanism.[24] Intense intergroup competition in product and labor markets, in turn, prevented the group system from degenerating into an exercise in mutual shirking.

3. Employment relations Concern for the long-term welfare of employees serves as a major constraint on the Japanese firm. Under the "lifetime" employment system, the mutual expectation of employer and employee is that the employee will trade below-market wages in the first half of his or her career in return for an implicit promise of continuous employment until mandatory retirement age and supra-market wages in the second half of his or her career. Employees within the system receive extensive training and education in a program of systematic job rotation and promotion. Because labor mobility is limited and the employee has in effect posted a bond at the outset of the employment relationship that will only be fully recouped upon retirement, employees have a significant vested interest in the continued viability of their firm.

While there is typically no written agreement to safeguard the employee's interests, a number of extra-legal protections provide substantial assurances that the employer will not opportunistically appropriate the gains generated by the employee's firm-specific human capital investment. First, since high-level corporate management is drawn from the ranks of career employees, managers are themselves long-term repeat players who realize that employee goodwill is crucial to the success of the business and who identify very closely with employees. Japanese managers rate market share, which is closely tied to employee welfare, ahead of more shareholder-oriented goals. Since the market for managerial talent is similarly limited and managers also make large firm-specific human capital investments, management is prone to emphasize growth as a means of diversifying risk. High rates of growth in the postwar period have allowed Japanese firms to operate heavily on trust because it is cheaper than reliance on explicit contracts.

The corporate culture in which the Japanese firm operates provides a second protection. *Ex ante*, the cost of writing an explicit contract to cover all the uncertainties inherent in an employment relationship of thirty or more years is prohibitive and makes such contracts rare. Moreover, the individual employee has virtually no power to control the ways in which the firm will adapt to unforeseen contingencies over the course of his or her career. Corporations are, however, reputation-bearing entities; a firm's favorable reputation provides prospective employees with the confidence to enter into a highly enduring and unspecified relationship with an employer. Corporate culture communicates to potential employees an important principle about how the firm responds to uncertainties. The organization will be characterized by the principle that it selects and articulates to the world in the form of its corporate culture. At the same time, the continuous articulation of the rule in the form of reputation allows the firm to monitor the principle. In this way, corporate culture serves as an important gap-filling and monitoring device to economize on transaction costs in complex environments.

Finally, employees are protected from a form of employer opportunism that is possible in a governance system more directly oriented toward the stock market–appropriation of employee human capital investments in takeover contexts. Whether appropriation of this sort actually occurs may be irrelevant. If employees believe that it occurs, the belief would be sufficient to deter some human capital investments. In a world without hostile takeovers such as has existed in postwar Japan (though whether it persists is a topic we explore in Chapter 7), one major source of potential employer opportunism is removed and employee commitment to the firm is enhanced.

4. Government-business relations   Government–business relations are a crucial facet of the Japanese corporate contract. In the abstract, interaction between the public and private sectors can be viewed in relational perspective. Detailed, binding regulations promulgated by bureaucracies are highly discrete. By proscribing detailed rules, procedures, and formal mechanisms, regulation typically is an attempt to carve economic and other activity into distinct regulatory universes, to treat each case separately "on the merits," and to allocate benefits and burdens *ex ante*. In other words, most regulation serves as a discrete contract between the regulators and the regulated.

Much regulatory activity in postwar Japan, however, was the antithesis of discrete contract. Private ordering facilitated by repeated, informal contacts between regulators and the regulated acts was a key element in the formation and enforcement of economic policy. As the lexicon invented to describe this approach suggests, the bureaucracy was viewed as being engaged in an ongoing process of accommodation with regulated actors, shaping and enforcing compromises rather than directing policy outcomes. As Frank Upham notes, the "consultative consensual character" of the postwar Japanese administrative process, with its exclusion of outsiders and insulation from legal attack, "creates an environment in which good relations are the key to success in dealing with the government . . . The end result is a relationship of diffuse and undefined mutual obligations . . ."[25]

Administrative guidance was a crucial facilitating mechanism in this private ordering process. Long enshrouded in mystery, administrative guidance is simply the informal enforcement of regulatory objectives. While the technique is not unique to Japan, it has attracted particular attention because it was such an important regulatory technique among Japanese regulators. Administrative guidance was the glue that held together repeated dealings between the public and private sectors in Japan. The ability of the regulated to participate in the regulatory process outweighed the disadvantages of occasional bureaucratic strong-arm tactics; the flexibility and discretion it afforded the regulators vastly surpassed the costs of reliance on such informal means to achieve administrative ends. Administrative guidance also protected these repeated dealings from internal and external legal challenges that, if successful, would particularize and rigidify the business–government relationship.

Administrative guidance was also highly efficient from the perspective of contracting costs. In a rapidly growing postwar Japanese economy, the demand for regulation expanded more quickly than regulators were equipped to handle. It was less costly to use the flexible, implicit contract of legally unenforceable administrative guidance over legislation and formal regulation. Securing voluntary compliance with ministry guidance saved the agencies considerable administrative and political costs that would otherwise have been incurred in proposing and amending laws in the Diet. At the same time, regulated entities obtained official approval for their activities flexibly and expeditiously in the face of a rapidly evolving business environment.

Private ordering was further facilitated by the practice of *amakudari*, in which bureaucrats take high-level private sector jobs at the end of their public careers, a process we explore in Chapter 8. These ex-bureaucrats become board members and high-level managers of their new host firms and provide critical access to the agencies with jurisdiction over their industry. Because *amakudari* gives bureaucrats a personal stake in not alienating the corporate sector under their jurisdiction, it helps to ensure that the government will not unilaterally rewrite the regulatory contract.

5. Board structure and relations   A sizeable gap between Japanese corporate law and practice historically has existed in the composition and role of the board of directors. In contrast to the German system of co-determination, Japanese law does not require employee participation at the board level. Yet, Japanese boards traditionally have been comprised almost exclusively of managers who have served the corporation throughout their career and were viewed as employee representatives. Legally, the Japanese board is charged with monitoring corporate activity and vested with the authority to make important managerial decisions. In fact, boards have not traditionally emphasized their monitoring role. Moreover, it was commonly understood that a few senior directors (acting as an informal management committee) or a representative director (who is virtually always the president) have the ultimate decisionmaking authority in the corporation, rather than the board as a whole. These discrepancies between law and practice recently led a blue ribbon corporate governance panel to conclude that "it is questionable whether the Japanese board of directors actually complies with the Commercial Code's stipulation that it function[s] as the body which decides on corporate will and exercises corporate oversight."[26]

The gaps between law and practice can be traced to beliefs about the board's proper function in the Japanese system. Election to the board has traditionally been viewed almost exclusively as the crowning achievement in a long career with the firm that begins upon graduation from college. Virtually all members of the board have traditionally been members of senior management (typically one from each of the company's major divisions). Indeed, until it was amended recently, the Commercial Code did not even recognize officers as a distinct corporate organ, suggesting that the concepts were indistinct. The fact that senior managers are almost never hired away from competitors or firms in other industries reinforces the perception that directors represent employees or, at most, divisions of the firm.

This belief system shaped the two defining characteristics of the traditional Japanese board, its large size and lack of independent directors and committees. A 1999 survey of all listed companies in Japan found that the boards of firms with more than 1,000 employees had an average of 17.7 directors. Among the same firms, 22 percent had twenty to twenty-four directors and 10 percent had twenty-five or more directors.[27] The friendly merger of two large Japanese banks once created a board of sixty-seven.[28]

II. DERIVATIVE SUITS

A. Historical Background

Before the Occupation commercial code revisions, Japan had no derivative suit mechanism. It did, however, have a rather weak substitute, borrowed from Germany in the 1899 Code, by which shareholders holding not less than one-tenth of the capital of the corporation could require the auditors of the corporation to bring suit against directors.[29] The mechanism was rarely used, perhaps because those shareholders who held 10 percent of a corporation's capital could enforce their rights through informal means of control. In addition, sparsity of use may also be attributed to strict rules regarding security for expenses (described below) and, as a further deterrent, a provision that if the suit failed, shareholders would be liable for damages to the company.

While the 1899 Commercial Code principles were liberal in their day, they did not fit SCAP's image of a free capitalist democracy in which corporations are controlled by average shareholders. One contemporary Occupation observer noted "stockholder suits to recover damages, to compel payment of dividends, or to remove management in such corporations are scarcely within the scope of Japanese conception."[30] Establishment of a workable derivative suit mechanism became a high priority for Lester Salwin and his fellow legal reformers, and the institution was implemented in 1950.

B. Mechanics

In Japan as in the United States, a shareholder may bring suit on behalf of the corporation against a director to enforce a director's duties to the corporation. The shareholder's right to sue "derives from" his or her shareholding, and any damages paid by the defendant are paid not to the shareholder, but to the corporation.

The similarities between Japan and the United States are great, but differences can be found in the details. In the United States, derivative suits may be brought against any third party; in Japan, they may only be brought against directors and other similarly situated parties.[31] While most U.S. states require that plaintiffs own shares contemporaneously with the conduct on which the suit against management is based, Japan requires only that a shareholder have held shares continuously for six months before bringing suit.[32]

In Japan, the loser pays court costs. If a plaintiff wins, because the damages accrue to the company, the Commercial Code (art. 268-2) provides that the company shall pay a "reasonable amount" of attorneys' fees upon plaintiff's motion. Absent extraordinary circumstances, defendants pay their own attorneys' fees.

C. Pre-1993 Price Incentives and Disincentives

Before 1993, five specific factors limited derivative suits: Attorneys' fees, filing fees, security-for-expenses, heavy information costs resulting from limited discovery, and an abuse of rights doctrine. Reviewing these factors is more than just an historical exercise; it is useful in determining *what* changes in *which* factors led to increase suits after 1993.

1. Attorney fees   Attorneys' fees are historically one of the most important factors in the setting of prices for derivative actions in Japan and the United States. In the United States, without the prospect of recouping attorneys' fees through judicial awards, many if not most U.S. derivative actions would never be brought. In some U.S. cases, attorneys' fees are the only relief awarded. In Japan, these fee awards are relatively inconsequential and, if anything, create a barrier to potential shareholder–plaintiffs.

In both Japan and the United States, the rules pertaining to attorneys' fees in the derivative action context differ somewhat from those that govern nonderivative cases. In Delaware and in most other U.S. jurisdictions, the "lodestar" method is the method of choice for resolving the dilemma. Using this method, the court focuses on the value of the attorney's time at the attorney's customary hourly rate, then adjusts this "lodestar figure" by a multiplier to account for a variety of factors, including, most importantly, the risk assumed by the attorney.[33] Delaware decisions, while not rejecting the lodestar method, lend support to the percentage-of-recovery method, by which attorneys can seek higher awards based on "results obtained."[34]

The Japanese approach is somewhat difficult to pin down. Article 268-2 of the Commercial Code provides that shareholders may demand that the company pay a "reasonable (*sōtō*) amount within the scope" of the attorney's actual fee. The language seems clear enough, but before 1993, no cases regarding this provision were litigated. Regardless, there is a general feeling in Japan that Japanese attorneys, who are rarely as handsomely paid as their American counterparts, should not be highly compensated for an action in which the client's actual monetary recovery is so meager.

The predictable result of the Japanese rule is to raise the shareholder–plaintiff's cost of bringing a derivative action. Plaintiffs must pay the attorney's initial fee before beginning the action. Should they be successful, the corporation might pay the plaintiff's attorney enough of that attorney's fee to make the action worthwhile. Even in that case, however, the plaintiffs are still responsible for whatever is deemed to be in excess of a "reasonable amount." Should the plaintiffs be unsuccessful, the entire legal bill falls into their lap.

The attorney in the Japanese system likewise has less economic incentive compared to his American counterpart because of the legal rules regarding attorneys' fees. In the United States, the plaintiff's attorney, in accordance with portfolio theory, attempts to diversify his or her practice by undertaking a portfolio of different investments in litigation in order to reduce the variance associated with expected return. Accordingly, the diversified attorney should be willing to pursue high-risk litigation as long as such litigation has the same expected value as other cases that have a higher possibility of success but a lower possible recovery.[35]

By contrast, in making the decision whether to undertake a particular derivative action, the Japanese attorney faces a completely different set of economic incentives. Because the legal rules pertaining to attorneys' fees are less liberal in Japan, the attorney has less incentive to undertake derivative actions relative to other forms of litigation. While other forms of litigation may have equal recovery rates and are equally risky "investments," the legal profession perceives such actions as less complicated than derivative actions. More importantly, the Japanese bar perceives derivative litigation to be more time-consuming than "traditional" litigation. Because the Japanese fee calculation does not factor in time spent on a case, the time-consuming nature of the cases impacts negatively on derivative litigation rates. Thus, the inability of the Japanese system to channel the rewards of private enforcement to the attorney effectively raises the price of derivative litigation relative to the price of the same action in the United States, not only for the plaintiff, but for the attorney as well.

2. Litigation fees   The traditional American rule regarding litigation fees is that each party bears its own expenses. In the derivative litigation context, however, most American commentators argue that such a rule would have a chilling effect on the system, as plaintiffs would not be able or willing to shoulder the burden of the expense.[36] Thus, in derivative actions and the other so-called "common fund" cases, shareholders often have a right of recovery of such expenses from the corporation.

Until 1993, the Japanese rule was remarkably different. As in most other civil law countries, the Japanese Code of Civil Procedure (art. 89) dictates that the loser bear the litigation costs of both parties. On its face the rule may have been only mildly ominous. What gave the rule its death knell quality is the amount of litigation fees required to pursue an action in the Japanese courts. To pursue an action, the plaintiff must buy revenue stamps (*inshi*) in an amount fixed by statute and attach them to the complaint. The amount of the stamps required depends solely on the amount of damages that the plaintiff claims.

Though ostensibly for the purpose of preventing frivolous "strike" suits, the actual effect of the pre-1993 Japanese litigation fee rules was to discourage all suits, as can be seen in the following example. Suppose that a shareholder holds 1,000 shares in a firm that has 100 million shares outstanding. The shareholder wants to sue the directors of the corporation for the return of ¥1 billion ($10 million). To bring the action in the court of first instance, the shareholder must buy revenue stamps in the amount of ¥3,117,600 (about $31,000), none of which is recoverable unless the shareholder eventually wins the case. In this example, the shareholder stands to gain a pro rata increase in the value of each of her shares only in the amount of ¥10, or a total gain on her 1,000 shares of ¥10,000 (about $100). Although the fees will be reimbursed if the shareholder wins, it is unlikely that a shareholder will bring an action that requires $24,000 "up front" for a return of only $80. Even worse, if the shareholder should lose, he or she forfeits all the fees for a return of zero, or more likely a negative return, as the shareholder must pay the directors' court costs as well as his or her own attorney's fees. Although the expected gains for a shareholder who holds a high percentage of a company's stock may be higher than in this example, that shareholder still must contemplate the utility of paying the litigation fees "up front."

3. Security for expenses   The requirement that a shareholder–plaintiff post a bond as security for expenses serves no purpose but to limit the number of derivative suits. The Japanese rule, modeled after that of California, allows the court, at the request of the defendant, to order the shareholder–plaintiff to furnish adequate security.[37] This rule requires the plaintiff to furnish security if the defendant can "render credible" the claim that the suit was brought in bad faith (*akui*).[38] Courts, however, have interpreted the rule liberally in favor of the defendant, finding bad faith when the plaintiff knows that the action will harm the director. Delaware has abolished the rule for the obvious reason that it chills both meritorious and nonmeritorious suits alike.

4. Access to information   To bring a derivative action, shareholders must have access to enough relevant information to know that an actionable event has occurred and to what extent that event infringes on their entitlements. The principal mechanisms by which such information is made available in the United States—disclosure subject to the securities laws, review by shareholders on demand, and after the action is filed, discovery—are weaker in Japan, increasing the costs, and thus decreasing the occurrence of derivative actions.

Beyond normal disclosure requirements, shareholders with at least 10 percent (pre-October 1993) or 3 percent (post-October 1993) of the outstanding stock[39] can gain access to financial records of the corporation through the right to inspect books and records delineated in Commercial Code art. 293-6 and the right to have the court appoint an inspector under art. 294. In most cases, however, and especially in large corporations, it is likely that any shareholder with the requisite percentage holdings already has access to any information he might desire, thus making the provision in its current form only mildly helpful. Furthermore, in order to have the court appoint an inspector, the shareholder must first show cause, which can often be shown only if the shareholder had access to the records in the first place.

5. Abuse-of-rights doctrine   Some form of an abuse-of-rights doctrine is present in most civil law systems. Though the nuances differ in different countries, the general theory is that individuals cannot use their legal rights with the sole intent of harming another, without any legitimate benefit accruing to themselves. When such action is taken, such person makes illegal ("abusive") use of his otherwise legal right.

In the derivative action context, the abuse-of-rights doctrine works exclusively to the detriment of shareholder–plaintiffs. The doctrine can be employed only in one context: As a defense by the directors. If the defense fails, the plaintiffs and the directors are still in the original position. If the defense succeeds, the director wins, and even worse, the plaintiffs may be liable for special damages to both the directors and the corporation because of the abuse.

D. Post-1993 Incentives

Among these obstacles, before 1993, the biggest roadblock to shareholder litigation was the filing fee. Before 1993, there was academic debate regarding the proper amount of litigation fees required for a derivative suit. Most scholars argued that the courts were right; fees should be determined by the sliding scale. But some argued that because the amount of damages to be paid to the suing shareholder (not the corporation) was indeterminate, the fee should be fixed at ¥8,200 (about $80), in accordance with a procedural rule that set damages at ¥950,000 in such cases.[40] In the 1993 *Nikkō Securities Case*,[41] the Tokyo High Court agreed with this logic, saving the plaintiff–shareholders approximately $2 million in fees. Several months later, following the Tokyo High Court's logic, the Diet revised the Commercial Code to lower the filing fee for all derivative actions to ¥8,200. It is this Commercial Code revision that marks the watershed in Japanese shareholder derivative litigation. As Table 2.1 shows, following the 1993 revisions, derivative litigation rates increased dramatically. Although plaintiffs and shareholder activists (and for the most part, the media) proclaimed a new age of corporate governance in which managers were responsible to shareholders, many managers complained that the suits were nuisance suits of groundless claims looking for cheap settlement.

Nuisance or not, change came. Corporations purchased directors' and officers' (D & O) liability insurance policies. Legal departments in large companies suddenly wielded new clout.[42] Lawyers invented new methods for giving managers power without putting them on the board, where they would risk liability.[43]

Still, shareholder–plaintiffs face an uphill battle. Shareholders in Japan, as in the United States, often lose because of the business judgment rule. Appropriately

Table 2.1. *Japanese derivative suits*

Year	Pending cases			New cases		
	District Court	High Court	Total	District Court	Tokyo District Court	Osaka District Court
1993	74	10	84	n.a.	18	6
1994	133	12	145	n.a.	35	3
1995	158	16	174	n.a.	22	5
1996	174	14	188	71	16	6
1997	203	16	219	83	36	6
1998	222	18	240	68	22	14
1999	258	28	286	95	30	10

Note: n.a. = not available.

Sources: Cumulative Supreme Court Secretariat data from Daihyō Soshō no Keizoku Kensū [Number of Derivative Suits], 194 Shōji Hōmu Shiryōban 193 (2000). Newly filed cases data officially unpublished, obtained in telephone interview, Supreme Court Secretariat, June 5, 2000. Tokyo District Court data from Hisaki Kobayashi, Tokyo Chisai ni okeru Shōji Jiken no Gaiyō [Outline of Commercial Suits in the Tokyo District Court], 1580 Shōji Hōmu 4 (2000). Osaka District Court data from Mitsuhiro Ikeda, Osaka Chisai ni okeru Shōji Jiken no Gaikyō [Outline of Commercial Litigation in Osaka District Court], 1585 Shōji Hōmu 4, 6 (2001).

or not, Japanese courts, usually composed of career judges with no business experience, are especially reluctant to second-guess the business judgment of directors. In the next section, we examine more precisely plaintiff success rates and other benefits of suit.

III. DIRECT BENEFITS TO SHAREHOLDERS?

Perhaps the easiest way to determine whether benefits accrue to shareholders is to examine success rates in court. To do so, we examined a database of derivative suits filed between 1993 and 1999 and published in the legal journal *Shiryōban Shōji Hōmu*. This database contains seventy-three derivative suits and is the most comprehensive published database available. Of the seventy-three cases listed, only two cases resulted in outright victory for plaintiffs. Only ten cases settled. Twenty cases either were decided for defendants or were withdrawn by the plaintiff in response to an adverse ruling. Forty-one cases were pending at the end of 2000, and only four of those forty-one pending cases were pending because of appeals by defendants of adverse judgments.

Still, despite this overall record, winning plaintiffs might profit from derivative suits. Although damages are paid to the corporation and not directly to shareholders, shareholders might receive direct economic benefits from derivative suits in the form of higher stock prices. Only if prices rise can the compensatory goals of derivative litigation be realized. If derivative litigation raises stock prices sufficiently, plaintiffs might be willing to sue in order to sell their shares later at increased prices.

To examine the potential direct benefits from derivative suits, we conducted several experiments using a modified *Shiryōban Shōji Hōmu* database. To measure stock price benefits, we narrowed down the seventy-three cases to the fifty-six cases filed against Tokyo Stock Exchange companies. Of these fifty-six cases, in two instances, different plaintiff groups filed suit against the same companies on the same date (IBJ and Nomura Securities). Three suits are against companies that have been delisted from the Tokyo Stock Exchange and as such do not have complete stock price data (two against Yamaichi Securities; one against Hokkaido Takushoku Bank). Removing these five suits leaves a total of fifty-one suits in the database. The companies involved in the fifty-one suits were on average larger than average Tokyo Stock Exchange firms.[44]

We performed several empirical tests using this database. First, as Roberta Romano did in her seminal article on U.S. derivative litigation, we used well-established event study methodology to measure the stock price effects of filing suit. In her event study of sixty-six derivative and class actions in the United States, Romano found that the average abnormal return on the day a suit is filed is positive and borderline significant, while the abnormal return of the day before suit is filed is significantly negative. Splitting the sample into derivative suits and class actions revealed that "derivative claims produce no significant impact" on either the day of filing or the preceding day.[45]

Table 2.2 shows the results of an event study of the stock price effects on the filing dates of the fifty-one Japanese firms.[46] The results of our regressions of Japanese firms differ little from Romano's study of U.S. firms: Japanese derivative suits do not result in statistically significant stock price movements. In some ways, this result is unsurprising, as moderate damage payments to a widely dispersed body of shareholders might not be expected to cause large price swings. But the lack of significant price adjustments (and in fact negative measures for all but one day) suggests a stronger claim: Shareholders apparently do not expect to receive gains of any sort or magnitude from filing, whether from awards of damages, from future specific deterrence, or from lawsuit-induced restructuring of corporate governance mechanisms.

In another important empirical study of derivative suits in the United States, Daniel Fischel and Michael Bradley examined the stock price reactions to management motions to dismiss derivative suits, composed of eighteen court-ordered terminations and six non-dismissals. Fischel and Bradley used event

Table 2.2. *Average abnormal returns on lawsuit filings (51 firms)*

Day or event window	Market-adjusted return (%)	z	% Positive
Day before lawsuit filed	−0.112	−0.032754	42.9
Day lawsuit filed	0.0597	0.278872	44.6
Day after lawsuit filed	−0.374	−1.57994	39.3
Day of suit + day after	−0.314	−0.91999	39.3

study data to make the claim that "neither termination nor continuation of a derivative stockholder suit has a significant effect on the wealth of the firm's stockholders."[47]

Again, we conducted a similar event study for Japan to measure the stock price effect of judicial screening. In Japan, the relevant screening mechanism is not the dismissal motion, but the judicial decision of whether to require plaintiffs to post a bond. Because of the expense of posting bond and the nature of the "bad faith" standard, a requirement that the shareholder–plaintiff post a bond is similar to a dismissal in the United States for failure to state a claim upon which relief can be granted pursuant to rule 12(b)(6) of the Federal Rules of Civil Procedure. Our sample contains thirteen separate event dates (for fifteen companies; in two cases the court ruled on two bond motions on the same day) in which the court ruled that plaintiffs were required to post bond and four cases in which the court denied management's motion to require the posting of bond.

The results of decisions not to require plaintiff to post bond have no statistically significant impact, and the sample is quite small in any event. But the results of the bond-required cases are intriguing. Although the day after the court's decision is insignificant, the day of the court's decision is significantly *positive* (average return $= 0.8208$, $z = 2.236$, 76.9 percent positive). In contrast to Bradley and Fischel's results, our calculations thus tentatively suggest that a small increase in shareholder wealth occurs when Japanese courts require plaintiffs to post bond. These results, based as they are on a small sample, are difficult to interpret. Perhaps the market believes that the suits are nuisance suits, and is pleased to be rid of them. Or perhaps given the "bad faith" standard, the market believes that the requiring of a bond is equal to a finding of no liability. Finally, given that the returns are positive on the day of the court decision for the tiny sample of non-dismissal cases, perhaps the market is simply reacting to *any* news regarding the case, regardless of the disposition.

Finally, we looked at final dispositions of cases. Of the fifty-one cases in the sample of Tokyo Stock Exchange firms, twenty-five cases were pending, and only two of those cases were defendants' appeals. Seventeen cases were decided for defendants. Although an examination of the stock price effects of awards to plaintiffs might be probative, plaintiffs won awards in only two cases in the sample, the Hazama political bribery case[48] and the Daiwa Bank illegal trading case. The two-day return in both cases individually and combined was insignificant, but the sample size alone is notable: In only two cases in the entire Tokyo Stock Exchange sample did plaintiffs win, and the Daiwa plaintiffs ultimately accepted a much lower award in settlement of the case during the appeals process. Like their U.S. counterparts, the success rate for shareholder–plaintiffs in court in Japan is, in a word, abysmal.

Because of the lack of final judicial dispositions, we focus on settlements. Only ten firms in the Tokyo Stock Exchange sample reported settlements. Although some cases surely settle quietly, no other cases in the Tokyo Stock Exchange sample were withdrawn in the absence of an adverse judicial ruling, suggesting that settlement truly is rare, at least in suits against directors of large companies. Again, this fact alone is significant. While most suits in the United States settle,[49] most suits in Japan apparently recover nothing. Although many factors can explain the difference (including that most suits are frivolous), one explanation might be that Japanese defendants are better able than U.S. defendants to determine that the expected value to plaintiffs of going to trial is negative, for at least five reasons. First, Japanese courts side with plaintiffs with relative infrequency. Second, the lack of a discovery mechanism creates informational asymmetries in which defendants know much more about the facts than plaintiffs. Third, although the *efficiency* of the Japanese "loser pays" rule is unclear, it at least strengthens the bargaining power of defendants. Fourth, D&O insurance in Japan covers fewer directors and has lower payout caps than in the United States, which may reduce directors' incentives to settle. Finally, the lack of an extensive body of derivative suit case law in Japan may reduce the ability to enter into a settlement in the shadow of the law.

Of the ten settling firms in the sample, we were unable to find a settlement amount for one firm, and removed it. Before examining the stock price effects, it is useful to compare settlement amounts and awards per share. Table 2.3 shows the average amounts per outstanding share that in theory should be gained from a settlement in each case, absent transaction costs.

The settlement data suggest three conclusions. First, cases only settle when directorial conduct is quite severe—apparently bad loans, bribery, bid-rigging, payments to sokaiya, and illegal accounting measures are prerequisites. To break down the fifty-one cases roughly by cause, the directors of every firm in the sample (eight separate suits) accused of paying sokaiya settled. In the four cases of bribery in the sample, two settled, and one was a victory for plaintiffs. One of the two accounting cases ("tobashi" accounting fraud and loss compensation) settled. Two of the five illegal trading cases (both against Daiwa Bank directors) were plaintiff victories in the lower court, but were settled during the appeals process. By contrast, only one of the fifteen cases involving bad loans settled, and in that case the loans were made to a raider with organized crime connections. In only one of the eleven cases involving alleged bad investments or acquisitions did plaintiffs win or obtain settlement. Plaintiffs neither won nor achieved settlement in the two HIV tainted-blood cases, the two labor cases, the lone real estate contract case, or the single nuclear power case.

Second, note the large discrepancy between damages claimed and settlement amounts. Although plaintiffs in the Ajinomoto and Takashimaya cases fared relatively well, on average, plaintiffs settled for less than one-half of 1 percent of damages claimed.

Finally, note the settlement amount per share. In theory, the amounts listed below, when paid by the directors to the relevant firms, should increase the price per share by a figure close to the relevant amounts (minus attorneys' fees paid by the corporation). Per-share recovery in Japan is even lower than it is in the United States—on average, about one-fourth of a cent in Japan (about 0.036 percent of

Table 2.3. *Settlement amounts per share*

Company	Issue	Damages claimed ¥ ($)	Settlement amount ¥ ($)	Stock price ¥ ($)	Settlement amount per share[a] ¥ ($)
Janome Sewing Machine	Bad loans	152 billion (1.52 billion)	2,000,000 (20,000)[b]	146 (1.46)	0.013 ($.00013)
Obayashi	Bribery	290 million (2.9 million)	20,000,000 (200,000)	536 (5.36)	0.027 (0.00027)
Takashimaya	Sokaiya	160 million (1.6 million)	170,000,000 (1,700,000)	1,300 (13.00)	0.545 (0.00545)
Nomura Securities	Sokaiya	828 million (8.28 million)[c]	380,000,000 (3,800,000)	850 (8.50)	0.1935 (0.001)
Ajinomoto	Sokaiya	120 million (1.2 million)	120,000,000 (1,200,000)	1,110 (11.10)	1.50 (0.015)
Hitachi	Bid-rigging	232 million (2.32 million)	100,000,000 (1,000,000)[d]	1,374 (13.74)	0.030 (0.00030)
Dai-Ichi Kangyo Bank	Sokaiya	2.2 billion (22 million)	127,000,000 (1,270,000)	852 (8.52)	0.041 (0.00041)
Cosmo Securities	Accounting	69.8 billion (698 million)	130,000,000 (1,300,000)	275 (2.75)	0.301 (0.00301)
Kajima	Bribery	280 million (2.8 million)	40,000,000 (400,000)	324 (3.24)	0.042 (0.00042)

[a] Calculated using outstanding share data from Toyo Keizai (ed.), Shikiho (1999).
[b] Settlement of only one director, who also agreed to return 6,000 shares.
[c] Consolidation of three suits.
[d] One defendant only.

the stock price), compared to 18¢ (about 2 percent of the stock price) in the United States.[50]

To test whether plaintiffs actually receive such gains, we conducted an event study on the nine firms listed in Table 2.3. The returns for both days were positive, with a two-day increase of 1.16 percent, but statistically insignificant ($t = 1.55$). An increase of 1.16 percent represents an average gain of approximately ¥8 per share, a trivial amount given the size of the firms involved.

The above evidence suggests that plaintiffs have little economic reason to file suit. We found no statistically significant abnormal returns upon filing suit or settlement. In fact, the only statistically significant returns found were those observed when plaintiffs were required to post bond, tentatively suggesting that shareholders find some suits frivolous and wasteful of corporate assets. In addition to the lack of price effects, few settlements occur, and when they occur, pro rata recovery is small.

The event study tests are by no means conclusive. The sample is relatively small and may not be representative of the entire market. The event dates that we examine may not necessarily be the proper period to examine, as investors may have anticipated filings, court opinions, and settlements long before the event window dates. As always, the market is noisy, longer event windows introduce even more noise, it is difficult to assess causation, and the question of what exactly event studies measure is open to debate. Still, using standard statistical methods, our results are relatively similar to those found by both Romano and Fischel and Bradley, suggesting that derivative suits, whether in the United States or Japan, produce few gains, or at least few immediate and direct gains, to shareholders.

IV. SO WHY SUE?

Shareholder litigation in Japan, like shareholder litigation in the United States, does not appear to be motivated by direct benefits to shareholders. But if not, why sue? Even if shareholder litigation results in intangible deterrence benefits, there should be little reason for individual shareholders to sue. In this section, we attempt to unravel the reasons behind Japanese shareholder litigation.

This section is the result of an examination of 140 derivative suits filed between 1993 and 1999. Of these 140 cases, seventy-three are listed in the *Shiryōban Shōji Hōmu* list used in Section III. The remaining sixty-seven cases were not used in the foregoing study because of insufficient stock price data; none of the firms are listed on the Tokyo Stock Exchange. Of these sixty-seven cases, twenty-three are not listed in the database but had published court opinions or other official documents. From attorneys, court offices, and other sources, we obtained briefs and other court records on twenty-nine cases. Through interviews, we gathered information related to fifteen additional cases.

A. Bar Benefits

One potential source of derivative litigation—and the leading cause of such suits in the United States—is plaintiffs' attorneys. If attorneys can win sufficient fee awards, suits will have a net positive value and will proceed regardless of whether plaintiffs directly receive large benefits. So long as an attorney can find a nominal shareholder willing to lend her name to the complaint, suits will be filed.

In Japan, determining exactly what benefits accrue to attorneys in derivative actions is difficult. Most attorneys' fee agreements are separate from settlement agreements and confidential, and there is no Japanese scholarship on this point. In this section, we first describe the basics of the Japanese legal profession and attorney compensation. We then turn to the specifics of attorneys' fees in derivative litigation, first in theory, and then in practice.

1. The market for attorneys   The structure of the Japanese legal profession is easy to summarize. Lawyers are few, most are in Tokyo, and they have a monopoly over most legal services. With half the population of the United States,

Japan has approximately 20,000 licensed attorneys in comparison to their roughly 900,000 American counterparts. This simple numerical comparison is misleading for a variety of reasons that we explore in Chapter 8, but the small number of attorneys in Japan matters in the derivative suit context because only licensed attorneys (and pro se plaintiffs) may bring such suits.

In cartel-like fashion, the Japanese Federation of Bar Associations publishes an attorneys' fee schedule (the "Fee Rules") that is adopted by local bar associations.[51] Attorneys' fees are generally paid by each litigant and have two components: A nonrefundable retainer (*chakushukin*), based on the amount of damages claimed, and a "success fee" (*hōshūkin*) based on the amount of damages actually received. Although not mandatory, many attorneys follow the cartel schedule to the letter, and most fees are reasonably close to the chart.[52] Table 2.4 shows the range of these fees established in the Fee Rules.

Consider how the Fee Rules would apply if the eight settled cases in the Tokyo Stock Exchange data set (see Table 2.3 above) went to court. In those cases, the average amount claimed was about ¥28 billion ($280 million), and the average damages award was ¥131 million (about $1.3 million). Pursuant to the Fee Rules, assuming that the base amounts are not considered "indeterminate" to the filing shareholder, the average retainer would have been ¥564 million (about $5.6 million), and the success fee approximately ¥12.6 million (about $126,000), for a total average fee of about $5.7 million. This figure suggests that *if* an attorney follows the Fee Rules, and *if* the court awards fees accordingly, compensation is lower than in the United States,[53] but is not trivial.

But also consider how the Fee Rules would apply in *all* cases, not just the settled ones. According to our calculations, the average amount of damages claimed in the fifty-one cases in the dataset is ¥39.32 billion, or about $400 million. If Japanese attorneys applied the Fee Rules to this amount, their average retainer—the fee that they would receive simply for filing the case, regardless of their success or even their subsequent laziness—would be over $7 million. That

Table 2.4. *Attorneys' fees pursuant to Fee Rules*

Plaintiff's damages	Retainer	Success fee
Up to ¥3 million (about $30,000)	8%	16%
From ¥3 million to ¥30 million (about $30,000–300,000)	5% + ¥90,000 ($900)	10% + ¥180,000 ($1,800)
From ¥30 million to ¥300 million (about $300,000 to $3 million)	3% + ¥690,000 ($6,900)	6% + ¥1,380,000 ($13,800)
Over ¥300 million ($3 million)	2% + ¥3,690,000 ($36,900)	4% + ¥7,380,000 ($73,800)
Indeterminate economic gain = damages fixed at ¥8 million	¥490,000 ($4,900)	¥980,000 ($9,800)

fee would be substantially higher than the average fee *initially* received by attorneys in the United States, who generally are compensated on a contingent basis.

2. Court-awarded derivative suit fees Pursuant to the Commercial Code, attorneys are entitled to a "reasonable amount" of attorneys' fees upon plaintiff's motion. But because of the lack of cases litigated to final judgment even after the 1993 Commercial Code revisions, it is difficult to determine precisely what constitutes a "reasonable amount."[54]

In 1998, the Kobe District Court decided the only case directly on point, *Kōno* v. *Kōno Chemical Co.*[55] In that case, the shareholder–plaintiffs argued that the amount of damages should be based on the Kobe Bar Association's version of the Fee Rules. The court agreed, finding that the appropriate base amount for calculating fees was the amount of damages requested, not "indeterminate" economic gain. The court then held that an amount approximately equal to that stated in the Fee Rules was "reasonable."

3. Settlement practice Settlement practice[56] suggests that attorneys in successful derivative suits are compensated beyond the $14,700 prescribed by the Fee Rules for "indeterminate damages" cases, but perhaps less than the full Fee Rules amounts authorized in the Kobe District Court's decision. The first in-court derivative action settlement was the *Nihon Sunrise* case, in which the parties settled in Tokyo High Court for ¥130 million ($1.3 million).[57]

The settlement agreement provided for attorneys' fees. Plaintiffs' attorneys stated that given the split of opinion regarding fees at the time of the settlement (1994), they were only able to negotiate a reduced total fee of 9 percent, or roughly ¥11.7 million ($117,000).[58] Under the Fee Rules, the retainer alone would have been nearly ¥10 million. Considering that this fee was to be shared among four elite attorneys for several months of work, it is a low amount in comparison both to U.S. fees and to fees that could be earned by those attorneys in Japan in non-derivative actions. Or to put it more bluntly, as the lead attorney in that case told us, "we really didn't make much on that thing at all."[59]

4. What do attorneys actually charge? Anecdotal evidence suggests that in practice, many derivative suit attorneys reduce their retainers. In the *Janome Sewing Machine* case,[60] for instance, in which damages claimed were ¥152 billion ($1.5 billion), attorneys reportedly accepted a retainer of only ¥3 million ($30,000). The retainer under the Fee Rules would have been over ¥3 billion ($30 million).[61] But attorney practice varies widely, and differences in practice and motivation may be observed between elite and non-elite lawyers.

a. Elite attorneys At least one group of attorneys consistently accepts derivative actions on a reduced-retainer basis. Founded in February 1996 and based in Osaka, the Shareholder Ombudsman (*Kabunushi Onbuzuman*) organization consists of about twenty elite lawyers, as well as accountants, academics, and investors. Shareholder Ombudsman has no recognizable equal, and has litigated several of the more high-profile cases in Japan, including actions against directors of Takashimaya Department Store, Sumitomo Corporation, Dai-Ichi Kangyo Bank, Nomura Securities, Yamaichi Securities, Ajinomoto, Japan Airlines, and Kobe Steel.

Shareholder Ombudsman member attorneys informed us that the group does not calculate its fee in accordance with the Fee Rules, choosing instead to charge a retainer of only ¥300,000–500,000 ($3,000–5,000). Although this is still a significant amount for many plaintiffs, the organization has ongoing relationships with several shareholders who regularly lend their names to cases. If the plaintiffs win, the corporation pays the attorneys' fee based on the Fee Rules. A portion of the fees goes to the attorneys involved with the case, but most money flows back to the organization. Although we were unable to gather data on all Shareholder Ombudsman cases, we obtained attorneys' fee amounts for three of the Table 4 settlements: Takashimaya, Ajinomoto, and Obayashi. The average settlement award in those cases was ¥103 million ($1 million), the fee under the fee rules would have been ¥19.17 million ($191,700), and the fee actually paid was ¥11.77 million, a figure representing about 11 percent of the settlement award and about 60 percent of the fee under the rules.[62]

b. Non-elite attorneys At the other end of the spectrum from Shareholder Ombudsman are a small handful—if that many—of attorneys who often are straightforward in their acceptance of derivative cases for reasons that more typically drive shareholder litigation in the United States—attorneys' fees. These attorneys are not elite lawyers like the Shareholder Ombudsman group, an expected result given the fee rule incentives for elite attorneys to take the best and easiest cases. After elite attorneys have taken the best, these non-elite attorneys are often stuck with the low-return, high-risk losers. We determined that only eleven of the 140 cases—besides those litigated by Shareholder Ombudsman elites—involved attorneys who appeared to use the case either for publicity or explicitly for non-discounted attorneys' fees, but that determination is highly subjective and relies mostly on information on reputation gleaned from interviews.

One Japanese attorney, Hideto Iida, has been involved in several large derivative cases, including suits against directors of Green Cross, Nomura Securities, and Sumitomo Corporation, but until recently, he had never won a case. It is possible to ascribe a non-monetary motivation to each of Iida's cases, especially given his low success rate. Consider Iida's statement to the *Wall Street Journal* that in order to find a plaintiff to sue Sumitomo, he "began dialing through his secret list of 10 big investors."[63] Iida might have begun dialing because he is rent-seeking, or because he has a passion for justice. Most observers emphasize the former over the latter; Iida is widely regarded by the media, Japanese corporate executives, and in fact by other attorneys who bring derivative suits as motivated by some combination of attorneys' fees and advertising.

Few attorneys are willing to take the chances that Iida has. But for the attorneys who can identify winners, there apparently is profit to be found here.

If potential profits to attorneys outweigh costs, we might expect attorneys to enter into Coasean transactions in which they award a portion of their fee to the plaintiffs to induce them to sue. We have seen confidential and (and presumably privileged) internal documentation of one case in which the attorneys gave the *plaintiff* approximately $2,000 from the attorneys' fee received from the corporation. Two plaintiffs that we interviewed regarding separate suits also spoke of such arrangements. Although the Commercial Code, the Attorneys' Law, and the Attorneys' Code of Ethics contain no specific prohibition of such a practice, and no disciplinary proceeding record on point exists, the fee-kickback practice does indeed rest on shaky legal ground. Such clandestine practicesarouse our suspicions that perhaps there are more incentives for attorneys and plaintiffs than meets the eye. It would not be surprising in some suits to find hidden economic benefits such as direct payments from directors to plaintiffs or various lawyer–client contingency arrangements.

B. Residual Explanations

Attorney motivations appear to have the greatest explanatory power in analyzing why Japanese shareholders sue. At least four other reasons play supporting roles: Non-monetary motives, sokaiya suits, insurance-settlement motivations, and public enforcement.

1. Non-monetary motives   Some suits appear to reflect little or no obvious individual economic motivation for any party. These suits are motivated by social movements, spite, moral disdain, altruism, fairness, justice, and desire for public vindication.

Perhaps the suits with the clearest non-monetary concerns are those brought by environmental activists. In the *Chubu Electric* case,[64] for instance, shareholders demanded that management pay back to the company ¥200 million ($2 million) that was given to a local fishery association as compensation for future fishing losses to result from the completion of a feasibility study for a nuclear power plant. The anti-nuclear plaintiffs argued that the payment was a bribe, and that there was little prospect of the feasibility study being completed. (The court disagreed.)

Activist cases aside, our interviews suggest three general non-monetary factors at work. First, some plaintiffs expressed anger over corporate scandals. Second, some saw suits as a method of expressing their moral opprobrium and sense of justice. Third, some took pride in their role as corporate cops, and seemed to enjoy contributing to the welfare of others.

It is difficult to assess exactly how many of the cases are linked to such motivations, or to what extent suits with ties to organized citizens' movements are motivated by non-monetary incentives. Some plaintiffs clearly *appear* to be suing for non-monetary reasons (given the data in Section II, many must), and anger can probably explain a residuum of suits in any system.

We interviewed ten individual plaintiffs suing directors of large public corporations. Although the sample is not entirely random, it is useful in sorting out plaintiff and attorney motivations. All ten stated that they were suing for some sort of non-monetary reason, usually to "teach those guys a lesson." Each plaintiff expected to incur no monetary costs, but expected to win or obtain a large settlement (eight of the cases involved criminal action by the director or a related party), and accordingly expected the company to pay their attorneys' fees and the directors to reimburse even their ¥8,200 in filing fees.

Of the ten plaintiffs, two stated that they expected to receive compensation in the form of a distribution from their attorneys—clear monetary incentives. One plaintiff was a large blockholder (suing his brother, no less) who expected to gain from an increase in the value of his shares—again, clear monetary incentives. The remaining seven plaintiffs have no clear monetary incentives. Only one plaintiff of the seven, a retired bank president who was the least forthcoming of our interviewees in volunteering answers, paid a "full price" retainer to his attorney. Four plaintiffs paid reduced retainers to their attorneys, and two paid no retainer at all. Each of these six plaintiffs told us that he would not have paid full price, and one explicitly offered this underlying reasoning: "I may be angry, but I'm not stupid. The only one who will profit here is my attorney, and he is in charge. I get no profit, and I have no say. I want those guys to pay, but I'm just along for the ride."

Other plaintiffs and attorneys made similar statements that suggest the dominant role of attorney incentives. One prominent attorney told us before our plaintiff interviews started,

Of course, they'll all tell you that they're suing because they want justice. Most of them actually do want justice, but who doesn't? We all want justice. Of course I coach them to make those statements to the media and so on, but most of them believe it anyway . . . The truth is that justice or no justice, attorneys want winning cases, and if they can't get a winner, they'll take what's left.

It is difficult to assess *conclusively* whether these ten suits proceeded because of anger, attorney incentives, or some combination of both. In three of the ten cases, plaintiffs had monetary motives, but the blockholder case surely is a rare one. In seven of the ten cases, plaintiffs had no monetary incentive to sue. The evidence presented earlier in this section strongly suggests the existence of attorney incentives, and plaintiff and attorney statements support that evidence. Given the interview evidence, the more tangible nature of attorney incentives, and a necessarily subjective judgment about the sincerity (or more accurately, the lack thereof) of the emotions expressed by some the plaintiffs whom we interviewed, we find a dominant role for attorney incentives to be more plausible in the majority of cases than the evidence for plaintiff non-monetary motivations.

2. *Sokaiya* A *sokaiya* (literally, "general meeting operator") is usually a nominal shareholder who either attempts to extort money from a company's managers

by threatening to disrupt its annual shareholders' meeting with embarrassing or hostile questions, or who works for a company's management to suppress dissent at the meeting. As we discuss in Chapter 5, sokaiya have historically flourished in Japan because the structure of Japanese corporate law and governance institutions lead to low levels of corporate disclosure. With the lowering of filing fees in 1993, a few sokaiya branched out to derivative suits as a form of business.

Perhaps the most famous of these "derivative-suit sokaiya" is the former sokaiya labeled in court opinions with the pseudonym "Akira Suzuki."[65] As the defendant directors in the Tokai Bank case explained in their motion to cause Suzuki to post a bond, "Due care must be given to the fact that the lowering of filing fees leads to shareholders who bring derivative suits for personal gain, derivative suits by those who hold grudges, and demonstration derivative suits by 'occupational special shareholders' (so-called sokaiya)."[66] In another derivative suit brought by Suzuki against the directors of Tokyo-Mitsubishi Bank, the court noted in its granting of plaintiffs' bond motion that Suzuki "has filed seven corporate suits, and in each of them he has either lost, withdrawn the suit, or lost the case when he refused to post bond; he does not have a single sincere lawsuit."[67]

It is unclear exactly how many sokaiya-related suits have been brought. The number appears to be relatively small; even the seven suits cited by the court as being brought by Suzuki do not appear to all be derivative suits. Of the 140 cases that we examined, ten appeared to have some sokaiya link.

Sokaiya whom we interviewed stated that while there is little *direct* profit in derivative suits (especially because they must chance civil liability for bringing frivolous claims), the lowering of filing fees has increased the credibility of their threats to file suit and to use the court as a public forum for sharing sensitive corporate information. Because of high response costs, corporations sometimes pay to rid themselves of nuisance suits. Because of the danger of public release of information, some corporations apparently pay for silence. These threats and settlements never become public documents, but can help sokaiya reap significant rewards.

3. Insurance   Japanese D&O liability insurance has gone from being unheard of to being widely used. In 1994, 400 companies had policies, an increase of 500 percent from 1993.[68] By 1999, 70–80 percent of listed companies were said to have policies, most in aggregate amounts of ¥100–500 million ($1–5 million), including all but three of the firms in our Tokyo Stock Exchange sample.[69] Because of relatively low risk in Japan, premiums are relatively low compared to the United States. According to the *Nihon Keizai Shinbun* newspaper in 1993

For companies listed in the second section of the Tokyo Stock Exchange, for coverage of ¥1 billion [$10 million], the premiums are generally only in the millions of yen ($ tens of thousands). If you consider this as a per-executive cost, the cost is about the same as the annual insurance premiums on a luxury car. For large firms in the first section, for coverage of ¥1 billion, even including their subsidiaries, the premium is only in the ten millions.[70]

Even in 1999, the per-executive annual cost of insurance is said to be ¥200,000–300,000 ($2,000–3,000). Still, because of the increase in the numbers of policies written, D&O insurance is increasingly profitable, with gross premiums rising from ¥1.7 billion ($17 million) in 1993 to ¥4.8 billion ($48 million) in 1997.[71]

Because of the increased prevalence of insurance, directors might face a moral hazard problem, and consequently commit more punishable acts. But note that while the number of polices written has skyrocketed, the *amounts* of coverage, at least pre-*Daiwa*, have remained relatively trivial, suggesting that insurance has not led to more punishable acts. Most Japanese companies also attempt to mitigate moral hazard problems by requiring directors to contribute personally a percentage of the premium (not necessarily an odious requirement if compensation is raised accordingly).

The increased prevalence of insurance might also suggest that plaintiffs are more willing to bring suits against management because settlements will be more forthcoming from insurance companies than they would be from individuals. While there may be some truth to this, if it were a widespread motivation, we might expect to see many more settlements than we currently observe.

4. Public and private enforcement A final factor enters the calculus of plaintiffs and attorneys when deciding whether to bring suits: Government enforcement, often in the form of criminal prosecution. In many cases, derivative suits "piggyback" on such enforcement actions. Government enforcement actions are an integral part of the calculus of plaintiffs and attorneys when deciding to bring suit.

Before the 1990s, shareholders wishing to sue faced an uphill battle in gathering information about defendants' conduct. Information disclosure is not terribly abundant, shareholder rights to view corporate records are predicated on the holder having at least 3 percent of the shares, cause must be shown to appoint an outside inspector, and pretrial discovery is nonexistent. Before international competition crept into Japan, this sort of arrangement, in which directors had great leeway in decisionmaking, was socially acceptable and even considered by some to be good business practice. But with growing international competition, the system was difficult to sustain politically, socially, and economically.

Beginning in the early 1990s, after the bursting of the Japanese real estate and stock market bubble that characterized the late 1980s, and with an influx of foreign business underway, prosecutors began aggressively to pursue individual wrongdoers in the corporate context. With increased criminal enforcement and public announcements of state-gathered evidence, potential shareholder–plaintiffs were able to gather more information about corporate activities, and specifically management misdeeds, than they had in the past. In effect, prosecutorial subpoena and investigative powers became a substitute for the lack of effective means of information gathering by shareholders.

Prosecutors became especially active in pursuing sokaiya rabble-rouser payment cases, securities violations, and, eventually, tainted-blood HIV cases.[72] Not coincidentally, the derivative suits brought against directors of large public corporations tend to raise the same common issues: "securities scandals, the construction contracting industry (bribery and bid-rigging scandals), payments to sokaiya to keep corporate secrets, tainted-blood HIV cases, and other large corporate scandals."[73] Once the prosecutors have obtained a guilty verdict, derivative suit settlement should be relatively easy: Plaintiffs use evidence gathered by the state, defendants often cave, and the judiciary, having found guilt in a criminal case, is unlikely to reach a different verdict in a civil case. Because prosecutors have a 99.9 percent success rate,[74] many plaintiffs simply initiate suit when the indictment is filed.

Increased prosecutorial action reduced the transaction costs to shareholders of identifying potential winning cases for derivative suits. If an attorney can identify a potential winner with some certainty, he may be more likely to forgo the retainer. Prosecutors help attorneys and plaintiffs pick these potential winners and avoid lemons.

Perhaps the best empirical evidence of a causal relation between public and private enforcement is a direct examination of the cases. Of the 140 cases that we examined, we were able to identify twenty in which criminal penalties were imposed, twenty involving pending criminal cases, and another thirteen in which the action in question was the subject of some sort of official investigation. In fifty of these fifty-three cases, criminal enforcement preceded civil enforcement. In the nine cases discussed in Section III in which plaintiffs recovered damages (one victory and eight settlements), all but one case involved criminal activity. In fact, because derivative litigation institutions are relatively weak in the absence of criminal wrongdoing, some commentators state—and our evidence at least suggests—that plaintiffs may *only* be successful in cases in which prosecutors go forward. As a prominent attorney writes, "Because the courts as a general rule hold that even mistaken business judgments will not be questioned in the absence of illegal acts, in judicial cases involving listed companies, the only shareholders who have litigated successfully have been those whose directors committed illegal acts."[75]

It could be that the increase in public and private enforcement are both caused by the same phenomenon: Increased managerial misdeeds during the bubble economy years. Although an increase in managerial misdeeds over the period may have occurred, we found that in practice, private action tends to follow prosecutorial action, and not the other way around. Civil suits are often filed immediately after the prosecutor indicts.[76] As one attorney told us, "I would only bring an action if the prosecutors acted first. That gives me a good chance of winning; without it, I have a good chance only of losing." The leading Japanese corporate law journal's editorial department echoes these sentiments, stating that by 1999, "[i]t is becoming normal for parties to reach a settlement agreement after the defendants have been found guilty in a criminal proceeding—probably because after it's clear that there is a violation of the law, it's useless to fight."[77]

To attempt to examine empirically the relationship between prosecutorial action and derivative litigation on a broader scale, we compared the prosecution and judicial disposition of white-collar crimes in Japan with Japanese derivative litigation rates. Because there are no reliable categorical data on "white-collar crime," we constructed two indexes using data on indictments and court cases. The Ministry of Justice publishes *Annual Report of Statistics on Prosecution*, which contains data on the number of criminal indictments by category. The Supreme Court General Secretariat similarly publishes *Annual Report of Judicial Statistics*, containing data on court cases. Using these sources, we examined data on indictments and court cases for three categories of offenses for the period 1988–98: "Civil" laws including the Commercial Code and the Bankruptcy Law, securities laws, and banking laws. The data are not comprehensive. They do not include, for instance, bribery of public officials or garden-variety embezzlement, which are covered by the Penal Code but are, nevertheless, crimes in which plaintiff–shareholders would be likely to have an interest. Still, they give a relatively accurate picture of the kinds of criminal actions in which shareholders normally would be interested and which are generally included in Japanese studies of white-collar crime:[78] Commercial Code violations (including payments to sokaiya, special embezzlement, receipt or demand of a bribe, and excessive issuance of shares), securities fraud, and banking fraud.

Our results can be quickly summarized. For almost every category of white-collar crime, both in terms of indictments and court cases, the 1993–98 annual average figures are substantially higher than the 1988–93 figures. The total figures for the post-1993 period are more than 60 percent higher for both indictments (226 compared to 361) and court cases (forty-four compared to seventy-nine) than the pre-1993 period.

Due care should be exercised in interpreting these data, as they are quite crude. But while it is impossible to show a direct causal relationship between public and private enforcement rates, the general statistics are consistent with the theory and the direct evidence, as the derivative action increase correlates with increases in criminal indictments and court cases not only in each individual category, but across both white-collar crime measures. The prosecution story is further supported by the fact that derivative litigation increased slightly even *before* the 1993 reduction of filing fees, while prosecution in that period rose as well.

CONCLUSION

Corporate governance in Japan is a product of formal and informal rules that shape the structure and monitoring of firms. In the postwar period, the law has sometimes been overshadowed by highly developed nonlegal institutions. Yet, as this chapter has shown, corporate actors are highly attuned to the legal environment. The rules for derivative suits matter. Make such suits expensive, and few shareholders will use this particular mechanism to monitor management (or even to extract rents from the firm). Lower the cost of filing suit, and Japanese shareholders (and their attorneys) will sue with greater frequency, even if their motives for doing so appear to be mixed.

The contribution of derivative suits to corporate governance, of course, is a separate, and controversial matter. In Japan, as in the United States, shareholders appear to receive few direct gains from derivative litigation. Rather, attorneys' fees, even in a system with very different fee structures than those of the United States, appear to drive most shareholder litigation in Japan. To be sure, some additional factors are helpful in explaining the cases. Plaintiffs and attorneys typically have multiple motivations, and a residuum of anger, spite, altruism, fairness, and justice appears in Japan as elsewhere. Sokaiya rabble-rousers sometimes bring losing suits to harass managers into paying blackmail. Some suits may be made more likely by the existence of D&O insurance. And public enforcement institutions help plaintiffs and attorneys avoid lemons: To find winning cases, plaintiffs and their attorneys initiate suit against indicted managers.

NOTES

1. Shareholder suits against directors can be divided into two types: Derivative and direct. Direct actions may be brought against the corporation or its directors by a shareholder for an alleged wrong that affects the shareholder directly. Any damages awarded accrue directly to the shareholders who bring the suit. In the United States, direct actions can be brought by shareholders either on their own behalf or on behalf of a class. In Japan, although the direct action is available, the class action is not.
2. See Roberta Romano, The Shareholder Suit: Litigation Without Foundation?, 7 J. L. Econ. & Org. 55, 58 (1991).
3. See Daihyō Soshō no Keizoku Kensō, 194 Shōji Hōmu Shiryōban 193 (2000).
4. *Nishimura* v. *Yasui*, Osaka District Court, 199 Shiryōban Shōji Hōmu 264 (Judgment of Sept. 20, 2000). For a summary translation, see Tsuyoshi Yamada, The Daiwa Bank Case, 15 Colum. J. Asian L. 193 (2002).
5. 488 A.2d 858 (Del. 1985).
6. John C. Coffee, The Unfaithful Champion: The Plaintiff as Monitor in Shareholder Litigation, 48 L. & Contemp. Prob. 5 (1985); Romano, *supra* note 2.
7. See, for example, William E. Nelson, Contract Litigation and the Elite Bar in New York City, 1960–1980, 39 Emory L.J. 413, 460 (1990) ("business litigiousness" as seen in derivative suits as part of American cultural litigiousness); Anthony Borden, The Shareholder Suit Charade, Am. Law., Dec. 67 (1989).
8. John O. Haley, Consensual Governance: A Study of Law, Culture, and the Political Economy of Postwar Japan, in 3 The Political Economy of Japan: Cultural and Social Dynamics 32, 38 (Shumpei Kumon and Henry Rosovsky eds., 1992).
9. Lester N. Salwin, The New Commercial Code of Japan: Symbol of Gradual Progress Toward Democratic Goals, 50 Geo. L.J. 478, 487 (1962).
10. The 1933 Illinois Business Corporation Act was by most accounts, "a landmark statute" and "the most modern of state statutes." William H. Painter, Introduction: Symposium on the 1983 Illinois Business Corporation Act, 1985 U. Ill. L. Rev. 635, 635 (1985); Charles W. Murdock, Why Illinois? A Comparison of Illinois and Delaware Corporate Jurisprudence, 19 S. Ill. U. L.J. 1, 1 (1994).
11. A major exception is the institution of statutory auditor (*kansayaku*). The statutory auditor is a distinctly Japanese corporate organ with roots in the German Aufsichtsrat. Pursuant to Commercial Code revisions passed May 22, 2002, corporations may eliminate

the statutory auditor if in its place they establish board nominating, compensation, and audit committees (each of which has three or more members) and make outside directors a majority of each.

12. Like corporate law, Japan's principal securities statute, the Securities Exchange Law (SEL) is also closely modeled after the US federal securities laws. Like the U.S. laws on which they are based, the SEL and related securities regulations emphasize investor protection and corporate disclosure. An independent enforcement agency modeled after the US Securities and Exchange Commission was established during the Occupation, although it was disbanded a short time later.

13. Directors are elected to the board at the general meeting of shareholders. Commercial Code art. 254(1). The board must consist of three members, id. art. 255, who serve terms of not more than two years, id. art. 256(1).

14. Under the Commercial Code, directors' conduct is governed by a duty of care, defined in relation to the Civil Code's mandate principles as the "care of a good manager," Commercial Code art. 254(3); Civil Code art. 644, and a duty of loyalty, Commercial Code art. 254-3. Japanese courts and scholars disagree over whether the duties of care and loyalty are coterminous or distinct. These duties are supplemented by duties to avoid both self-dealing, Commercial Code art. 265, and competition with the corporation, Commercial Code art. 264.

15. Commercial Code art. 232-2 (shareholder proposals); Commercial Code arts. 264, 265, 266 (interested director transactions).; SEL art. 194 (proxy rules); Kabushiki kaisha no kansa nado ni kansuru shōhō no tokurei ni kansuru hōritsu [Law for Special Exceptions to the Commercial Code Concerning Audits, etc. of Joint Stock Companies], Law No. 22 of 1974, art. 21-2 and 21-3 (proxy rules).

16. SEL arts. 1, 166, 164, 24, 2405, 24-5(3), 193-2, 27-2 to 27-22.

17. Adolf A. Berle, Jr. and Gardiner C. Means, The Modern Corporation and Private Property (1932).

18. Hugh Patrick, The Relevance of Japanese Finance and its Main Bank System, in The Japanese Main Bank System 353, 359 (Masahiko Aoki and Hugh Patrick eds., 1994).

19. Paul Sheard, The Main Bank System and Corporate Monitoring and Control in Japan, 11 J. Econ. Behavior 399 (1989).

20. See Masahiko Aoki et al., The Japanese Main Bank System: An Introductory Overview, in The Japanese Main Bank System, *supra* note 18, at 7.

21. See Stephen D. Prowse, Institutional Investment Patterns and Corporate Financial Behavior in the United States and Japan, 27 J. Fin. Econ. 43 (1990).

22. The main bank also provided a range of services to its clients that in other economies would be performed by investment banks, venture capitalists, and credit rating agencies. The main bank also performed a signaling function analogous to that of a credit rating agency, as prospective creditors relied on the main bank's superior information in determining whether to extend credit to a particular firm. James E. Hodder and Adrian E. Tschoegl, Corporate Finance in Japan, in Japanese Capital Markets: New Developments in Regulations and Institutions 133, 140 (Shinji Takagi ed., 1993).

23. See Keizai Hakusho [White Paper on the Economy] 231 (Keizai Kikakuchō ed., 1992).

24. Kunio Ito, M&A to kabushiki mochiai no honshitsu [M&A and the Essence of Cross-Shareholding], Kin'yū Ja-naru, Dec. 1989, at 11.

25. Frank K. Upham, Law and Social Change in Postwar Japan 203–4 (1987).

26. Corporate Governance Comm., Corporate Governance Forum of Japan, Corporate Governance Principles–A Japanese View 49 (1998).

27. William M. Mercer Companies LLC, Torishimariyaku Inobeishon [Director Innovation] 20–1 (1999). A study by Steven Kaplan found that Japanese firms had a median of twenty-one directors, while US firms had a median of fifteen. Steven N. Kaplan and J. Mark Ramseyer, Those Japanese Firms with Their Disdain for Shareholders: Another Fable for the Academy, 74 Wash. U. L.Q. 403, 410 (1996).
28. The Skies Are Darkening over Japan's Big Bank Mergers, The Economist, May 27, 2000, at 75.
29. Commercial Code, unamended 1899 provisions, art. 178 (renumbered and revised in 1938 reforms as Shoho, unamended 1938 provisions, art. 267), reprinted in Kyūhōrei Shū [Old Laws and Ordinances] 329 (1968). See Masahiro Kitazawa, Kabunushi no Daihyō Soshō [Shareholder Derivative Actions], in 6 Shinpan Chūshaku Kaishahō [Company Law Commentary], New Edition 354, 355 (Akio Takeuchi et al. eds., 1987).
30. US Dept. of State, Report of the Mission on Japanese Combines, in 14 Far Eastern Series 22 (1946).
31. For Delaware, see *Grobow* v. *Perot*, 539 A.2d 180 (Del. 1988); for Japan, Commercial Code art. 196.
32. Commercial Code art. 267(1). In contrast to the complicated demand rules developed by the Delaware courts, Japan requires universal demand. See, for example, *Grimes* v. *Donald*, 673 A.2d 1207 (Del. 1996) (Delaware); American Law Institute, Principles of Corporate Governance: Analysis and Recommendations § 7.03 (ALI); Commercial Code art. 267 (Japan).
33. The seminal case for this approach is *Lindy Bros. Builders* v. *American Radiator & Standard Sanitary Corp.*, 487 F.2d 161 (3d Cir. 1973).
34. *Sugarland Indus., Inc.* v. *Thomas*, 420 A.2d 142, 150 (Del. 1980).
35. See John C. Coffee, Jr., Understanding the Plaintiff's Attorney: The Implications of Economic Theory for Private Enforcement of Law Through Class and Derivative Actions, 86 Colum. L. Rev. 669, 712 (1986).
36. Robert C. Clark, Corporate Law 659 (1986).
37. Commercial Code art. 267(4). The bond is paid to the corporation if the suit proves to be unmeritorious. A plaintiff may also be required to post a bond if he has no office or domicile in Japan. Civil Code art. 107(1).
38. Commercial Code arts. 267(5) and 106(2).
39. After an amendment to the Commercial Code in 2001, the threshold for access to books and records is 3% of voting rights, rather than outstanding stock.
40. See, for example, Akira Kawatani, Minji Soshōhō Inshi no Kenkyū [A Study of Civil Litigation Revenue Stamps] 78 (1962). The relevant law is Minji Soshō Hiyō Tō ni Kansuru Hōritsu [Law Concerning Civil Litigation Costs], Law No. 40 of 1974, art. 4(2).
41. *Asai* v. *Iwasaki*, Tokyo District Court, 797 Hanrei Times 382 (Aug. 11, 1992), rev'd, Tokyo High Court, 823 Hanrei Times 131 (Mar. 30, 1993).
42. Hideaki Kubori and Naoto Nakamura, Kabunushi Daihyō Soshō to Yakuin no Sekinin [Shareholder Derivative Suits and Officer Liablity] 188 (1993).
43. See Shōji Hōmu Kenkyūkai, Shikkō Yakuin Saido ni Kansuru Anke-to Shūkei Kekka [Composite Results of Poll Regarding Executive Officer System], 182 Shiryōban Shōji Hōmu 26 (1999)(finding adoption by forty-five of sixty-three responding companies of 140 polled); Shikkō Yakuin Dōnyū Kasoku [Acceleration of Introduction of Executive Officer System], Nihon Keizai Shinbun, June 25, 1999, at 3 (179 companies adopted).
44. In millions of yen, assets of sample firm 11,867,884, assets of average Tokyo Stock Exchange firm 1,126,664; total capitalization of sample firm 619,763, total capitalization

of average TSE firm 133,458; sales of sample firm 2,491,933; sales of average TSE firm 480,664. TSE listing requirements require four million listed shares, ¥1 billion in shareholders' equity, and a minimum of 800 shareholders.

45. Romano, *supra* note 2, at 67. See also Sanjai Bhagat et al., The Shareholder Wealth Implications of Corporate Lawsuits, Fin. Management, Winter 1998, at 5 (finding negative returns on filing date when corporation is defendant, but not in corporate governance suits); Mark L. Cross et al., The Impact of Directors and Officers' Liability Suits on Firm Value, 45 J. Risk & Ins. 128 (1989) (finding negative impact on firm value from suit).

46. We use standard event study methodology, with market model parameter estimates measured 240 days beginning 300 days before the event date, and a two-day window. See Ronald J. Gilson and Bernard S. Black, The Law and Finance of Corporate Acquisitions 204 (2d ed. 1995); Stephen J. Brown and Jerold B. Warner, Using Daily Stock Returns: The Case of Event Studies, 14 J. Fin. Econ. 3 (1985). We experimented with several other methodologies, including adding industry controls, adjusting the market model to include periods after the event window, and controlling for window variance.

47. Daniel R. Fischel and Michael Bradley, The Role of Liability Rules and the Derivative Suit in Corporate Law: A Theoretical and Empirical Analysis, 71 Cornell L. Rev. 261, 280–1 (1986).

48. *Matsumura* v. *Otsuru* (The Hazama Case), Tokyo District Court, 130 Shiryōban Shōji Hōmu 94 (Dec. 22, 1994).

49. Romano, *supra* note 2, at 60; see also Thomas M. Jones, An Empirical Examination of the Resolution of Shareholder Derivative and Class Action Lawsuits, 60 Boston U. L. Rev. 542, 545 (1980) (most suits result in some recovery for shareholders).

50. See Romano, *supra* note 2, at 62. Japanese firms, including all firms in the settling sample, frequently trade in minimum units of 1,000 shares. Occasionally securities houses repackage the expensive shares as covered warrants, or "mini-stocks" for small investors, but stockholder rights do not attach. Because of the unit share system, per-shareholder gain in Japan may be higher.

51. Nichibenren, Hōshū Tō Kijun Kitei [Regulations Concerning The Standards for Attorneys' Fees, etc.], Oct. 1, 1995 (hereinafter Fee Rules).

52. Although empirical data on fee practices are lacking, many attorneys are said to charge a retainer of about 10% and a success fee of about 15%, except in cases with very high damages. See Songai Baishōgaku Santei Kijun [Standards for Computation of Damages] 14 (Tokyo San Bengoshikai Kōtsu Jiko Shori Iinkai ed., 1993); Zensuke Ishimura and Yuriko Kaminaga, Attorneys and Cases Involving Automobile Accidents, 9 Law in Japan 83, 106–8 (1976).

53. See Janet C. Alexander, Do the Merits Matter? A Study of Settlements in Securities Class Actions, 43 Stan. L. Rev. 497, 541 (1991); Romano, *supra* n. 2, at 63 (20–30%).

54. See Shinsaku Iwahara et al., Zadankai, Kabunushi Daihyō Soshō Seido to Zaizen to Kongo no Mondaiten [Roundtable, Improvement of the Shareholder Derivative Suit Mechanism and Future Problems], 1329 Shōji Hōmu 4, 17–18 (1993).

55. *Kōno* v. *Kōno Chemical Co.*, Kobe District Court, 1674 Hanrei Jihō 156 (Judgment of Oct. 1, 1998).

56. Japanese law does not require judicial approval of settlements or notice to shareholders of settlement. See generally Tatsuo Ikeda and Masahiro Nakagawa, Kabunushi Daihyō Soshō ni Okeru Wakai [Settlement of Derivative Actions], 1062 Jurisuto 66 (1995).

57. *Yoshitake* v. *Todani* (Nihon Sunrise Case), Tokyo District Court, 1354 Shōji Hōmu 134 (Judgment of Mar. 31, 1994); *Yoshitake* v. *Todani* (Nihon Sunrise Case), Tokyo High Court, 1480 Hanrei Jihō 154 (Judgment of Sept. 21, 1993).

58. Naoya Endō et al., Nihon Sanraizu Kabunushi Daihyō Soshō Jiken no Ichiban Hanketsu to Wakai [Nihon Sunrise Derivative Suit First Judgment and Settlement], 1363 Shōji Hōmu 51, 61–2 (1994).

59. Interview with Naoya Endō, Nov. 11, 1999. Unfortunately, public settlement agreements such as this one are rare. We examined twelve reported settlement agreements and found no mention of attorneys' fees other than an occasional general provision as to which party was to bear "litigation costs." For whatever reason, attorneys apparently prefer to have attorneys' fee arrangements documented in separate agreements that are not readily available.

60. *Suzuki* v. *Yasuda* (Janome Sewing Machine Case), Tokyo District Court, 125 Shiryōban Shōji Hōmu 184 (Judgment of July 8, 1994).

61. Mitsue Aizawa et al., Zadankai, Kabunushi Daihyō Soshō no Tetsuzukihōteki Kentō [Roundtable on Examination of Shareholder Derivative Suit Procedural Law], 1062 Jurisuto 8, 15 (1995) (statement of Mitsue Aizawa).

62. The relation of fees paid to fees under the Fee Rules was not uniform; while the Ajinomoto settlement was exactly as dictated by the Fee Rules, Obayashi was lower, and Takashimaya was higher (based largely on the fact that the defendants agreed to a higher settlement award than damages initially claimed to include newly incurred damages).

63. Robert Steiner, A Legal Gadfly Goes After Sumitomo, Wall Street Journal, June 26, 1996, at A15.

64. *Nakagawa* v. *Matsunaga* (Chubu Electric Power Co. Case), Nagoya High Court, 169 Shiryōban Shōji Hōmu 240 (Judgment of Nov. 17, 1999).

65. The name "Akira Suzuki" is somewhat similar to "John Doe" in the United States. Pseudonyms are commonly used by private case reporters when editors believe that the facts of the case are sensitive.

66. Motion of Defendants, Oct. 18, 1993, *Suzuki* v. *Itō* (Tokai Bank Case), Nagoya District Court, in 175 Bessatsu Shōji Hōmu 450, 452 (1995).

67. *Suzuki* v. *Ifu* (Tokyo-Mitsubishi Bank Case), Tokyo District Court, 196 Bessatsu Shōji Hōmu 322, 324 (Judgment of June 25, 1996).

68. Kiyoshi Kitagawa, Kabunushi Daihyō Shoshō: Torishimariyaku no Sekinin Seido no Genjō to Kadai [Shareholder Derivative Suits: The Current State of Director Liability], 1397 Shōji Hōmu 27, 32 (1995).

69. Hideaki Kubori et al., Torishimariyaku no Sekinin [Director Liability] 71 (1999); Kyogaku Baishō, Bōei e Kigyō Hashiru [Companies Run to Defenses Following Huge Damage Award], Nihon Keizai Shinbun, Oct. 23, 2000, at 5.

70. Kabunushi no Hanran 56 (Nihon Keizai Shinbun ed. 1993); see also Kabunushi Daihyō Soshō to Kaisha Yakuin Baishō Sekinin Hoken no Kaisetsu [Commentary on Shareholder Derivative Suits and D&O Insurance] 21 (Mitsui Kaijō Kasai Hoken Kabushiki Kaisha ed., 1994) (Mitsui Marine & Fire Insurance publication listing annual premiums of ¥500,000 for an entire board of twenty directors, or ¥25,000 ($250) per director). Note that these amounts are far lower than the damages awarded in the Daiwa case (¥83 billion). Coverage limits in 2000 were said to be in the range of ¥2–3 billion. See Daiwagin Kabunushi Daihyō Soshō, Chisai Hanketsu, [District

Court Judgment in Daiwa Bank Derivative Suit], Nihon Keizai Shinbun, Sept. 21, 2000, at 3.

71. Kubori et al., *supra* n. 70, at 71.
72. See, for example, Osamu Sakuma, Kooporeeto Gabanansu to Keijihō [Corporate Governance and Criminal Law], 1542 Shōji Hōmu 23 (1999). As Eric Feldman notes, the decision to prosecute in the HIV cases was spurred on by other civil actions. Eric A. Feldman, The Ritual of Rights in Japan: Law, Society and Health Policy 128 (2000).
73. See Toshikazu Suenaga, Kooporeeto Gananansu to Kenzensei Kakuho [Corporate Governance and Securing Stability], 1542 Shōji Hōmu 14, 19 (1999).
74. See J. Mark Ramseyer and Eric B. Rasmusen, Why is the Japanese Conviction Rate so High?, 30 J. Legal Stud. 53, 55 (2001).
75. Hideaki Kubori, Kachō Kurasu no Chikara o Ikaseru Nihonkei no Kigyō Tōji o Kangaeyō [Let's Think about a Japanese-style Corporate Governance System that is Invigorated by the Power of Middle Management], 898 Nikkei Bus. 43, 45 (July 7, 1997).
76. This fact may help explain why the filing of a derivative suit has little impact on stock returns, as the market may have already incorporated such information into the price.
77. Henshūbu, '99nen Shōji Hōmu Hairaito: Kigyō Hōmu ni totte Kotoshi ha Donna Toshi datta no ka? [1999 Corporate Law Highlights: What Sort of Year was this for Corporate Legal Practice?], 1547 Shōji Hōmu 15, 20 (1999).
78. See, for example, Kuniji Shibahara, Keizai Keihō [The Law of Economic Crime] (2000).

3

Venture Capital

INTRODUCTION

"Corporate governance" usually refers to the rather narrow, if important, agency problem on which we focused in Chapter 2: Monitoring and disciplining corporate management. But corporate governance institutions have far broader impact. Among other things, they help condition the climate for entrepreneurship and the growth of new firms.

Today, the economic importance of funding entrepreneurs is largely taken for granted. One commentator calls the venture capital market and firms financed by it "among the crown jewels of the American economy."[1] Just a few years ago, however, the preoccupation with agency problems blinded scholars and policy-makers to some potentially critical shortcomings in the Japanese institutional framework for corporate governance. Through the first half of the 1990s, for example, many scholars implied that Japan's corporate governance institutions were superior to those of the United States, because monitoring by concentrated shareholders, particularly large and powerful financial institutions, helped solve agency problems better than the dispersed-shareholder–weak-financial-institution model prevalent in the United States. Even to this day, despite the importance of entrepreneurial finance, few attempts have been made to assess corporate governance systems in terms of their ability to encourage and fund economic innovation and to promote corporate adaptability.

In this chapter, we explore the linkage between corporate governance and innovation by comparing the institutional environments for venture capital in the United States and Japan. We draw a link between corporate governance institutions and the vitality of venture capital markets. We examine data that show both quantitative and qualitative differences between the venture capital markets in the United States and Japan, and explain the differences as a function of distinct corporate governance traits in the two countries. Ultimately, we conclude that the venture capital market in Japan has been constrained by the very features of Japanese corporate governance that, until fairly recently, were viewed with envy by commentators focusing narrowly on agency costs and monitoring management.

We isolate five traits of the institutional environment for corporate governance that contribute to the success of the U.S. venture capital market: The existence of large, independent sources of venture capital funding, liquidity, highly developed legal and contractual incentive structures, labor mobility, and risk tolerance. We show that these traits are relatively weak in the bank-centered institutional environment for Japanese corporate governance.

A caveat at the outset: Our point is not to rework the shopworn argument that Japanese firms are imitative rather than innovative, and that entrepreneurialism is lacking in Japanese economic actors. These arguments, sometimes linked to the claim that omniscient bureaucrats deserve credit for Japanese economic success, have been challenged persuasively by informed commentators.[2] Any economy as successful as Japan's (at least in comparative historical perspective, if not recently) must be dynamic, innovative, and infused with entrepreneurial drive. Rather, we assert that different kinds of entrepreneurialism and innovation may emerge in different economies. The premise underlying this chapter is simply that an active venture capital market drives a particular strain of entrepreneurship and innovation that is economically valuable, and that certain institutional settings do a better job of facilitating a venture capital market than others.

As in the case of derivative suits discussed in Chapter 2, we will show that institutional obstacles blocking the attainment of a desired economic goal motivated legal changes in recent years. As in Chapter 2, actors appear to have responded to these changes, though the venture capital market in Japan remains underdeveloped. Indeed, it may be fair to state that thus far, the focus on venture capital and start-up firms has had greater impact on the way corporate law is produced in Japan than in transforming the venture capital market.

The chapter is organized into five sections. Section I examines the practical and theoretical significance of the venture capital market by situating venture capital within the comparative corporate governance debate. Section II contrasts the size and operation of the venture capital markets in the United States and Japan. The data show that the world's two largest economies have developed different ways to mobilize entrepreneurialism and innovation. Section III explains the differences by isolating five traits of the U.S. corporate governance system that facilitate an active venture capital market. These traits appear to be linked to the market orientation of American corporate governance, and are not prevalent in Japan's bank-centered system. Section IV examines recent Japanese legal reforms designed to jump-start the venture capital market, and analyzes the role of these reforms in the new market for the production of corporate law in Japan. Section V examines two normative implications of the comparison. First, the development of venture capital markets requires not only an active stock market, but also the concomitant legal and social practices found in a stock market-oriented corporate governance system. Second, the focus on venture capital provides a cautionary tale (for both the United States and Japan) about undertaking piecemeal corporate governance reforms based on limited assessments of foreign practices.

I. VENTURE CAPITAL'S SIGNIFICANCE IN CORPORATE GOVERNANCE

Although venture capital financing occupies only a small fraction of corporate finance in the United States, it is an almost essential form of financing for high-risk, entrepreneurial ventures. Venture-capital-backed firms contribute significantly to job growth, exports, R&D expenditures, and corporate tax payments.[3] The ability of venture-capital-backed firms to quickly exploit market opportunities is reflected in their superior stock performance compared to firms that did not receive venture capital funding.[4] Moreover, venture capital is often pivotal to the development of new industries.[5]

From a theoretical perspective, the competitive edge and innovative capacities of venture-capital-backed firms make the venture capital market a logical subject on which to extend the focus of comparative corporate law scholarship. A key insight from comparative corporate governance literature is that corporate laws and institutions may persist not because they have withstood a Darwinian struggle for survival (thereby demonstrating their efficiency), but because chance events have selected and then locked them into a particular path.[6] The mechanisms that lead to path dependence in corporate practices and institutions include network externalities, learning effects, and cognitive biases. Path dependence is, thus, shorthand for a fairly uncontroversial claim: That historical, ideological, and behavioral settings matter because they set the path upon which institutions are formed. Scholars have shown that the "modern corporation" Adolf Berle and Gardiner Means described for the United States in the 1930s in their classic *The Modern Corporation and Private Property* was more the product of political ideology and historical circumstance than the pinnacle of economic development.[7]

The historical and political contingency of governance systems means that alternative institutions to govern business organizations are not only possible, but also inevitable. In one line of influential research, scholars classified governance systems in developed economies as either bank centered or market centered.[8] Japan and Germany are the most prominent examples of the former, the United States the latter. Since we have already discussed the main features of Japanese corporate governance in Chapter 2, we omit further description here. By contrast, a market-centered governance system is tied to the one-dimensional relationship between suppliers of equity capital (shareholders) and corporate managers. This is a less comprehensive and more transient form of monitoring, because few of the shareholders have a stake in the firm large enough to incur the costs of the monitoring effort. A market-centered system expands opportunities for exit and increases the relative number of impersonal, discrete exchanges among corporate constituents. There is greater resort to explicit contracts and other formal legal mechanisms of corporate accountability. Hostile takeover bidders, independent directors, and the courts—all "outsiders" in relation to the firm—figure prominently in this form of governance. In effect, these outsiders substitute for the multidimensional "internal" monitoring that occurs among exchange partners in a bank-oriented governance system.

Underlying the bank-centered, market-centered dichotomy are differences in the ways these two systems respond to a single type of problem: Aligning the incentives of major corporate constituents—principally suppliers of capital and managers. A second crucial task of governance systems linked to a different aspect of efficiency, however, has been neglected. This is the ability of an organization to respond quickly to changes in the competitive environment, a feature Douglass North calls "adaptive efficiency." As described by North,

[a]daptive efficiency . . . is concerned with the kinds of rules that shape the way an economy evolves through time. It is also concerned with the willingness of society to acquire knowledge and learning, to induce innovation, to undertake risk and creative activity of all sorts, as well as to resolve problems and bottlenecks of the society through time.[9]

This neglected aspect of efficiency has important implications for competitiveness and economic change. Engaging in searches and experimentation, and learning from the resulting feedback, are keys to the evolution of an economic system.[10] Yet, because "the overall institutional structure plays the key role in the degree that the society and the economy will encourage the trials, experiments, and innovations that we can characterize as adaptively efficient,"[11] path dependence means that not all governance systems are likely to be equally successful at encouraging adaptive efficiency. Indeed, as legal scholar Ronald Gilson has pointed out, corporate governance systems in major economies appear to involve a tradeoff between credible commitment to stability on the one hand and adaptability on the other.[12]

As recent economic history shows, adaptive efficiency is enhanced by an institutional structure that fosters an active venture capital market. Entrepreneurial innovations take place outside the confines of established firms, and often outside the boundaries of existing industries.[13] Through their screening and funding decisions, venture capitalists provide crucial feedback on the viability of economic experiments. As catalysts and risk takers in support of entrepreneurial innovation, venture capitalists play a unique role in the process of value creation and economic evolution.

As we explore below, the bank-centered, market-centered dichotomy appears to explain rather well differences, not only in responses to agency costs, but also in approaches to entrepreneurial finance and corporate innovation.

II. A PROFILE OF THE VENTURE CAPITAL MARKETS IN THE UNITED STATES AND JAPAN

In this section, we examine data from the United States and Japan to construct simple, contrasting profiles of the venture capital markets in the two countries. To summarize the differences at the outset, U.S. venture capital funds are larger and more independent, hold larger equity stakes in and take a more active role in the management of portfolio companies, make more early stage investments, and invest more heavily in new technologies than their Japanese counterparts. We first provide a snapshot of Japan and the United States in the mid-1990s, before the explosion of interest in Silicon Valley during the U.S. bubble, and prior to a number of institutional reforms in Japan designed to create a more vibrant market for entrepreneurial finance. In the next part, we explore more recent institutional and market developments transpiring in the wake of the situation described here.

A. Size

The contrast between the world's two largest economies in their approach to entrepreneurship is striking. For example, in a 2002 sample of thirty-seven countries (representing 92 percent of world GDP), U.S. domestic venture capital investments as a percentage of GDP are larger in any country other than Korea, Israel, and Canada. Although only 20 percent of the venture-capital-backed companies are in the United States, they garner almost 70 percent of the venture capital invested in all the sample countries.[14] By contrast, Japan ranks last among G7 countries in entrepreneurial activity, and near the bottom of the thirty-seven-country sample in terms of both venture capital invested as a percentage of GDP, and venture capital invested per company.[15]

To fully understand why Japan ranks so low on these scales, it is instructive to explore in detail the situation before Japan embarked on institutional reforms to jump-start its venture capital industry. For example, in 1993, 637 U.S. venture capital firms disbursed over $3 billion in funds, while 121 Japanese venture capital firms disbursed only ¥76 billion ($760 million). Other indications of a considerably more active venture capital market in the United States than in Japan a decade ago were the far larger number of start-up companies and the number of companies listed on the over-the-counter (OTC) market. The size differential is summarized in Table 3.1.[16]

These figures, however, captured only a small portion of the differences between the two venture capital markets in the early 1990s. In addition to quantitative differences, significant structural and operational differences have traditionally distinguished the venture capital markets of the United States and Japan.

B. United States

Venture capital in the United States "is best defined as *active* investment in private companies with high growth potential."[17] Venture capitalists in the United States

Table 3.1. *Relative size of the U.S. and Japanese venture capital markets (early 1990s)*

	US	Japan	Japan/U.S.
Number of venture capital firms	637	121	1/5
Total amount invested	$35 billion	$1 billion	1/3
Annual investment	$3.1 billion	$760 million	1/4
Number of start-ups	670,000	90,000	1/7
New public companies	619	149	1/4
Companies listed on NASDAQ/Japan OTC market	4,902	563	1/9
Public companies	8,296	2,773	1/3
Public companies as % of all companies	0.18	0.21	1.2

Source: 1072 Jurisuto 71 (1995) (data from 1993–94).

provide intensive oversight of the firms in their portfolios. Venture capitalists usually take concentrated equity investments in their portfolio companies and participate actively in the governance of such firms through service on the board of directors, informal company visits, and involvement in strategic decisions.[18] According to a leading study, the lead venture capitalist averages a 19 percent ownership stake in the portfolio company at the time of the initial public offering (IPO), and the aggregate holdings by all venture capitalists represent, on average, 34 percent of the outstanding shares of the portfolio company.[19] Venture capitalists play a key role on the board of directors of their portfolio companies, holding approximately one-third of the board seats prior to the IPO. [20] In addition, venture capitalists in the United States retain the right to appoint and remove key personnel and provide entrepreneurs with access to investment bankers, lawyers, and other consultants.[21]

The structure of venture capital investments and the contract between the venture capital provider and the venture business facilitate active monitoring of portfolio companies. The incentives of investor and entrepreneur are aligned by the contractual relationships between the venture capitalist and the principals who invest in the venture capital fund, and between the venture capitalist and the entrepreneur. The characteristics of these arrangements, discussed in Section III, render the U.S. venture capitalist an active partner and monitor of the portfolio firm. As a leading commentator notes, "[t]hese characteristics reflect a clever and successful mechanism for managing projects with high potential but also a high degree of uncertainty."[22]

In addition to active investment in portfolio firms, a second set of defining characteristics of the U.S. venture capital market is independence and willingness to make early-stage investments in new technologies and products. Most U.S. venture capital firms are independent private partnerships. Since 1980, this category has accounted for at least 72 percent of the capital under management.[23] Private and public pension funds dominate as the source of capital commitments. Since 1984, pension funds have accounted for at least 38 percent of all capital raised.[24] The other principal sources of venture capital commitments include financial institutions (25 percent of all commitments in 2001, though averaging closer to 10 percent in the 1990s), endowments and foundations (22 percent of commitments in 2001), and families and individuals (9 percent).[25] Operating outside of, but parallel to, the venture capital funds are wealthy individuals known as "angels" who also play a key role in the supply of seed capital to start-up ventures.[26]

Seed, start-up, and other early-stage investments account for approximately 25 percent of all venture capital firm disbursements, while later-stage and expansion funds represent approximately 75 percent of all disbursements.[27] Although investments by industry class fluctuate over time, U.S. venture capital investments tend to be concentrated in computer software and hardware, health care and biotechnology, and communications.[28]

C. Japan

In both structure and operation, the Japanese venture capital market offers a striking contrast to the U.S. industry just described. The characteristics of the Japanese venture capital market bear the strong influence of a bank-oriented governance system. In the mid-1990s, for example, more than half of the venture capital firms in Japan were affiliated with banks, securities firms, or insurance companies.[29] Even as of 2000, despite a doubling in the number of venture capital firms in Japan over the past decade (from 120 to 245), over 70 percent of the top 100 Japanese venture capital firms were subsidiaries of banks and securities companies.[30] The dominance of banks and other financial institutions in Japanese venture capital can also be seen in terms of funding. In 1994, for example, banks provided 24 percent of all venture capital funds, while insurance companies provided 14 percent. In 2001, banks provided 30 percent and insurance companies 14 percent.[31] Two major suppliers of capital to start-up firms in the United States are virtually absent from Japan: Pension funds until recently did not invest in venture capital at all (and still only contribute about 1–2 percent of all funding); and despite vast personal financial wealth, there are almost no angels in Japan.[32]

In contrast to venture capital practices in the United States, Japanese venture capital firms have traditionally not taken significant equity stakes in their portfolio companies. A Japan Fair Trade Commission survey of seventy-two venture capital firms in the mid-1990s showed that twenty-seven firms (38 percent of the total) did not own more than 10 percent of the equity of any company in their portfolio.[33] Thirty-seven companies (51 percent) owned more than 10 percent of the stock of between one and ten portfolio companies. The lack of large equity positions by Japanese venture capital providers is confirmed by the survey finding that the average "control stock ratio" among venture capital firms was only 1.1 percent.[34]

Unlike the equity-oriented investment of U.S. venture capitalists, Japanese venture capital disbursements have been heavily weighted toward loans made to a relatively small number of borrowers. Small equity investments are made in a large number of firms. In 1993, loans to 715 firms accounted for 58 percent of total venture capital disbursements. Equity investments were made in 8,864 firms, representing 42 percent of total disbursements. The value of stock owned as a percentage of total asset value was over 50 percent for only fourteen of seventy-two firms surveyed by the Japan Fair Trade Commission. Twenty-five venture capital firms reported stock value of 0–10 percent of total asset value.[35]

Finally, the timing and placement of Japanese venture capital investments has not followed the U.S. pattern. Japanese venture capital has traditionally been characterized by intermediate-stage "mezzanine" financing of relatively mature industries. Early-stage financing accounted for only 16 percent of all disbursements in 1994.[36] In contrast to the U.S. venture capital industry, Japanese

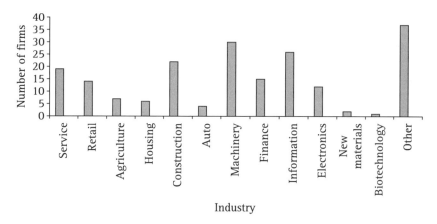

Figure 3.1. *Businesses in which Japanese venture capital firms own more than 10% of the outstanding stock*

Source: 1410 Shōji Hōmu 2, 5 (1995).

venture capital firms have historically not invested heavily in businesses conducting research and development on new materials or biotechnology.[37] Instead, they have invested most heavily in manufacturing, wholesale and retail sales, and the service industry.[38] As shown in Figure 3.1, stock ownership of Japanese venture capital firms has traditionally been concentrated in machinery-related, information-related, and the construction and real estate industries.

III. THE GENETIC CODES FOR VENTURE CAPITAL IN THE UNITED STATES AND JAPAN

Entrepreneurial change occurs within the formal and informal constraints of existing institutions. Put differently, the institutional structure creates and defines the opportunities available to the entrepreneur. In this section, we analyze key traits of the U.S. venture capital market in order to contrast the incentives for venture-capital-backed innovation supplied by the institutional settings for corporate governance in the United States and Japan. Again, we focus our comparison initially on the institutional settings in the 1990s. More recent institutional changes and responses are discussed in Section IV.

Five traits of the active venture capital market in the United States can be distilled or derived from Section II: The existence of large, independent sources of funding, liquidity, highly developed incentive structures, labor mobility, and risk tolerance. Independent sources of funding concern the extent to which funding for innovation is liberated from potential constraints tied to existing financial structures and corporate cultures. Liquidity involves an exit strategy for the venture capital provider, the existence of which is crucial to the investment decision. Incentives entail contractual and structural mechanisms to motivate and align the interests of the relevant players in the venture capital process. Labor mobility—implicit but, nonetheless, crucial to the success of venture capitalism in the United States—facilitates the supply of managerial and technical expertise to operate venture businesses. Risk tolerance affects the willingness of venture capital participants to engage in high-risk, high-return activities.

Each of these traits is at least loosely linked to the stock market-orientation of American corporate governance practices. The Japanese venture capital industry, operating within a bank-centered institutional setting, displays each of these traits only weakly or not at all.

A. Large, Independent Sources of Funding

The amount of funds available for investment is obviously of critical importance to the vitality of a venture capital market. Japan lags far behind the United States and Europe in venture capital investments, and the gap is growing. In 2001, the amount invested in Japan was 1/30 of that in the United States, and 1/14 that in Europe.

Beyond sheer size, however, sources of funding substantively shape the operation of the venture capital market. Venture capitalists can be expected to behave differently—to have different investment and exit strategies and performance expectations—depending on their relationship with their principal investors.[39] The independence of major sources of venture capital funds allows the venture capitalist to concentrate on nurturing the most promising new firms and harvesting investments in the most profitable manner. Almost inevitably, the venture capital market will be affected if the interests of large bank and securities firm investors in venture capital funds are reflected in the activities of venture capitalists.

Pension funds play an important role in the U.S. venture capital market, not only because they are the single largest source of capital, but also because the capital is provided to independent venture capitalists. Pension fund managers invest in venture capital funds for purposes of diversification; investments in venture capital partnerships often constitute an important part of the high-risk, high-return portion of the manager's portfolio. As such, the pension manager's investment decision reflects a calculation about the skill of the venture capitalist in ferreting out opportunities that promise a high rate of return.

Legal rules in the United States have facilitated the large size and independence of venture capital funds by permitting pension funds to invest in venture capital funds. The pool of venture capital under management increased sixfold from 1978 to 1990 after the Department of Labor released a policy statement permitting pension funds to invest in venture partnerships.[40] Regulations under the Employee Retirement Income Security Act (ERISA) ensure that pension money is employed in the *active* management of venture capital-backed firms.[41]

The scarcity of independent venture capital firms and the complete absence of pension money in the Japanese venture capital market until very recently[42] have affected the placement and staging of Japanese venture capital. The investment decisions of venture capital firms affiliated with banks and securities firms may differ from those of independent venture capital providers. This is particularly likely in Japan because the staff of venture capital firms affiliated with banks and securities companies are drawn from the parent companies. The venture capital firm thus retains the parent company orientation. The parent company imprint is particularly strong on bank-affiliated firms, because bank employees are rotated through venture capital affiliates for relatively short periods of time. As a result, commentators have suggested that Japanese banks view venture capital investments principally as a way to increase loan and fee income, while securities companies review venture capital investments chiefly for their potential to generate underwriting fees when the venture businesses go public.[43]

The data support these claims. Historically, a large percentage of Japanese venture capital funds was supplied in the form of loans,[44] reflecting the banking orientation of Japanese finance. Moreover, venture capital funding has traditionally been invested in relatively mature firms with potential to issue shares publicly a short time after the infusion of venture capital,[45] an obvious benefit to the securities firms that serve as underwriters.

The placement and staging of Japanese venture capital disbursements suggest that the venture capital market's ability to serve as an engine of innovation is diminished by the link to established banking and financial networks. In contrast to the use of venture capital in the United States to fund new, high-risk technologies, venture capital in Japan has traditionally funded well-established, comparatively low technology industries such as real estate and retail. Moreover, the use of Japanese venture capital for mezzanine rather than start-up funding means that by definition it cannot serve as the main catalyst for the development of new technologies and services, because seed and start-up funds must be supplied by a different source.

In Japan, banks have traditionally been the source of financing for high-risk, in-house corporate innovation. It might be argued that bank financing of risky, innovative projects fully substitutes for the venture capital market, eliminating the significance of any underdevelopment in the venture capital market in Japan. Such bank financing, however, does not appear to be a close substitute for venture capital because it has been concentrated in the postwar period on large corporate borrowers linked to the lending bank through *keiretsu* affiliations. This leaves less risk capital for small, entrepreneurial borrowers, and ties the funding of innovation to preexisting corporate networks and cultures.

B. Liquidity

Exit is crucial to the operation of a venture capital market. Venture capitalists provide management consulting information and reputational capital along with monetary capital to portfolio companies. Once a portfolio company succeeds, the non-capital contributions can be utilized more efficiently by other early-stage companies. As legal scholars Bernard Black and Ronald Gilson point out, "because the economies of scope . . . link financial and nonfinancial contributions, recycling the venture capitalist's non-capital contributions also requires the venture capitalist to exit—to recycle its financial contribution from successful companies to early-stage companies."[46] In addition, exit enhances the efficiency of the relationship between the venture capitalist and the investors in the venture capital fund. Exit by the venture capitalist provides a benchmark for evaluating his skills, and allows capital providers to recycle their investments from less to more successful venture capitalists.

The opportunity for a venture capitalist to exit the investment is typically provided either by an IPO or the acquisition of the portfolio company by another firm. Black and Gilson have argued that the availability of exit by an IPO is crucial to the success of the venture capital market due to the structure of the implied incentive contract between the venture capitalist and the entrepreneur: Because entrepreneurs value control over their enterprises, the potential for the venture capitalist to exit by means of an IPO and return significant control to the entrepreneur provides incentives to the entrepreneur in a way that other forms of exit cannot. Thus, Black and Gilson conclude that "the potential for exit through an IPO, possible in a stock market-centered capital market, allows the venture capitalist and the entrepreneur to contract implicitly over control in a manner that is not easily duplicatable in a bank-centered capital market."[47]

Consistent with Black and Gilson's claim, Japan's bank-centered system has historically limited the potential for exit through an IPO. This is reflected both in data on the number of firms listed on Japan's OTC market and the lengthy process of listing a company on the OTC market. In the early 1990s, the start-up to IPO process took 4.7 years on average in the United States; the similar process took well over 15 years in Japan.[48] In Japan, 92 percent of the companies whose shares were traded on the OTC market around this time were fifteen years old or older, and only one percent of such firms was less than ten years old; in the United States, 42 percent of the NASDAQ-traded firms at this time were less than ten years old.[49]

A principal reason for the bottleneck was Ministry of Finance (MOF) regulation of the financial markets. Equity finance has historically been limited, as would be expected in a bank-oriented corporate system. Moreover, regulators traditionally reserved the equity market for large companies, reflecting a policy determination that small issuers pose too great a risk to investors. Strict listing requirements, which until the mid-1990s included profitability guidelines and minimum net asset requirements for all firms, eliminated from the IPO market firms with growth potential that need equity financing to cover start-up costs. Many companies that met the formal listing standards failed to pass the informal and more stringent "practical listing standards" that were applied by the OTC self-regulatory body under the ultimate guidance of MOF.[50] Even more drastically, from 1992 to 1995 MOF imposed weekly limits on the supply of IPOs to the market in order to support share prices on the Tokyo Stock Exchange. These limits were enforced regardless of the quality of the issuer or the public demand for its securities.

Meeting the exacting listing requirements of the OTC market was all the more time-consuming because the emphasis on established, group-affiliated firms made it particularly difficult to expand a new business rapidly.[51] New companies lacked the affiliations with established corporate networks important to obtaining bank and equity financing, talented employees and managers, and upstream and downstream business partners in Japan.

Recent U.S. experience suggests that when the IPO exit option narrows, acquisitions can pick up the slack. For example, in 2001, when adverse market conditions affected the IPO market, a record 322 venture-backed companies were acquired for $15.3 billion.[52] In Japan, as with IPO exits, acquisitions have provided only a narrow exit opportunity in Japan. For example, less than 15 percent of exits (about 185 companies) were in the form of mergers and acquisitions in 2002.[53] Again, the reasons can be traced to characteristics of Japanese corporate governance. As we examine in detail in Chapter 7, the market for corporate control has historically been severely limited. While negotiated transactions of the type involved in the acquisition of a venture business are not prevented by Japanese corporate law, a variety of legal and nonlegal frictions have traditionally made mergers difficult and exceedingly rare in comparison not only to the United States, but also to most developed countries.

C. Incentives

Incentive structures are needed on three levels of the venture capital process. Providers of capital must have incentives to invest in venture capital funds. Venture capitalists need incentives to invest the fund's capital in a particular portfolio firm. And entrepreneurs who found start-up firms must have incentives to work toward the success of the venture and to accept diminished control over the enterprise in return for the infusion of venture capital. In the United States, these incentives are provided by a distinctive set of structural and contractual mechanisms.

Most U.S. venture capital funds are structured as limited partnerships. In this structure, the venture capitalist serves as general partner and other investors serve as limited partners. The venture capital firm itself is structured as a management company responsible for managing several pools of capital, each of which is a legally separate limited partnership. The limited partnership structure prevails in the industry because it provides the appropriate legal and tax incentives for investors in the fund. Limited partners enjoy limited liability, provided they do not assume a high degree of managerial input in the partnership. Tax treatment is favorable because limited partnership income is not subject to taxation at the partnership level. Venture capitalists are able to minimize distributional conflicts between themselves as active investors and the passive investors in the fund by limiting the life of the partnership (thus requiring periodic performance review), building contractual mechanisms into the partnership agreement to minimize conflicts of interest, and creating compensation schemes heavily dependent on investment returns.[54]

While the venture capital process may evolve into a highly relational contract between venture capitalist and entrepreneur, it does not begin as one. In fact, at the time of the investment decision, the venture capital process is a deal between strangers: Information asymmetries are great, uncertainty is high, and mutual wariness about opportunism abounds between the venture capitalist and the entrepreneur. To overcome these problems, industry standards have developed which provide an extensive set of contractual incentives and protections to venture capitalists in their relationships with entrepreneurs.

Venture capitalists utilize complex contractual arrangements to align the interests of the entrepreneur–manager with those of the providers of venture capital. The basic document that governs the relationship between the venture capital provider and the entrepreneur is the stock purchase agreement. This agreement will typically provide for staged financing as well as registration rights, information rights, and board representation for the venture capitalist. These provisions minimize agency costs and information asymmetries that exist between the capital provider and the venture manager by allowing the venture capitalist to remain in effective control of the venture and to maintain liquidity of the investment.

Under most stock purchase agreements, the venture capital investment is made as a purchase of convertible preferred stock. If the venture does well, the venture capitalist benefits through capital gains on the sale of the underlying common stock when the investment is harvested. Conversely, the terms of the convertible preferred stock ensure that the entrepreneur bears a disproportionate share of the risk of failure. These terms typically include a liquidation preference, redemption rights, and anti-dilution protection. The liquidation preference provides downside protection in the form of a return of the venture capitalist's investment (to the extent of available assets) should the portfolio company fail; redemption rights supply an exit mechanism to protect the venture capitalist in the event of mediocre performance by the portfolio company; and anti-dilution protections ensure that the venture capitalist will maintain control of the venture.

In return, the entrepreneur–managers receive a critically important infusion of capital, along with reputational capital and managerial assistance. To tie managerial compensation to the success of the venture and to ensure continued employment with the firm, the entrepreneurial team typically accepts modest cash salaries in return for stock options. Because the stock options vest over time, if key employees are terminated or quit, they will have worked for below-market monetary compensation while forfeiting their equity stake in the venture. Stock option plans may also enable managers to recoup control of the firm when the venture capitalist exits in an IPO.

Complex organizational and contractual structures mirroring those just discussed also operate between the general partner and the investors in the fund. Control mechanisms, compensation arrangements for the general partner, mandatory distribution requirements, and the fixed term for the fund all work to overcome contracting problems that might otherwise make investors reluctant to part with their money. Moreover, the two contracts—between the venture capitalist and portfolio company, and between the investor and the venture capital fund—are intertwined, so that each supports the other, improving the efficiency of both.[55]

Few of these organizational and incentive structures have traditionally been utilized in Japan, because they were underdeveloped or unavailable. While it would be an overstatement to explain the absence of sophisticated incentive structures as a *result* of Japan's bank-centered governance system, as shown below, the underdevelopment of the institutional and legal framework needed to support venture capital investments bears the strong imprint of a corporate finance environment long dominated by banks. Also responsible are historically contingent legal obstacles and the influence of informal contracting practices that flourish in close-knit transacting networks.

Until reforms discussed in the next section of the chapter, no available organizational form in Japan offered venture capital providers both flow-through tax treatment and limited liability. Financial policies protective of the banking industry and other regulatory obstacles provide a partial explanation. A Japanese counterpart of the limited partnership organizational form exists, but rules adopted by the Japanese tax authorities impose a withholding tax when there are ten or more limited partners, rendering this organizational form costly when used by a large number of investors.[56] A fund organized in the corporate form is costly due to double taxation. The trust form would be attractive, since it offers flow-through tax treatment, and the trust agreement could in theory provide for limited liability.[57] In practice, however, the trust form has not been available because a license is required to serve as a trustee, and MOF has, until recently, limited access to the trust business to a small number of banks in accordance with its policy of financial market segmentation.[58]

A commonly used organizational form for venture capital investment in Japan is the partnership for investment purposes [*tōshi jigyō kumiai*], which is roughly equivalent to the U.S. general partnership.[59] This is the vehicle by which institutional investors supply venture capital in Japan. The investment firm partnership offers flow-through tax treatment but does not provide limited liability to any of its members. The lack of limited liability in this organizational form, as well as stringent regulation of pension fund investments prior to recent financial reforms, accounts for the total absence of pension money in the Japanese venture capital market until just a few years ago.

As in the United States, the relationship between Japanese venture capital providers and managers of portfolio companies is governed by contract. The Japanese contract, however, differs substantially from the stock purchase agreement and equity terms used in the United States. In Japan, long-term consulting agreements are typically concluded between venture capital providers and venture businesses. These agreements provide for management support in the form of introductions of personnel, assistance in creating real estate and sales linkages, and related services.[60] In addition, the agreements provide that as the venture business nears the IPO phase, the venture capital firm will arrange for a managing underwriter, accountants, and other experts to assist in the public offering. These simple agreements, however, do not contain the extensive mix of incentives and protections found in the United States: Contractual protections are considered to be of limited value if the venture business is failing, and venture capitalists are constrained by existing Japanese business practices from seeking more thorough contractual control over the management of venture businesses.[61] Moreover, extensive contractual protections and incentives are less critical where venture capital investments are made, as is typically the case in Japan, of mezzanine rather than seed or start-up funds.

Similarly, equity instruments utilized in the Japanese venture capital industry do not contain the features that have become industry standards in the United States. As might be expected in an economy long accustomed to bank finance, until very recently there was little financial innovation involving equity instruments. There is virtually no history of convertible preferred stock usage in Japan. In the 1990s, virtually all equity investments in the Japanese venture capital market took the form of common stock. Warrants and convertible bonds accounted for less than 10 percent of the total funds supplied by venture capital firms as of 1993.[62]

Legal barriers shaped by historical circumstance account for the passivity of Japanese venture capitalists. The Japanese Anti-Monopoly Law enacted after the Second World War prohibited holding companies as a means of preventing the reemergence of the family controlled conglomerates known as *zaibatsu* that dominated the prewar economy.[63] Until the ban on holding companies was relaxed at the end of 1997, venture funds had to limit their stock ownership in portfolio firms to avoid classification as holding companies. For similar policy reasons, until the mid-1990s, regulations also prohibited persons affiliated with venture capital funds from serving as a manager of a venture business.

Other legal barriers linked to the historical (American) concern with economic concentration hinder the structuring of managerial incentive schemes in Japan. Until the mid-1990s, Japanese corporate law prohibited the repurchase of a company's own shares, including for future use in connection with stock options. Thus, new shares were required to be issued upon the exercise of an option. Yet, shareholders had to approve an issuance of shares at a price lower than the current market price, and this approval only remained valid for six months.[64] These provisions made the issuance of stock options so cumbersome as to be practically unworkable. Sony, one of Japan's most innovative firms, devised a complex structure involving bonds with detachable warrants to circumvent these restrictions on incentive stock plans. In 1995, the legal regime was partially liberalized through amendments to legislation that permitted the shareholders' authorization to remain valid for ten years, and provided for favorable tax treatment of options.[65] However, only "specified new businesses" which received the approval of the Ministry of International Trade and Industry were permitted to make use of this "liberalized" regime. In 1996, only thirty-one businesses had received approval to issue stock options under this statute.[66]

D. Labor Mobility

Although venture capitalists furnish reputational capital and management consulting services to venture businesses, there is no substitute for the entrepreneurial team that founds, operates, and manages the venture. An active venture capital market thus requires a liquid market for human, as well as monetary capital.

As we saw in the previous chapter, highly ingrained institutional and cultural patterns central to Japanese corporate governance dramatically limit the market for human capital in Japan. Under Japan's "lifetime" employment system, job turnover among white-collar workers is low, and the market for lateral hires is virtually closed.

In theory, the lifetime employment system might not necessarily pose a major obstacle to venture capital in Japan. This system only applies to Japan's largest firms, which by definition are not the focus of the venture capital industry. The entire postwar Japanese labor market, however, was shaped by the widely held public perception that long-term, large-firm employment was more prestigious and desirable than small-firm employment. Until the onset of significantly more complex and less stable employment patterns in the late 1990s, the career aspiration of a significant percentage of the college-educated Japanese population was to be employed essentially for the duration of one's career by a major industrial firm, financial institution, or governmental ministry that oversees the financial or industrial sector.[67] By contrast, a comparatively small percentage of the Japanese population harbors entrepreneurial aspirations. According to one survey, only 10 percent of the Japanese engineering graduates polled wanted to found their own firm in the future, as compared to 25 percent of the American engineering graduates polled.[68]

Another spillover from the lifetime employment system that limits labor mobility is the Japanese pension system. Until recently, pension rules contemplated only defined contribution plans, in which the employer promises a specific package of benefits to the employee upon retirement. These benefits are not portable from one firm to another, and severe financial penalties can be incurred for departure prior to normal retirement age. Managerial spinoffs from large firms to start-up firms were thus limited by the firm-specific nature of the pension system.

As a result of these factors, the market for managerial and research talent has traditionally been highly illiquid. International comparisons have indicated far lower job turnover and far higher expectation of remaining in present employment among Japanese employees compared to other nationalities.[69] The data on research personnel show extreme immobility: One study shows that among ninety-eight engineers at NEC, Fujitsu, and Toshiba, only 3 percent had experience working at a different firm.[70] In the same study, of 109 engineers at Data General, DEC, and Honeywell, 49 percent had experience working at a different firm.

E. Risk Tolerance

Venture capital, at least as it is known in the United States, is, by its very nature, a high-risk, high-return investment. Venture capitalists in the United States seek to invest in projects with an expected rate of return of 30–50 percent per year.[71] As a Congressional report notes, the affinity of the venture capital community for funding young, innovative companies places it "centerstage of the riskiest . . . segment" of the U.S. capital markets.[72] Worldwide, about 30 percent of the firms in which venture capital is invested fail.[73] Risk tolerance is thus another essential trait of an active venture capital market.

Risk tolerance is nurtured in the American system of corporate governance, which poses substantial risks to human and monetary capital. The active market for corporate control places employees and managers at risk. Notwithstanding occasional backlashes against mergers and corporate downsizing, prevailing thought is that these risks have a healthy disciplining effect on corporate actors. Meanwhile, a one-dimensional monitoring system limits the range of protections available to investors; participants in the American corporate governance system are not as tightly bound by the web of relationships that constrains corporate actors in Japan. Risks to monetary capital are instead covered principally through liquidity and diversification. Indeed, a basic rationale for the prevalence of flexible enabling statutes in U.S. corporate law is to facilitate entry and exit and to protect expectations in the event of changed circumstances. A major reason why "judges are now at the center of the American system of corporate governance"[74] is that American corporate actors proceed on the available information and allow the courts to fill gaps *ex post*. Risk tolerance is thus a latent characteristic of American corporate governance culture.[75]

This trait of U.S. corporate culture has not been prevalent in Japan. On the contrary, extensive inter-corporate linkages among banks and firms in postwar Japan absorbed risk and reduced uncertainty.[76] In this sense, an element of "insurance" was implicit in postwar Japanese industrial and financial organization in its heyday.[77] As discussed in the next chapter, corporate and regulatory actors have traditionally engaged in lengthy "preclearance" efforts to obtain the approval of all interested parties before undertaking an activity. Bureaucrats display a high degree of paternalism in their regulatory activities, and it is not uncommon for the private sector to complain to regulators about adverse market developments. Many Japanese commentators have suggested that as a result, the principle of self-responsibility is lacking among Japanese investors.

This cautious corporate culture handicaps the development of a truly active venture capital market in Japan. Data indicate that Japanese venture capital has traditionally been far less risky than its American counterpart. While about a third of the U.S. firms in which venture capital is invested fail, in 1993 only 9 of the 1,090 firms in which Japan's largest venture capital fund had invested failed within the preceding year.[78] But diminished risk comes at a cost. As the data in Section II show, Japanese venture capitalists have tended to invest in industries that are already fairly mature, and shied away from frontier technologies. Low risk tolerance slows venture capital's engine of adaptive efficiency.

IV. INSTITUTIONAL CHANGE AND DEVELOPMENTS IN THE VC MARKET

By the mid-1990s, both the depths of Japan's economic problems and the emergence of Silicon Valley as a major U.S. success story had focused the attention of Japanese policymakers and business people on the economic potential of venture capital. A series of measures were taken in the ensuing years to create an institutional climate more conducive to the venture capital market and the firms they support. This part briefly surveys those changes, as well as recent developments in the industry. Attributing causation between reform and response, of course, is very difficult, particularly since the reforms are recent and macroeconomic variables no doubt affect the market significantly. Our aim is simply to highlight the recent evolution in this under-studied aspect of Japanese economic activity. Regardless of their economic impact, the focus on venture capital by important business and policymaking groups has had a profound effect on the making of corporate law in Japan, a process we explain below.

Recent institutional reforms in the area of venture capital have addressed four out of five of what we called the "genetic codes" for venture capital in the previous section. Funding sources were liberalized with the relaxation of regulations on pension fund investments. The Ministry of Health, Labor and Welfare eliminated the so-called 5-3-3-2 rule, which specified the permissible investment allocation of pension funds (and did not include venture capital). This change should not only increase total investment in venture capital, but also increase funding of independent venture capital firms. Indeed, as measured by investment amount per investor, pension funds have already surpassed banks and other financial institutions,[79] although as noted above, pension money still occupies a negligible portion of total venture capital investments.

The venture capital market has grown in terms of both number of firms and amount invested. In 1993, 121 venture capital firms dispersed ¥76 billion ($760 million). Today, there are about 245 venture capital firms in Japan, investing ¥1.3 trillion ($1.3 billion) in 2002—huge increases in percentage terms, though from a very low base. Independent venture capital firms appear to be making inroads against venture capital firms affiliated with banks and other financial institutions. Numerically, more than half of all Japanese Venture Capital firms are now independent of financial institutions, although the independent firms tend to be comparatively small.[80]

A variety of changes have been made to improve liquidity by expanding financing and exit options for early-stage Japanese firms. A 2001 amendment to the Commercial Code eliminated a ¥50,000 ($500) minimum par value requirement for issued shares, and a requirement that per share net asset value following a stock split exceed ¥50,000. These requirements had inhibited liquidity and made it difficult to issue stock options. Several restrictions on equity financing in the year prior to an IPO were also lifted in 2001. Even more importantly, in 1999, two new equity markets specializing in financing of earlier-stage, high-growth companies were established. Both markets, a special section of the Tokyo Stock Exchange called the Market of the High Growth and Emerging Stocks (MOTHERS), and NASDAQ Japan offered less stringent listing standards than had traditionally been applied by the existing exchanges. IPO exits have increased, and the amount of funds raised per IPO is up significantly from the mid-1990s.[81] (NASDAQ Japan announced its closure in the fall of 2002, hurt by the bursting of the Internet bubble and problems with its partner, the Osaka Stock Exchange.)

The government has taken steps to increase the portability of pensions, in part as a way to spur greater labor mobility. In 2001, a law was enacted to allow companies to adopt defined contribution plans similar to U.S. 401(k) plans. Company plans are now fully portable for most employees. To date, the new pension structure has not been widely adopted. A decade of recession, however, has changed employment practices and increased labor mobility. At the very least, expectations of career-long employment with a single firm have diminished as the core group of workers protected by the lifetime employment system shrinks, layoffs are announced, and the ranks of part-time workers swell.

As noted above, two key missing components of the Japanese venture capital support structure were an organizational form like the limited partnership and a viable framework for the issuance of stock options. Both of these shortcomings were addressed legislatively. In 1998, the Investment Enterprise Limited Liability Association Law became effective. This new form of business organization provides limited liability and flow-through tax treatment for investors in qualifying venture capital funds. Since the law became effective, thirty funds, almost half of those established since the law's enactment, have adopted that form.[82]

Probably the single most important institutional reform is in the area of stock options. Beginning with an amendment to the Commercial Code in 1997, the legal regime for stock options has been liberalized in stages, so that today it is similar to that prevailing in the United States. The 1997 amendment is particularly significant because for the first time in postwar history, a Commercial Code amendment was initiated by politicians rather than bureaucrats working through the Ministry of Justice (MOJ) Legislative Reform Council. The business community prevailed upon Diet members to bypass the traditional, ponderous process in which a small group of academics selected by the MOJ considered, sometimes for years, specific changes to the Code prior to their enactment.[83] In addition to politicians and business groups, the Ministry of Economy, Trade, and Industry (METI, the predecessor of Ministry of International Trade and Industry or MITI) has also become actively involved in corporate law reform, particularly as it relates to new firms. Over the past several years, it has promoted a number of special statutes seeking to create a more favorable environment for business start-ups. These statutes will likely be incorporated into the Commercial Code in the future. Thus, in effect, the Legislative Reform Council now has active competitors in the corporate law reform process: Politicians working closely with business interests, and METI. The result of this competitive pressure is more "demand driven" corporate law amendments, made at an accelerated pace.

In sum, since the snapshot of the industry in the mid-1990s presented in the previous section, the Japanese venture capital market has grown larger and more independent. Investment allocation is shifting from manufacturing, construction, and retail to information technology and biotechnology businesses.[84] Investments are moving toward earlier stages, and investments in equity are eroding the traditional emphasis on loans. Whereas in 1993 loans constituted 58 percent of venture capital disbursements, in 2002 equity investments were 80 percent of the total.[85] Most of these changes, however, are either marginal or have started from a very low baseline. As noted at the outset, Japan still ranks at or near the bottom in many cross-country measures of entrepreneurial activity. Some progress has been made, and it seems reasonable to attribute at least some of this progress to improvements in the institutional environment. But as of this writing, a vibrant venture capital market remains an elusive goal for Japan.

V. IMPLICATIONS

What does the experience of the United States suggest for Japan and other countries currently without highly developed venture capital markets? What does the analysis contribute to the comparative corporate governance debate?

A. Creating a Venture Capital Market

An influential comparative study of venture capital by Black and Gilson begins with the plausible assumption that entrepreneurs have a preference for control.[86] Approaching the issue from a demand-side perspective, Black and Gilson ask under what circumstances an entrepreneur would surrender control in return for the capital and non-capital assets provided by the venture capitalist. They argue entrepreneurs do so when there is potential to regain control if the firm succeeds and the venture capitalist exits in an IPO. Because other means of exit do not return control to the entrepreneur, Black and Gilson conclude that bank-oriented systems lack an institution (a developed stock market) crucial to the incentive structure at the heart of the entrepreneurial process.

One implication of this analysis is that countries seeking to develop venture capital markets must nurture an IPO market. Alternatively or in the interim, it may be possible to piggyback on the U.S. IPO market as a way to jump-start a venture capital industry.

The Japanese experience, however, indicates that the link between an IPO market and the vitality of the venture capital market is less direct than meets the eye. The analysis in Section III demonstrates that the relationship between corporate governance systems and venture capital markets is complex and multifaceted. Components of the institutional mix which affect the *supply* of venture capital are equally or more important than the stock market's ability to return control to the entrepreneur. The barriers to a more active venture capital market in Japan are more formidable than simply lifting restrictive regulations on the OTC market and expanding the number of IPOs. Moreover, piggybacking on the U.S. IPO market may be a viable solution for firms in countries that have the right institutional mix save one: A developed stock market. Importing an exit strategy, however, may not work in corporate governance systems in which innovation is tied to larger systems of financial and industrial organization, labor markets are illiquid, contracting practices and organizational forms are inconsistent with the creation of sophisticated formal incentive structures, or risk tolerance is low. To date, entrepreneurs from only a single country—Israel—appear to have successfully piggybacked on the NASDAQ as a means of bypassing local institutional obstacles.[87]

From a more sanguine perspective, however, one clear lesson from comparative corporate governance studies is that little is inevitable in economic life; alternatives are possible. Japan may yet demonstrate that alternative venture capital markets are possible. For example, it is plausible that a venture capital market could emerge in which capital providers recycle their investments by arranging for the integration of maturing venture businesses into existing networks of firms. Venture capitalists could take the place of banks as the nuclei of groups of new firms engaged in intensive monitoring and information sharing. Indeed, the emergence of the so-called "Internet *keiretsu*" in the late 1990s suggests this very possibility. Precisely replicating the U.S. template may not be necessary to the creation of a vibrant market for entrepreneurial finance. At present, however, Japan does not provide a clearly marked, successful alternative path for the development of a venture capital market.

B. Reassessing the Comparative Corporate Governance Debate

Douglass North has written that "[t]echnological change and institutional change are the basic keys to societal and economic evolution and both exhibit the characteristics of path dependence."[88] Focusing on venture capital as an engine of change demonstrates that corporate governance scholarship is itself path dependent. Preoccupied with the narrow task of minimizing agency costs in the corporate form of joint economic activity, scholars in the 1990s became fixated on the ways bank-centered systems solve agency problems. At the height of American fascination with Japanese corporate governance, much was made of the Japanese legal environment that permitted banks to play a significant role in the monitoring of corporate management—a phenomenon some have called "romanticizing" bank monitoring.

This venture capital focus, however, provides a cautionary tale—for both countries—about transplanting foreign legal institutions and corporate practices. As this chapter reveals, precisely the legal, regulatory, and social environment that enabled bank-centered monitoring in Japan simultaneously handicapped the development of an active venture capital industry. For U.S. policymakers, changing the rules of the game to facilitate one improvement may have had quite negative consequences in other areas.

Subsequently, given the relative economic success of the United States vis-à-vis Japan, the latter country has sought, through piecemeal importation of law, to invigorate its venture capital market. The results to date are moderately encouraging, but not spectacular. It turns out that replicating the U.S. template for venture capital is difficult because the institutional structure supporting it is highly complex and interrelated.[89] Transplanting stock options, IPO standards, and organizational forms into vastly different social structures, labor markets, and regulatory systems is bound to be of limited utility. Transformation of Japanese venture capital markets probably must await further progress in larger, ongoing transformations of corporate, social, and legal systems. The process is underway, but far from complete.

CONCLUSION

Focusing on venture capital casts the debate over bank- versus market-oriented governance systems in a new light. The institutions supporting American governance fortuitously facilitate a complex contracting structure that makes venture capital flourish. By contrast, entrepreneurial finance and the firms it funds, while increasingly crucial to Japanese economic competitiveness and vitality, have been constrained by the institutional framework supporting its postwar corporate governance system. In a pattern that will be seen throughout the book, Japanese policymakers responded to the problem fairly aggressively with changes to the institutional environment. Ensuing developments suggest that these changes are necessary, but not sufficient, to transform Japan's setting for entrepreneurial activity.

NOTES

1. Ronald J. Gilson, Engineering a Venture Capital Market: Replicating the US Template, in Global Markets, Domestic Institutions: Corporate Law and Governance in a New Era of Cross-Border Deals 507 (Curtis J. Milhaupt ed., 2003).
2. See, for example, Ryuhei Wakasugi, Organizational Structure and Behavior in Research and Development, in Business Enterprise in Japan: Views of Leading Japanese Economists 159 (Kenichi Imai and Ryutaro Komiya eds., 1994) (challenging the claim that the distinctive features of Japanese R&D can be completely explained by technology followership and a social system which supports such followership); Mitsuo Matsushita, International Trade and Competition Law in Japan 276–7 (1993) (concluding that "the post-war success of Japanese industry should be attributed primarily to the entrepreneurship of industries rather than the industrial policies of the government").
3. See William D. Bygrave and Jeffry A. Timmons, Venture Capital at the Crossroads 1–4 (1992).
4. Marcia Vickers, Nothing Ventured, Less Gain, New York Times, April 21, 1996, at F3 (citing study by Securities Data Company showing that of the companies that have gone

public since 1986, offerings backed by venture capital rose an average of 135.1%, while others gained an average of 32.5%). The superior stock performance of venture capital-backed firms could also reflect reputational effects and the success of the "screening" function performed by venture capitalists in deciding which firms to support.

5. See Bygrave and Timmons, *supra* note 3, at 95–123 (explaining venture capital's role in fostering the semiconductor, computer, and biotechnology industries).

6. On the impact of these phenomena, see W. Brian Arthur, Increasing Returns and Path Dependence in the Economy 116–18 (1994).

7. The seminal work is Mark J. Roe, A Political Theory of American Corporate Finance, 91 Colum. L. Rev. 10 (1991).

8. See, for example, Erik Berglof, Capital Structure as a Mechanism of Control: A Comparison of Financial Systems, in The Firm as a Nexus of Treaties 237 (Masahiko Aoki, Bo Gustafsson, and Oliver Williamson eds., 1990).

9. Douglass C. North, Institutions, Institutional Change and Economic Performance 80 (1990).

10. Richard R. Nelson and Sidney G. Winter, An Evolutionary Theory of Economic Change 402 (1982). Nelson and Winter argue that "flexibility, experimentation, and ability to change direction as a result of what is learned are placed high on the list of desiderata for proposed institutional regimes." Id. at 394.

11. North, *supra* note 9, at 81.

12. Ronald J. Gilson, Corporate Governance and Economic Efficiency: When Do Institutions Matter?, 74 Wash. U.L.Q. 327, 334–45 (1996).

13. Innovation, of course, also can also occur within large firms. In Japan, for example, innovation typically takes place within the boundaries of large, well established firms and is funded by banks. We argue in Section III infra that this type of "in-house" innovation, however, is likely to be tied to existing industries, markets, and corporate cultures, diminishing its contribution to adaptive efficiency.

14. See Global Entrepreneurship Monitor, 2002 Executive Report 25, fig. 21 (2002).

15. See id. at 8, 25–6, figs. 21, 23.

16. Table 1 is not weighted for the size differential between the economies of the United States and Japan. At then-prevailing exchange rates, Japanese GDP was about 80% of U.S. GDP.

17. William A. Sahlman, Insights from the Venture Capital Model of Project Governance, 29 Bus. Econ. 35, 35 (1994) (hereinafter Sahlman, Insights) (emphasis added).

18. See, for example, Josh Lerner, Venture Capitalists and the Oversight of Private Firms, 50 J. Fin. 301 (1995).

19. Christopher B. Barry, et al., The Role of Venture Capital in the Creation of Public Companies, 27 J. Fin. Econ. 447, 448 (1990) (hereinafter Barry et al., Role of Venture Capital).

20. Id. at 448; Sahlman, Insights, *supra* note 17.

21. Paul Gompers and Josh Lerner, The Use of Covenants: An Empirical Analysis of Venture Partnership Agreements 3 (Harvard Business School Working Paper No. 95-047, Jan. 1995).

22. Sahlman, Insights, *supra* note 17, at 36.

23. Thomson Financial, National Venture Capital Association Yearbook 10 (2002) (hereinafter 2002 Yearbook).

24. Id.

25. Id.

26. Approximately 250,000 individuals invest $10 billion annually in 30,000 ventures in the United States. Regina Fazio Maruca, Venture Capital: The Invisible Angels, Harv. Bus. Rev., July–Aug. (1993), at 8 (citing study by the Center for Venture Research).
27. 2002 Yearbook, *supra* note 23, at 11.
28. See, for example, id. at 12.
29. Yuji Tanahashi, Bencha bijinesu no shinkō to bencha kyapitaru no yakuwari [Promoting Venture Businesses and the Role of Venture Capital], 1072 Jurisuto 64, 67 (1995) (from table 4). Of the 121 Japanese venture capital firms in the mid-1990s, twenty-two were affiliates of major banks, fifteen were affiliated with securities firms, forty were affiliated with regional banks, ten were affiliated with insurance companies, four were foreign owned, and thirty were classified as "other."
30. Nikkei Financial Journal, July 7, 2000.
31. Venture Enterprise Center, Survey of Venture Capital Investment 1 (2003).
32. As of 2002, only about 0.7% of Japanese adults were informal investors in start-up ventures. This compares with about 4.5% of U.S. adults. Global Enterprise Monitor, *supra* note 18, at 30, fig. 27.
33. Kazuyuki Funahashi, Bencha kyapitaru no jittai chōsa [Venture Capital Survey], 1410 Shōji hōmu 2, 4 (1995).
34. Id. Control stock ratio is the ratio of stock of "controlled companies" owned by the venture capital firm to the firm's total assets. A portfolio company is deemed to be "controlled" by a venture capital firm if it owns (a) 50% or more of the portfolio company's outstanding stock or (b) 10–50% of the outstanding stock and otherwise exercises control over the portfolio firm.
35. Funahashi, *supra* note 33, at 5 (table 2).
36. Tūshō sangyō shō [Ministry of International Trade and Industry], Tsūshō hakusho [White Paper on Trade] 199 (1995). Later stage financing accounts for 21%; 63% is classified as "other." Id.
37. Funahashi, *supra* note 33, at 4.
38. Yuji Tanahashi, Bencha bijinesu no shinkō to bencha kyapitaru no yakuwari [Promoting Venture Businesses and the Role of Venture Capital], 1072 Jurisuto 64, 68 (1995).
39. Christopher B. Barry, New Directions in Research on Venture Capital Finance, 23 Fin. Mgmt. 3, 13 (1994).
40. Joshua Lerner, Venture Capitalists and the Decision to Go Public, 35 J. Fin. Econ. 293, 295 (1994).
41. Pub. L. No. 93-406, 88 Stat. 829 (codified as amended at 29 U.S.C. §§ 1001-461, and in scattered sections of titles 5, 18, 26, 31, and 42 U.S.C.). Under the Department of Labor's "Plan Asset Regulation" promulgated under ERISA, investment entities are subjected to substantial regulatory burdens if their assets are treated as "plan assets" of employee benefit plans that invest in the entity. However, a specific exemption is provided for the assets of a "venture capital operating company" (VCOC). In order to qualify as a VCOC, the company must, on an annual basis, (a) have at least 50% of its assets invested in venture capital investments in which the VCOC retains "management rights" (defined as contractual rights which entitle the VCOC to substantially participate in or influence the conduct of the management of the portfolio company), and (b) actually exercise its management rights with respect to at least one such portfolio company in the ordinary course of its business. See 29 C.F.R. § 2510.3-101 (2002).

42. Until recently, the legal and regulatory environment in Japan effectively barred pension fund participation in the venture capital industry. The exposure of pension funds to unlimited liability under prevailing organizational forms in the venture capital industry made this form of investment undesirable from a legal standpoint. Moreover, the Health and Welfare Ministry, which regulates pension funds, adhered to investment policies that effectively placed venture capital off limits as an investment. Equally important in damming the flow of pension money into venture capital funds were the protective policies of Japanese financial regulators. For many years, MOF did not permit insurance companies or trust banks (the only institutions permitted to manage pension money until a series of recent financial reforms) to invest in venture capital funds.

43. See Hiroyuki Nishimura and Masato Ishizawa, Industry, Bureaucrats Strive to Turn Venture Capital Puddle into Deep Pool, Nikkei Weekly, Aug. 1, 1994, available in LEXIS, News Library, Non-US File.

44. See Tanahashi, *supra* note 38, at 69 (table 1).

45. Emiko Terazono, Survey of Venture and Development Capital, Financial Times, Sept. 24, 1993, available in LEXIS, News Library, Non-US File.

46. Bernard S. Black and Ronald J. Gilson, Venture Capital and the Structure of Capital Markets: Banks versus Stock Markets, 47 J. Fin. Econ. 243, 255 (1998).

47. Id. at 274.

48. There is conflicting data on exactly how much time was required, with figures ranging from seventeen years, see Tanahashi, *supra* note 38, at 71, to twenty-nine years, see Emiko Terazono, Venture Capital Becomes a Scarce Resource, Financial Times, Sept. 30, 1992, available in LEXIS, News Library, Non-US File.

49. James W. Borton, Venture Firms Eye Japan's Deep Pockets, Japan Economic Journal, Aug. 12, 1989, available in LEXIS, News Library, Non-US file.

50. See, for example, Bencha kigyō no keiei to shien [Management and Support of Venture Firms] 145–6 (Shuichi Matsuda ed., 1994).

51. For example, one study showed a 33% increase in sales volume of the twenty fastest growing firms on the Japanese OTC market, compared to 183% for the comparable US firms. See Matsuda, *supra* note 50, at 96.

52. 2002 Yearbook, *supra* note 23, at 77.

53. Survey of Venture Capital Investment, *supra* note 31, at 2.

54. See William A. Sahlman, The Structure and Governance of Venture-Capital Organizations, 27 J. Fin. Econ. 473, 489–503 (1990) (hereinafter Sahlman, Venture-Capital Organizations); Gilson, *supra* note 1.

55. Gilson, *supra* note 1.

56. The "undisclosed partnership" [tokumei kumiai] is roughly analogous to the limited partnership. See Commercial Code arts. 535–542. The tax law imposing withholding tax is Shotokuzeihō [Income Tax Law], Law No. 33 of 1965, arts. 210–211; Shotokuzeihō shikōrei [Income Tax Law Enforcement Order], arts. 327, 288.

57. See Shintakuhō [Trust Law], Law No. 62 of 1921, art. 36(3).

58. See Kin'yū kikan no shintaku gyōmu no keneito ni kansuru hōritsu [Law Concerning the Conduct of the Trust Business by Financial Institutions], Law. No. 43 of 1943.

59. See Shōhō [Commercial Code], Law No. 48 of 1899, arts. 667–688 (containing provisions for the voluntary partnership under the Civil Code [minpō jō no nin'i kumiai]).

60. Kazunori Ozaki, Bencha kyapitaru no kinō to yakuwari [The Function and Role of Venture Capital], 110 Shihon shijo, 21, 25 (1994).

61. Interview with Kazunori Ozaki, Director, Japan Associated Finance Co., Ltd. (JAFCO), in Tokyo Japan (July 2, 1996) (JAFCO is one of Japan's largest venture capital firms).

62. Tanahashi, *supra* note 38, at 69, table 1.

63. Shiteki dokusen no kinshi oyobi kōsei torihiki no kakuho ni kansuru hōritsu [Law Concerning the Prohibition of Private Monopolies and the Maintenance of Fair Trade], Law No. 54 of 1947, art. 9.

64. Id., art. 280–2.

65. Aratana jigyō katsudō no sokushin no tame no kankei hōritsu no seibi ni kansuru hōritsu [Law on the Preparation of Legislation Related to the Promotion of New Business Activities], Law No. 128 of 1995.

66. Kiyoshi Kitagawa, Kaisei shinki jigyōhō no gaiyō [Overview of the Revised New Business Law] (I), 1415 Shōji Hōmu 2, 3 (1996).

67. See, for example, Matsuda, *supra* note 50, at 258 (reporting that 17.4% of Japanese college students surveyed wanted to work for large firms after graduation and 13% wanted to become high-level public officials; 12.7% of U.S. college students surveyed wanted to work for large firms; none wanted to become public officials). In another survey, 40% of the Japanese engineering graduates polled wanted to obtain a successful career within their existing firm, as compared with just over 20% of the Americans polled. See Yoshinori Tamura and Koichi Hirata, Tentō tokosoku shijo to bencha kigyō [Special OTC Market and Venture Firms] 14 (1995). Other international comparisons confirm the relative immobility inherent in Japanese employment practices. See id. at 15.

68. Cited in Tanahashi, *supra* note 38, at 66.

69. See Tamura and Hirada, *supra* note 67, at 15. Japanese corporate presidents have worked for their firms for a median thirty-nine years compared to twenty-eight years for U.S. CEOs. When a Japanese president leaves his job, 68.5% of the time he becomes chairman of the board of the same company. Steven N. Kaplan and J. Mark Ramseyer, Those Japanese Firms with their Disdain for Shareholders: Another Fable for the Academy, 74 Wash. U. L.Q. 403, 414 (1996).

70. Kiyonori Sakakibara and D. Eleanor Westney, Comparative Study of the Training, Careers, and Organization of Engineers in the Computer Industry in the United States and Japan, 20 Hitotsubashi J. Com. & Mgmt. 1, 5 (1985).

71. Sahlman, Insights, *supra* note 17, at 36; J. William Petty et al., Harvesting the Entrepreneurial Venture: A Time for Creating Value, 7 J. Ap. Fin. 48, 56 (1994).

72. Joint Econ. Comm., 98th Cong., 2nd Sess., Venture Capital and Innovation 22 (Joint Comm. Print 1984).

73. Shinichi Kishima, Japan Stock Paralysis Chance for Venture Capital, Reuters, Mar. 16, 1993, available in LEXIS, News Library, Non-US file.

74. Jonathan R. Macey, Courts and Corporations: A Comment on Coffee, 89 Colum. L. Rev. 1692, 1701 (1989).

75. The link between American institutions and attitudes toward risk in commercial enterprises was recognized long ago. See Stuart Banner, Anglo-American Securities Regulation: Cultural and Political Roots, 1690–860, 195 (1998) (explaining that Tocqueville attributed American proclivities toward stock speculation to the form of government, which he thought acclimatized citizens to risk).

76. See, for example, Ken-ichi Imai, Japan's Corporate Networks, in 3 The Political Economy of Japan: Cultural and Social Dynamics 198, 208–18 (Shumpei Kumon and Henry Rosovksy eds., 1992); Iwao Nakatani, The Economic Role of Financial

Corporate Grouping, in The Economic Analysis of the Japanese Firm 227 (Masahiko Aoki ed., 1984) (arguing that risk sharing is a major motivation for the formation of Japanese business groups).

77. Literature on implicit insurance contracting in Japan is voluminous. See, for example, Nakatani, id.; Paul Sheard, Interlocking Shareholdings and Corporate Governance, in The Japanese Firm: Sources of Competitive Strength 310 (Masahiko Aoki and Ronald Dore eds., 1994).

78. Shinichi Kishima, Japan Stock Paralysis Chance for Venture Capital, Reuters, Mar. 16, 1993, available in LEXIS, News Library, Non-US file.

79. Survey of Venture Capital Investment, *supra* note 31, at 20.

80. Nippon Technical Venture website, available at http://www.ntvp.com. See also Scot Kojola, Venture Capital in Japan: Institutional Changes Create Opportunities for Growth, but is it Enough? Unpublished paper (2003).

81. Tokyo Stock Exchange website, available at http://www.tse.or.jp/english/listing/companies/statistics_m.pdf.

82. VEC, Main Points of Survey Report on Actual State of Venture Capital Investments, available at http://www.vec.or.jp/investment_e.html.

83. Hideki Kanda, Reforms in Corporate Law and Financial Regulation in Japan. Unpublished manuscript (2000). Since 1997, the business community, working through their political allies in the Liberal Democratic Party, has had a much larger voice in the corporate law reform process. Other recent examples of direct business and political input in the production of corporate law include the 2001 amendment permitting firms to limit the personal liability of directors for breach of duty, and withdrawal of a MOJ draft amendment requiring the appointment of at least one outside director to the board of large corporations.

84. Survey of Venture Capital Investment, *supra* note 31, at 23–4.

85. Id. at 3.

86. Black and Gilson, *supra* note 46.

87. See Edward B. Rock, Greenhorns, Yankees and Cosmopolitans: Venture Capital, IPOs, Foreign Firms, and U.S. Markets, 2 Theoretical Inq. L. 711 (2001).

88. North, *supra* note 9, at 103.

89. For an in-depth examination of the features of the U.S. template and an analysis of several foreign attempts to replicate it, see Gilson, *supra* note 1.

4

The "*Jusen* Problem"

The depths of Japan's bad debt problem are by now universally known. Excellent works have been devoted to analyzing the banking crisis and possible path of recovery for the industry.[1] Yet, perhaps because they are usually conducted by economists, analyses of how the Japanese financial industry fell into crisis seldom devote in-depth coverage to the role of Japanese regulatory style in the creation and resolution of that country's financial crisis. For a book such as this one, devoted to the impact of formal and informal rules on the Japanese economy, perhaps no episode in postwar history deserves more careful treatment than the collapse and resolution of Japan's home mortgage lending ("*jusen*") industry, the first of several Japanese financial crises in the 1990s and early 2000s.

The *jusen* problem arose when a special class of home mortgage lending companies abandoned their original mandate and lent heavily to real estate developers and speculators during the bubble economy. Directly at stake in the *jusen* problem was as much as ¥13 trillion ($130 billion) in unrecoverable loans. Moreover, the *jusen* companies were an integral part of a bad debt problem that may have totaled ¥80 trillion ($800 billion) at its peak, twice the size of America's S&L disaster measured as a percentage of GDP. The struggle to resolve the *jusen* crisis and to allocate the massive resulting losses captured the attention of regulators, politicians, and taxpayers, as well as the entire world financial community, from late 1995 to the summer of 1996. As explored at the end of the chapter, in subtle but significant ways, the ramifications of the *jusen* problem are still being felt.

The creation and resolution of the problem is one of the most striking examples of regulatory failure, intense political and bureaucratic activity, strategic interest group bargaining, and large-scale dispute resolution in recent Japanese history. For decades, commentators have debated the substance and success of Japanese regulatory methods, and the role of the bureaucracy, politics, and law in Japanese economic activity. The debate has raised more questions than it has answered: For example, what role do interest groups, politicians, and bureaucrats play in the political economy of Japan? To what extent have Japanese regulatory methods contributed to Japan's economic strength, and more recently to its financial woes? And the debate has largely bypassed other crucial issues, such as the strategic use of law to further the bargaining positions of Japanese interest groups.

This chapter adds fresh insights to this debate based on a detailed study of regulatory interaction in the Japanese financial industry during a time of unprecedented disruption and dissention. In the Introduction, we approvingly noted the adage that "There is no way to substitute pure theory for a knowledge of history."[2] This chapter is principally devoted to a recounting of recent history as a means of understanding Japanese postwar regulatory practices. Yet, we believe some simple theory helps sharpen the telling of that history. In this chapter, Japanese regulatory interaction is modeled as a network of (mostly informal) interrelated institutions that facilitate coordinated public–private decisionmaking—a system of financial governance we call a "regulatory cartel."[3] Briefly, as the term is used here, a regulatory cartel is an interlinked system for cooperative decisionmaking and enforcement among the public and private sectors, which operates according to reasonably well-understood substantive and procedural rules, and which has as its purpose and effect the control of entry, production, and price, not only within specified industries, but also across industrial sectors.

The term "regulatory cartel" is not intended to be pejorative; rather, the concept is employed here because it captures (imperfectly, but nonetheless powerfully) the dynamics of decisionmaking and enforcement that characterized Japanese finance in its heyday. Simply put, the *jusen* problem was an outgrowth of the incentives generated by this regulatory cartel. The implications of the model go beyond the *jusen* problem, however. The model helps to explain the relatively infrequent use of formal procedures and legal institutions in postwar Japanese finance, and offers insights into the nature of legal change in a mature, post-industrial Japan.

The chapter is organized into five sections. Drawing on cartel theory, Section I creates a simple model of regulatory interaction in Japanese finance composed of two sets of norms that have governed both the bargaining dynamics and substantive outcomes of Japanese financial regulation in the postwar period. Section II provides an overview of the *jusen* problem. Section III examines the efforts by regulated groups, regulators, and politicians to resolve the problem, with special attention devoted to bargaining strategies and the use and non-use of law in fashioning a solution. Section IV discusses the series of legal and institutional reforms implemented in the wake of the *jusen* problem, which constitute important facets of the template for Japanese financial regulation today. Section V shows that the *jusen* problem and its resolution are consistent with the model of regulatory interaction developed here, and shows that the response to the *jusen* problem illustrates the slow process of transition underway in Japanese financial regulation.

I. REGULATORY INTERACTION IN JAPANESE FINANCE

Cartel theory offers useful insights into both the process and content of financial regulation in postwar Japan. We use it here in a simple model of public–private interaction to explain Japanese financial regulation.

A. Japanese Finance as a Regulatory Cartel

The model is composed of two sets of norms, which we call "bargaining norms" and "substantive norms." Bargaining norms arise out of the institutional context of Japanese finance. They shape the structure of negotiations and the resolution of disputes in the financial industry, thereby determining the process by which regulation is made and enforced. The dynamics unleashed by these bargaining norms in turn generate a second set of norms that substantively shape the operation of the financial industry. Substantive norms govern primary conduct and encourage or discourage particular forms of behavior. Together, these norms constituted the rules of the game in Japanese finance until their graduate demise, a process ongoing to this day.

The essence of a cartel is coordinated decisionmaking.[4] In standard cartel theory, the object of agreement is price, output, or allocation of markets. In Japanese finance, the object of coordinated decisionmaking is the substantive terms of regulation. Japanese finance can profitably be viewed as a "regulatory cartel" in which both the regulated and the regulators cooperate in order to enforce market segmentation, control entry, regulate output, and allocate the gains of the cartel's activities among the various participants. We describe the Japanese system as a "regulatory" cartel because in place of the private rule-making, enforcement, and dispute resolution activities that characterize a typical industrial cartel in standard economic theory, the functions of control of output and entry are vested in government agencies as well as in private sector cooperation. The Japanese regulatory cartel, moreover, is characterized, not only by control of output and entry within a particular product market, but also by cross-market connections, functioning either at the administrative or the political level, which sometimes bring non-competing industries into contact with one another within the framework of an economy-wide network of regulated industries.

Coordinated decisionmaking, particularly over long periods of time, is not a naturally occurring phenomenon; it requires constant and extensive information exchange, intensive cooperation, and effective dispute resolution. In Japan, coordinated decisionmaking on matters of financial regulation, particularly prior to reforms in the late 1990s designed to separate policy making and enforcement functions in the Ministry of Finance (MOF), was facilitated by extensive ministerial compartmentalization and "patterning." That is, bureaucratic compartmentalization is extensively replicated elsewhere in the policy-making apparatus. In MOF's pre-reform institutional design, separate and relatively autonomous bureaus oversaw the banking and securities industries. Individual bureaus were further subdivided into sections that mirrored specific segments of the regulated industries, such as trust banking. These arrangements infused bureaucratic decisions with private party input from below, and channeled issue-specific political interests from above. Simultaneously, they provided mechanisms for public–private interaction, dispute resolution, and consensus-building.

The concentrated and compartmentalized nature of Japanese financial oversight had important effects on the formulation of policy and the resolution of disputes. MOF's sweeping mandate to regulate virtually the entire financial industry reduced the number of issues requiring cross-jurisdictional adjustment, and facilitated interest balancing. As one American scholar of Japanese finance observed, "[b]ecause MOF is a single institution, it is able to forge decisions that take into account its various sections."[5] Indeed, MOF's policies often seemed calculated principally to balance the interests of competing groups under its jurisdiction.

The structure of the financial industry itself facilitated policy coordination among competitors in the same sector. Both the banking and securities industries were and continue to be led by a small group of major players serving as front-line contacts with the regulators. The major firms often led their industries by example after consultation with senior Finance Ministry officials. Leadership is also provided by *gyōkai dantai*—powerful industry associations led by the same major firms. These respective roles are played by the largest of the city banks and the Federation of Japanese Bankers Associations in the banking industry and by the "Big Four" securities firms (down to three after the demise, in 1997, of Yamaichi Securities) and the Securities Industry Association in the securities industry. Consultations and conflict resolution within an industry and between an industry and its regulator often occur through the medium of the industry associations.

Employment patterns in the banking and securities industries enhanced information exchange and identity of interests between the major industry players and MOF officials. Specific bank and securities firm employees at each stage of the corporate hierarchy were often assigned to remain in daily contact with their counterparts at the relevant MOF bureau, a practice that is now declining. The large firms benefited from these practices through close, ongoing contacts with the regulators; ministry officials, in turn, obtained information, advice, and favors from the major firms.

For smaller firms especially, another important employment-related practice is *amakudari*, in which bureaucrats parachute into lucrative private-sector positions at the end of their careers in public service. While the prevalence of the practice varies across Japanese industries, historically it was widespread in finance. The traditional rationale behind *amakudari* is that retired bureaucrats provide an important link between the new host firm and the ex-official's former agency. Lacking such established links, smaller firms disproportionately hired retired bureaucrats. It was believed that a firm's contact base, information flow, and public image of stability and competence would all be enhanced by hiring an ex-official. (In Chapter 8, we explore *amakudari* further, and show that the practice has waned considerably in recent years, as deregulation, bureaucratic scandals, and other factors have undermined the rationale for hiring ex-officials.)

Yet another institution that facilitates coordinated public–private interaction is the *shingikai* (consultative committee). Statutorily created *shingikai* are attached to and appointed by administrative agencies. Their principal ostensible role is to examine significant policy issues under the charge of their parent agencies. Although the *shingikai* are often derided as ornamental rubber stamps, to dismiss them as meaningless would be a serious mistake. In fact, the *shingikai* perform an important role in facilitating group decisionmaking and resolving disputes. This they accomplish in a number of ways. They provide a supplementary channel for public–private interaction beyond the means previously described. They serve as listening posts for ministry officials while shielding the bureaucrats from direct exposure to interest group influences, and they give affected interests a stake in policy outcomes, since interested parties have participated in the process of policy formulation. Above all, they are a means of adjusting conflicting interests within the affected ministry.

At the top of the policymaking network, a distinctive political mechanism infuses the regulatory process with interest-group concerns. LDP legislators coalesce into issue-specific groups called *zoku* (tribes), which exert influence on the ministries. The *zoku* legislators work to support industries in their districts by developing a special relationship with the relevant bureaucracy. Once the relationship is established, they lobby for policy proposals, mediate between the bureaucracy and interest groups, and participate in the pertinent LDP policymaking process. Once again patterning is evident, as the *zoku* legislators are arranged hierarchically according to their degree of influence with the ministry and specialized according to the bureau or section of the ministry where they operate.

This segmented and hierarchical institutional design gave rise to the following set of bargaining norms that controlled consensus formation and conflict resolution in postwar Japanese finance:

1. *Internal Cooperation*: If possible, policy conflicts or issues were to be resolved within the group principally affected, without percolation up to the next level. Large firms and industry associations led the coordination process.

2. *Brokerage and Facilitation*: If internal resolution proved impossible, policy conflicts or issues percolated up to the next major level of authority—typically the appropriate bureau within the ministry responsible—with brokerage and facilitation services provided by that higher-level authority. Such services could include extensive consultations with affected groups, sponsorship of negotiations, informal persuasion, interest balancing, and public relations efforts.

3. *Negotiated Inter-jurisdictional Resolution*: If policy conflicts or issues spilled over between jurisdictional lines, they were resolved through negotiations between higher level authorities, if possible. The higher level authorities were the Administrative Vice Minister and other upper echelon career officials within a single ministry if the issue affected two industries under the jurisdiction of the same ministry. If the issue affected two industries under the jurisdiction of different ministries, the higher-level authorities were the ministers of the two ministries.

4. *Channeled Political Intervention*: If resolution through inter-jurisdictional negotiations was unsuccessful, policy conflicts or issues were resolved through overt political intervention in the bargaining process. Often, political intervention

would take the form of pressure applied by *zoku* legislators at the bureau or section level of the relevant ministry.

These bargaining norms represent approaches the regulatory cartel undertook to deal with increasingly difficult problems. It should be noted that when a problem proved incapable of resolution at one level so that the system moved to the next level of bargaining, the process would not necessarily cease at the previous level. The relevant actors could continue discussions at the previous level, even after impasse, on the theory that consensus might still be possible at the lower level once the higher-level bargaining process has commenced, or at least that continuing lower-level discussions could facilitate the bargaining at higher levels. Accordingly, as a problem became more complex and difficult to resolve, several levels of bargaining were likely to occur simultaneously.

These bargaining norms and the institutional design which generated them supplied the infrastructure for regulatory coordination in Japanese finance. For example, a policy conflict or issue involving only the banking industry was resolved internally by the banking industry if possible, typically through the mechanism of the Federation of Bankers Associations. If an internal solution was not possible, the Banking Bureau would broker a resolution of the issue. If the issue affected the securities industry as well, resolution would implicate both the Banking and Securities Bureaus. If possible, such problems were worked out between the director generals of these bureaus, with input from the industry associations and major firms in the industries. Particularly thorny issues affecting both industries were resolved at the ministry level in consultation with the Administrative Vice Minister. The most problematic issues, and those most likely to be resolved through overt political intervention, were those involving industries under the jurisdiction of more than one ministry.[6] Such issues were resolved through high-level inter-ministerial consultation. The operations of senior political leaders and *zoku* legislators was evident in these cases.

The practice of *nemawashi* (laying the groundwork for a consensus-based decision) can best be viewed as the organic manipulation of the institutional machinery by actors subject to these bargaining norms. Discussions led by industry associations and major firms are held at the industry level to formulate an initial policy position; bureaucrats broker deals and facilitate negotiations among competing interests with an eye on political realities; *shingikai* are assembled to coordinate and legitimate compromises; and *zoku* legislators are mobilized when the process does not appear to be generating a result favorable to specific interest groups.

B. The Dynamics of Cartel-like Cooperation and the Creation of Substantive Norms

Borrowing again from cartel theory, we next show that the dynamics set in motion by these bargaining norms have had substantive effects on Japanese financial regulation. Colloquially, commentators have dubbed the propensity of Japanese regulators to protect all members of the financial industry—however weak—the "convoy policy." It is useful to disaggregate this policy into several distinct, legally unenforceable but widely followed practices (norms). These norms, in turn, flow directly from the impulses generated by the regulatory cartel.

Cartel theory predicts that once a mutual understanding has been reached as to price and division of output, the second task of cartel members is to "promote mutual confidence that there will be adherence to these decisions."[7] Adherence to the group's decisions is problematic because cartels are inherently unstable. Since each individual member of a cartel will be better off if it can provide consumers slightly better terms than those offered by other cartel members, there are powerful incentives to cheat on the cartel. Simply put, the raw allocations of profits, power, and prestige that accompany cartel-like behavior constantly threaten to undermine the cooperation essential to continued functioning of the cartel. Those with the most to gain (or the least to lose) by operating outside of the agreed system will have incentives to discontinue cooperation. Thus, institutional settings and bargaining norms that facilitate coordinated group decisionmaking simultaneously unleash powerful incentives for individual members to defect from the group.

As members of a cartel, players in Japanese finance were subject to the same centrifugal forces. In order to deal with incentives that are self-destructive to the group, substantive norms were generated by the bargaining dynamics in Japanese finance.

1. *Survival of the weakest.* Policies (rates) are set to permit the survival of the weakest member of the group. The weakest member of the group is often the one most likely to defect from the group's norms because the benefit this member obtains from abiding by those norms may be outweighed by the benefit it can obtain through defection. Because defection by one member can threaten the entire structure, the weakest member has a credible threat that places it in a strong bargaining position vis-à-vis its counterparts. In consequence, the substantive norms of the group are likely to protect the weakest member in order to ensure this member's continuing loyalty to the group.

The norm of survival of the weakest benefits the stronger as well as the weak members. In addition to enhancing the durability of the cartel as a whole, the survival of the weakest norm may support pricing arrangements that allow the weakest member to stay in business, while allowing more efficient producers to earn supercompetitive profits.

2. *No exit (no failure).* A corollary of the principle of survival of the weakest is that of no exit: No group member is allowed to exit (fail).[8] This enhances stability both by preventing failure by weaker members and by increasing public confidence in the management of the group.

3. *Responsibility and equitable subordination.* When the danger of financial failure grows, the parent or principal source of funding for the failing entity is

expected to take responsibility by extending financial assistance and by subordinating its claims to those of other creditors, even if not legally required to do so. This norm encourages monitoring by stronger group members, by imposing both monetary and reputational costs on stronger players who allow smaller players under their jurisdiction to fall into difficulty.

4. *Implicit government insurance.* The preceding norms lead naturally to a substantive norm of implicit insurance provided by the government. If strong members are expected to assist weaker members and if no member of the group is allowed to fail, some entity must backstop the strong members. Thus, an implicit grant of government insurance is inherent in the operation of the other norms. Put differently, the responsibility and equitable subordination norm extends even to the government.

We believe that the best explanation for the existence of these norms is the incentive to cheat on the regulatory cartel. Together, the substantive norms instill confidence in and prevent exit from the group, enhance group stability, and encourage monitoring of weaker group members by stronger members.

C. The Effects of Cartel-like Cooperation in Finance

Viewing the bargaining and substantive norms as animated by cartel-like dynamics provides a powerful explanation for the observable behavior of regulators and regulated in the Japanese banking industry for most of the postwar period. Due to its central position in the decisionmaking matrix, control over group entry, and role as ultimate guarantor of the financial system, MOF served as an enforcer of the regulatory cartel (subject to potential intervention by the LDP if MOF proved unable to resolve a conflict). The function of the cartel was to coordinate decisionmaking on the regulation of the financial industry and to maintain both group member and public confidence in those decisions.

As with cartel behavior generally, a central aim of cooperation in this regulatory system was to generate and allocate rents: Votes and political patronage were allocated among political elites; regulatory property rights and concomitant distributions of power, prestige, and budgetary appropriations were allocated among separate ministries; similar rights were allocated among intra-ministry bureaus; licenses to engage in lucrative activities were allocated among industries; and profits were allocated among large and small firms.

The cartel perspective helps explain the traditionally infrequent resort to formal legal institutions in Japanese finance, and we believe, in Japan generally. Informal "*ex ante* monitoring" or "preclearance"[9] is the process by which the decisions of the regulatory cartel were made and enforced. Until recently, courts were virtually never involved in Japanese finance because they are competing enforcement agents whose basic attributes undermine cooperation and politically attuned interest balancing. Institutionally, courts lie outside the network of consensus-building mechanisms that facilitate the regulatory cartel. Courts deal only with litigants, who almost by definition are one-time players that have strong incentives to defect from a cooperative game. Similarly, formal administrative procedures are designed to protect the integrity of bureaucratic decisionmaking and to provide redress for those aggrieved by agency action. There are far fewer occasions to use such procedures where public–private interaction takes place among a limited number of repeat players following informal norms that govern the regulatory process.

Cartel-like regulatory interaction in Japanese finance had substantial positive effects and considerable staying power. It provided stability in times of stress caused by high growth, led to enormous public confidence in the abilities of bureaucratic elites to manage the economy wisely and in the public interest, and virtually eliminated costly resort to formal legal institutions and divisive litigation in the formulation and enforcement of financial regulation. Plausible arguments might be made that *ex ante* monitoring is justified on efficiency grounds over formal rule making.[10]

However, as the *jusen* problem dramatically illustrates, cartel-like regulatory activities produced harmful effects as well. Such activities are non-transparent by definition, making it difficult to discern the rationale supporting policy decisions and the process by which decisions are reached. The possibility of corruption or undue influence cannot be entirely discounted. Cartel-like activities are rigid to the extent that they protect vested interests and remain impervious to outside influences. Perhaps most seriously, the need to prevent cheating by barring exit from the group creates enormous moral hazard by forcing the government implicitly to underwrite risky behavior. Over time, the incentives generated by informal, cartel-like regulation can create an environment in which individual actors rationally pursuing their own interests lead to disaster for the system as a whole. This, in essence, is the story of the *jusen* problem.

II. THE *JUSEN* PROBLEM

We now turn from a general explication of the bargaining and substantive norms of Japanese finance to the causes of the *jusen* problem itself.

A. Establishment and Monitoring of the *Jusen* Companies

The *jusen* companies were established in the early 1970s, principally for the purpose of providing housing loans to individuals. From the time of their establishment, the *jusen* companies fell into a curious regulatory lacuna. As nondepository institutions, the *jusen* companies did not fall directly under MOF's jurisdiction as regulator of the nation's banks. Nor were the *jusen* companies engaged in the insurance or securities businesses, which would have similarly brought them under MOF's broad ambit. And they were certainly not engaged in other activities, such as imports and exports, that could have brought them under the jurisdiction of another agency such as the Ministry of International Trade and Industry. In the case of the *jusen* companies, policymakers reached the conclusion—curious in hindsight—that these companies should not be directly regulated by any agency. The *shingikai* advising the Minister of Finance on the creation of a separate class of mortgage lending institutions recommended that the *jusen* companies not be treated as an integral part of the financial system. The panel's 1973 report states, "At least for the present time, there is little need to regulate the *jusen* companies from the standpoint of protecting consumers. Rather, it is appropriate for the time being to observe what type of housing finance institution best suits our national circumstances."[11]

At least in theory the *jusen* companies did not escape all regulatory oversight; the formal basis for their regulation, however, was indirect and opaque. As businesses engaged in lending, the *jusen* companies were subject to a registration requirement[12] and to the "investigative" authority of MOF.[13] For reasons that have never been made clear, however, the relevant statutes distinguished between MOF's authority to "investigate" the business and finances of the *jusen* companies, and its power to "inspect" other registered businesses engaged in lending. MOF officials asserted that the former power was weaker, but the exact import of the distinction is not apparent from the relevant statutes. Regardless of the legal distinction, MOF apparently did not exercise *any* regulatory authority over the *jusen* companies from the time of their establishment until 1991.

Further obscuring the *jusen* regulatory picture is the practice of *amakudari*. The *jusen* companies were attractive landing places for MOF officials. As of 1995, thirteen directors of the *jusen* companies were former MOF officials.[14] All of these retired bureaucrats held senior positions in their new companies. Ten of the twenty-six men who served as presidents of the *jusen* companies were former MOF officials. Seven of the eleven chairpersons were retired MOF officials. And twelve of ninety-five representative directors were originally employed by MOF.[15] These figures lend support to popular speculation that MOF encouraged the establishment of the *jusen* companies, in part because they would provide attractive second career opportunities for financial bureaucrats.

Amakudari created an insidious set of incentives in relation to regulation of the *jusen* companies. Current MOF officials were loath to criticize their former superiors at the ministry who had retired and were now managing the *jusen* companies. Moreover, there was little reason to exercise MOF's attenuated formal regulatory authority when so many informal channels to *jusen* management already existed. MOF was clearly in a position to monitor and influence the *jusen* companies through the major banks, insurance companies, and securities firms that were their founding institutions, all of which fell under MOF's jurisdiction. As shown below, however, to the extent that MOF exercised any such influence, it contributed to rather than alleviated the monitoring problems that beset the *jusen* companies. As a result, the *jusen* companies remained essentially unregulated entities from the time of their establishment until the seriousness of their financial situation became apparent in the early 1990s.

For distinct reasons, shareholder and director monitoring of the *jusen* companies were also ineffective at preventing risky lending behavior. The founding institutions held most of the stock of the *jusen* companies, and almost 90 percent of the directors of the *jusen* companies were dispatched from the founding institutions.[16] In Japanese financial circles, there is an understanding that some activities which would be unacceptable if performed directly by a major financial institution are permissible if performed indirectly through an intermediary. The *jusen* companies provided just such a buffer, even though they remained under the influence of the founding institutions.

This business climate led to a practice known in Japan as "introduction finance" and other practices that increased the risk of the *jusen* companies' loan portfolios. High-risk or unsavory borrowers who would not have qualified for loans from major banks were "introduced" by the founding institutions to their *jusen* company affiliates, often for a substantial finders' fee. Over half of the loan business of some *jusen* companies consisted of this type of introduction finance.[17] There is also widespread understanding in the Japanese financial community that the *jusen* companies were forced to take nonperforming assets off the books of the founding institutions, and were used to evade lending limits applicable to the parent banks.

The lack of close monitoring by the shareholders and directors of the *jusen* companies was also a product of the times. As discussed below, most of the riskiest and most questionable business practices of the *jusen* companies coincided with Japan's bubble economy, one of the most remarkable examples of financial speculation in history. Speculative behavior and lax oversight were exemplified by, but by no means limited to, the *jusen* companies.

In short, the *jusen* companies were not closely monitored by their regulators, shareholders, or directors.

B. Financial Liberalization and the Business of the *Jusen* Companies

As noted above, the *jusen* companies were founded to provide home mortgages to individuals. At the time of their establishment, commercial banks were not eager to engage directly in this line of business. In 1971, banks provided just 29 percent of all individual home mortgage loans.[18] Gradually, however, financial liberalization changed the landscape of Japanese banking. Regulatory constraints that had limited access to the capital markets and held corporate borrowers in long-term relationships with their bankers began to weaken. As banks began to lose corporate finance business to the capital markets in the mid-1970s and 1980s, the home mortgage lending business became more attractive. By 1980, the banks' share of the home mortgage lending market had grown to 39 percent.[19] This newfound banking business grew at the expense of the *jusen* companies. From a peak of just over 7 percent of the market in 1980, the *jusen* companies' share of the home finance business fell to 5 percent in 1985, and then shrank at a rate of about 1 percent per year from 1985 to 1988, falling to less than 2 percent in 1993.[20]

To compensate for the loss of the home mortgage lending business to the founding institutions and other banks, the *jusen* companies abandoned their original mandate and began lending heavily to corporate borrowers. In 1980, the *jusen* companies lent just ¥15 billion ($150 million) to corporations compared to ¥317 billion ($3.17 billion) in lending to individuals.[21] In 1986, the percentages of corporate and individual lending were almost equal. By 1988, the *jusen* companies were lending almost twice as much to corporations as to individuals. And by 1990, corporate lending had reached ¥973 billion ($9.73 billion), against just ¥265 billion ($2.65 billion) in lending to individuals.[22] Many of these corporate borrowers were real estate developers and speculators too small for the capital markets, and of insufficient credit quality for the banks.

Thus, although the *jusen* companies were established to engage in home mortgage lending, they changed their focus to corporate lending as the home mortgage business was largely lost to commercial banks in the decade after their founding.

C. The Agricultural Credit Cooperative System and the *Jusen* Companies' Source of Funds

At the same time as their core business was being eroded, the *jusen* companies began borrowing huge sums from agricultural cooperatives, which constitute a separate financial system and a potent political force in Japan. These cooperatives were established in virtually every village in Japan shortly after the end of the Second World War to provide financing for agricultural development. The political power of the cooperatives derives from the importance of agricultural policy in Japan and the vote gathering capacity of the system for the LDP. As a network of farm institutions with millions of members spread throughout every electoral district in Japan, the agricultural cooperatives are a powerful political medium. Although organized ostensibly for technological and financial purposes, the cooperatives provided a ready-made channel through which the interests of the farmers could express themselves in the political process. The farmers, moreover, are an interest group which in Japan, as in the United States, has inherent advantages in the political process: They are dispersed throughout the country and, because they have a large, nondiversified investment in their businesses, the value of which is heavily dependent on government policies, they tend to be politically active both in voting and in campaign contributions.[23] Not surprisingly, the *zoku* legislators who focus on agricultural interests, called *nōrinzoku*, are among the most powerful and effective.

As the economics of Japanese agriculture changed, the credit cooperatives drifted away from their initial function of serving the credit needs of farmers. Farmers' demand for credit fell as the percentage of Japanese GNP occupied by agriculture declined. And as the income of farmers diversified and increased, the deposits of the credit cooperatives grew dramatically. To resolve the mismatch between liabilities and assets, the agricultural cooperatives increasingly turned to the *jusen* companies. Consequently, agricultural cooperative loans to the *jusen* companies increased almost sixfold between 1985 and 1992.

D. The Bubble Economy and its Impact on the *Jusen* Companies

The final step in the creation of the *jusen* problem was Japan's bubble economy, which lasted from 1988 to 90. The bubble economy had a profound effect on the *jusen* institutions. One important ingredient was the sudden riches that came into the hands of Japan's farmers, already quite prosperous as a result of favorable government policies towards agriculture and extensive outside income. Many farmers, especially in the areas abutting major cities, found that they could sell their properties and become instantly wealthy. They began to sell agricultural land to developers in large numbers, depositing much of the proceeds in their local agricultural credit cooperative. Investment in these cooperatives was by no means an irrational decision: They were convenient, well known, paid a good rate of return, and appeared to be perfectly safe. Thus, large amounts of new money flowed into the local agricultural cooperatives. Deposits in the local cooperatives jumped from ¥39 trillion ($390 billion) in 1985 to ¥61 trillion ($600 billion) in 1991.

The massive inflow of funds to the local cooperatives was accompanied by stagnant or even decreasing loan demand for traditional farming credit. The net effect of the bubble economy on the agricultural cooperatives, therefore, was to create a mountain of cash looking for a profitable investment. The *jusen* companies appeared to be perfect candidates for such investments. Cooperative lending to the *jusen* firms became particularly pronounced after the bubble economy began to collapse in 1990. In that year, lending surged from ¥2.9 trillion ($29 billion) to ¥4.9 trillion ($49 billion). This spike can be traced directly to a MOF administrative circular issued in March of 1990.[24] The administrative guidance was designed to rein in lending for speculative real estate transactions, which was contributing to dramatic asset inflation. The circular provided that each bank should restrict the growth in its real estate lending to no more than the growth in its overall loan portfolio.[25] To help enforce the restrictions, in the same circular, the banks were advised to notify MOF of all loans made to the real estate, construction, or non-bank industries.

There were two crucial omissions in this administrative guidance that would play a major role in agricultural cooperative and *jusen* financing over the next five years. First, while a companion circular addressed to the agricultural cooperatives similarly limited the growth of their direct real estate lending, they were not required to report loans made to the real estate, construction, or non-bank industries. Second, no restrictions of any kind were placed on real estate lending by the *jusen* companies. The practical effect of these omissions was to create a financing pipeline from the agricultural cooperatives, through the *jusen* companies, to the real estate industry. The agricultural cooperatives could lend unlimited amounts to the *jusen* companies[26] without so much as a reporting requirement; the *jusen* companies, in turn, could lend unlimited sums borrowed from the agricultural cooperatives to real estate developers and speculators. There was a dramatic increase in *jusen* borrowing from the agricultural cooperatives after the March 1990 administrative guidance.

When the bubble burst, the quality of real estate loan assets held by the *jusen* companies deteriorated substantially, and corporate bankruptcies skyrocketed. As a result of these developments, it had become clear as early as 1991 that the *jusen* companies were in serious financial difficulty. Land and stock prices had begun a steep descent, and corporate borrowers were encountering increasing financial problems. MOF undertook its first on-site investigation of the *jusen* companies in 1991. The investigation showed that the seven *jusen* companies held a total of ¥4.6 trillion ($46 billion) in nonperforming loans, equivalent to 38 percent of their total loan portfolio.[27] The *jusen* companies were in serious trouble, but the worst was yet to come.

III. RESOLVING THE PROBLEM

In this Section, we examine the attempts to resolve the nonperforming loan problem of the *jusen* companies. While we defer our analysis of these attempts to Section IV, the narrative below clearly illustrates the stress this problem placed on the bargaining and substantive norms of cooperation and coordinated decision-making, and the failure of traditional methods to address adequately a problem of this magnitude. Indeed, as will be shown, reliance on the norms actually exacerbated the problem, leading to a crisis in 1995. Ultimately, the bargaining and substantive norms were employed only in modified form in the *jusen* context, and a partial infrastructure was put in place to move Japanese financial regulation toward a new, more legally oriented and transparent set of standards.

A. Initial Attempts to Restructure *Jusen* Loans

In view of the serious financial condition of the *jusen* companies, five-year restructuring plans for each company were devised under MOF supervision in late 1991 and early 1992. These plans involved reductions in lending, interest rate reductions on loans made by the founding institutions, loan support from non-founding lenders, and cost-cutting measures.[28]

These plans, however, failed to improve the financial condition of the *jusen* companies. In fact, their condition continued to deteriorate, and by early 1993 it was necessary to formulate a second restructuring plan. MOF rejected a Sanwa Bank proposal to undertake a full-scale restructuring of the *jusen* company it had founded, and instead orchestrated the formulation of a new, ten-year restructuring plan for each of the *jusen* companies, using Sanwa's *jusen* affiliate as a model.

The centerpiece of these second restructurings was interest rate reduction. The founding institutions completely eliminated the interest charged on their loans to the *jusen* companies. Other bank lenders reduced their interest rate to 2.5 percent, the official Bank of Japan discount rate at the time. The agricultural credit cooperatives reduced their interest rate to 4.5 percent, their cost of funds at the time.[29]

During the process of consensus-building among the regulators and interested private parties that preceded the second restructuring, a memorandum was exchanged that would become controversial when the *jusen* problem developed into a crisis two years later. At a meeting in February of 1993, the Director General of MOF's Banking Bureau provided a memorandum to his counterpart in the Economic Affairs Bureau of MAFF. The memorandum, a masterpiece of bureaucratic obfuscation, can be interpreted as providing that the founding institutions, backed by MOF assurances, would guarantee the principal amount of all loans made by the agricultural cooperatives to the *jusen* companies. The critical passage of the memorandum states:

The founding financial institutions will take responsibility for dealing with the restructuring plan of [the relevant *jusen* company] (MOF will take responsibility for guiding [the parties involved] so that no burdens will be imposed on the agriculture-related institutions... beyond those contemplated by the current measures).[30]

The exact import of this language is unclear; indeed, the passage is pregnant with studied ambiguity. To be sure, the founding institutions do not explicitly guarantee the agricultural cooperatives' loans to their *jusen* company affiliates. Nor does MOF explicitly provide such a guarantee on behalf of the founding institutions. Indeed, as a regulatory agency, MOF possesses no legal authority to issue such a guarantee in the name of private financial institutions. Yet, the passage is open to the interpretation that MOF was providing assurances that the agricultural cooperatives' losses in connection with the *jusen* company workouts would be limited to interest rate reductions under the restructuring plans. Given the traditional rules under which players in Japanese finance have operated, and given MOF's influence over the institutions involved, it is not unreasonable to assume that MOF had the informal power to make good on such a commitment, if indeed one was made.

The February 1993 memorandum would appear to represent a significant concession by MOF, since MOF appeared to be making some kind of commitment that the assets of the founding institutions would stand behind the agriculture-related institutions' *jusen* loans. Why would MOF, supposedly a champion of banking interests, agree to such terms? Part of the answer appears to be the fact that the agricultural cooperatives had the power to destroy the *jusen* companies by withdrawing their loans. Thus, it is possible that MOF needed to issue this extraordinary memorandum because it feared a withdrawal of agricultural cooperative money from the *jusen* companies. By 1992, the agricultural cooperatives had become a vital source of funding for the *jusen* companies, accounting for ¥5.6 trillion ($56 billion) out of ¥14 trillion ($140 billion) in total loans. Foreign lenders had already begun to withdraw their funding in anticipation of serious problems. If the agricultural cooperatives had similarly ceased lending, the *jusen* companies would have quickly collapsed. This threat was mitigated, to some extent, by the fact that if the *jusen* companies collapsed as a result of withdrawals by the agricultural cooperatives, the cooperatives would not, in fact, be able to withdraw all their funds, and the remaining investments in the *jusen* companies would lose much of their value. The threat, nevertheless, had some credibility because the cooperatives had less to lose from the collapse of the *jusen* companies than did either the founding institutions or MOF. For the founding institutions, collapse of the *jusen* firms would represent both a large financial loss and also a reduction in prestige and public confidence. For MOF, a *jusen* collapse would be extremely embarrassing because of MOF's role in creating these companies and staffing them with *amakudari* officials. Moreover, a *jusen* collapse would have raised questions both in Japan and around the world about the stability of the Japanese financial sector generally.

In the face of this situation, although MOF could not issue a guarantee, it also could not afford to lose the support of the agricultural cooperatives. The result was conscious ambiguity. When the memorandum surfaced publicly two years later, the finance and agriculture ministry officials involved disputed its significance.[31]

This ambiguity was a natural byproduct of the intense negotiations that ensued between MOF and MAFF officials. MOF was under tremendous conflicting pressures from the farm lobby and MAFF on the one hand, and the banks under its jurisdiction on the other. At the time, the memorandum must have seemed a brilliant solution to the problem, and one that was fully consistent with the substantive norms of Japanese financial regulation, including the government's implicit role as ultimate guarantor of the financial system.

Indeed, the second restructuring vividly illustrates the bargaining and substantive norms of Japanese financial regulation in action. In this case, a serious problem that spilled over jurisdictional lines was resolved through inter-ministerial negotiations, following intense mobilization of industry and political forces on both sides. MOF officials, at the center of this activity, facilitated a solution based on accepted substantive principles. Consistent with the survival of the weakest norm, the agricultural cooperatives were granted the most favorable deal in the restructuring. The founding institutions, under the responsibility norm, took on far more than their pro rata share of the burden of interest rate reductions. The first *jusen* company to be established, which was founded by a major bank with close relations to MOF, was used as the model to be followed in the restructuring of the other *jusen* companies.

The second "restructuring" of the *jusen* companies was also a classic example of regulatory "forbearance": An attempt to buy time in the hope that economic conditions would improve, lifting the *jusen* companies out of their financial problems. Under this policy of forbearance, however, the nonperforming assets of the *jusen* companies multiplied rapidly. The nonperforming assets of the seven *jusen* companies increased by 75 percent during the four years between MOF's first on-site investigation of the *jusen* companies and a second on-site investigation in August of 1995.[32] Real estate prices did not recover as forecast by MOF, and a serious financial situation turned desperate. By March 1995, the *jusen* companies had borrowed a total of almost ¥13 trillion ($130 billion) and had made loans of ¥10.72 trillion ($107 billion). Even according to MOF's calculations, considered by independent analysts to be optimistic, ¥8.13 trillion ($81 billion) of these loans were nonperforming; and ¥6.27 trillion ($63 billion) of these nonperforming loans were deemed to be completely unrecoverable.[33]

By March 1995, almost 75 percent (¥9.697 trillion, $97 billion out of a total of ¥13.060 trillion, $130 billion) of the combined assets of all seven *jusen* companies were nonperforming. Almost 60 percent (almost ¥6.3 trillion, $63 billion) of the loans made by the *jusen* companies were completely unrecoverable. All seven of the *jusen* companies were insolvent by September of 1995.

In spite of, or perhaps more accurately due to, the initial attempts to deal with the *jusen* companies' nonperforming loans, the *jusen* problem had reached catastrophic proportions.

B. Pressure Builds

By the summer of 1995, the *jusen* problem had taken on practical and symbolic significance at the center of the bad debt crisis facing the Japanese financial system, particularly because the *jusen* companies were the first class of Japanese financial institutions that simply could not continue to operate under their current weight of nonperforming loans.

An interim report of the Financial System Stabilization Committee, part of a standing MOF advisory panel, explained that because

> *Jusen* companies hold a large amount of problem loans and many financial institutions give financing to *Jusen* companies, the *Jusen* problem can have a significant influence on the stability of the financial system as a whole. Thus, the *Jusen* problem has become symbolic in the non-performing loan problem and should be urgently addressed.[34]

A number of other factors added to the sense of crisis surrounding the Japanese financial system. The Daiwa Bank scandal (see Chapter 2) and persistent doubts about the accuracy of MOF's estimates of the amount of nonperforming loans held by Japanese financial institutions diminished its credibility as a regulator. Moreover, the international financial community began to perceive an unusual systemic risk in Japanese finance arising from the no failure norm and the informal purchase and assumption transactions (in which a strong bank purchases the assets and assumes the liabilities of an insolvent bank) MOF had used to enforce the norm. The concern was that MOF, in an effort to rescue troubled financial institutions at any cost, would jeopardize the health of otherwise strong institutions by forcing them to acquire institutions that should have been allowed to fail.

The international financial markets began to exact a price for these concerns in the form of the "Japan Premium," an additional risk premium charged by non-Japanese banks on loans to Japanese banks in international money markets. In September of 1995, the Japan Premium was fifty basis points (0.5 percent), a significant premium given the razor-thin margins of international money markets. The Japan Premium was particularly galling to major Japanese banks, because no matter how strong they were financially, the international financial markets were penalizing them for their country's bad debt crisis and financial regulatory style. The Japan Premium was also intensely embarrassing to the Japanese government and its economic agencies.

The coalescence of these domestic and international forces created a public outcry over the *jusen* problem reminiscent of America's S&L crisis in the late 1980s, and made the formulation of concrete measures to deal effectively with the jusen problem not only unavoidable, but also urgent.

C. Early Negotiations

To develop actual measures addressing the *jusen* problem, the Financial System Stabilization Committee chose to rely on time-honored Japanese methods. Its interim report urged the *jusen* companies and the founding institutions to "play substantive roles in agreeing on the basic future policies and disposal scheme of problem loans."[35] The Committee encouraged discussions among the interested parties, particularly between the founding institutions and the agricultural credit cooperatives, and requested that all parties concerned "make as many concessions as possible, with due recognition of their own responsibilities in the *Jusen* problem, considering the historical background and other relevant factors."[36] Simultaneously, the report encouraged the regulators to promote the formation of consensus among the parties in creating an overall framework for the solution of the problem.

To address the *jusen* issue specifically, MOF initiated negotiations between the founding institutions and the agricultural credit cooperatives in the fall of 1995 in order to divide the approximately ¥7.5 trillion ($75 billion) of immediate losses connected with the *jusen* companies. While there are an infinite number of potential ways to apportion the losses, the actual theories discussed followed a few stylized models, reflecting disparate views about responsibility for the *jusen* problem in light of the substantive norms of Japanese finance.

The agricultural institutions asserted that the founders should bear the entire amount of the losses (the "founder liability argument"). They stressed that the founding institutions had established, managed, and dominated the operation of the *jusen* companies, and thus should bear full responsibility for their downfall. Moreover, the agricultural institutions pointed to the memorandum exchanged in 1993 as proof that their loans to the *jusen* companies were guaranteed by the founding institutions and ultimately by MOF. The founder liability argument is a clear expression of the "responsibility" norm.

The founding institutions, standing to lose the most under straightforward application of the substantive norms of Japanese finance, sought to defect from the traditional arrangement and relied on common bankruptcy principles in staking out their position. The founding institutions countered that the *jusen* companies were separate legal entities, and there was no basis for treating some creditors more favorably than others. Thus, all lenders should share the losses in proportion to their loans to the *jusen* companies (the "lender liability argument").

A third position, intermediate between the first two, held that the founding institutions' responsibility should be limited to the value of their own loans to the *jusen* companies. Under this "modified founder liability" theory, the founding

Table 4.1. *Possible loss allocation methods and their impact on lenders to the* jusen *companies (unit: trillion ¥)*

Lending group	Loans made to *jusen*	Lender liability[a]	Founder liability[b]	Modified founder liability[c]
Founding institutions	3.5	2.1	7.5	3.5
Other lenders	3.8	2.2	–	1.7
Agricultural cooperatives	5.5	3.2	–	2.3
Total	12.8	7.5[d]	7.5[d]	7.5[d]

Notes:
[a] All lenders to *jusen* companies bear losses in proportion to total losses/total loans.
[b] Founding institutions bear all losses.
[c] Founding institutions write off all loans to *jusen* companies. Agricultural cooperatives and other lenders bear remaining losses in proportion to their loans to *jusen* companies.
[d] Total losses include ¥6.27 trillion in unrecoverable loans and ¥1.24 trillion of nonperforming loans.
Source: 1413 Shōji hōmu 19, 21 (1996).

institutions would write off all their loans to the *jusen* companies, and all other lenders would bear losses in proportion to their *jusen* loans.

As Table 4.1 illustrates, the loss allocation method chosen would have a profound financial impact on the three distinct groups of financial institutions involved in lending to the *jusen* companies—founding institutions, agricultural credit cooperatives, and other bank lenders. The negotiations, then, represented not posturing based on abstract theories of liability, but concrete and desperate attempts to avoid trillions of yen in losses.

The enormous sums of money at stake amplified the debate over who bore responsibility for the failure of the *jusen* companies. To take the most dramatic example, as Table 4.1 indicates, there is a ¥5.4 trillion ($54 billion) difference between the loss that the founding institutions would collectively bear under a "founder liability" theory of loss allocation, and the corresponding loss under a pro rata "lender liability" theory. Under a pro rata lender liability theory of loss allocation as would be applicable in a formal bankruptcy proceeding, the agricultural cooperatives, as the largest lenders to the *jusen* companies, would bear the largest share of the losses. Conversely, the founding institutions would bear the lightest burden in formal bankruptcy proceedings.

Negotiations to resolve the loss allocation controversy proceeded on several levels simultaneously. At the center of attempts to resolve the problem were the MOF-sponsored talks between the founding institutions and the agricultural cooperatives. The ruling coalition formed a Securities and Finance Project Team to monitor the negotiations. When consensus among the principals to the negotiations proved elusive, an LDP *Jusen* Problem Study Group was established to generate political momentum toward a solution. By November 1995, senior MOF officials had entered into full-scale bilateral negotiations with their counterparts at MAFF on the issue of loss allocation. And beneath the surface, a battle by proxy was being fought on behalf of the agricultural cooperatives by the *nōrinzoku* politicians on the one hand, and by politicians aligned with MOF in support of the banks on the other. The associations representing the various agriculture-affiliated financial institutions visited MOF to report on the negotiations and to request that MOF guide the founding institutions toward accepting full responsibility for the *jusen* losses.[37]

These behind-the-scenes maneuvers prompted a public debate over the use of informal methods rather than legal procedures to resolve the *jusen* problem. Editorials began to appear in Japanese newspapers calling for an end to "regulation in secret rooms" and urging resort to the legal process to resolve the problem.[38] Pressured by a chorus of founder liability arguments, representatives of the Federation of Japanese Bankers Associations began to issue public reminders that the founding institutions could force the *jusen* companies into bankruptcy.[39] The suggestion brought protests from the agriculture-affiliated institutions, and was greeted unenthusiastically by MOF officials, who publicly stressed the need for the interested parties to resolve the problem among themselves.[40] Less publicly, MOF was busy shaping the contours of its own plan to resolve the problem.

The utter lack of agreement among the principals on the issue of loss allocation during the MOF-sponsored meetings caused MOF to devise the basic outlines of its own *jusen* resolution plan[41] and increased political involvement in the policymaking process. On December 1, 1995 a policy coordination council of the ruling coalition issued guidelines on the resolution of the *jusen* problem. The guidelines called for a simultaneous liquidation of all seven *jusen* companies, immediate write-offs of unrecoverable assets and the transfer of other assets to a special purpose *jusen* resolution vehicle. The guidelines stressed that the use of public funds should be limited to "absolutely unavoidable circumstances" and emphasized that "it is necessary to ensure transparency, and to clarify the responsibility of each party" for the *jusen* problem.[42] Although the guidelines were silent on the crucial issue of loss allocation, they suggested a heavy burden for the founding institutions in recommending that "the financial strength of the parties should be carefully considered" in crafting the final plan.[43]

MOF officials quickly sought to capitalize on the political authority of the guidelines. Finance Minister Masayoshi Takemura indicated that MOF would respect the guidelines while working toward a final proposal. According to Takemura, in issuing the guidelines the government was not "reaching a conclusion" on the *jusen* problem; rather, the regulators would play a mediative role by standing between the parties if talks among the principals stalled.[44] Simultaneously, Yoshimasa Nishimura, the Director General of MOF's Banking Bureau, summoned the presidents of two major banks to MOF and requested that the founding institutions accept the guidelines and assent to a version of the modified lender liability allocation that would involve a ¥1.5 trillion ($15 billion) contribution from the agricultural affiliates and some supplemental funds from the founding institutions beyond the ¥3.5 trillion ($35 billion) in loan write-offs.[45]

Once again, however, both sides rebuffed MOF's initiatives. The agricultural cooperatives refused to accept a loss of the magnitude required by a modified lender liability formula. Founding institutions refused to consider sustaining losses in excess of the amounts they had lent to the *jusen* companies.

As the struggle to apportion losses dragged on, strategic bargaining "in the shadow of the law" began to shape the pace and structure of the final outcome. Restless politicians threatened resort to the legal system if a liquidation plan including a loss allocation scheme were not finalized by December 18,[46] although it is unclear what standing the politicians would have had to initiate legal proceedings. Continually pressed by MOF to bear a share of the losses beyond their ¥3.5 trillion in loans, the founding institutions began to argue that sustaining any greater losses would invite shareholder derivative litigation.[47] Similarly, the founding institutions rejected any suggestion that they cover secondary losses, again raising the danger of shareholder derivative litigation.[48] Reacting angrily to MOF's pressure on the banks, the chairman of the Federation of Japanese Bankers Associations issued an explicit threat to force the *jusen* companies into bankruptcy if MOF continued to press the founding institutions to bear a larger share of the losses.[49] MOF steadfastly rejected the idea of a legal solution, reiterating its position that a deal worked out among the parties was the best way to achieve a prompt resolution of the *jusen* problem.[50]

D. The Government's *Jusen* Resolution Plan

The confrontation over loss allocation came to a head on December 14, 1995. On that date, the agricultural cooperatives rejected MOF's proposal for the cooperatives to cover ¥1.2 trillion ($12 billion) of first stage losses, and offered just ¥530 billion ($5.3 billion) as their maximum possible contribution. This would force the use of public funds to cover first stage losses, and probably led to a high-level rift within MOF between the Budget and Banking Bureaus. After all-night consultations among three high-ranking career MOF officials, it was determined that public funds would be needed to fill the shortfall in first stage loss coverage.[51] Although the exact chain of events leading to the decision to use public funds in the first stage of the *jusen* cleanup are uncertain to this day, press accounts suggest that only a high-level political decision could have altered MOF's plan and forced the introduction of public funds to cover first stage losses.[52]

A few days later, representatives of MOF, MAFF, and the ruling coalition adopted a document entitled "On the Resolution of the *Jusen* Problem"[53] in an attempt to lay the groundwork for the injection of public money into the *jusen* resolution framework. Adoption of the document by these three parties indicates high-level coordination among the ministries and political leaders in the formulation of the final resolution plan. The document called for increased transparency through the publication of data on the operations of the *jusen* companies, and for a clarification of regulatory and private-sector responsibility for the creation of the *jusen* problem. The document skirted the issue of agricultural cooperative responsibility, but did call for a major restructuring of the agricultural finance system.

The document set out for the first time an authoritative plan to allocate *jusen* losses. First stage losses to be realized immediately would be limited to ¥6.4 trillion ($64 billion). The losses would be covered principally by the founding institutions and other lenders: Founding institutions would write off the entire amount of their loans to the *jusen* companies (¥3.5 trillion, $35 billion), and make a capital contribution and low-interest loan to a *jusen* resolution corporation (later officially named the Housing Loan Administration, HLA) that would assume and attempt to collect on the assets transferred to it. The other lending banks would write off ¥1.7 trillion ($17 billion) and make a low-interest loan and capital contribution to the HLA. The agricultural cooperatives would be called upon to "cooperate in *contributing* ¥530 billion [$5.3 billion]" to the HLA and in making a low-interest loan to the HLA "premised on the repayment of all of their loans to the *jusen* companies."[54] The word "contribute" was used so that the agricultural cooperatives could publicly maintain that they were not responsible for the *jusen* problem and were voluntarily participating in the *jusen* resolution plan in a spirit of public service.

This loss allocation formula fell short of covering even the reduced first-stage loss of ¥6.4 trillion. Thus, the document called for the government to contribute ¥680 billion from the fiscal year 1996 budget into a newly established account at the Deposit Insurance Corporation (DIC) to fund the shortfall. An additional ¥5 billion ($50 million) of public funds would be used for a capital contribution to the DIC to strengthen its operations. In addition, the document provided that the new DIC account would be used to "cover a portion of any losses that result after the assets are transferred [to the HLA]. The government will take appropriate measures if a loss appears in this account." [55] As clarified by MOF officials later, this passage means that taxpayer money would be used to cover half of all secondary losses that arise in the future as the HLA disposes of assets.[56] The cabinet adopted this resolution plan on December 19, 1995.

The final report of the Financial System Research Council, issued on December 22, offers perhaps the most thoughtful official perspective on the *jusen* resolution.[57] After stressing the importance of a prompt solution to the problem, the report emphasizes the fundamentally private nature of the *jusen* problem, and thus the appropriateness of a solution worked out through discussions among the principals.[58] But the report notes the difficulties experienced in resolving the problem through private consultations, and suggests that regulatory intervention was needed to address the *jusen* problem on a macro level and to restore confidence in the Japanese financial system. Thus the use of public funds, while exceptional, was unavoidable: "This Research Council," states the report, "believes that the government has no choice but to decide upon these temporary and extraordinary measures, which include the use of public funds . . . In order to obtain the understanding of the public, we believe it is indispensable to thoroughly clarify" responsibility for the *jusen* problem.[59]

The report calls for the regulatory authorities to "examine past regulatory policy in regard to the creation of the bubble and the bad debt problem . . . and to construct a new and highly transparent financial system while improving future financial regulation." [60]

Thoughtful official perspectives notwithstanding, the government's plan was promptly lambasted by the press and touched off a major public outcry against the use of public funds to resolve the crisis. An editorial in *Nihon Keizai Shimbun* captured the main criticisms of the plan and the process by which it was formulated.[61] The editorial vented the suspicion that the final loss allocation formula was the product of a cynical political decision made under the influence of *nōrinzoku* politicians to rescue the agricultural cooperatives at taxpayer expense. The editorial criticized the back room deals involved, and called for a thorough vetting of responsibility for the *jusen* problem, starting with the regulatory authorities. Finally, it suggested that some of MOF's conduct in shaping the resolution plan was inconsistent with the rule of law.

E. The Secondary Loss Dispute

After struggling for five months to obtain agreement on the division of the current losses on unrecoverable assets, the government immediately faced another hurdle: How to cover the secondary losses that would inevitably arise as the HLA attempted to recover on the ¥6.6 trillion ($66 billion) of assets that would be transferred to it for management and collection. MOF officials attempted to persuade the founding institutions to contribute capital and low-interest loans to a new fund to be established within the DIC to cover secondary losses. The founding institutions, however, attached conditions to their participation. They requested legal support for the plan, in order to shield their managers from shareholder litigation. They also wanted assurances that the loans would be guaranteed and that the agricultural cooperatives would participate.[62]

MOF ultimately prevailed. On January 24, 1996, MOF published its final outline on coverage of secondary losses. That plan had two components. First, each of the three groups of lenders to the *jusen* companies would contribute ¥2.2 trillion ($22 billion) in the form of low-interest loans to the HLA. The ¥6.6 trillion would be used to purchase the assets of the *jusen* companies to be recovered by the HLA. The principal of these loans would be guaranteed by the DIC. Second, the plan called for legislation establishing a "Financial System Stabilization Fund" of up to ¥1 trillion ($10 billion) within DIC, funded by the institutions that had lent to the *jusen* companies.[63] The fund would be managed by the DIC. Half of all secondary losses would be covered out of public funds and half out of earnings on the Financial System Stabilization Fund. If returns on the fund turn out to be insufficient to cover half the losses, then the remaining losses will be borne by the DIC as the guarantor of borrowings made by the HLA. The establishment of the Financial System Stabilization Fund would be codified legislatively to protect the contributing institutions against shareholder derivative litigation.

F. Diet Debate

Deliberations on the resolution package began in the Diet's Lower House Budget Committee at the end of January 1996. A principal focus of the discussions was the basis for the December 1995 loss allocation formula, which called for a ¥685 billion injection of taxpayer funds. Diet members were particularly interested in learning how the amount of the agricultural cooperatives' "contribution" had been determined. In testimony before the Diet, the Minister of Agriculture provided two explanations. First, he claimed that the figure represented the maximum amount that the agricultural cooperatives could afford without suffering serious financial damage. He explained that ¥200 billion of the ¥530 billion total agricultural contribution would be made by the prefectural cooperatives, which would push twenty of the forty-seven such institutions into the red.[64] Second, the figure was said to represent the unrealized portion of the agricultural cooperatives' loss on interest rate reduction from the 1993 restructuring plan.[65] The leading opposition party criticized these explanations as inconsistent *post hoc* rationalizations.[66]

The Agriculture Minister's reluctance to admit that the figure was simply the result of a political compromise has never been fully explained. No doubt it stemmed in part from a desire to avoid further criticism of the plan as a politically motivated bailout of the agriculture cooperatives. But it may also have stemmed from a deeper inclination to maintain at least the appearance that only "acceptable" models of dispute resolution had been followed in ending the crisis. It may have been important to be viewed as abiding by the norm against financial institution failure, and to rationalize the agricultural cooperatives' "contribution" in the context of the preexisting, consensus-based 1993 restructuring formula. Publicly admitting to an overt political deal may have stripped the plan of the internal logic and aura of legitimacy needed to hold the fragile consensus together.

G. *Jusen* Resolution and Financial Reform Legislation

In early June of 1996, after 137 days of Diet wrangling, which included an extraordinary sit-in by opposition parties, a special committee of the Lower House approved a package of bills to implement both the *jusen* resolution and other financial reforms. Following the committee's approval of the bills, the three coalition parties released a statement signaling their intent to secure additional contributions from financial institutions to reduce the public's burden, and calling for the establishment of a transparent system of financial regulation based on strict monitoring and market-based regulations, the early establishment of an organization to liquidate the *jusen* companies and recover loans, and a prompt restructuring of the agricultural cooperative system. The package of financial bills codifying the government's *jusen* liquidation plan, including the expenditure of public funds and the establishment of the HLA to carry out the liquidation of the *jusen* companies and the recovery of their assets,[67] was passed just before the expiration of the Diet session in mid-June.

H. Supplemental Loss-Coverage Fund

Passage of the legislation capped the *jusen* debate but did not disarm public anger. No sooner had the legislation designed to heighten transparency and reduce MOF discretion been enacted than MOF began strong-arming the financial institutions into providing additional funds to lessen the burden on the Japanese taxpayers. The ministry's plan was to create yet another special fund through contributions from the financial institutions and the Bank of Japan, the earnings on which would defray the ¥685 billion fiscal outlay required to cover first stage losses.

MOF and other government officials had begun laying the groundwork for convincing financial institutions to bear a larger share of the losses in the previous month. For example, Finance Minister Kubo stated "the [founding] banks should voluntarily consider additional contributions, also taking into account their social role."[68] The government also began considering steps to shield the banks from shareholder derivative suits that might be filed for contributing shareholder assets to the government fund.[69] These measures included a formal request from MOF to the banks for additional funds, as well as a Diet declaration seeking contributions and pledging that the fund would be used to help preserve the stability of the Japanese financial system.[70]

Although the financial institutions vehemently fought the proposal to make even further contributions toward the *jusen* resolution scheme, MOF ultimately prevailed. The financial institutions and the Bank of Japan agreed to contribute additional monies to a fund designed to offset the ¥685 billion in taxpayer money used to cover first stage losses.

The final cost of the *jusen* problem to the Japanese taxpayers, however, will not be known for another decade, when the HLA completes its work. Much more than the earnings from the Financial System Stabilization Fund may be needed to cover secondary losses, depending on land prices and interest rates.

The delay in final accounting is probably not an accident. By putting off the day of reckoning into the distant future, the actors on the political stage at the time were able to deflect the intense public criticism that would have come their way if the final tally had been estimated immediately, especially given Japan's economic woes and the freshness of the *jusen* debacle in public consciousness. When the costs are finally known, things are likely to be different. A new generation of voters will have emerged for whom the *jusen* fiasco is an obscure episode in their economic history. While the final resolution costs may present a political problem for someone, those who face the problem will be different from the politicians, bureaucrats, and interest group leaders who crafted the resolution plan of 1995–96.

IV. INSTITUTIONAL REFORMS

Looking back, the *jusen* debacle was the beginning of a process of re-engineering Japanese financial regulation—a process that gathered momentum with subsequent "Big Bang" reforms (discussed below). Legislation passed in the immediate aftermath of the *jusen* problem sought to decrease the discretion of MOF in dealing with ailing financial firms and increase the effect of the market on financial industry participants. This legislation appears to have been formulated, at least in part, on the initiative of the Bank of Japan, which was waiting for an opportune moment to press for broad financial reforms.

These reform measures include two major changes relating to the treatment of failing financial institutions. First, a system of "prompt corrective action" based on objective criteria was instituted to deal with financial institutions in failing health.[71] Similar to US legislation enacted in the wake of the S&L crisis,[72] this law is designed to prevent politically palatable but economically costly regulatory "forbearance." Under the law, when the soundness of a financial institution, as measured by objective criteria such as capital adequacy ratios, deteriorates beyond certain benchmarks, financial regulators are required to undertake increasingly stringent measures to minimize the danger to depositors. Second, another bill confers upon regulators the authority to petition the initiation of corporate reorganization or bankruptcy procedures with respect to financial institutions.[73]

With the introduction of these measures, in a major departure from past Japanese financial practices, some financial institutions would be allowed to fail. To prepare for this eventuality, another bill was designed to make systemic improvements in the deposit insurance system.[74] In the event of a financial institution's failure, the DIC would be able to provide depositors with a cash payment, outside of court procedures, of an amount equivalent to their estimated return in bankruptcy. A similar bill was enacted to strengthen the deposit insurance system for agricultural credit cooperatives. Ostensibly to provide time for the public to assess the financial health of particular depository institutions, however, the government guaranteed all deposits (including those above the statutory payoff cost limit of ¥10 million ($100,000)) for five years. As the guarantee was about to expire in 2001, the financial system had still not recovered, so the blanket guarantee was extended, and a phased withdrawal over a period of several years was instituted.

In addition to deposit insurance reforms, the politics surrounding the government's handling of the *jusen* crisis rekindled long-simmering debates on two institutional reforms: Removing financial inspection and supervisory responsibilities from MOF and increasing the independence of the Bank of Japan. Reform in both areas was accomplished in 1997.

In December of 1996, the LDP and its non-cabinet allies approved a plan that transferred financial inspection and supervisory authority from MOF to the Financial Supervisory Agency (FSA), a body established under the Prime Minister's office. This agency has supervisory authority over all financial institutions. The former Banking and Securities Bureaus of MOF were consolidated into a single unit of the Finance Bureau. Management of crises in the financial sector is shared by MOF and the FSA. Thus, Japan's current supervisory structure is a direct outgrowth of the *jusen* problem.

Simultaneously, the *jusen* matter lent momentum to a movement to reduce MOF's influence over the Bank of Japan. Critics had maintained for some time that the Bank of Japan enjoyed less independence than the central banks of the United States and western European countries, and that MOF's influence over the Bank was behind the easy monetary policies that helped to create the bubble economy in the late 1980s.

The task of recommending specific legislation to revise the Bank of Japan Law was delegated to a subcommittee of the Financial System Research Council. The Council's report concluded that many provisions of the then-current Bank of Japan Law were inconsistent with "today's economy and finance given the progress of marketization and globalization." [75] The report noted that public interest in monetary policy had increased as a result of the bubble economy and subsequent nonperforming loan problems, and concluded that "[i]n these circumstances, for the Bank of Japan to gain credibility from the public and financial markets, it is indispensable to reform the entire policy making framework with emphasis on securing central bank independence and the transparency of policy making." [76] Legislation to implement the recommendations of the Council was enacted in 1997,[77] and the Bank of Japan gained formal independence from MOF.

V. ANALYSIS AND CONCLUSIONS

The rise and fall of the *jusen* companies illustrates both the operation of the traditional (informal) norms of Japanese public–private ordering which we have described as a "regulatory cartel," as well as the beginning of a process in which these traditional norms began breaking down and being replaced by more explicit, transparent, and legally oriented rules of the game.

Several salient features of Japanese financial regulation were prominently represented in the *jusen* controversy. The *jusen* problem arose in part because of limited competition. Indeed, the *jusen* companies were created explicitly to serve a narrowly defined market share that was not being met by other financial institutions. The problems these institutions encountered were also partly due to constraints on market entry: The *jusen* companies were given dispensation to engage in real estate finance at a time when other financial firms were being administratively dissuaded from doing so; and agricultural cooperatives were allowed to lend to the *jusen* companies without restriction at a time when other financial institutions faced regulatory constraints on such lending. The entire negotiation process followed from the institutional design of Japanese finance discussed in Section I, and the interaction among interested groups was carefully calibrated to influence the relevant decisionmakers within MOF and MAFF.

Convoy-style "survival of the weakest" regulation and avoidance of failure were the hallmarks of each of the three *jusen* rescue or resolution plans. These plans displayed remarkable concern for the agricultural cooperatives, which themselves were cleverly manipulating the convoy system by claiming to be financially strapped, unsophisticated dupes of the commercial banking industry. The process displayed a high degree of informality, even at great cost to the participants, as evidenced by the fact that the founding institutions accepted a nonlegal *jusen* resolution process that cost them over a trillion yen ($10 billion) more than, in theory, they would have had to pay under formal bankruptcy procedures.[78] MOF relied exclusively on nonlegal measures, such as pressuring bank executives to resign and securing nonbinding contributions to special loss-coverage funds, in response to the crisis. As critics of the process pointed out, legal procedures and rules played little role in the resolution of what was essentially a private insolvency matter. Yet, the influence of legal norms was not absent: When the negotiations turned unfavorable to the banks that had founded most of the *jusen* companies, their industry representatives repeatedly threatened to place the *jusen* companies in legal bankruptcy proceedings, and argued that the banks could not accept the traditional approach of founder liability because of the risk of shareholder derivative litigation. Despite pervasive resort to informal processes, the banks were bargaining in the shadow of the law.

It is also evident that those charged with resolving the *jusen* problem attempted to follow the traditional rules of the game as outlined in Section I. The bargaining process, for example, followed well-established norms. By 1991, when the *jusen* problem first surfaced, it was too late for the individual *jusen* companies to resolve their problems alone. They, therefore, turned to MOF, which provided brokerage and facilitation services to devise five-year recovery plans for each institution. As losses continued to mount, it became evident that major lenders, including the agricultural cooperatives, might be asked to incur losses as part of a rescue effort, and a second restructuring was attempted. Here, the conflict increasingly spilled across industry and jurisdictional boundaries, as the agricultural cooperatives (under the principal jurisdiction of MAFF) sought to distance themselves from the founding institutions (all of which fell under the jurisdiction of MOF) and to emphasize their supposedly more limited role as unsophisticated investors in the *jusen* companies. These spillover effects triggered the bargaining norm of negotiated inter-jurisdictional resolution. Because two industries—banking and agriculture—were involved, MOF entered into discussions with MAFF in which the ministries acted as representatives of their respective industries. When even this proved inadequate, the fourth norm of channeled political intervention came into play. The ruling coalition formed a project team to monitor the negotiations, the LDP organized a *Jusen* Problem Study Group to press for a solution, and *zoku* legislators lobbied on behalf of banks or agricultural interests. There is speculation that even the Prime Minister eventually entered the picture as negotiations reached an eleventh-hour phase. As the matter approached a crisis, negotiations were underway in one form or another at all levels of the bargaining hierarchy. In the end, a resolution plan developed through administratively brokered negotiations among private parties was jointly endorsed by MOF, MAFF, and the ruling coalition—the expected outcome of a bargaining process involving a complex, wide-ranging problem.

The resolution generated by this process was, in general, consistent with the substantive norms we identified in Section I. Above all, the principle of survival of the weakest was maintained. The agriculture cooperatives were extremely nimble at casting themselves in the role of the weakest party. Consistent with this norm, the cooperatives used their alleged weakness to give credibility to a threat of defection: They threatened to withdraw their money from the *jusen* companies, and thus plunge these institutions to a chaotic insolvency that would cast a cloud on the entire Japanese financial system. The no-exit policy was maintained, to a degree, although the *jusen* companies had to be sacrificed. There was simply no way that these institutions could have been rescued, given the enormous losses on their balance sheets. But the agricultural cooperatives were saved at the expense of the banks and the Japanese taxpayers,[79] even though many argued that the cooperatives should have been required to bear their pro rata share of the losses, regardless of the financial impact. Taxpayer funds were allocated to cover first-stage losses, and much more may be required to cover second-stage losses. The government also explicitly committed to ensure all bank deposits for a period of five years, and the Bank of Japan reduced interest rates to virtually unheard of levels, in part in an attempt to prop up the nation's sagging banking industry. Thus, responsibility and equitable subordination—norms applicable even to the government—were a hallmark of the resolution plan.

In an extreme disaster such as the *jusen* debacle, the responsibility and equitable subordination norm can conflict with the principle of survival of the weakest: MOF, in pushing the major banks to accept full founder liability to rescue troubled institutions, might have unduly weakened the pillars of the Japanese financial system. Indeed, this was the major concern underlying the Japan Premium imposed on Japanese banks by the international financial community. By allocating losses among the three principal groups of lenders to the *jusen* companies roughly according to financial strength, the regulatory cartel arrived at a solution that enabled all players—other than the *jusen* companies themselves—to survive.

Although the *jusen* resolution plan, thus fit quite well within the framework of traditional Japanese public–private decisionmaking, severe strains in the system were evident. Every bit of effort the regulatory cartel could muster was needed to achieve a rough form of consensus on the *jusen* resolution plan. The enormity of the losses simply precluded a cooperative *ex ante* agreement. While the agricultural cooperatives were satisfied to proceed under the traditional substantive norms of Japanese finance, the major banks balked at the obligation to shoulder the enormous losses dictated by adherence to those norms. As noted above, the founding institutions used the threat of legal process against the other players repeatedly as a sword to gain bargaining advantages in the negotiations, and the specter of shareholder derivative litigation as a shield to deflect pressure to accept full founder liability. While the banks may not have intended to carry out their threats, the very fact that they were made suggests that resort to formal legal resolution proceedings was a credible solution to the *jusen* problem. Enormous cracks in the foundation of governance by consensus were revealed in the bargaining process.

Equally significant is the public outrage over the underlying causes and resolution of the *jusen* problem. This outrage, fueled by an increasingly critical media, was directed toward the nonlegal, non-transparent "back room deals" and favoritism towards politically powerful groups that characterized both the operation and demise of the *jusen* companies. Japan observers may be hard pressed to recall a comparable display of public disenchantment with the *modus operandi* of political, bureaucratic, and business leaders.

As a result, the *jusen* issue provoked serious reconsideration of the traditional norms by thoughtful Japanese, both within and outside of the government. Indeed, the *jusen* problem is illustrative of the process of transition currently underway in Japan. Traditional substantive norms were applied in modified form, and a partial foundation was laid to reorient Japanese financial regulation toward greater transparency and procedural integrity. To be sure, these changes, like subsequent developments, have been incremental, gradual, and painful. In fact, it is interesting to note that the MOF and Bank of Japan reforms implemented in the wake of the *jusen* problem were carried out according to the traditional preclearance style of lawmaking, in which committees of experts were selected to reach consensus on the legislation, and no revisions were made to the bills by the Diet. Japan's financial problems may not presage a "comforting convergence with an American economic model," [80] but the *jusen* episode does indicate the willingness of international financial markets to punish players who adhere to the traditional norms of Japanese financial regulation over more widely accepted and accessible standards of regulation. In this sense, Japanese finance is slowly converging with more internationally recognized rules of the game. "Big Bang" reforms subsequent to the resolution of the *jusen* problem have moved Japanese finance further away from the regulatory cartel model.[81] For example, market segmentation eroded, leading in 2001 to the complete elimination of restrictions that separated the banking, securities, and insurance industries. Corporate fund raising options were expanded with the introduction of new bond products, new stock exchange listing and initial public offering standards, and the promotion of asset-backed securities. Disclosure and enforcement were improved through a variety of measures. Deregulation of this sort hastens the breakdown of the old system by reducing the incentive for banks and other regulated firms to negotiate on a continuous basis with MOF, and eliminating many of the benefits of abiding by the regulatory cartel.

The regulatory cartel did have the appearance of working well in the era of high economic growth and stable expectations. In those times, the primary role of the cartel was to divide up an expanding pie. Persons outside the cartel may not have received their share of the increase, but because their lot was also improving public anger remained muted. Groups within the cartel found it relatively easy to bargain over the spoils when the pie was increasing. It was possible to give in a little to a competing interest when all groups were profiting handsomely in any event. Moreover, given the repeat nature of dealings within the cartel, a group whose interests were slighted somewhat in one round could rest assured that there would be other occasions in which it would come out ahead.

Many groups benefited from the governance-by-consensus model epitomized by the regulatory cartel in Japanese finance. This mode of decisionmaking and dispute resolution helps to account for the growth—for a time, at least—of remarkably powerful financial institutions in Japan, and the appearance (if diminishing reality) of an extremely stable financial system guided by an able bureaucracy. At the same time, governance by consensus was efficient in a period of rapid economic growth; and it freed Japanese financial and corporate actors from the concern that heavy reliance on formal legal rules and procedures might hinder economic growth and beneficial modes of industrial organization.

In times of low economic growth, however, the traditional Japanese methods of governance do not operate well. Those outside the framework for consensus-building become disenchanted by the privileges enjoyed by those with influence. And even those who enjoy a seat at the bargaining table find themselves hard pressed to reach agreement on the allocation of a stable or shrinking, rather than an expanding, pie. These problems were evident in the *jusen* controversy and succeeding rounds of financial crisis, where the actors had to divide up "bads" such as economic losses and political opprobrium. Although the process did result in a resolution of the *jusen* problem, the extreme difficulties faced along the way were the first signs that continued operation of the regulatory cartel was untenable.

Regrettably, however, public anger over the *jusen* debacle caused Japanese policymakers to become even more timid in their response to the country's mounting nonperforming loan problems. Thus, some of the regulatory forbearance that has stalled resolution of Japan's financial problems to this day can be traced to backlash from the episode recounted in this chapter.

As of this writing, it is still not possible to say that market-oriented financial oversight and norms have fully replaced the regulatory cartel, although recent episodes of bank failure have been handled in a manner that differs markedly from the *jusen* resolution. Ultimately, the *jusen* problem and its aftermath will be seen as the beginning of the end of the regulatory cartel—the watershed moment in the complete transformation of Japanese finance—whenever that day finally arrives.

NOTES

1. See, for example, Takeo Hoshi and Anil K. Kashyap, Corporate Financing and Governance in Japan (2001).
2. Robert Higgs, Crisis and Leviathan 259 (1987).

3. The term "regulatory cartel" was coined in Curtis J. Milhaupt and Geoffrey P. Miller, Cooperation, Conflict and Convergence in Japanese Finance: Evidence from the *"Jusen"* Problem, 29 L. & Poly. Int. Bus. 1 (1997), on which this chapter is based.

4. See Phillip Areeda and Donald F. Turner, 2 Antitrust Law 280 (1978). For a classic exposition of cartel organization, see George Stigler, The Theory of Price (4th edn. 1987).

5. Frances McCall Rosenbluth, Financial Politics in Contemporary Japan 20 (1989) (footnote omitted).

6. For case studies demonstrating that Japanese financial policy making proceeds far less smoothly when MOF shares financial oversight with another ministry, see James Horne, Japan's Financial Markets: Conflict and Consensus in Policymaking 214–15 (1985); Rosenbluth, *supra* note 4, at 167–208.

7. George A. Hay, Oligopoly, Shared Monopoly, and Antitrust Law, in Economic Analysis and Antitrust Law 160, 162 (Terry Calvani and John Siegfried eds., 1988).

8. An exception exists where a weak firm is merged into a stronger firm.

9. See, for example, Hideki Kanda, Politics, Formalism, and the Elusive Goal of Investor Protection: Regulation of Structured Investment Funds in Japan, 12 U. Pa. J. Int'l Bus. L. 569, 582 (1991); David G. Litt et al., Politics, Bureaucracies, and Financial Markets: Bank Entry into Commercial Paper Underwriting in the United States and Japan, 139 U. Pa. L. Rev. 369 (1990).

10. See Kanda, *supra* note 9; Hideki Kanda, Finance Bureaucracy and the Regulation of Financial Markets, in Japan: Economic Success and Legal System 305, 312–15 (Harald Baum ed., 1997).

11. Kin'yū seido chōsakai tōshin [Report of the Financial System Research Council], Minkan jūtaku kin'yū no arikata ni tsuite [On the Goals of the Private Housing Finance System], (Dec. 15, 1973), excerpts reprinted in Okurashō, Nōrinsuisanshō [MOF, Ministry of Agriculture] Jūsentō kankei shiryō [Jusen Related Data] 7 (1996) [hereinafter Jusen Data].

12. Kashi kingyō no kiseitō ni kansuru hōritsu [Lending Business Law], Law No. 32 of 1983, Appendix, art. 9.

13. Kashi kingyō no kiseitō ni kansuru hōritsu shikōrei [Lending Business Law Enforcement Order], Order No. 181 of 1983, art. 1(4) (giving MOF authority to "investigate" the business and finances of all registered firms engaged in the lending business).

14. Jusen Data, *supra* note 11, at 159.

15. Id.

16. See id.

17. Jūsen mondai "kisō kōza" ["Basic Course" on the Jusen Problem], Kin'yū bijinesu, April 1996, at 30, 32.

18. Jusen Data, *supra* note 11, at 5.

19. Id.

20. Id.

21. Id., at 40.

22. Id.

23. Compare the similarly disproportionate political power of American farmers, who share similar characteristics. See, for example, Geoffrey P. Miller, Public Choice at the Dawn of the Special Interest State: The Story of Butter and Margarine, 77 Calif. L. Rev. 83 (1989).

24. Tōchi kanren yūshi no yokosei ni tsuite [Regarding Restrictions on Land-Related Finance], MOF Banking Bureau Circular No. 555, March 27, 1990, reprinted in Jusen Data, *supra* note 11, at 10.
25. Id.
26. MAFF took the position that the *jusen* companies were fundamentally home mortgage lenders and therefore loans to the *jusen* companies did not constitute real estate loans of the type covered by the administrative guidance. This interpretation, of course, fails to acknowledge that by 1990, a large percentage of *jusen* loans were being made to real estate companies, not individual home buyers.
27. Kin'yū bijinesu, *supra* note 17, at 31.
28. *Jusen* Data, *supra* note 11, at 50.
29. See id., at 51.
30. Reprinted in id., at 14.
31. See "Ganpon hoshō" no kaishaku tairitsu [Conflicting Interpretations of "Guarantee of Principal"], Nihon keizai shimbun, Feb. 16, 1996, at 1 (reporting Diet testimony of former MAFF official asserting that the memorandum was a guarantee of agricultural cooperatives' principal, and testimony of former MOF official asserting that it did not constitute a guarantee).
32. Jūsen furyō saiken, '91 nen ni 67% [*Jusen* Bad Loans: 67% in '91], Nihon keizai shimbun, Feb. 6, 1996, at 1.
33. *Jusen* Data, *supra* note 11, at 41. Of the total, ¥8.74 trillion in loans had been made to corporate borrowers and ¥1.98 trillion in loans had been made to individuals.
34. Interim Report by the Financial System Stabilization Committee of the Financial System Research Council, Sept. 27, 1995, at 7 (English translation).
35. Id. at 3.
36. Id. at 8.
37. Jūsen shori de ōkurashō ni bōtaikō e no shidō wo yōsei [(Agricultural Affiliates) Request that MOF Give Guidance to the Founding Institutions in the *Jusen* Workout], Nihon keizai shimbun, Nov. 18, 1995, at 4.
38. See Jūsen mondai wa misshistu gōysei yame hōteki shōri wo [Stop the Secret Room Regulation, Resolve the *Jusen* Problem Legally], Nihon keizai shimbun, Nov. 21, 1995 (criticizing the handling of the *jusen* problem as symbolic of Japan's non-transparent methods of financial regulation).
39. See Hōteki seiri hatsugen ni kōgi [Protesting a Legal Solution], Nihon keizai shimbun, Nov. 23, 1995, at 5.
40. See id.
41. Under MOF's plan, losses on nonperforming loans would be divided into two stages: "First-stage losses" would be realized immediately when the performing assets of the *jusen* companies were separated from the nonperforming assets and transferred to a newly created vehicle established for the purpose of assuming and collecting the loans. The financial institutions involved would cover all of the first-stage losses. Losses that arose from the subsequent efforts to dispose of the assets transferred to the *jusen* resolution vehicle ("secondary losses") would be covered in part by the lending institutions, and partly from public funds.
42. Cited in Jūsen mondai no shōri ni tsuite [On the Resolution of the *Jusen* Problem], reprinted in *Jusen* Data, *supra* note 11, at 15.
43. Id. There is no question that the founding institutions were the strongest group financially.

44. Jūsen mondai, yotō no gaidorain sonchō [MOF will Respect the Ruling Parties' Guidelines on the *Jusen* Problem], Nihon keizai shimbun, Dec. 1, 1995, evening ed at 3.

45. "Shusei bōtai" kyōryoku wo bōtaikō shunō ni ōkurasho yōsei [MOF Requests the Heads of Founding Banks to Cooperate in "Modified Founder" (Liability)], Nihon keizai shimbun, Dec. 1, 1995, at 1.

46. Jūsen shori, 18 nichi hōkoku wo [(Calling for) *Jusen* Resolution Report on the 18th], Nihon keizai shimbun, Dec. 16, 1995, at 1.

47. Okura, nōsuishō de saishū chōsei [MOF and MAFF Enter into Final Adjustment], Nihon keizai shimbun, Dec. 2, 1995, at 3.

48. Niji sonshitsu no futan kyohi [Rejecting the Secondary Loss Proposal], Nihon keizai shimbun, Dec. 18, 1995, at 1.

49. Kashutsu zandaka kosu futan mitomezu [(Founding Institutions) will not Accept a Share of Losses in Excess of the Loan Amount], Nihon keizai shimbun, Dec. 6, 1995, at 7.

50. Hōteki seiri ni shinchō shisei [Cautious Stance on a Legal Solution], Nihon keizai shimbun, Dec. 14, 1995, at 3.

51. Jūsen shingi: koko ga shōten: nōrinkei futan gaku [Examining the *Jusen*: Focus on the Amount of the Agricultural Affiliates' Burden], Nihon keizai shimbun, Jan. 31, 1996, at 3.

52. Id. (concluding that the agricultural affiliates originally planned to cover ¥1 trillion of losses, but that a high-level political decision was made to reduce the burden to ¥530 billion at some point between Dec. 4th and 14th).

53. On the Resolution of the *Jusen* Problem, *supra* note 41.

54. Id. (emphasis added).

55. Id.

56. See Niji sonshitsu, kuni ga hanbun futan [Government to Bear Half of the Secondary Losses], Nihon keizai shimbun, Dec. 24, 1995, at 3.

57. Kin'yū seido chōsa kai [Financial System Research Council], Kin'yū shisutemu anteika no tame no shoshisaku−shijō kiritsu ni motozuku atarashii kin'yū shisutemu no kochiku [Policies to Stabilize the Financial System: Building a New Financial System Based on Market Principles], reprinted in 1085 Jurisuto 39 (1996).

58. Id. at 45.

59. Id. at 46.

60. Id.

61. See, for example, Rūru itsudatsushita jūsen no seiji ketchaku [A Political *Jusen* Decision Lacking in Rules], Nihon keizai shimbun, Dec. 20, 1995, at 2.

62. Jūsen 2 ji sonshitsu shori saku de ōkurashō [MOF (Planning) Policy to Cover Secondary Losses], Nihon keizai shimbun, Jan. 21, 1996, at 3.

63. Jūsen saishū shorian no yōshi [Main Points of the Final *Jusen* Resolution Plan], Nihon keizai shimbun, Jan. 23, 1996, at 5.

64. Kamiawanu jūsen rongi [Frictionless *Jusen* Debate], Nihon keizai shimbun, Jan. 31, 1996, at 3.

65. ¥530 billion is roughly the amount of interest to be forgiven over the seven years that had remained on the agricultural cooperatives' restructured loans to the *jusen* companies, discounted to present value.

66. "Jūsen" tōben mujun darake [Inconsistencies Abound in "*Jusen*" Responses], Nihon keizai shimbun, Feb. 7, 1996, at 5.

67. Tokutei jūsen kin'yū kikan senmon gaisha no saimu saiken no shori no sokushintō ni kansuru tokubetsu sochihō [Special Measures Law to Promote the Resolution of the

Assets and Liabilities of the *Jusen* Companies], Law No. 93 of 1996. A related bill suspends prescription on loans made by *jusen* companies. Tokutei jūsen kin'yū kikan senmon gaisha ga yūsuru saiken no jikō no teishitō ni kansuru tokubetsu sochihō [Special Measures Law to Suspend the Prescription of Loans Held by *Jusen* Companies], Law No. 98 of 1996.

68. Hashimoto Positive on Step to Deter Suits over "*Jusen*," Japan Economic Newswire, May 28, 1996, available in LEXIS, News Library, Non-US file.

69. Id.

70. MOF Prepares Measures to Avoid Lawsuits over "*Jusen*," Japan Economic Newswire, June 12, 1996, available in LEXIS, News Library, Non-US File.

71. Kin'yū kikantō no keiei no kenzensei kakuhō no tame no kankei hōritsu no seibi ni kansuru hōritsu [Bill to Implement Measures for Ensuring the Sound Management of Financial Institutions], Law No. 94 of 1996.

72. See Federal Deposit Insurance Corporation Improvements Act §131 (codified at 12 U.S.C. § 1831o(a)(2)).

73. Kin'yū kikan no kōsei tetsuzuki no tokureitō ni kansuru hōritsu [Bill to Implement Special Procedures for Reorganizing Financial Institutions], Law No. 95 of 1996. The bill also amends the Corporate Reorganization Law so that it can be applied to the resolution of failed cooperative-type financial institutions, and empowers the DIC to act as the agent of depositors whose rights will be represented and exercised by the DIC in court procedures.

74. Yokin hokenhō no ichibu wo kaisei suru hōritsu [Bill to Amend the Deposit Insurance Law], Law No. 96 of 1996. For an analysis of Japan's deposit insurance system, see Curtis J. Milhaupt, Japan's Experience with Deposit Insurance and Failing Banks: Implications for Financial Regulatory Design?, 17 Monetary & Econ. Stud. 21 (1999).

75. Financial System Research Council, Report on the Revision of the Bank of Japan Law 1 (Feb. 6, 1997).

76. Id.

77. See Nihon ginkō hō [Bank of Japan Law], Law. No. 67 of 1942, as amended.

78. See *supra* Table 4.1. Accepting the informal resolution plan over formal bankruptcy proceedings cost the founding institutions approximately ¥1.4 trillion ($14 billion), less the legal costs of the proceedings.

79. The reduction in the agricultural cooperatives' share of the losses from ¥3.2 trillion ($32 billion) under a pro rata formula (theoretically possible though not formally considered) to ¥530 billion ($5.3 billion) under the resolution plan adopted caused a corresponding increase in the losses sustained by the founding institutions, other lenders, and the Japanese taxpayers, and necessitated deferring ¥1.24 trillion ($12.4 billion) of losses to the second stage, where once again taxpayers and non-agricultural lenders will bear most of the burden.

80. See Edward J. Lincoln, Japan Hasn't Really Failed, New York Times, Feb. 22, 1997, at 17.

81. For a thorough analysis of the Big Bang and its impact, see Hoshi and Kashyap, *supra* note 1, at 289–98.

5

Sokaiya

As public outrage over the *jusen* debacle faded, it was soon replaced by another corporate governance issue: the Sokaiya. Corporate extortion by "sokaiya" gangster–racketeers historically has been widespread in Japan. Although sokaiya (literally, "general meeting operators") take several forms, a sokaiya, as we discussed in the derivative suit context, is typically defined as a nominal shareholder who *either* attempts to extort money from a company by threatening to disrupt its annual shareholders' meeting *or* works for a company to suppress opposition at the meeting. Surprisingly, Japanese executives pay sokaiya despite the fact that payment can result in civil and criminal liability not only for sokaiya, but for the executive as well.

In the late 1990s, scandals involving some of Japan's largest and most prestigious financial institutions thrust sokaiya into international headlines and to the center of the comparative corporate governance debate. In spring 1997, prosecutors revealed that Dai-Ichi Kangyo Bank (DKB), the fifth-largest corporation in the world, had paid sokaiya Ryuichi Koike a total of $120 million in secured loans for his services. Koike then admitted that he used these funds to acquire a stake–significantly, exactly the number of shares needed to give him the right to make proposals at shareholders' meetings–in each of Japan's "Big Four" securities brokerages. The brokerages subsequently paid Koike a combined total of nearly $8 million to keep their meetings quiet. The "Koike scandal" led to mass board resignations, to the arrest of thirty-five executives, to the suicide of a former DKB chairperson, and ultimately to the dissolution of Yamaichi Securities and the collapse of the Japanese stock market. Six months later, eight executives of Hitachi, Toshiba, and three Mitsubishi group companies were arrested (and as of this writing, all but one have been convicted) for paying sokaiya amounts ranging from $21,000 to $90,000–ostensibly for the use of a beach house–to keep their meetings quiet. Fewer than six months after that, prosecutors revealed that the exorbitant brochure-advertising fees that certain Mitsubishi group companies had paid a former flight attendant were actually disguised payments to her husband, a thirty-year sokaiya veteran, to keep meetings quiet. In August 1998, two extortionists were arrested for leasing office plants (at prices to make a florist blush) to Japan Airlines in exchange for meeting protection, and Toyota and Nissan soon admitted that they had done the same. Scandals and incidents continued at a slower pace in the 2000s in large firms like Nippon Shinpan, Yakult, Seibu Railways, Hankyu Department Stores,

Kobe Steel, Sumikura Industrial, and Kubota Corporation. The largest scandal, at Nippon Shinpan consumer credit company, involved payoffs of $800,000.

These recent incidents appear to be part of a much larger phenomenon. Since criminal penalties were clearly imposed on payments to sokaiya in 1982, executives of thirty-three corporations—almost all of which are household names in Japan, and only one of which is not listed on the Tokyo Stock Exchange—have been convicted of making payments to sokaiya. In a 1997 survey of large Japanese firms including giants such as NTT, Toyota, and Matsushita, nearly 90 percent indicated that they had been approached by sokaiya with extortionist demands of one kind or another.[1] Another recent survey of 2,000 firms (1,200 responding) found that 77 percent had paid sokaiya.[2] This generous corporate support is said to have kept in business 1,000 sokaiya in the 90s, with stock in nearly 12,000 companies, and about half that number in 2003.

From the American corporate perspective, making payments to sokaiya probably falls somewhere between unusual and crazy. The nearest U.S. equivalent to the recent Japanese scandals would be if directors and managers of Citicorp, Ford, General Electric, Motorola, Intel, Sara Lee, Macy's, Bloomingdales, Merrill Lynch, Lehman Brothers, and Morgan Stanley were all arrested in the same year for paying members of the Gambino and Lucchese crime families to keep their shareholders' meetings short. Petty extortion and blackmail are of course universal. But payment on such a grand scale despite potential personal civil and criminal liability for such a seemingly needless service of keeping meetings short and quiet is nearly unthinkable in the United States.

Many commentators claim that socio-cultural factors provide a compelling explanation for sokaiya activity in Japan, and for its absence in the United States. In the United States, with its historical tradition of political democracy, the concern is not the length of the meeting or the decibel level of shareholders, but the ability of shareholders to participate in the corporate democratic process. By contrast, in Japan, a shareholders' meeting is supposed to be a harmonious model of business decorum, and management will pay potential disturbers of the peace to stay away, or at least to be quiet, so as not to cause the firm and its executives to lose face.[3]

But corporate democracy in Japan and the United States function essentially the same way—through proxy machinery, not shareholders' meetings. And which U.S. executive would not prefer a "harmonious" meeting to a chaotic one? In this chapter, we argue that a better explanation for the behavior of extortionists and managers in Japan and the United States lies in the choice sets that are determined by institutions. Specifically, we argue, first, that Japanese institutions lead to low levels of corporate disclosure. Because extortion correlates positively to secrecy, inadequate disclosure creates blackmail material that can be used by sokaiya any day of the year. Second, we show empirically that long shareholders' meetings in Japan send negative market signals that lead to stock price drops. Japanese executives pay sokaiya to avoid these negative returns. Conversely, sokaiya do not emerge in the United States because U.S. institutions facilitate more public disclosure of information, provide legal and profitable alternative uses for negative information, and do not otherwise give signaling value to meeting length. Concisely stated, Japanese firms historically have chosen to pay sokaiya, while their U.S. counterparts have not, because in Japan, institutions make paying sokaiya less costly than the alternative choices of (*a*) disclosure of negative information or (*b*) long meetings.

In exploring the relationship among institutions, information, and extortion, this chapter offers insights in two broad areas of legal and economic theory. First, this chapter examines the role of law and other institutions in facilitating the emergence of corruption. The Japanese thicket of formal and informal regulation tends to create an environment in which corruption flourishes relative to the less heavily regulated (but more private litigation-oriented) U.S. system.

Second, despite an abundance of theoretical literature on blackmail by scholars like Coase, Nozick, and Posner,[4] case studies of actual instances of blackmail are relatively sparse. Judge Posner argues that real-life examples are few because blackmail is in fact a rare crime—rare, he posits, because when blackmail is a crime, rational blackmailees will refuse to pay.[5] This chapter shows that in certain institutional contexts, blackmail can actually become a relatively commonplace activity even among rational actors.

For those readers with a proclivity for sensationalism, if blackmail is not enough, we also add that the sokaiya story is often worthy of pulp fiction. It is about murder: Two suspicious ones in 1997. It is about dramatic suicides: In 1997 and 1998, a former bank chairperson, a Diet member, and a high-ranking bureaucrat, each hung himself on the day before he was to be arrested or questioned about sokaiya activity. It is about confessions and redemptions too numerous to count. And yes, it is about sex: Executives sometimes pay sokaiya to silence the announcement of their extramarital (or at least imprudent) affairs.

Section I describes sokaiya, discusses strategies for dealing with them, and analyzes laws designed to eliminate their activities. Section II analyzes the institutions that shape Japanese and U.S. corporate information markets and shows how the Japanese system leads to blackmail. Section III tests and analyzes the relationship between meeting length and stock returns.

I. A CORPORATE EXTORTION PRIMER

The question of why sokaiya successfully extort Japanese companies in spite of the law, while sokaiya apparently do not arise in the United States even in the absence of legal prohibitions, principally involves three factors: Sokaiya, corporations, and corporate law.

A. Sokaiya

Although sokaiya play a variety of roles, they usually come in one of three varieties. First, there are fighters. Japanese managers have long known that one of the easiest ways to ensure an orderly shareholders' meeting is to hire thugs to intimidate shareholders who want to speak.[6] This rent-a-thug image is fueled by well-publicized melees of the early 1970s at Chisso corporation, where sokaiya physically suppressed environmental activists,[7] and at Mitsubishi Heavy Industries, where sokaiya fought to a bloody finish with shareholders who protested the company's production of military weapons for the Vietnam War.[8] Relatively few incidents of physical shareholder repression have surfaced since that time—perhaps because sokaiya moved into other more profitable lines of business or perhaps because shareholders began to get the message through more subtle hints of violence.

Second, a few elite sokaiya are paid to keep other more dangerous sokaiya away from meetings. These sokaiya use various means to accomplish the task: sometimes intimidation, sometimes influence peddling, sometimes outright payment. These sokaiya sometimes become corporate insiders, advising companies as to how to deal with other troublemakers, how to organize meetings, and how to circumvent the law. As one such sokaiya (who prefers the title "consultant") told one of us, "Sokaiya problem? What sokaiya problem? I show up. I give advice. I help. I do the same thing that a lawyer would do. And I'm cheaper, too. What's the problem with that?"

Finally, and most commonly, many sokaiya make a living through blackmail. Sometimes sokaiya blackmail by threatening to reveal sensitive information at the public forum of shareholders' meetings. Sometimes the blackmail is not related to meetings at all. A favorite sokaiya tactic is to request that a corporation subscribe to magazines published by the sokaiya, the underlying threat being that if the company does not subscribe, scandalous stories about the company will appear in the magazine.[9] Other popular tactics include organizing expensive golf tournaments, leasing potted plants, and holding karaoke-singing contests. Still others style themselves as "shareholder activists," accepting fees for their notions on how to improve corporate governance (with implicit threats of exposure if not paid). Japanese police arrest approximately 200 sokaiya (and related actors) each year on various extortion charges, but blackmail persists.

Blackmail *might* flourish in Japan—not just among sokaiya but also in society as a whole—because of broad legal and social differences. But this does not seem to be the case. In a recent study, Richard Posner found only 124 reported published opinions (among 3 million in the Westlaw database) in blackmail cases in the United States in the last century.[10] We have serious doubts—as does Posner—about the reliability of using the number of judicial opinions as a measure of blackmail activity. But because good alternatives are scarce, and a comparison would be nice, we adopt a similar approach for Japan. We searched for all blackmail opinions in *Hanrei Taikei*, a ten-disk CD-ROM database that is the Japanese functional equivalent of Westlaw. Like Posner, we have no doubt that the search might have missed some cases. Still, after reading through all the extortion cases returned by the search, we were only able to classify fifteen of them as informational blackmail—a small number indeed, and easily comparable with the U.S.

number given the disparity in database size. The information used for blackmail in Japan was much the same as one would expect to find (and occasionally finds) in the United States—a former in-house lawyer threatens to expose a religious organization's secrets,[11] a witness threatens to expose a criminal act,[12] a child with no legal father threatens to expose a dead man as his father if not paid off by the heirs,[13] a local newspaper threatens to publish the results of a popularity poll discrediting a local doctor unless he pays up.[14] Nothing is uniquely Japanese here.

Nor is there anything particularly Japanese about the three primary sokaiya activities—violence, meeting management, and corporate blackmail. In a widely reported incident, for instance, an "investigative reporter" in Philadelphia threatened to publish damaging stories about companies if they did not hire him as a "consultant."[15] Intimidation and penny stock manipulation also occur in the United States—often allegedly carried out by organized crime syndicates. And meetings in the United States, like anywhere else, sometimes get out of hand. The main difference between Japan and the United States is thus not the scope of activity, but the scale.

B. The Companies

When confronted by a sokaiya, companies have two primary options: Pay or resist.

1. Pay A company's general affairs department usually handles payments to sokaiya. Before 1982, many companies had their affiliated sokaiya form a queue at the door of that department on the day of, or the day before, their shareholders' meeting. All on line received envelopes full of cash. Recent compensation schemes are more sophisticated. The 1997 Koike scandal involved off-the-books loans to a company owned by Koike's brother (DKB), purchases and repurchases of expensive golf club memberships (Daiwa Securities), and compensation for losses incurred through Koike's discretionary "VIP" account (Nomura Securities), futures accounts (Nikko Securities), and Singapore International Monetary Exchange Nikkei index accounts (Yamaichi Securities).

Estimates of how much money companies actually pay sokaiya vary. One study finds that typical sokaiya earn $20–200 per firm, twice a year.[16] One firm's general affairs department chief states that his company's regular policy at one time was to pay small-time sokaiya ¥100,000 ($10,000) per year, and to pay its "expert" sokaiya ¥300,000–500,000 ($3,000–5,000) per month, with bonuses of ¥2–3 million ($20,000–30,000) around the time of the meeting. The firm's annual sokaiya budget was ¥500 million ($5 million) for 2,000 sokaiya, which results in an average payment of $2,500 per sokaiya.[17]

Other evidence comes from the 1997 Koike scandal. As a result of the scandal, Nomura Securities admitted paying ¥70 million ($700,000) annually for subscriptions to 700 magazines.[18] Soon thereafter, the media reported that each of

Japan's large city banks subscribed to an average of 1,000 such magazines at a cost of ¥100 million ($1 million) annually.[19] Finally, a late 1998 National Tax Agency investigation of the firms involved in the scandal found that DKB and the Big Four securities houses had paid thirty-five sokaiya in addition to Koike a total of ¥1.1 billion ($10.1 million) over a five-year period, for an annual take of nearly $300,000 per sokaiya.[20]

One way to estimate the amounts that companies pay is to calculate the average amount cited in court cases. From 1983 to 1998, Japanese courts sentenced executives from thirty-three firms (some firms in more than one incident) who made payments to a total of 135 sokaiya. The total amount of the payments to sokaiya by these thirty-three firms is ¥12.9 billion ($129 million), representing a disbursement of about ¥92 million ($920,000) per sokaiya or ¥375 million ($3.75 million) per firm. The highest amount received by a single sokaiya was ¥11.78 billion ($118 million); the lowest, ¥50,000 ($500).[21] On one hand, these figures may understate firms' total payments, as many firms have relationships with more than one sokaiya. But on the other, these figures may overstate the payments, as prosecutors may let smaller payments slide, choosing to litigate only the large cases.

In short, it is difficult to determine how much firms pay sokaiya. Many of the managers that we interviewed suggested that one reason that this may be so is that firms pay sokaiya varying amounts depending on their relationship with the company, the quality of their information, the credibility of their threat, and their skills in performing other services for the company. Although sokaiya can earn handsome profits, for a large firm typical of the type that sokaiya visit, even the aggregate amounts may not be too terribly high.

2. *Resist*   Of course, not all firms pay sokaiya. Those who do not pay either (*a*) are not bothered by sokaiya, (*b*) turn threatening sokaiya over to prosecutors, who pursue them on extortion charges,[22] or (*c*) simply ignore sokaiya threats. Although the third strategy may seem to be the easiest course, a few executives who ignored sokaiya threats have become subject to acts of violence. One survey conducted by a National Police Agency (NPA) administrator found ten acts of violence against corporate officials during a one-year period alone. At least three of these incidents—assaults on executives of Tokai Bank, Fuji Film, and Sumitomo Bank—are linked to the refusal of those companies' executives to pay sokaiya.[23] Assault on executives is by no means uniquely Japanese—such incidents undoubtedly occur in the United States with some regularity, and perhaps even more frequently than in Japan. In Japan, however, the specific links to corporate extortion are often more clear.

C. The Law

Payments to sokaiya to suppress shareholders' rights have been illegal since the Commercial Code was promulgated in 1950. Under section 494 of the Code, it is illegal to make an "improper solicitation" with respect to the "exercise of shareholder rights." "Improper solicitation," courts have held, includes paying sokaiya to prevent others from "fairly speaking or fairly exercising their vote."[24]

But this formulation of the law raised multiple problems for prosecutors and civil plaintiffs. How could a prosecutor or plaintiff prove that an improper solicitation was made, or that such a solicitation was made with respect to the "exercise of shareholder rights" and not for some other purpose? Faced with these issues and growing concerns about corporate gangsters in an internationalizing Japan, the Japanese legislature in 1981 enacted a full-scale revision of the Commercial Code aimed specifically at the elimination of sokaiya. Effective October 1982, prosecutors need no longer prove an "improper solicitation." Instead, they need only prove that a "benefit" was offered with respect to the exercise of shareholder rights, and, in civil cases, if the benefit is "gratuitously offered" to a "specific shareholder," it is presumed that it is offered with respect to those rights.[25]

The revisions also imposed clear civil and criminal penalties on both sokaiya and management. As for civil penalties, the revised Commercial Code (art. 294-2) provided that sokaiya must return to the company any benefits received. The director, officer, or other manager who made the payment to the sokaiya must also return the same to the company (art. 266). If the company does not file suit to recover the payment, a shareholder may, as we discussed in Chapter 2, bring a derivative action to recover the amounts (art. 294-2). The new Code (art. 497) also introduced criminal penalties—up to six months' imprisonment or fines of up to ¥300,000 ($3,000) for both the offeror of the benefit (management) and the recipient (sokaiya).

The "sokaiya provisions" of the Commercial Code create incentives against payments to sokaiya, and may have contributed to the decline in the estimated sokaiya population from about 6,000 pre-1982 to about 1,000 in 1997.[26] But the provisions have at least three readily apparent problems. First, in the Japanese criminal system, statutes of limitations are linked directly to the length of the sentence to be imposed. The six-month sentence specified by the Code carries a statute of limitations of only three years.[27] Second, in civil cases, the presumption that a benefit, if gratuitously offered, is made in connection with shareholders' rights, only arises if the payment is made to a shareholder. If the sokaiya is a non-shareholder, the presumption does not arise; and as the pre-1982 situation indicates, it is difficult to prove a case without it. Third, while the sokaiya provisions may influence the behavior of the typical sokaiya who accepts payment for his shareholders' meeting services, they do not address the sokaiya magazine subscription phenomenon, which can be a significant sphere of sokaiya activity.

The Japanese judiciary has added an additional reason why the sokaiya provisions may not have the full impact that they otherwise could. In the scores of individual executive cases adjudicated between 1982 and 1998, only four sokaiya (in the Noritake, Ajinomoto, and two in the Mitsubishi group cases) actually were sentenced to prison. All others received suspended sentences. In no case did any of the executives who were convicted in those incidents receive jail time—they *all* received suspended sentences. This is not an aberration from the Japanese criminal justice system as a whole, which sends fewer than 5 percent of its suspects to prisons, compared to over 30 percent in the United States,[28] but it does show that the sokaiya provisions are not being enforced to their fullest extent.

II. INFORMATION

Some sokaiya blackmail has nothing to do with shareholders' meetings. This is clearly evidenced by year-round sokaiya magazine subscriptions and implied in relevant case law.[29] To put it another way, what would be the expected result if holding Japanese shareholders' meetings suddenly were made illegal? After executives sobered up from the tremendous parties that they surely would throw in celebration, sokaiya activity would continue as usual. Information with blackmail potential would still be available, and executives would still be vulnerable. The sokaiyas' broadcast of information would simply switch to some other forum.

In this section, we analyze the Japanese corporate information regime and its role in creating a blackmail-conducive market regardless of whether shareholders' meetings occur. In Section A, we discuss the types of information that sokaiya use for blackmail. In Section B, we discuss some reasons why Japanese corporate law, corporate governance, and regulatory institutions might discourage public disclosure of such information. In Section C, we explain how sokaiya might obtain the information, and how as an extortion "firm" they are able to use it for profit. In Section D, we outline the incentives that lead to sokaiya concentration in certain industries and types of firms. Section E examines legal methods by which negative information can be used to profit, and shows that because several methods that exist in the United States either do not exist in Japan or are extremely limited, sokaiya turn to blackmail. Finally, Section F offers a brief comparative test of the institutions-information theory.

A. Types of Information

The U.S. corporate governance system and U.S. corporate law regime, which we define broadly to include regulatory institutions, makes available more useful information to independent investors, reducing the marginal costs to investors of information acquisition. In contrast, the Japanese system often keeps such information—most importantly, negative information—secret. Sokaiya normally blackmail corporations with three types of information: Financial and accounting data, potentially scandalous information relating to corporate malfeasance, and private information about management.

1. Financial and accounting data It is widely recognized that Japanese corporations do not disclose as much information as their U.S. counterparts.[30] Although some changes have occurred in recent years, a review of a Japanese corporation's annual report in comparison to a U.S. report reveals some prominent differences. First, a Japanese report contains no mention of management compensation, as required in the United States.[31] Second, Japanese reports historically do not break down sales by industry or business line, so it is difficult to determine a firm's profitability. Third, assets a Japanese firm holds in the form of securities are booked at the price at which the firm bought the shares, and not the current market price. Finally, a Japanese financial statement usually is not specific about the method that the company uses to depreciate its assets. The aggregate result is that the annual report, which is mandatory in both systems, contains significantly less useful information in Japan than in the United States.

A recent survey by the Organization for Economic Cooperation and Development (OECD) further illustrates the point. The OECD studied the consolidated financial statements of several large public corporations and rated their disclosure of operating results relative to OECD guidelines as full or partial. Of fifty-three U.S. firms studied, thirty-four had full disclosure, and nineteen had partial. The twenty-five British firms in the survey ranked similarly with nineteen full, six partial. Of the twenty-three Japanese firms surveyed, the results were nearly opposite: Only two firms had full disclosure, while twenty-one firms had only partial disclosure.[32] A similar survey by the Investor Responsibility Research Center found that on average, Japanese listed corporations were required by law to disclose only 40 percent of the information that is required in the United States.[33]

Enter the sokaiya. A skilled sokaiya can expertly deconstruct a balance sheet, querying discrepancies, errors, and omissions. Though the same may be true of analysts in the United States, sokaiya have more secrets to expose in Japan because less information is initially disclosed.[34]

2. Past bad acts   More often, sokaiya use information regarding past corporate misdeeds to blackmail corporate executives. Sometimes the acts are illegal; sometimes they are merely embarrassing. A list of bad acts that sokaiya typically use for blackmail would include silently settled products liability claims, hiring and employment issues, bid-rigging, poor management practices, and other unreported liabilities.

It is difficult to determine whether Japanese firms on average commit more "bad acts" than U.S. firms or if more bad acts simply are kept secret. If the former is true, it is probably so because Japanese overregulation creates incentives for firms to commit bad acts. An obvious case is that of now-defunct Yamaichi Securities. Yamaichi competed in what is perhaps the most heavily regulated sector of the Japanese economy: The securities industry. Unlike the United States, where brokerage fees were deregulated in 1975, commissions on securities transactions in Japan remained fixed until 1998. In order to maintain the accounts of its largest customers, Yamaichi agreed to perform "*tobashi*" transactions, the illegal practice of repurchasing shares that have declined so that favored customers do not have to report losses. Sokaiya learned of the arrangement and used it to blackmail Yamaichi.

Various inefficiencies in Japanese corporate law may account for other corporate secrets. Minimum stock price regulations, strict rules on stock transfer restrictions, and longstanding virtual bans on a firm buying its own stock or even creating a holding company (both of which have now been eliminated) all created roadblocks around which corporations had to "improvise." It should come as little surprise that the improvisations occasionally are improper enough to invite blackmail.

3. Personal information Sometimes the information that sokaiya use to blackmail companies is purely personal in nature—an executive's extramarital affair, a director's criminal son, a manager's questionable background—all make excellent blackmail fodder. It is unclear whether the amount of this sort of blackmail paid in Japan exceeds that paid in the United States. If more is paid in Japan by corporations, two reasons may help explain why.

First, executives in Japan receive lower average salaries than do their U.S. counterparts.[35] It may be that executive blackmail based on personal information is more easily paid by individuals in the United States, while in Japan an executive may feel that he has no choice but to turn to his company for financial assistance. Or, stated another way, payment of personal blackmail is part of a Japanese executive's compensation package, while in the United States, blackmail payment responsibility is allocated to the executive, to be paid out of her salary. This may be a partial explanation for the $600,000 difference in average CEO compensation between Japan and the United States—in Japan, the $600,000 goes directly to the sokaiya. Without such payment, qualified CEOs might not accept the job.

Second, personal blackmail in Japan easily piggybacks on corporate blackmail. Because firms are already paying sokaiya based on corporate information, it is not difficult for an executive to request that payment be made to a particular sokaiya without announcing the reason for the payment, or by asserting that the payment is for the suppression of corporate secrets. Because corporate blackmail is not as prevalent in the United States, the payment of personal blackmail by the firm is more difficult.

B. Information Concealment: The Role of Government and Governance

To facilitate the non-disclosure of negative information, a system would need at least three elements. First, it would need an organizational structure that would tend to prevent negative information from being unwillingly released. Second, it would require minimal enforcement of disclosure requirements so that firms would (a) not get caught keeping secrets and (b) if caught, would not be too severely punished. Third, it would need some mechanism through which economy-wide (or at least industry-wide) unraveling effects could be deterred. In Japan, firms appear to benefit from all three elements.

1. Maintaining secrecy Three aspects of the Japanese corporate governance system help to maintain secrecy better than in the United States. First, the cross-shareholding (*keiretsu*) system common in the Japanese economy lessens the need for market-wide disclosure. If a small number of institutional shareholders hold a large percentage of a company's stock, there is lessened incentive to share information outside of that limited group. Unlike the widely dispersed owners of U.S. firms, Japanese cross-shareholders can obtain information as a result of their inside position, and therefore extensive public disclosure is unnecessary.

Second, most large Japanese firms are affiliated with a main bank. Main banks are in some ways similar to non-financial cross-shareholders, as their inside position reduces the need for public disclosure. More so than in the United States, the Japanese main bank system is also characterized by repeated contractual arrangements between bank and client. This pattern of repeated deals may lead to more limited disclosure of information than if firms were more often engaged in searches for competitive terms among multiple (non-main) banks.

Finally, Japanese boards of directors are composed almost exclusively of insiders. Although the existence of an outside director may not necessarily result in an increase in shareholder wealth,[36] the presence of outside directors might result in a greater flow of information to sources outside of the firm. This might be especially true in Japan, where relatively inactive labor markets mean that a firm's directors (and auditors) are generally lifelong members of the firm.

It could be argued that Japanese corporate governance gives firms *little* reason to pay sokaiya. The story would go something like this: A company's core group of shareholders is relatively stable and usually does not sell its shares. Knowing this, a company should not care if negative information is publicly released, and thus has little reason to pay sokaiya to prevent its release. But precisely because cross-shareholding accounts for a relatively large percentage of a firm's stock, trading in a firm's account by "non-stable" shareholders—outside investors—can greatly influence the firm's stock price. According to one estimate, individual shareholders control 75 percent of the total Tokyo Stock Exchange float.[37] Firms have incentives to pay to ensure that negative information does not leave the corporate group and reach these investors.

2. Enforcement   The Japanese disclosure regime is characterized by a lack of enforcement of disclosure laws by civil or criminal means relative to the level of enforcement in the United States. The U.S. Securities and Exchange Commission investigates an average of 150–200 cases annually. By contrast, from 1992 to 1995, the Japanese Securities and Exchange Surveillance Commission (SESC) investigated only six. The SESC made Japanese headlines when it filed a record five criminal complaints in the 1996–97 fiscal year, and again in 1997–98 when it filed a grand total of seven (four of which were the DKB-Nomura sokaiya cases).

Virtually no securities fraud litigation, civil or criminal, occurs in Japan. Japan has no class action mechanism. Another potential enforcement mechanism, the shareholder derivative suit, has only recently become active, as we saw in Chapter 2.

The relative lack of enforcement in Japan implies that firms wishing to keep secrets should be able to do so more easily in Japan than in the United States.

Although these secrets may be simple financial disclosure misstatements or omissions, more often they tend to relate to questionable—or illegal—corporate acts. The more robust inspection and enforcement system of the United States, combined with incentives toward disclosure to avoid private litigation,[38] encourages early production of potential secrets and tends to expose those that are intended to be concealed.

3. Deterring disclosure   Even in the absence of mandatory disclosure provisions, competitive markets should still produce something close to the right level of information to investors. Firms with positive outlooks have every reason to disclose their rosy futures. Those firms with the next most favorable information then disclose, and the unraveling process continues until all firms disclose except for those firms with the worst information. At this point, investors can draw inferences about those firms' financial outlook from their silence. In Japan, this "unraveling effect" appears not to occur as frequently or as deeply as it does in the United States.

But the unraveling effect can be slowed or stopped. Unraveling depends on "whether the uninformed party knows what kind of information the other party has and might wish to conceal."[39] The broad range of Japanese corporate secrets may limit unraveling as investors cannot be sure what type of information to seek. Some deterrence of the unraveling effect probably also results from direct coordination among managers of "competitive" firms.[40]

But most importantly, corporate Japan may have mitigated the unraveling effect by relying on an institution—the bureaucracy—to monitor firms and keep disclosure at preset levels, in effect creating an "information cartel." Although bureaucratic influence may come from a variety of different sources, we focus in particular on the most prominent ministry (particularly in recent sokaiya scandals), the Ministry of Finance (MOF). MOF historically serves as regulator, protector, and promoter of the financial services industry and securities markets.[41] In many cases, MOF chooses protection and promotion over regulation. Events of the 1990s tend to confirm what had always been widely suspected:

On July 24, 1995, Daiwa Bank learned that trader Toshihide Iguchi had incurred $1.1 billion in losses over eleven years from trading U.S. Treasury securities in its New York branch. The Bank informed MOF of the developments on August 8. MOF did not give any information to its U.S. counterparts (and of course gave none to investors) until the Bank issued a formal report to Japanese and U.S. authorities on September 18.[42]

In November 1997, Yamaichi Securities collapsed, largely because of off-the-book debts of ¥260 billion ($2.6 billion) incurred through "tobashi," the practice of shifting losses so that they are never realized by favored customers. In February 1998, the chief of MOF's Securities Bureau at the time admitted in Diet testimony that Yamaichi's President informed him of the losses in 1991. Yamaichi's internal investigation team's final report (based on testimony from Yamaichi's then-President) states that MOF instructed the firm to conceal the losses in overseas accounts.[43]

In January 1998, two MOF financial inspectors were arrested on charges that they took bribes from Sumitomo Bank, Tokyo-Mitsubishi Bank, Sanwa Bank, Dai-Ichi Kangyo Bank, Asahi Bank, and Hokkaido Takushoku Bank in return for revealing *inspection plans* to the "MOF-tan" (a manager in charge of MOF relations) at those banks. During and after a subsequent investigation, a senior investigator committed suicide, the Minister and Vice-Minister were forced to resign, and 112 officials were disciplined for "excessive" wining and dining.[44]

In January 1998, Koichi Miyakawa, a former MOF financial inspector, admitted to prosecutors that he learned of illegal loans by Dai-Ichi Kangyo Bank to sokaiya Ryuichi Koike in 1994 and deleted information regarding those loans from his official report.[45]

Examples abound; many more vignettes can be pulled from the *jusen* home mortgage lending company collapse that we discussed in Chapter 4 and Ministry efforts to minimize the scale of outstanding bank debts. Abuses occur in the U.S. regulatory context as well. But in the Japanese context more so than in the United States, it is easy to find examples of MOF's apparent tendency to withhold information from investors.

The reasons why MOF might withhold information are plentiful, and suggest that the incidents recounted above are not mere aberrations. Sometimes the goal may be market stability. Sometimes MOF may withhold information in order to prevent firms from failing—a goal that can be observed in the United States in cases like the 1979 Chrysler Corporation rescue or the 1998 Long-Term Capital Management bailout, but that practice is supported more openly and invoked more frequently in Japan. Private interest, rather than public policy, is also likely; recent scandals suggest that bribery, at least in the form of lavish entertainment if not cash, may be widespread. Even if outright bribery is limited to a few high-profile cases (which, unfortunately, appears not to be the case), it is no secret that bureaucrats' careers are determined by legislators, who receive large contributions from large corporations. Also a potential contributing factor is the practice of *amakudari*, through which former bureaucrats, as we discuss in Chapter 8, retire to high-paying positions in the very companies that they formerly monitored, supported, and promoted. As Mark Ramseyer and Frances Rosenbluth note, "ex-bureaucrats will rarely be able to obtain pork through a simple phone call. [Instead,] the government may choose to compensate the ex-bureaucrat's employer through anticompetitive constraints rather than simple grants."[46]

Although anticompetitive constraints normally imply rigged prices, it probably also means rigged disclosure. The case is easy to overstate, and we do not assert that MOF or any other agency purposely limits disclosure as a matter of policy (though they might). But through small steps and individual actions, MOF and other agencies can be effectively employed as institutional solutions to collective action problems, ensuring that "excessive" disclosure does not occur, and allowing all firms to profit while maintaining minimum disclosure policies. This, in essence, is another illustration of the "regulatory cartel" we discussed in chapter 4.

C. Information Acquisition: Organized Crime Syndicates

A blackmail threat is only credible if the blackmailer has sensitive information and the means to expose it. Sokaiya are often able to acquire both by means of relationships to the *yakuza* (Japan's organized crime syndicates) and related groups.

Japanese organized crime figures are more numerous and more pervasive in everyday Japanese life than their mafia counterparts in the United States. In the corporate context, as we discuss more fully in the next chapter, firms turn to sokaiya to handle activities for which they either are not equipped to handle or are not willing to undertake directly. Companies can hire organized crime syndicates to enforce judgments, a skill at which gangs appear to be more adept than the legal system. Construction firms reportedly use such syndicates to monitor bid-rigging for public works projects. For securities firms, one common use of gangsters is said to be in the manipulation of stock prices, especially in the ramping of prices for new issues. For real estate firms, such syndicates can be used to intimidate stubborn holdout owners into vacating land at a low price, a niche created, at least in part, by Japanese landlord–tenant law, which heavily favors tenants. For lenders, sokaiya can assist with debt collection or may even purchase bad debts so that banks do not have to write them off.

The problem for the corporation is that once it turns to the organized crime for private law enforcement, the organizations, via sokaiya, can then use information gathered in performing the services to blackmail the company. If information with blackmail potential is not readily available, a sokaiya can pay low-level employees or disgruntled ex-employees for information regarding sensitive rumors and the like. And the company knows that the sokaiya can follow through on the threat of exposure—after all, it is the expertise of organized crime syndicates in such matters that leads corporations to turn to them in the first place.

Mob ties help sokaiya in other ways. First, and perhaps obviously, yakuza can impose occasional threats of physical violence when necessary. Second, mob ties also help sokaiya maintain their monopoly over information that has blackmail potential. Crime syndicates limit new entrants to the field, keeping out those without mob ties and occasionally engaging in turf wars with rival gangs. Organized crime organizations also deter overreaching by their own members, as groups internally limit the number of their members who engage in corporate racketeering.

As noted in Section I, not all sokaiya are involved in blackmail. Some fill important roles of silencing dissenters, whether they are shareholders or other sokaiya. In this sense, sokaiya are classic racketeers, mixing extortion with enforcement of illegal monopolies. Indeed, threats of physical violence against management appear to be more rare than one might otherwise expect. Many sokaiya, rather than working against the company, simply reinforce existing collusion between managers and large shareholders, providing services for which many managers pay.

Nor do all sokaiya have organized crime connections. A small group of sokaiya intelligentsia makes its living blackmailing corporations with information derived from standard securities analyses of firms' financial statements and other public documents. This group, which even includes a couple of corporate law professors, makes money more on analytical acumen than mob ties. Their tactics are more subtle, as they often send their written findings to the corporations, with attached cover letters, suggesting that perhaps the companies might wish to purchase the information in lieu of more widespread publication.

D. Information, Reputation, and Regulation

Sokaiya choose their targets knowing that Japanese corporate secrecy has a dual effect. First, the lack of publicly available information in Japan means that the secrets that sokaiya can unearth have more blackmail potential than more public "secrets" of the United States. Second, the non-availability of information means that the release of such information poses a greater threat to the Japanese corporation than to its U.S. counterpart, as investors in Japanese markets should be more likely to attach meaning to relatively immaterial information than they would in U.S. markets.

This analysis implies that sokaiya will target firms with specific characteristics. A list of firms that pay sokaiya should be composed largely of (*a*) firms with secrets and (*b*) firms to whom the release of information would be the most damaging. Of course there is no such list. But a substitute does exist—a list of firms implicated in sokaiya payment scandals. Since 1982, executives of thirty-three companies have been sentenced for sokaiya payments (a 100 percent conviction rate). Of these thirty-three total firms, seven, or over 20 percent, are very large food, convenience, and department stores—among the largest firms in the world. Another seven, including four with two sokaiya arrest incidents, are financial institutions. Combined, these two industry categories account for fourteen of the thirty-three—nearly half—of the firms with sokaiya arrest incidents. The same industry categories account for only 13 percent of Tokyo Stock Exchange firms, and for an even smaller percentage of all public Japanese firms.

This industry breakdown shows that reputation plays an important role in determining which firms tend to pay sokaiya. Firms whose reputation is most easily shattered, those that stand to lose the most from scandal, will value reputation more highly than other firms will. The applicability to financial institutions is clear; they operate in an industry in which public trust is essential, to success. Department stores in Japan function under similar constraints. Japanese department stores sell food, a commodity in which trust is essential, and serve a broad customer base among which rumors cannot easily be dispelled (as compared with a company with only a few clients). Moreover, there is little variation in Japanese department stores (among other things, most house the same smaller boutiques that pay rent), so consumers easily can switch. Finally, the margins in retail in Japan, and especially in food retail, are comparatively very thin, and the market is quite competitive: In Japan, there are 120 retailers and forty-six food retailers per 10,000 persons; in the United States the corresponding numbers are fifty-nine and seven per 10,000.[47] This thin-margin environment in which multiple competitors are often selling identical products may lead some Japanese department stores to value their reputation more highly than corresponding U.S. firms.

The degree to which industry is regulated also seems to determine sokaiya targets. As chapter 4 illustrated, MOF plays a predominant role in the financial services industry. In the retail industry, the Ministry of International Trade and Industry (MITI) is in charge, heavily regulating retail stores with inefficient requirements relating to floor space, vacation days (a minimum of twenty-four days per year) and even requiring local merchant consent to the creation of new large stores.[48] Heavy regulation may lead to questionable practices, the knowledge of which can be used for subsequent blackmail, or it may be a conduit for deterring the informational unraveling effect.

Certain classes of firms are not on the list of sokaiya incidents. Electrical utilities, for instance, may have little reason to pay (though they still might), as customers normally purchase electricity with less regard to the degree of trust that they hold in the firm than they would for purchases of food or financial services—and with an oligopoly of ten firms (compared to 3,000 in the United States) controlling the industry, customers may have little choice.[49] Similarly, no small firms appear on the list, as many of those firms have little or no reputation to protect, are not subject to heavy regulation, and may not be cost-effective targets for sokaiya, as the cost of detection is presumably the same as it is for deriving greater benefits from large firms. Thus, although the world press expressed shock and surprise over the fact that recent scandals involved Japan's elite institutions, those are exactly the type of firms that would be expected to pay sokaiya.

E. Uses for Negative Information, or Why Don't They Just . . .?

Why do sokaiya choose to blackmail executives with negative information as opposed to using it to profit in some legal manner? While extortion-like uses for negative information can arise in all systems, institutions determine the form of the extortion. In the United States, three potential uses for negative information—securities lawsuits, financial instruments, and publication—are readily apparent. In Japan, however, these sources of profit are much more limited, and holders of negative information thus turn to extortion, whether as sokaiya or by selling information to sokaiya.

1. Lawsuits Negative information in the United States is often used for profit by securities plaintiffs, or more specifically, by their attorneys.[50] In the United States, as a Congressional committee noted, securities class litigation is "lawyer-driven" and often carried out by "professional plaintiffs" who own nominal interests in many different companies and who stand willing to lend their names to class actions in exchange for an extra "bounty" payment upon settlement.[51] In such a system, nominal professional plaintiffs perform the same economic function as sokaiya—they simply exercise their claim legally after disclosure, while sokaiya make their claim illegally before the information can be disclosed.

Congress attempted to modify the U.S. system through the Private Securities Litigation Reform Act of 1995, which requires plaintiffs to file complaints that describe their transactions in the security at issue, disclose any prior securities class action in which they sought to serve as a class representative, and promise not to accept a bounty payment.[52] But in Japan, this particular policy issue would never arise. The class action system does not exist. The Japanese derivative suit mechanism, as we discussed above, creates lower monetary incentives for shareholders and their attorneys than in the United States. Without a legal mechanism through which to profit from negative information, an illegal one emerged.

2. Financial instruments   Investors can profit on undisclosed negative information by the use of financial instruments such as put options or short sales. A stock option, for instance, gives the holder the right, but not the obligation, to purchase ("call") or to sell ("put") the underlying share at a predetermined price ("strike price"). A person who has dirt on a company can profit by purchasing puts with a strike price that is greater than the market price is expected to be after the release of negative information. The holder then waits for the market to discover the negative information (perhaps encouraging the discovery by disseminating it himself or herself), watches the market price fall, and sells the put at the predetermined higher-than-market price.

Why do sokaiya in Japan not simply use their negative information to turn a profit by using stock options or short-selling? It would not invoke the criminal penalties that blackmail entails. All a sokaiya would have to do to profit is buy the appropriate financial instruments and release the negative information to the market—as some investors in both United States and Japan often do as a matter of strategy. Or, even more simply, if meeting length correlates to stock price, a sophisticated sokaiya-investor conceivably could profit simply by purchasing puts (or short-selling) in a portfolio of firms, each of whose meetings he or she disturbs, and waiting for the puts to become "in the money" after the disruption.

But due to heavy regulation, both options and short sales historically have been more difficult, more costly, and much less popular in Japan than in the United States. Single-stock option trading (as opposed to market index options) was only introduced on the Japanese stock exchanges in July 1997. If the relevant firm offers options, a sokaiya who wants to purchase an option on a Japanese issue must come up with capital to fund the purchase. The sokaiya must then carefully calculate the maturity date after which the negative information is to be released, as Japanese options are European-style (only exercisable on a predetermined maturity date) as opposed to American-style (exercisable any time during the life of the option), and the available maturity dates are fixed. The broker must then be paid a hefty commission. If the option is exercised, the broker is also paid a significant margin.[53] The sokaiya-investor must pay capital gains tax on the profit (normally withheld by the broker), as well as a securities transaction tax.[54]

A similar story applies to short sales. Japanese law historically prohibited true short sales.[55] But investors can short stocks via a margin transaction, modeled on the U.S. system, in which they post collateral through a margin account but do not actually take possession of the underlying shares. To enter into such a margin transaction, a margin account must first be established. Most Japanese brokerages require an initial margin account deposit of ¥20–50 million ($200,000–500,000).[56] Most brokerages will not open a margin account for a customer who does not transact significant other securities business, as short-selling is usually conducted only as part of a hedging strategy, and suitability rules apply as they do in the United States. If a margin account can be established, a sokaiya-investor must then post additional collateral—up to 80 percent of the value of the transaction—for each short sale that is entered into.[57] Brokerages do not handle small-scale margin transactions; most historically have minimum transactional requirements of ¥1 million ($10,000). Not all stocks are available for short-sales, and, as always, taxes must be paid.

Transaction costs aside, sokaiya blackmail has at least three advantages over trading. First, short sales or options generate income only once for each negative exposed nugget of information. But income earned from blackmail can be repeated at least once a year with continued threats of exposure. At some point, to be sure, the information and the threat can go stale, but until that time, sokaiya may prefer blackmail because less complete and accurate information may be required to generate steady income. If a group of repeat-player sokaiya share blackmail information as a common-pool resource, internal norms may further reduce incentives for short-selling for individual gain. Of course, blackmail and trading are not mutually exclusive. A sokaiya could blackmail the company, short the stock, announce the information, and reap a dual profit—but then he would be unable to reap future profits using either method.

Second, sokaiya blackmail may be less risky. A holder of a short position or a put option has no way of determining whether, when, or to what extent market prices will actually fall. Short-sellers face additional risks. "Uptick" rules that prohibit short sales in a falling market prevent sokaiya from shorting after the release of the information.[58] If multiple sokaiya attempt to short-sell, purchases required to cover their repayment obligations can actually drive prices up. Blackmail, on the other hand, involves almost certain payment, and provided that the sokaiya sticks with regular clients and abides by the rules of the game, the risk of arrest is minimal.

Finally, in a market of low informational availability, many companies may actually prefer blackmail to the use of financial instruments. Shorting is a viable investment strategy only if negative information is to be released. Companies have no desire to see negative information released. Accordingly, some should be willing to pay potential short-selling sokaiya significant sums not to short.

3. Publication   When cooperation leads to efficiency gains that the market fails to capture, private ordering economic institutions will emerge. Perhaps the cooperation of sokaiya with managers constitute such a "private order" institution. But if there is so much valuable negative information out there, why do securities agencies, newspapers, or some other third party not profit from it legally by selling it to investors?

Part of the answer may lie in the players in the game. The most likely distributors of the information would be securities houses and their affiliated research groups. But these groups may not always have the proper incentives to research and convey to customers negative information. Japanese securities firms traditionally earn the bulk of their profits through commissions rather than on trading on their own accounts. Accordingly, their goal is to influence customers to buy more securities and pay more commissions. Moreover, as recent scandals have shown, the securities houses themselves are often so deeply mired in sokaiya activity that pointing out the mistakes of others could simply be a suicide request.

The media may constitute another likely source of negative information distributorship. But the Japanese media has long been known for its press club that rewards positive publicity for the news source over exposé reporting. Moreover, many Japanese media with enough capital to publish news of hidden corporate wrongdoing are often owned by or affiliated substantially with the very large corporations on whom they would be reporting. They could report instead on their corporate owners' competitors, but opening your competitors' closets while your own are full of skeletons does not seem to be a prudent course of action.

Not all media are part of the press club; most notably, the stock-in-and trade of weekly magazines is lurid political, celebrity, and corporate dirt. These publications have not been shy about printing accusations, sometimes with little regard for accuracy. But in the corporate context, the weeklies traditionally have not printed many scoops, choosing instead to explore the unsavory details of corporate scandal after major revelations have been made in other contexts. A combination of reasons might explain why, including fear of liability, lack of in-house expertise and resources, relative lack of reader interest, and a fixed policy of no payments to informers at most weeklies. Thus, while the weeklies occasionally break stories (especially those involving sex), they historically have not competed directly with sokaiya.

This leaves one particular group of actors with enough capital and consumer trust to fill the gap—foreign securities firms. Although foreign firms have been in Japan since 1961, their activity was relatively limited until the bubble economy that began in the mid-1980s. As new entrants to the market, establishing a reputation among Japanese securities customers was relatively difficult, and such firms were forced to be much more active in trading for the own accounts than their Japanese counterparts which could rely on churning alone. But as foreign firms lured foreign customers to Japanese markets and developed reputations in Japanese domestic markets, that picture began to change, and now the top four foreign firms conduct more retail trading than do the Japanese top four.

These foreign firms already may have affected sokaiya activity. The decline in sokaiya from 6,000 pre-1982 to about 1,000 in 1997 and 420 in 2002 is often cited as a result of enforcement of the 1982 sokaiya provisions. But very little actually changed in 1982—sokaiya activity was illegal before 1982, and a handful of arrests in the following years does not amount to rigorous enforcement. A better explanation for the decline of sokaiya may be the relatively unbiased dissemination of information by foreign firms in Japan. With fewer ties to listed firms and an initial reliance on trading wholesale rather than retail for profit, foreign firms are often said to be less reluctant to distribute (accurate) negative information about listed firms.[59] Foreign firms can make legitimate use of negative information on which sokaiya would otherwise profit. As the foreign retail presence increases, their distribution of negative information to investors may further drive sokaiya out of business.

F. A Brief Comparative Test

If institutions determine how negative information is used, we would expect to see sokaiya-like actors in similar institutional environments. As it turns out, sokaiya-like actors are not unique to Japan. In South Korea, "*chongheoggun*" are "hecklers" who "demand money from companies in exchange for pro-management services or speeches during [shareholders'] meetings."[60] Some commentators argue that their influence is even stronger in Korea than in Japan—the only difference between the two actors being that Japanese sokaiya are under greater scrutiny from the world press.

Although not identical, the similarity between Japanese and Korean institutions and organizations is more than cosmetic. Korean firms are arguably even more heavily regulated than Japanese firms. Korean *chaebol* look a lot like Japanese *keiretsu* and other cross-shareholding arrangements, and *chaebol* is written with the same Chinese characters used in Japanese for *zaibatsu*, Japan's prewar conglomerates. Similar institutions lead to similar results.

It could be that sokaiya simply plague Asian systems. But how, then, could Italian "*disturbatori*" be explained? *Disturbatori* are "professional claques that get paid under the table not to disrupt a company's annual shareholders' meeting"[61]—in other words, Italian sokaiya. Elementary geography rules out migration as an explanation, and only with artful manipulation can Italian cultural history be compared to that of Japan or South Korea. But Italian institutions are quite similar to those of Japan and South Korea. Italy has no labels like *keiretsu* or *chaebol* for its corporate system, but its largest organizations are structured in the form of pyramidal groups of financial and operational firms.[62] As in Japan and Korea, the state plays an inordinate role in corporate governance, and corruption scandals occur with some regularity. The mafia parallel to yakuza is inescapable. And like Japan, "as a rule, minority shareholders are excluded not only from participation in the company's life, but, quite frequently, from . . . true and correct information on its activity."[63] This sketch is brief to be sure, but it is significant that such an unusual actor as the sokaiya emerges in three systems with similar institutions, while it does not emerge in the United States and similar systems.

III. FILIBUSTER BLACKMAIL

Section II showed how Japanese institutions can give rise to sokaiya blackmail that is not necessarily dependent on shareholders' meetings; the prevention of information-based scandal is crucial to understanding sokaiya. But shareholders' meetings also seem to play a critical role in the sokaiya framework. Every published judicial opinion relating to sokaiya incidents since 1982 mentions shareholders' meetings as at least a partial impetus for payment. Magazine subscriptions aside, most of the payments to sokaiya come just before a firm's shareholders' meeting. And sokaiyas' use of *shitsumonjo*—a written list of expository questions to be raised at the meeting that sokaiya submit to management to induce payment—also underscores meeting importance.

Two reasons explain the annual concentration of sokaiya payments. First, if management had to pay sokaiya year-round, accounting would be more difficult, and the risk of detection would increase. Second, annual payments are a mechanism by which the sokaiya can precommit to limited extortion. The sokaiya's implicit message to the firm is "pay me this one time and you won't see me again until next year." Absent such a structure, a sokaiya has an incentive to come back more often, and the more often he comes back, the more likely the firm is to refuse to pay.

But precommitment alone cannot fully explain sokaiya behavior. Many sokaiya are not precommitted to annual payments. And those sokaiya who solicit annually may actually not be choosing to precommit, as the payment schedule appears to be dictated at least in part by management. But even if the precommitment explanation for annual payments were valid, it does not explain why sokaiya and managers would choose annual *meetings* as a focus of payment when other less costly, less detectable alternatives (such as year-end gift-giving season) are available.

Why shareholders' meetings? Do the firms not know that in most cases, a shareholders' meeting is nothing but, as Berle aptly described it, "a kind of ancient, meaningless ritual like some of the ceremonies that go on with the mace in the House of Lords?"[64] Why do managers pay sokaiya to keep their meetings short and quiet? Who cares if a "meaningless ritual" of a meeting runs long? To answer these questions, we first look at the role of shareholders' meetings in Japan and the United States. We then conduct an empirical test to see whether the length of a shareholders' meeting matters. Finally, we offer three explanations of the results of the test, and reject three others.

A. The Role of Shareholders' Meetings

In both Japan and the United States, shareholders' meetings are usually mean-ingless rituals that have all the entertainment value of watching wet paint dry. Occasionally they become lively, such as in the context of contests for corporate control, the occasional shareholder activist proposal, or shareholder protest situations. But for the most part they have little to do with accountability or governance, as corporate democracy in the form of majority shareholder rule generally settles contentious issues before the meeting. Still, shareholders' meetings are required by law and stock exchange rules to be held annually both in Japan and the United States, and managers begrudgingly comply.

In Japan, however, meetings take on heightened significance. One of the rea-sons why this is so, paradoxically, is the sokaiya. In the early 1970s, author Saburō Shiroyama, perhaps the most famous of all Japanese business novelists and the author of a wildly popular fictional account of an aging sokaiya's last stand,[65] had one of those ideas that must have sounded great at the time. If all companies would merely hold their meetings on the same day, Shiroyama rea-soned, the sokaiya could be defeated. Sokaiya resources would be limited, as they could not possibly attend all meetings at once, and police resources could be maximized because they would only have to be mobilized for that one day. The Japanese NPA liked the idea (they had been toying with it themselves), and decided to promote it. The timing and national coordination of the meetings would be no problem, as MOF already had in place a policy of encouraging firms to end their fiscal years on March 31 (the close of the government's fiscal year) for easier national bookkeeping. Police conferred with the large commercial banks—a perennial sokaiya target—and the banks agreed to hold their meetings on the same day in June.[66] As the years went by, an increasing number of firms began to hold their meetings on the designated day in June. In 1998, 2,325 firms, including a peak of 95 percent of all firms listed on the first section of the Tokyo Stock Exchange, held their meetings on "meeting day."

Though "meeting day" may reduce sokaiyas' ability to attend multiple meet-ings, it has significant drawbacks. First, if sokaiya cannot attend multiple meetings, neither can ordinary shareholders who have shares in several corpora-tions. Second, having meetings on the same day significantly increases media scrutiny of those meetings. Whereas previous media coverage had been sporadic, now almost every company with potentially scandalous material comes under the public eye, turning shareholders' meetings into something of a national referen-dum on effective corporate governance. Thanks to meeting day, a sokaiya's dis-ruption of a meeting will be well publicized, and all the sokaiya has to do the following year to receive payments is to point to his success in disrupting a meeting the previous year ("Hey, do you want me to do that to *you?*").

But almost all actors have independent incentives to support the meeting day idea. Police can concentrate their resources to protect almost all firms on a single day, a job made easy by the fact that meeting disrupters are spread thin.

Firms like meeting day (the more firms, the better), as it deters disrupters of all sorts, including both sokaiya and shareholders with legitimate grievances. Even sokaiya might support the plan, as they will be paid regardless of when firms have their meetings, and if they decide to actually disrupt, police forces are spread thin as well. The only actor who would likely not support meeting day is the individual investor, who cannot overcome collective action constraints to have his or her voice heard.

Yet, even before the establishment of a unitary meeting day, investors looked closely at shareholders' meetings in Japan. As in the United States, sometimes the reason to pay attention was because of dramatic incidents, such as Boone Pickens's failed takeover attempt of Koito Manufacturing in 1990–91 (he was shouted down several times at meetings by sokaiya). But more often than not, meetings were still relatively dull affairs. The reason that investors—and managers—paid attention to shareholders' meetings was to monitor the length of the meeting.

Meeting time in Japan is all-important. The top story of the evening news on meeting day is usually the length of large firms' meetings. After their meetings, each of Japan's large commercial banks traditionally was required to call the Banking Department of MOF to report its meeting time.[67] As the manager of one of those banks' general affairs departments told us, "This really puts us in a bind. If our meeting is too short, MOF thinks it's because we're paying sokaiya. If it's too long, they say, 'What's wrong? You got bad loans outstanding or something?'" As a consequence, most firms try to hit the magic number of 30 minutes for their meetings—and most succeed. In 1997, at the height of sokaiya scandals, average meeting length on meeting day was 29 minutes, over 95 percent of meetings ended in less than an hour, and no questions were asked at 87.5 percent of meetings.[68]

Companies employ a variety of strategies to keep meetings short. Some, of course, pay sokaiya. This tactic seems to work; firms that pay sokaiya tend to have short, orderly shareholders' meetings, while those that do not pay have long ones. Three recent stories illustrate the point. First, Sony, often held to be a model of good corporate governance practices in Japan, publicly announced in 1983 that to comply with the new sokaiya provisions, it unequivocally would have no further relations with sokaiya. Sokaiya responded by questioning Sony executives for over 13 hours at its 1984 meeting. The market responded negatively, "chilling" a two-month rise in Sony's stock price.[69] Second, in contrast, Nomura Securities' most potentially volatile meeting was its 1995 gathering, in which it (*a*) announced a record $500 million loss and (*b*) reinstated as directors its former chairperson and president, who had resigned four years earlier to take responsibility for sokaiya and loss compensation scandals. Nomura paid sokaiya Ryuichi Koike for his silence at the firm's 1995 meeting. The meeting lasted half an hour. Finally, department store Matsuzakaya's 1994 and 1995 meetings lasted 4 hours and 3 hours, respectively. Matsuzakaya executives began paying sokaiya in 1996. Its 1996 meeting lasted 19 minutes; its 1997 meeting, 38 minutes.[70]

Paying sokaiya is not the only possible strategy. Many firms hold their "real," but not official shareholders' meeting—a gathering of representatives from the firm's largest shareholding corporations and banks—well in advance of the legal meeting to iron out potential problems before they can arise. Others stack the deck by seating employee shareholders in the front row. The job of such employees is essentially that of one type of sokaiya—move the meeting along quickly with shouts of "no objection!" and loud cheering. Though the Japanese Supreme Court stated in 1996 that such a seating arrangement infringes upon shareholder rights,[71] allegations of abuse continue.

Meeting time might be important simply because of "meeting day." Executives in any country would prefer short meetings to long ones—even General Motors has measures in place to keep its meeting short, and almost all firms have policies to control unruly parties.[72] Perhaps the effect is simply concentrated by meeting day into an all-out race to the bottom. But this account cannot be a complete explanation, as meeting time was *always* a subject of media and investor interest, even for firms not holding their meetings on meeting day. To be sure, there is something of a chicken-and-egg phenomenon: sokaiya-induced increased scrutiny on meeting day leads to meeting time significance, which leads to more sokaiya activity. Still, sokaiya activity and meeting time significance existed for at least 100 years before meeting day was established.

Meeting day or no meeting day, managers will only pay to keep meetings short if the benefit of having a short meeting exceeds the costs required to keep it short. In the next section, we try to determine what benefit, if any, short meetings provide.

B. An Empirical Test

To determine the "prices" of long and short meetings, we conducted the following event study, using the same standard methodology that we used in Chapter 2. We hypothesize that if long meetings are more damaging than short meetings, on average, firms that have long meetings will have significantly negative stock returns. This is by no means a foregone conclusion. Investors might reward firms that have long meetings because those meetings tend to show that management is not paying sokaiya to keep its meetings short. Investors might also simply ignore meetings altogether, or some combination of these three forces could cancel each other out. Still, the fact that managers pay to have short meetings implies that on average, the stock price of companies that have long meetings will fall, and the stock price of companies that have short meetings will rise.

To test the hypothesis, we use the following method. A publication named *Shiryōban Shōji Hōmu* (loosely, "Corporate Law Data Book") publishes an accurate list of the length of the shareholders' meetings of virtually every large Japanese firm—1,927 firms in 1997, and a total of 12,301 observations for the period 1990–97, a period of intense sokaiya activity. From these lists, we constructed a data set of all long meetings held on meeting day (when 95 percent of firms hold their annual meetings) by first-section Tokyo Stock Exchange firms during the eight-year period from 1990 to 1997. We define "long" as 1 hour or longer. A review of the *Shiryōban Shōji Hōmu* data yielded 285 such long meetings. Of the firms that held these 285 meetings, all but five had complete stock price data in the Datastream electronic database, yielding a total of 280 observations. We then used event study methodology to test the price effects on the firms' stock in the year of their long meeting for the two-day period beginning the day of the meeting.

It would be nice to run a study on similar data from on U.S. firms. These data, unfortunately, do not exist—once again highlighting the importance of meeting times in Japan. Still, important conclusions about the U.S. system can be drawn from existing data. First, studies have shown that in general, predictable, information-laden events (such as dividend signals) create market risk. Risk-averse investors who invest in firms at the time of those predictable events are compensated with higher returns on their investments. Based on this theory, one study of 500 U.S. corporations found that on average, those corporations had significant positive returns of 0.56 percent on the day of their shareholders' meetings.[73] Given the large number of U.S. companies that routinely have meetings of over 2 hours (at some firms, meetings are lengthy entertainment events), the study suggests that meeting time is not a significant factor in U.S. investment decisions. It also suggests that in Japan or the United States, a shareholders' meeting of *any* length should generally be expected to produce, on average, small, but *positive* returns.

Our results are intriguing. First, the average market-adjusted returns for the entire sample of 280 firms are relatively unexciting. They show that the market-adjusted returns of the 280 firms, on average, declined by 0.06 percent over the two-day period. This statistically insignificant decline is practically equal to the performance of the market as a whole.[74]

We then split the sample into two groups: Repeaters (142 firms) and non-repeaters (138 firms).[75] We define "repeater" as those firms in the data set of long meetings whose meetings in the year *preceding* their long meeting also exceeded 1 hour. All other firms are non-repeaters. The reasoning behind this division is that if a firm regularly has long meetings, investors eventually learn that there is no information being signaled by the length of the firm's meeting. Electrical utilities, for instance, almost always have very long meetings; they were the only repeater firms in 1991, 1992, and 1994 to have meetings longer than 2 hours. But these meetings run long because of anti-nuclear protests, not sokaiya. And some meetings of Japanese firms with good investor relations programs run long for the same planned reasons that they might in the United States: Speeches, entertainment, and hors d'oeuvres. Realizing this, the market should not react to the length of repeaters' meetings. We find that repeaters in fact average a slight, though insignificant, increase in market-adjusted returns during the meeting day window.

The real story in this event study is the set of firms that have long meetings out of the blue; that is, the non-repeaters. In the year of their long meetings, these firms, on average, have statistically significant ($z = 2.11$) market-adjusted returns of −0.59 percent. The significance of this return is apparent not only from the result of the relatively complex *z* test, but also by the simple observation that the average aggregate return in each of the eight years in the sample was negative (if meeting time were not a factor, the distribution of negative and positive returns should be roughly equal). Stated concretely, the data show that during the period 1990–97, if a company that did not regularly have long meetings suddenly had a long meeting, that company lost, on average, 0.59 percent of its value (adjusted for market risk and variation in the Tokyo Stock Price Index) during the two-day period beginning the day it held its meeting.[76]

Faced with these stock price effects, how might each actor—managers, sokaiya, and shareholders—behave? Managers have incentives to pay sokaiya to keep meetings short, whether the payments are made to keep sokaiya quiet at meetings or as compensation for sokaiya suppression of "legitimate" shareholder voice. Sokaiya clearly have incentives to disrupt meetings, and given negative returns for long meetings, it may not be necessary that all of their information is always true or even always secret, so long as they can make the meeting run long and collect enough true information over time to maintain the signal's validity. Finally and somewhat perversely, investors should in some cases welcome payments to sokaiya, as sokaiya, for a relatively trivial fee, can prevent an average loss in shareholder wealth of 0.59 percent. Even if the payments by management to sokaiya are made not for the purpose of increasing shareholder wealth, but for entrenching management, the effect on shareholder wealth is the same.

Investors, thus, prefer to buy the stock of those companies that have short meetings. Of course, this pleases companies that usually have short meetings. But some companies—presumably those with such low information disclosure that shareholders can only acquire relevant information by asking lengthy questions at shareholders' meetings—will tend to have long meetings. These companies have clear incentives to pool with (mimic) companies that have short meetings. Paying sokaiya helps them do so.

Japanese managers that we interviewed were aware of the stock price drops that long meetings, or at least meetings that run long although they were intended to be short, can bring. As one manger from the legal department of a large manufacturing firm stated,

We used to have short meetings every year—20–30 minutes or so. We worked hard at this—employees in the front row yelling "Banzai," the general affairs department paying people money, whatever it took. Then one year it was decided that we should not control the meeting so tightly. The meeting lasted an hour and a half—no big ruckus, just a bunch of pesky questions. That afternoon, our stock dropped 20 points. The next year we went back to short meetings.

While this statement conflicts with some of the perceived wisdom about Japanese corporations, it has empirical support. Studies by Steven Kaplan and others show that Japanese managers attempt to maximize shareholder wealth, as "the fortunes of Japanese top executives . . . are positively correlated with stock performance. . . ."[77] As the threat of shareholder litigation increased in 1993, managers had further reason to follow stock prices.

C. Interpreting the Data

The data clearly show that meeting length correlates to stock price. But the *cause* of the stock price drop is open to interpretation. It is unlikely that stock prices always fall whenever some yahoo stands up in a meeting and heckles management. Rather, the correlation of stock price to meeting length can be explained by some combination of the following three explanations.

1. Disclosure Because Japanese firms often suppress information, meeting length correlates to the amount of negative information disclosed at meetings in response to shareholder questions. A firm with a short meeting is one with few secrets, while a firm with a long meeting is one with undisclosed problems that come to light only in the relatively uncontrollable atmosphere of the shareholders' meeting. In other words, meeting length *per se* is not important—the important factor is the disclosure of negative information in response to shareholder inquiries (which simply happens to result in long meetings). A short meeting is thus preferable not simply because it is short, but because a short meeting means less disclosure of negative information.

When investors react negatively to disclosure, they may also be reacting more generally to the potential for exposure of scandal. Investors know that due to Japanese overregulation, companies must sometimes take illegal—but *efficient*— actions in order to be competitive. As long as such actions are rarely discovered or prosecuted, investors want companies to take such actions, as they lead to higher returns. Accordingly, investors seek to avoid the scandal of exposure. Negative disclosure at meetings may thus result in negative returns based not only on the specific disclosed information, but also based on management's inability to control future scandals. Given the competitive constraints faced by many firms (such as the department stores described earlier), preventing scandal might be more important in Japan than in many other systems.

2. Signaling In some cases, meeting length may not correspond to negative information uncovered at meetings. If potential investors in Japanese markets cannot get certain information from mandatory or voluntary disclosure, perhaps they can get clues on how to price stock from actions that the company takes. Such actions, whether intentional or not, can send signals to potential investors about the company's economic health. Investors can then base their investment decisions on the information that is revealed by the signals.

In Japan, recognized signals are sparse. The most commonly cited example of a signal is the payment of a dividend: A firm that increases its dividend signals that it anticipates an improving cash flow, and a firm that decreases its dividend signals that it anticipates a future cash flow problem. In Japan, unlike the United States, dividends usually have no correlation to earnings. Japanese firms base dividends on a fixed percentage of par value, such as the typical 10 percent annual yield on a share of ¥50 value, or ¥5, making Japanese dividends "void of an informational content."[78] Three other major signals are open-market stock repurchases, the granting of stock options to executives, and stock splits. But during the time period covered by our statistical tests the Japanese Commercial Code drastically restricted a company's ability to undertake any of these actions.[79]

Faced with non-disclosure and a dearth of reliable signals, one way that shareholders in Japan can make investment decisions is to look at firms' meeting times as indicia of corporate health. Investors cannot attend all meetings and make accurate judgments regarding the informational content of the meeting. But they know that management strives to have short meetings, and that meetings accordingly would only run long if something went "wrong." Investors can thus use meeting time (gleaned from news reports or market rumor) as a proxy for the level of disclosure of previously suppressed negative information.

3. Control of meetings   Finally, negative returns could result because executive inability to control meetings signals executive inability to manage companies. The same phenomenon may occur in the United States, but it may be more pronounced in Japan. In Japan, lifetime employment patterns tend to produce executives who are relatively insulated from the world outside the corporation (at least from control contests and labor markets), and are said to wield great authority within the firm. In such a system, executive failure in controlling the length of a shareholders' meeting may be viewed by investors either as heretofore-unseen managerial incompetence, or as a signal of a lack of internal support. In either case, long meetings serve as verdicts against management, which leads to negative returns.

Given management goals and disclosure policies, most of the stock price drop probably can be explained by the disclosure story and the signaling story, but the control story is quite plausible. Certainly managerial *belief* in the control story may be a significant motive for payment to sokaiya, regardless of whether it actually explains the negative returns. In any event, the disclosure, signaling, and control stories are better explanations of the observed correlation between meeting length and returns than the following three alternatives:

a   *The bubble.* The data come from a period of economic stagnation following the burst of the Japanese "bubble" economy in the late 1980s. Perhaps the negative average abnormal return can be explained by the downturn; in good times, investors may care less about negative information—and hence meeting time. But this interpretation, in fact, supports the informational disclosure story, as it implies that meeting time matters more when more suppressed negative information exists. As land prices plummeted, banks began to reveal huge outstanding bad loans, and the entire home mortgage industry began to fall apart, firms had more information on which sokaiya could prey. The rash of sokaiya arrests in 1997–98 may simply be examples of the fallout from the bubble's collapse. In good times—which Japan has not seen now for quite some time—one might still expect a negative return from firms with long meetings, though perhaps of a lesser magnitude.

b *Sokaiya manipulation.* Perhaps the negative returns are caused directly by sokaiya. Some sokaiya (or their accomplices in organized crime syndicates) are experienced stock price manipulators. To make their threats credible, they might intentionally buy large stakes in the companies whose meetings they plan to disrupt, disrupt the meetings, then sell the shares, sending stock prices down. They could then point to the stock price decline as evidence of their "success." Although this story is theoretically possible, we have never actually heard of such tactics, and we think for good reason. These are not the penny stocks or small initial public offerings that normally are manipulated; they are the shares of huge corporations. In order to move stock prices suddenly with no institutional backing, ordinary sokaiya would be required to use more of their own funds than they receive in blackmail payments from the company, an especially unlikely scenario given that the plan has a relatively high probability of failure. The handful of elite sokaiya who actually might be able to acquire the necessary funds are so connected with the companies that they have little incentive to overreach. Even if they were to attempt such a transaction, they probably would be thwarted by Japan's version of the Williams Act (SEL arts. 27-23 to 27-30), which requires disclosure of holdings of over 5 percent of public companies.

c *Decisions and planned disclosures.* Finally, perhaps the negative returns arise because long meetings occur when major decisions are reached, proxy votes fail, major disclosures are made independently by management, or similar other events occur. The story then would be that share prices fall because a long meeting signals shareholder dissatisfaction with management. But executives in Japan normally have total control over decisions and announcements made at meetings. Given large, stable, "friendly" shareholders, in Japan, even more so than in the United States, decisions are made before the meeting by proxies, and the meetings themselves are usually just rituals. And announcement timing can almost always be manipulated to avoid inopportune disclosure.

More importantly, in order for such an account to be true, there would need to be a correlation between negative decisions or announcements and meeting length. There is no reason why such a correlation would exist; on average, it should take just as long to reach a positive decision as a negative one. The results of the following test support the point. The *Nihon Keizai Shinbun* (*Nikkei*), Japan's equivalent to the *Wall Street Journal*, runs stories about the shareholders' meetings of major firms on meeting day (evening edition) and on the day following meeting day (morning edition). We examined these two sets of newspapers for each year during the ten-year period beginning in 1988. During this period, *Nikkei* reported on fifty-six meetings that lasted more than 1 hour. The length of the meeting is reported in the newspaper. One would expect Japan's *Wall Street Journal* to print stories on firms that reached significant decisions or made significant announcements at its meetings. However, stories involving only eleven of these fifty-six firms reported that the meetings involved decisions or planned announcements (negative *or* positive). Three of those eleven were decisions regarding shareholder proposals from environmental activists that were doomed to failure from the start and surely were news to no one. Removing these three firms shows that forty-eight of fifty-six stories about firms whose meetings exceeded one hour, or 86 percent, reported that the meeting ran long not because of information-laden decisions or announcements, but due to investor questions, disruptions, and the like. This is a very strong indication that long meetings on average are not evidence of, and do not signal, negative decisions or planned announcements, and that the more plausible explanations are disclosure, signaling, and control.

CONCLUSION

Why would rational executives of highly successful Japanese firms pay sokaiya racketeers to keep their shareholders' meetings short? This chapter has shown that sometimes they pay sokaiya for blackmail, hardly a uniquely Japanese phenomenon, but one that might have particular characteristics in the Japanese economic context. But sometimes the blackmail actually does center around shareholders' meetings. The econometric data presented in this chapter suggest that because meeting length is correlated to share prices, payments to sokaiya to keep meetings short can increase shareholder wealth.

This wealth maximization potential is a direct product of Japanese corporate law, regulation, and corporate governance, which facilitate barren information markets. Sokaiya—often armed with mob connections that make their threats perfectly clear—simply take advantage of the fact that little information is disseminated. U.S. corporate blackmail apparently does not reach the scale of that of Japan because the U.S. federal system, relatively unfettered by inefficient corporate law, heavy regulation, and other anti-competitive institutions, makes publicly available more information with blackmail potential.

The sokaiya payment institution persists because, given other existing institutions, almost all actors have reason to choose it over alternative choices. Obviously sokaiya can profit with little chance of detection. Managers and shareholders benefit, too. The Japanese press sometimes describes sokaiya-paying managers as gutless and cowardly. Managers counterattack with cries that they bravely pay sokaiya "for the good of the company."[80] We will make no attempt here to judge managerial cowardice or bravery. But the data suggest that managers' behavior may at least be wealth-maximizing, as managers appear to pay sokaiya when it is cheaper than information disclosure. On this issue, managerial and shareholder interests are aligned. Given that the system is one of non-disclosure, shareholders (and perhaps society as a whole) may derive further benefit from sokaiya activity, as sokaiya may serve as monitors of management behavior, forcing managers to calculate the cost of sokaiya bribes into the cost of their actions. And if the MOF wants to prevent firms from failing, it too may have incentives to support sokaiya activity.

The institutional incentive structure implies that recent Japanese legislative efforts to curtail sokaiya activity may be of limited efficacy. In November 1997, the Japanese legislature enacted revisions to the Commercial Code designed (once again) to eliminate sokaiya.[81] The new provisions increased criminal penalties for payment from imprisonment of six months or a $3,000 fine to three years or $30,000, imposed criminal liability for sokaiya who demand payment (as opposed to liability only for receiving payment), and increased penalties for related wrongdoing such as money laundering and making false statements to regulators. This legislation may have had some marginal effect. But even after the law was enacted (and several months after the most publicized scandals), 60 percent of surveyed directors, 79 percent of auditors, and 75 percent of managers still said that they would be unable to cut sokaiya ties in ten years.[82]

The 1997 legislation, like the 1982 legislation, ignored the broader institutional factors behind sokaiya activity, and as such is highly unlikely to result in the "consciousness revolution among management" that then Prime Minister Hashimoto announced when introducing the bill.[83] If a concerted effort toward the elimination of sokaiya is to be undertaken, a better way to proceed might be to employ mechanisms to increase the flow of information from companies to the market, such as loosening inefficient regulations, making keiretsu relationships more transparent, and controlling bureaucratic orchestration of disclosure. As we will discuss more fully in Chapters 7 and 8, some of these changes have occurred, are still occurring, and may drive sokaiya numbers below even their 2002 all-time low of 420. At the same time, many companies have undertaken efforts to improve their shareholder relations, and by 2003, only 68 percent of Tokyo Stock Exchange firms held their meetings on meeting day. Still, even in the changed institutional environment, some firms continue to find payment preferable to disclosure, and remaining sokaiya continue to profit.

NOTES

1. Taihan, Sōkaiya kara Sesshoku [Most Have Contact From Sokaiya], Mainichi Shinbun, June 15, 1997, at 1.
2. Fushōji de Nigeru na [Don't Run Away from Scandal], 896 Nikkei Bus. 38, 45 (June 9, 1997).
3. See, for example, David E. Kaplan and Alec Dubro, Yakuza 170, 173 (1986); Yoichiro Taniguchi, Japan's Company Law and the Promotion of Corporate Democracy: A Futile Attempt?, 27 Colum. J. of Transnat'l L. 195, 201 (1988).
4. Respectively, Ronald H. Coase, Blackmail, 74 Va. L. Rev. 655 (1988); Robert Nozick, Anarchy, State, and Utopia 84 (1974); and William M. Landes and Richard A. Posner, The Private Enforcement of Law, 4 J. Legal Stud. 1, 42–4 (1975).

5. Richard A. Posner, Blackmail, Privacy, and Freedom of Contract, 141 U. Penn. L. Rev. 1817, 1841 (1993). Posner later argues more precisely that blackmail between strangers is rare, while blackmail between acquaintances is "common but largely undetectable." Id., Overcoming Law 550 (1995).

6. The Tokyo District Court defines sokaiya as "one who holds a few shares of stock in many companies, and at the request of one of these companies, professionally attends the general meeting of that company for the express purpose of assisting the company in holding the meeting and passing all company-proposed resolutions." *Japan v. Hobo*, 7 Kakeishū 1712 (Tokyo D. Ct. Aug. 27, 1965).

7. *Goto v. Chisso, K. K.*, 736 Hanji 20 (Osaka D. Ct. Mar. 28, 1947), aff'd, 945 Hanji 23 (Osaka High Ct., Sept. 27, 1979), aff'd 1082 Hanji 9 (Sup. Ct., June 7, 1983).

8. See Toyoharu Kanda, Sōkaiya no 100 Nen [100 Years of Sokaiya] 91–9 (1991).

9. While some magazines are read by individual investors, securities analysts, and reporters for relatively scandalous but popular weekly magazines, most are sham publications that have no subscribers but the blackmailees. The real threat in such a case is exposure at the shareholders' meeting, and the subscription fee is simply a method of attempting to hide the payment. Recently internet publication is popular, see www.iijnet.or.jp/rondan (homepage of Rondan Doyukai, a forty-member "activist shareholder" group whose members have been arrested in the Ito-Yokado, Ajinomoto, and Kirin Beer scandals). See also www.sokaiya.com (forum for persons with grievances against companies to raise complaints in "virtual shareholders' meetings").

10. Posner, *supra* note 5, at 1841.

11. *Japan v. Yamazaki*, 1160 Hanji 3 (Tokyo D. Ct., Mar. 26, 1985).

12. *Japan v. Ichida*, 94 Saibanshū 151 (Sup. Ct., Apr. 6, 1954).

13. *Japan v. Yoshida*, 14 Daihan Keishū 1199 (Sup. Ct., Nov. 14, 1935).

14. *Japan v. Sugai*, 12 Daihan Keishū 1807 (Sup. Ct., Oct. 16, 1933).

15. See James Lindgren, Unraveling the Paradox of Blackmail, 84 Colum. L. Rev. 670, 683 (1984).

16. Kaplan and Dubro, *supra* note 3, at 170.

17. Rieki Kyōyo 2000 Nin ni Nen 5 Oku [Provision of Benefits of ¥500 million Annually to 2000 People], Yomiuri Shinbun, June 26, 1997, at 39.

18. 700 Shi Kōdoku Yamemasu [Canceling Subscriptions for 700 Magazines], Asahi Shinbun, July 10, 1997, at 35.

19. See Sōkaiya to Zetsuen Sengen [Oath to Break Ties with Sokaiya], Yomiuri Shinbun, July 11, 1997, at 1.

20. See Koike Hikoku Igai ni 11 Oku En [1.1 Billion Yen to Sokaiya other than Koike Defendant], Asahi Shinbun, Dec. 25, 1998, at 23. The breakdown is as follows: Nomura: Nine sokaiya, ¥370 million; Daiwa: Five sokaiya, ¥70 million; Nikko: four sokaiya, ¥80 million; Yamaichi: Five sokaiya, ¥280 million; DKB: Twenty-two sokiaya, ¥300 million.

21. The data are skewed by the large amount paid by Dai-Ichi Kangyo Bank. Removing this figure yields an average of about ¥6 million ($60,000) per sokaiya or ¥25 million ($250,000) per firm.

22. See, for example, *Japan v. Ishihara*, 23 Keishū 1469 (Sup. Ct., Sept. 25, 1961).

23. Eiichi Takano, Kigyō Taishō Bōryoku Jian no Taisaku Oyobi Sōkaiya nado no Dōkō to Torishimari Jōkyō [The Policy to Prevent Violence Against Enterprise and the Current Status and Elimination of the Sokaiya], 1355 Shōji Hōmu 31, 36 (1994).

24. *Japan* v. *Hobo*, 7 Kakeishū 1712 (Tokyo D. Ct. Aug 27, 1965), rev'd, 501 Hanji 34 (Tokyo High Ct., Oct. 17, 1967), aff'd, 57 Hanji 3 (Sup. Ct. Oct. 16, 1969).
25. Commercial Code arts. 294-2, 497. Although this language is broad enough to encompass a wide range of "benefits" to shareholders, courts interpret the language narrowly so that in effect only payments to typical sokaiya are outlawed. See *Suzuki* v. *Kumagaya*, 559 Hanji 275 (Fukui D. Ct., Mar. 29, 1988).
26. See, for example, Sōkaiya no Shinsō, Shūkan Daiyamondo, June 10, 1997, at 24, 25.
27. Code of Criminal Procedure art. 250. Tax violations that may result from payments carry a statute of limitations of five years. Id.
28. Daniel H. Foote, The Benevolent Paternalism of Japanese Criminal Justice, 80 Calif. L. Rev. 317 (1992).
29. See, for example, *Japan* v. *Ohishi*, 70 Shiryōban Shōji Hōmu 47 (Fukuoka D. Ct., May 11, 1990); *Japan* v. *Ozawa*, 70 Shiryōban Shōji Hōmu 48 (Fukuoka D. Ct., June 15, 1990).
30. See, for example, Jill Lorraine McKinnon, The Historical Development and Operational Form of Corporate Reporting Regulation in Japan 322-3 (1986); Howard D. Sherman and Bruce Andrew Babcock, Redressing Structural Imbalances in Japanese Corporate Governance: An International Perspective, in Japanese Corporate Governance: A Comparative study of Systems in Japan and the United States 63, 103, 149-50 n. 9 (David Kaufman ed., 1994).
31. The Commercial Code requires aggregate directors compensation to be approved by the shareholders (article 269), but contains no provision for officers.
32. Organization for Economic Cooperation and Development, Disclosure of Information by Multinational Enterprises, Working Document by the Working Group on Accounting Standards, No. 6 (1989).
33. Stephen M. Davis, Shareholder Rights Abroad: A Handbook for the Global Investor 64, 136 (1989).
34. Japanese firms whose shares trade in the United States might be expected to have relatively few sokaiya payments based on this type of information because they are subject to US disclosure standards. But of the 152 Japanese firms whose shares trade in the United States, twelve have been involved in sokaiya incidents. (Data from www.bankofny.com/adr) But these firms trade using "level 1" or "level 2" ADRs, which require less disclosure than is required of US firms.
35. See, for example, Paul Milgrom and John Roberts, Economics, Organization & Management 425-6 (1992).
36. Stuart Rosenstein and Jeffrey G. Wyatt, Inside Directors, Board Effectiveness, and Shareholder Wealth, 44 J. Fin. Econ. 229 (1997).
37. Aron Viner, Inside Japanese Financial Markets 101-2 (1988) (citing Yamaichi Research Institute data).
38. See Douglas J. Skinner, Why Firms Voluntarily Disclose Bad News, 32 J. Acct. Res. 38 (1994) (early voluntary disclosure (*a*) makes it difficult for plaintiffs to argue that the information was withheld and (*b*) limits the damages that may arise from a lengthy period of nondisclosure).
39. Douglas G. Baird et al., Game Theory and the Law 96 (1994).
40. See, for example, Yukio Noguchi, Ajinomoto Moto Sōmubuchō Zangeroku [Confessions of a Former Ajinomoto General Affairs Department Chief], Shinchō 45, Jan. 5, 1998, at 170, 177 ("I exchanged information with the heads of general affairs departments of other firms.").

41. See Curtis J. Milhaupt, Managing the Market: The Ministry of Finance and Securities Regulation in Japan, 30 Stan. J. Int'l L. 423, 444–60 (1994).
42. The derivative suit to which the incident gave rise is discussed in Chapter 2.
43. See, for example, Yamaichi "Tobashi" Jogen Mitomeru [Acknowledgment of "Tobashi" Advice to Yamaichi], Nihon Keizai Shinbun, Feb. 5, 1998, at 1.
44. See, for example, Mitsuzaka Kuraso Kyō Jinin [Finance Minister Mitsuzaka to Resign Today], Nihon Keizai Shinbun, Jan. 28, 1998, at 1.

   If a MOF-tan does not know the day of the MOF inspection, he or she will be fired. Because inspections occur in January, April, and October, you always know. Inspections take 33 to 35 days, so they are inevitably scheduled so as to avoid the March [fiscal year-end] accounting season, June shareholders' meetings, summer vacations, and the end and beginning of each year. The timing of the inspection is fixed, too, usually occurring not in the first, but in the second week of the month. It is best to know which branch the inspectors will visit, but even if you do not know, it is no big deal. A month or more before an investigation is supposed to begin, MOF gives you a "MOF Inspection Guide." If you made preparations in accordance with the Guide, everything was always fine. . . . At one bank, the MOF-tan and others knew not only the inspection dates of other banks, but also knew exactly which inspectors would show up. His reputation was so big that other MOF-tan would go to him for information. Even at my bank, we obtained the inspection data on five or six of our rival banks. Moto MOF-tan no Jukkai: Raibaru Kō no Kensa Shiryō ha Te ni Haireteita [Recollections of a Former MOF-tan: We Obtained Inspection Data on Rival Banks], Diamond Wkly, Mar. 7, 1998, at 35.

45. See, for example, Kensa Jōhō Nyūshu Hakaru [Scheme to Obtain Inspection Information], Nihon Keizai Shinbun, Jan. 27, 1997 (evening edition), at 17.
46. J. Mark Ramseyer and Frances McCall Rosenbluth, Japan's Political Marketplace 119 (1993).
47. Japan data: Commercial Survey 1994 (1995). US data: US Department of Commerce, Statistical Abstract of the United States 1996 762–3 (1996).
48. See generally Frank Upham, Privatizing Regulation: The Implementation of the Large-Scale Retail Stores Law, in Political Dynamics in Contemporary Japan 264–94 (Gary D. Allinson and Yasunori Sone eds., 1993).
49. See Kenji Tagusagawa, Reflection on Discussions Concerning Deregulation of the Electrical Power Industry, Japan Development Bank Research Report No. 63 (Dec. 1996). Electrical utilities may also be reluctant to pay because of continued ramifications from the Chisso incident, and perhaps because they prefer dealing with environmentalists than with sokaiya.
50. See Janet Cooper Alexander, Do the Merits Matter? A Study of Settlements in Securities Class Actions, 43 Stan. L. Rev. 497 (1991); Roberta Romano, The Shareholder Suit: Litigation Without Foundation, 7 J. L. Econ. & Org. 55 (1991).
51. Conference Report on Securities Litigation Reform, H.R. Rep. No. 369, 104th Congress, 1st Sess. 31, reprinted in 1995 U.S.C.C.A.N. 730, 731–4; Report on the Private Securities Litigation Reform Act of 1995, S. Rep. No. 98, 104th Congress, 1st Sess. 6 (1995), reprinted in 1995 U.S.C.C.A.N. 679, 685.
52. 15 U.S.C. § 78u-4(a)(2)(A).

53. Calculated as (trade price + stock price × 30%) × one transaction unit of shares × number of options. Credit Lyonnais Securities (Japan) Fact Sheet, Single Stock Options Markets in Japan (undated, issued 1997).

54. See Japan Securities Research Institute, Securities Market in Japan 1998 256–71 (1998).

55. Securities and Exchange Law (SEL), Law No. 25 of 1948, Art. 162 (prohibiting sales of securities that one does not own).

56. See, for example, Q & A Shōken 100 no Jōshiki [100 Common Sense Q & A's regarding Securities] 114–15 (Nihon Keizai Shinbunsha ed., 1997).

57. SEL art. 49; Tokyo Stock Exchange, Jutaku Keiyaku Kisoku [Trust Contract Rules] 13-2.

58. SEL art. 162; Shōken Torihiki Iinkai (S.E.C.), Yūka Shōken no Karauri ni Kansuru Kisoku [Regulations on Short Sales of Securities], Rule No. 16 of 1948.

59. See, for example, When Merrill Lynch Acts, Financial Sector Should Listen, Nikkei Wkly, Jan. 12, 1998, at 16.

60. Byung Jong Lee, Pro Heckling Season in South Korea Stirs Investor Resentment, Wall Street Journal, Mar. 5, 1990, at 1; see also Michael Lewis, The Real Asian Miracle, New York Times Magazine, May 31, 1998, at 34 (recounting Samsung shareholders' meeting that ran over 13 hours due to questioning of "sweet deals" of chairman).

61. James Hansem, Italy's 'Disturbers' Quiet Down, Int'l Herald Tribune, Nov. 30, 1993, at 1.

62. See Jonathan R. Macey, Italian Corporate Governance: One American's Perspective, 1998 Col. Bus. L. Rev. 121 (1998); Alessandro Sembenetti, Signalling, Financial Hierarchy and Agency Theory as Explanations for Dividend Behavior: Evidence from Italian Firm Data, 14 Managerial & Decision Econ. 37, 39 (1993).

63. Gian Bruno Bruni, Shareholders' Rights—Italy (unpublished manuscript presented at Int'l Bar. Assoc. Biennial conference, Berlin, 1996).

64. A. A. Berle, Jr., Economic Power and the Free Society 7 (1957).

65. Saburō Shiroyama, Sōkaiya Kinjō [Kinjo the Sokaiya] (1963), published in English as Kinjo the Corporate Bouncer and Other Stories from Japanese Business 58 (Tamae Prindle ed. & trans., 1989). See Frank Baldwin, The Idioms of Contemporary Japan VII: Sokaiya, 7 Japan Interpreter 502 (1974) (noting Shiroyama's role).

66. Some meeting coordination may already have been in place among large banks and corporations. See Tooru Inoue, Kaisha–Kabunushi–Sokaiya [Corporations, Shareholders, Sokaiya], 340 Jurisuto 58, 59 (1966).

67. See "Kegasenu Taimen" Tukare [Striking Out at "Loss of Honor"], Mainichi Shinbun, June 2, 1997, at 13.

68. 160 Shiryōban Shōji Hōmu 82 (1997); 1475 Shōji Hōmu 105 (1997).

69. Marason Sōkai ni Iyake [Disgust with the Marathon Meeting], Nihon Keizai Shinbun, Feb. 1, 1984, at 17.

70. See Matsuzakaya Torishimariyaku to Sōkaiya o Taiho, [Matsuzakaya Director and Sokaiya Arrested], Mainichi Shinbun, Oct. 20, 1997, at 1.

71. *Takahashi* v. *Shikoku Denryoku*, 1440 Shōji Hōmu 39 (Sup. Ct., Nov. 12, 1996).

72. See James Bennet, 10-Minute Clock Keeps Shots Low at G.M. Meeting, New York Times, May 27, 1995, at 35.

73. James A. Brickley, Interpreting Common Stock Returns around Proxy Statement Disclosures and Annual Shareholder Meetings, 21 J. Fin. & Quantitative Analysis 343 (1986).

74. For comparison, we used the same methodology on a sample of 280 first-section Tokyo Stock Exchange firms, chosen randomly, that had short meetings—less than an hour—on meeting day. Strictly speaking, this test is not necessary (because almost all firms have short meetings, the market model is a proxy for those firms), but the data provide an easy comparison. As one would predict, the returns are practically equal to the market return (-0.08 percent, $z = 0.05$). Similarly, it might also be of interest to examine event study data on all firms to see the full distribution of the correlation of meeting time to stock price change. But investors probably care little about the difference between a 15-minute meeting and a 30-minutes meeting, so data on all firms is unlikely to yield new insights. Moreover, because the events are clustered (they all occur on the same meeting day), the high cross-correlation between stocks means that traditional event study methodology is no longer applicable, and alternatives are problematic.

75. We also split the sample into long meetings (1 hour) and extraordinarily long meetings (2 hour), and found no significant results.

76. A loss of 0.59 percent may not sound large. But if the company in question is, for instance, Sony, a 0.59 percent market and risk-adjusted price decrease translates into a decrease in shareholder wealth of approximately $22 million. It also is worth noting that a company never actually "makes up" the decrease. Prices may subsequently increase, but these increases are the result either of new information being incorporated into prices or overall market movement.

77. Steven N. Kaplan, Top Executive Rewards and Firm Performance: A Comparison of Japan and the United States, 102 J. Pol. Econ. 510, 542–3 (1994); see also Steven N. Kaplan and Bernadette A. Minton, Appointments of Outsiders to Japanese Boards: Determinants and Implications for Managers, 36 J. Fin. Econ. 225 (1994). Further studies uniformly confirm Kaplan's data, with some studies finding even stronger correlation. See, for example, Yukiko Abe, Chief Executive Turnover and Firm Performance in Japan, J. Japanese & Int'l Econ. 2 (1997); Jun-Koo Kang and Anil Shivdasani, Firm Performance, Corporate Governance, and Top Executive Turnover in Japan, 38 J. Fin. Econ. 29 (1995).

78. Ali M. Fatemi and Alireza Tourani Rad, Stock Return Variation and Expected Dividends: The Far Eastern Experience, in Studies in the Financial Markets of the Pacific Basin 107 (Theodore Bos and Thomas A. Fethersten eds., vol. 11B, 1994).

79. Prior to amendments in the late 1990s, with some limited exceptions, the Code banned a firm from buying or redeeming its own stock. Commercial Code arts. 210–211; cf. N.Y. Bus. Corp. L. § 513 (permissive New York rules); Del. Gen. Corp. L. § 160 (same in Delaware). Before June 1, 1997, executive stock options were virtually impossible to award. Stock splits are theoretically permitted by the Code, see Commercial Code art. 218, but they are discouraged by the Code's requirement that after any split, a company's net assets must be at least ¥50,000 ($500) per share. See Commercial Code arts. 293–4(1), 293–3(2), 218(2), cf. Del. Gen. Corp. L. 173.

80. As convicted former Ajinomoto general affairs manager stated recently in an apparently heartfelt and decidedly poignant essay. Noguchi, *supra* note 40, at 173.

81. Shōhō oyobi Kabushiki Kaisha no Kansa Tō ni Kansuru Shōhō no Tokurei ni Kansuru Hōritsu no Ichibu o Kaisei Suru Hōritsu, Law No. 107 of 1997.

82. Many Execs Say Ties with Extortionists Will Continue, Japan Econ. Newswire, Mar. 25, 1998, available in Lexis.

83. Sangikai Giroku [Lower House Proceedings], 141st Session, Nov. 14, 1997, at 3.

6

Organized Crime

As the previous chapter suggested, organized crime flourishes in Japan. It thrives not only in gray areas such as corporate trouble making and blatantly illegal markets like prostitution and drug trade. It also prospers in more legitimate markets like golf course development, banking and securities, and disaster relief. The infiltration of the economy by organized criminal gangs is no secret; their members are easily identified, and their headquarters often display the firm's symbols on the front door.

Why did organized crime emerge in Japan, why does it persist, and what is its function in the Japanese economy? Despite a growing recognition of the vulnerability of developing societies and emerging democracies to the problem of organized crime, and continued study of the phenomenon in mature economies, no consensus exists even on the definition of organized crime,[1] much less on the more theoretically fundamental and practically significant questions. Without a richer understanding of the phenomenon, organized crime will continue to thrive because the roots of the problem will remain unexposed.

This chapter draws on new institutional economics literature and extensive empirical analysis to show that the structure and activities of organized criminal groups are significantly shaped by the state. Organized crime in Japan (as elsewhere), we argue, is the dark side of private ordering—an entrepreneurial response to inefficiencies in the property rights and enforcement framework supplied by the state.

A substantial literature has exposed the bright side of private ordering.[2] Many scholars have shown that over a wide range of human activity, informal norms provide efficient and effective mechanisms to govern conduct. Occasionally a commentator will note that not all private ordering arrangements result in efficient norms, or that private ordering is subject to the same collective action problems that plague formal lawmaking processes.[3] These cautionary asides in the literature, however, are rare and have never been developed into a robust theory of the organized, private exploitation of defects in state structures. We seek to provide analytical and empirical support for such a theory by focusing on a simple fact: In order to be effective, private ordering often requires the participation of intermediaries who possess information, time, and skill—intermediaries we refer to as rights-enforcement agents and information agents. In the United States, these roles are typically filled by lawyers or other organized professionals, who, to borrow legal scholar Ronald Gilson's famous phrase, function as "transaction cost engineers."[4] When property rights and enforcement institutions are misaligned, however, these agents may emerge from sources operating outside the bounds of established legal and social norms. Illicit entrepreneurs, then, substitute for state-supplied or state-sanctioned public services, especially as alternative enforcers of property rights. This "dark-side private ordering" provides a convincing explanation for the emergence and role of organized crime in both developed and developing economies.

Japan provides unusually fertile ground for our study. Private ordering is often seen as a key component of Japanese policy success in such diverse areas as crime prevention, civil dispute resolution, and labor relations.[5] Counterintuitively, however, Japan shares important parallels with transition economies: It has an institutional environment rife with incentives for the creation of alternative (illicit) enforcement mechanisms and a very active network of organized criminal groups. Yet, unlike virtually any other country, Japan also provides a wealth of relevant but unexplored data on organized crime. As explored below, the Japanese experience offers insights into organized crime in environments as diverse as Russia and Sicily.

Multiple regression analysis of the data from Japan supports substantial anecdotal evidence that members of organized crime in that country play an active entrepreneurial role in substituting for state-supplied property rights and enforcement mechanisms in such areas as dispute mediation, real estate foreclosure, corporate monitoring, lending, and (unorganized) crime control. We offer additional empirical evidence suggesting that the success of organized crime prevention may rest more heavily on the design of state-supplied institutions than on traditional anti-crime strategies. Our empirical analysis thus supports a significant normative claim: To combat organized crime most effectively, a state should alter its institutional incentive structure and introduce additional rights-enforcement agents.

Although we rely on the Japanese experience for data, our discussion has more universal import. The state acts as an institutional designer in any economy, determining, among other things, which business activities will be criminalized and which will be actively encouraged. How the state performs in this capacity affects the development not only of legitimate organizations, but also of illicit ones as well. In the spectrum of property rights structures and regulated business activities, Japan lies between the United States and more heavily state-controlled systems such as the former Soviet Union. Each of these systems features its own brand of organized crime, reflecting the institutional environment in which it evolved. The universal point emerging from our study is that where the state fails to get the institutions "right," it invites dark-side private ordering to fill in the gaps.

To gain a better understanding of the role of organized crime in an economy, we adopt two heuristics. First, we use the term "organized criminal firms" to emphasize the fundamentally entrepreneurial role of organized crime. Second, as more fully developed below, we characterize the private enforcement activities of organized criminal firms as "illicit entrepreneurialism" because it takes place outside the bounds of state ordering, in the shadow of violence.

The chapter proceeds as follows. In Section I, we survey the theory of organized crime, which is characterized by lack of agreement on fundamental principles and a shortage of empirical grounding. In Section II, we illustrate the close linkage between rights-enforcement and organized crime in Japan in such areas as bankruptcy, property, debtor–creditor relations, and corporate law. Section III presents a formal model to test empirically the relationship between state institutions and illicit entrepreneurialism in Japan. Our regression analysis results are consistent with the theory that organized criminal firms in Japan substitute for state institutions in such key areas as dispute resolution, crime control, and finance. Section IV examines the implications of the Japanese experience and applies those lessons to economies in transition.

I. ORGANIZED CRIME THEORY

We begin by stepping back from Japan to examine the literature on organized crime. It displays a marked lack of consensus on fundamental issues. As noted above, there is little agreement even on a definition of organized crime, less still on the question of why the phenomenon exists. The result, as one commentator notes, "is a patchwork of ideas, only loosely related to each other and having little consequence for empirical research."[6]

Economic theory has traditionally emphasized the monopoly that organized crime enjoys over illegal products and services. Thus, criminals organize themselves into firms for the same reasons that "legitimate" firms organize: To reap economies of scale or monopoly rents. Organized criminal firm monopolies tend to arise in the same ways as traditional monopolies—economies of scale may dictate that only one firm can effectively serve the market, small producers may merge, and barriers to entry may be created by government regulation and restrictions. The primary means for achieving success, economists hold, is extortion.[7]

Sociological literature, by contrast, traditionally has focused on the cultural or ethnic linkages that dictate the structure and cohesiveness of organized crime groups, largely bypassing the more fundamental question of why such groups emerge. More recently, sociologists have argued that the primary market for organized crime services is in "unstable transactions in which trust is scarce and fragile," and, more generally, that organized criminal firms arise in societies characterized by a lack of trust.[8] Thus, for example, the rise in organized crime in Eastern Europe and Russia is explained as an outgrowth of Communism, which is said to have systematically destroyed trust in government.[9]

Neither approach, however, is wholly satisfying. First, consider the sociologists' recent fascination with trust. Many of the services that organized criminal firms offer around the world involve not risky black or gray market transactions, but intervention in transactions that ought to be "stable," in that they are formally supported by the legal system—debt collection or labor dispute resolution, for example. Even more damaging to the proposed correlation between low trust and organized crime is the case of Japan. Japan has extensive organized crime, yet, Japan's social system is often viewed as founded on trust. Francis Fukuyama, for instance, defines Japan as a "high-trust society" in which social capital is in abundant supply.[10] Cross-country empirical analyses of trust confirm that characterization and generally cast doubt on the utility of mistrust as a key explanatory variable in the origins of organized crime.[11]

Turn, now, to the traditional economic approach. Theorists have cast doubt both on the idea that organized crime relies primarily on extortion, and that monopoly is the best concept to understand the activities of organized criminals. In the past several years, observers have begun to change their perspective on the services provided by organized criminals and the relationship between organized crime and the state. Focusing on Sicily, for example, Diego Gambetta argues that organized criminals deal not in extortion, but in protection, including the protection of contracts in the form of dispute settlement. Even more interestingly, he argues that rather than being a monopoly, organized crime competes with the state to provide this service.[12]

This recent turn in the literature is intriguing on several levels. First, it is consistent with an extensive body of literature emphasizing the entrepreneurial nature of organized crime, and thus the general applicability of economic principles to firms engaged in illicit as well as legitimate activities.[13] Second, it implicitly suggests that the state's institutional structure supplies incentives for illicit firms just as it does for legitimate enterprises; thus, firm adaptation is the central problem of economic organization in illegal as well as legal markets. Finally, the stylized histories of regions as diverse as post-feudal Sicily and post-Soviet Russia, which Gambetta and others rely upon in developing their arguments, contain interesting parallels with Japanese history, suggesting that societies currently experiencing significant organized crime problems began from a common starting point.

Institutional analysis—properly informed by empirical research—is a way to unite the insights provided by existing approaches to organized crime. As Gambetta posits with his theory of substitutes for state enforcement, and implicit in the economic ideas of firm organization, organized criminal firms often arise shortly after the historical establishment of formal property rights regimes.[14] Post-feudal Japan, for instance, like post-feudal Italy and post-Soviet Russia, is characterized by dramatic increases in formal property rights. Similar to these other countries, post-feudal Japan also is characterized by a weakness of complementary enforcement mechanisms. The Japanese transition out of feudalism left a void for private transaction-makers and rights-enforcers that was filled by a hodgepodge of groups, which in Japan included an amalgam of disenfranchised samurai, hoodlums, and poor peasants. This mismatch between property rights and enforcement mechanisms leads to organized crime—the dark side of private ordering. In order to develop and provide empirical support for this emergent view of organized crime, we thus focus on the institutional environment that provides fertile ground for illicit entrepreneurialism.

Although there is nothing inherently "illicit" about private ordering, there are several reasons to be concerned about the particular brand of entrepreneurialism discussed in this chapter. First, the "legitimate" activity of organized criminal firms is often used to launder income from illegal activities and to hide it from tax officials. Second, the activities of organized criminal firms are often accompanied by the threat or use of violence. Third, as a growing body of theoretical literature suggests, private and segmented enforcement of property rights can lead to the entrenchment of small-scale inefficient monopolies, high transaction costs, and a "tragedy of coercion" in which savings from the provision of collective services are dissipated in contests both among firms and between firms and the state.[15] Finally, regardless of efficiency concerns, private ordering by organized criminal firms is qualitatively different from conventional private ordering by contract or arbitration. While both avoid resort to governmental institutions, only the latter operates within constraints that are *inherently* legal, because they are legitimized by the same political theory that supports the governing order generally. Similarly, while the activities of both organized criminal groups and the state are backed by coercive force, only the violence of the legal system is rooted in a deeper conception of public order. The means and ends of organized criminal firms, by contrast, are determined solely in the private interest of the members themselves. Pervasive organized criminal involvement in private ordering, thus, not only increases the level of violence in society, it is also antithetical to the rule of law.

II. RIGHTS ENFORCEMENT AND ORGANIZED CRIME IN JAPAN

We have suggested a close linkage between flaws in a state's institutional framework for property rights enforcement and the emergence of entrepreneurs who capitalize on opportunities for "illegitimate" private ordering. In this section, we begin to explore this hypothesis by turning to Japan. As noted in the Introduction, Japan exhibits an institutional environment rife with incentives for the emergence and prosperity of such entrepreneurs. It also has a network of organized criminal firms whose activities closely track the opportunities provided by this institutional environment. Here, we informally examine the linkage between the two phenomena.

A. Rights Enforcement

Japan has experienced two property rights booms in the past one hundred years. As with the transition economies of today, both periods of property rights transformation in Japan are characterized by a significant expansion in the types of property rights recognized by the state, and major increases both in the number of people owning assets and in the number of economic transactions.

The first Japanese property rights boom occurred in the Meiji Period (1868–1911), when the country made a rapid transition from an agrarian, feudal society to a modern, industrialized economy. Legal reform, which included the transplantation of European codes and the enactment of a written constitution, was seen as one key to the modernization effort. Formally, at least, legal reform limited state intervention in private affairs and brought Japanese citizens a panoply of new property rights and protections under the law. A new land tax system eliminated multiple and community forms of land ownership, thereby establishing a more modern property rights regime. The expansion of property rights led to a significant increase in enforcement-related transactions. For example, a new tax system spawned large increases in debt and mortgage foreclosures.[16]

The second boom took place during the Allied Occupation following the Second World War. Occupation reformers, like the Meiji oligarchs before them, sought to re-engineer the Japanese political and socio-economic order through a massive transformation of the institutional framework. Occupation reformers designed a new constitution containing a more extensive list of recognized economic rights and more protections against governmental interference in private affairs. They fundamentally revised the system of agrarian land tenure to transfer ownership from absentee landowners to operators, and regulated the relationship between landowners and tenants.[17] Occupation officials forcibly disbanded the family-owned *zaibatsu* conglomerates that had dominated the economy in the early twentieth century and distributed their shares more broadly to the public. As we saw in Chapter 2, they revised the corporate code in a further effort to promote "corporate democracy" by strengthening the rights of minority shareholders. To protect and enforce these new rights, they reorganized the legal profession, granted it a greater degree of independence from government oversight, and instilled its members with a mission to safeguard individual liberties.

The expansion of property rights accompanying these two phases of wholesale institutional transformation, however, was not matched by the development of complementary enforcement mechanisms. This gap did not prove to be wholly problematic, of course, as Japan's subsequent economic success attests. Unlike the experience of Russia to date, the Japanese business community, with support from the state, developed a highly workable set of rules to govern economic exchange that held up without heavy reliance on formal enforcement mechanisms. Indeed, scholars of Japanese law seeking to explain Japan's prosperity and stability often focus on the pervasive and beneficial aspects of private ordering in Japan. John Haley, for example, has argued that the weakness of formal enforcement mechanisms in the hands of the economic regulators has forced the government to bargain with the private sector, allowing market solutions to prevail over bureaucratic fiat.[18]

As in modern transition economies, however, private ordering to overcome property rights defects in Japan can be problematic. In this section, we analyze several areas of rights enforcement in Japan that provide fertile ground for activity by organized criminal firms. We defer until Section II.B discussion of the ways in which organized criminal firms actually exploit these opportunities. One caveat: Our aim is not to pass normative judgment on Japanese institutions. All countries suffer to some extent from inefficiencies in formal structures. Indeed, this commonality is the basis for the relevance of Japan's experience with organized crime for other countries. To the extent that Japan is unusual, it is so only in the *degree* to which state mechanisms permit or encourage resort to private alternatives. Moreover, as explained below, in many areas bright-side private ordering has provided unusually effective partial substitutes for the Japanese state.

1. Bankruptcy Financially troubled corporations in Japan face a plethora of legal options. Firms seeking to liquidate can choose between bankruptcy and special liquidation. Firms seeking to reorganize historically could choose from no less than four separate procedures: Corporate reorganization, corporate arrangement, composition, and compulsory composition. Civil rehabilitation, introduced in 2001, replaced the composition option. The multiplicity of legal regimes is the result of a process of continuous borrowing from other countries, without any attempt to eliminate or streamline existing procedures.[19]

While the menu of formal options is laudably plentiful, truly workable procedures are virtually nonexistent. Neither liquidation procedure, for example, is as broad as Chapter 7 of the U.S. Bankruptcy Code in its inclusion of secured claims (particularly significant since virtually all lending in Japan is done on a secured basis), because secured creditors may exercise their rights outside of the liquidation process. Moreover, special liquidation procedures differ little from private settlements, since court supervision is minimal.[20] The reorganization procedures were similarly unappealing at least until the enactment of the civil rehabilitation regime. For example, corporate reorganization, which is based on the old Chapter 10 of the U.S. Bankruptcy Act, is a "rigid proceeding for large publicly held stock corporations and almost always entails a change of management."[21] Corporate arrangement is often unworkable when there are recalcitrant secured creditors because the stay of secured claims in such proceedings is discretionary.[22] Composition, the most frequently used procedure until its 2001 replacement by civil rehabilitation, had *no* provisions to stay the enforcement of secured claims. Compulsory compositions are reorganization plans proposed *after* a bankruptcy adjudication, and are exceedingly rare due to the difficulty of securing agreement following the conclusion of the bankruptcy process. As a result, until very recently, relatively few reorganizations of troubled firms in Japan took place within the legal system.

In lieu of formal insolvency, two relatively efficient private systems have historically dealt with financially troubled firms. The first is the "main bank" system, in which a bank serves as the largest lender and a principal shareholder of a corporate client. As a central repository of information on the borrower, the main bank has traditionally played an important role in rendering assistance in case of managerial crisis or financial failure. Until recently, there was a strong presumption on the part of the main bank, the troubled firm, other creditors, and even government regulators that the main bank would intervene to initiate an informal restructuring process. Often, such intervention would entail extending financial assistance, issuing guarantees to other creditors, and even absorbing a share of the losses exceeding the bank's loan share.[23] While this institution typically functioned only with respect to the largest borrowers, it redirected some of the most complex bankruptcies—those involving major creditor coordination problems—away from the legal system. In similar fashion, the traditional operation of the main bank system provided a substitute for the information agents—accountants and credit rating agencies—who specialize in corporate monitoring and disclosure for the benefit of corporate claimants seeking to protect their rights in more capital market-driven financial systems.

The second mechanism that siphons cases away from the legal system is a private sanction operated by local bank clearinghouses. Under a well-developed informal system, if a firm dishonors two promissory notes within a six-month period, member banks of the local clearinghouse suspend all current account transactions and loans with the firm for a two-year period. This "suspension of bank transaction" procedure, which constitutes a virtual death penalty for firms that experience it, triggers the vast majority of all business failures in Japan. As a result, firms go to great lengths to avoid dishonoring the second note, often by arranging for a main bank to sponsor their obligations. As shown below, however, these are not the only informal mechanisms used to resolve financial distress in Japan.

2. Debt collection   Japan's Attorneys' Law indirectly grants a monopoly on debt collection to licensed attorneys.[24] Indeed, debt collection ranks as a bread-and-butter role of the Japanese bar. The monopoly may be lucrative for Japanese attorneys, but it creates problems in the economy. For example, the nonperforming loan crisis afflicting Japanese banks throughout the past decade has been exacerbated by the lack of professionals capable of assisting in the loan foreclosure and collection process. To address this problem, a narrow exception to the Attorneys' Law was created in 1998, allowing the formation of "servicer" companies to engage in debt collection. Yet, even here the law did not completely infringe on lawyers' turf; the law requires that at least one member of the board of directors of a servicer company be a licensed attorney.[25] Although lawyers have a monopoly within the legal system, as the next section explores, they have dark-side competition.

3. Landlord–tenant issues   Japanese law is exceedingly protective of tenants' rights. As described by Mark Ramseyer and Minoru Nakazato, "[b]y judicial interpretation, almost all leases in Japan—no matter how many recitals to the contrary—give the tenant an interest close to a life estate."[26] As a result, redeveloping property can be a nightmare. To be sure, land owners can and do contract around some of the resulting obstacles by paying large sums to encourage the departure of unwanted tenants, charging large, nonrefundable fees to initiate a lease, or by simply building properties that encourage short-term tenancies.

As shown in the next section, however, the menu of options for developers seeking to dislodge uncooperative tenants is not limited to these relatively benign tactics.

4. Shareholders' rights The corporate governance framework that we outlined in Chapter 2 deserves highlighting here. As we discussed, the corporate form is characterized by a fundamental issue: Shareholders, who bear the economic risks of their investment, must delegate authority for actually running the firm to a class of professional managers, who typically lack a sufficient economic stake in the company to fully internalize the costs of their decisions. Japanese corporate law attempts to address this problem legally through the shareholder derivative suit. But as we also saw in Chapter 2, until recently it was virtually moribund. Derivative suits were rare in Japan for the same reason that the bankruptcy regime was not heavily utilized: Enforcement problems raised the cost of the procedure relative to private alternatives.

Once again, private ordering works to mitigate the frictions apparent in the formal system by providing effective substitutes for the legal regime. The concentration of large blocks of stock in the hands of banks and other institutional investors, and the organization of many firms into *keiretsu* corporate groups, provides mechanisms of voice for many Japanese shareholders that are far less costly and more effective than shareholder derivative litigation. But that bright-side private ordering does not fully satisfy the demand for corporate monitoring services. As shown below, illicit entrepreneurs have emerged to exploit the costly formal structures and lack of state-sanctioned rights-enforcement agents.

5. Rights-enforcement agents and dispute intermediaries Lawyers, like accountants, credit-rating agencies, and the press are crucial for rights enforcement. Ronald Gilson has shown, for example, that business lawyers in the United States create value by serving as "transaction cost engineers": Lawyers are the principal architects of a sophisticated transactional structure that constrains uncertainty-based opportunism and alleviates information problems in economic exchange, helping to bridge gaps between buyers and sellers of assets for a broad range of market transactions.[27] Similarly, lawyers perform a key function as reputational intermediaries in settling disputes.[28] Accountants, credit-rating agencies, and investment bankers perform roughly comparable roles by producing, evaluating, and certifying data in their own respective specialties.

Japan has only a fraction of the licensed attorneys found in the United States. The dearth of Japanese attorneys is a direct result of the national bar exam, which, as we discuss in more depth in Chapter 8, is graded on a curve that permits only about 2 percent of the roughly 50,000 annual takers to pass. Thus, Japan, with half the population of the United States, has approximately 20,000 licensed attorneys in comparison to their roughly 900,000 American counterparts. While this simple numerical comparison is misleading for a variety of reasons, the small number of attorneys in Japan is significant in those areas such as debt collection and courtroom advocacy where Japanese law grants a monopoly to licensed attorneys.

Perhaps less well known is the scarcity of other sophisticated agents capable of assisting in the rights-enforcement process. The Japanese accounting profession, for example, was rocked by a spate of scandals and improprieties that exposed serious flaws in its disclosure standards and practices. Client relationships often cloud the accuracy of disclosure. Moreover, the independence of the profession has been compromised by its relationship to financial regulators. Similarly, for regulatory reasons, Japan has few independent domestic credit-rating agencies, none of which enjoys a long history of operations.[29] Even bailiffs, the public servants in charge of enforcing civil judgments, have been historically scarce: Japan has only 521 such officers, while England, with a population smaller than Japan's, has five times that number.[30]

Thus, most of the institutional inefficiencies in Japan outlined above are exacerbated by a shortage of attorneys and other professionals qualified to function as rights-enforcement or information agents and reputational intermediaries on behalf of property rights holders. Simply put, Japan has relatively few transaction cost engineers sanctioned by the state. Though the scarcity is not intrinsically problematic, we hypothesize that the lack of access to sophisticated professional assistance in Japan at least partially explains the frequency of resort to extra-legal mechanisms of enforcement in that country.

6. Financial repression and entrepreneurial finance   The state affects economic activity not only by licensing professionals and defining and enforcing property rights, but also by supplying incentives for private actors through regulatory design. Perhaps no area of Japanese economic activity illustrates this principle better than finance, three aspects of which are most pertinent for our purposes. First, for reasons that have been explored exhaustively in the corporate governance literature, the Japanese financial system is bank oriented, with the stock market historically serving a less important role in corporate finance, due at least in part to regulatory constraints. Banks traditionally serviced large firms, which were seen as the engines of economic growth in the post-Second World War period. Second, the Bank of Japan's historical policy of low interest rates and credit rationing has resulted in excess demand for business loans, at least in comparison to the United States.[31] Accordingly, many businesses that need credit do not receive it, or do not receive it on competitive terms. Finally, the regulatory environment has historically encouraged the use of collateral in corporate finance.[32] A crucial aspect of a bank's credit decision is thus its assessment of the value of collateral offered by a potential borrower. Firms with marketable assets (or *keiretsu* affiliations) get loans; entrepreneurs with good ideas but few tangible assets get turned away. While access to bank funds for start-up firms in the United States is not dramatically different, the problems for Japanese entrepreneurs are compounded by a lack of viable alternatives to bank finance. Heavy regulation of IPOs, restrictions on the issuance of stock options, and antitrust barriers to the formation of desirable business structures have stunted the development of entrepreneurial finance in Japan, as we discussed in

Chapter 3. Many frustrated entrepreneurs therefore turn either to government-affiliated banks, or, as explored below, to less savory sources of funding.

B. Japanese Organized Crime

It is useful to examine some of the salient features of Japanese organized criminal firms to facilitate comparison with organized crime in other systems, as well as to begin testing the theories presented in the previous section. Some observers have found "striking similarities between [Japanese] gangs and La Cosa Nostra groups in the United States."[33] Although some of the similarity can be observed in sociological terms—"[b]oth instill a deep sense of obligation, empathy, devotion, and loyalty toward other group members"[34]—the underlying causes of the similarities appear to be largely historical and economic. The basic traits of Japanese organized criminal firms—membership, trademarks, structure, activities, police relations, and enforcement—differ little from the characteristics of firms in other systems. Notwithstanding these core similarities, however, to a remarkable degree Japanese organized crime is a visible, highly structured element of society, carefully attuned to the environment in which it operates.

1. Membership and income   Most new criminal firm recruits are poorly educated, single males around age 20. Nearly half have lost one or both parents, and nearly one-third come from the ranks of adolescent motorcycle gangs.[35] In his study of these gangs, anthropologist Ikuya Sato reports that firms recruit new members by "[t]hreats and flattery," inviting prospective members to "visit our office."[36] He also notes that, at least among motorcycle gang members, joining an organized criminal firm is something one does for economic reasons, and is not regarded as something done for a thrill.

Firm membership has at least one easily identifiable privilege: Income. Although skepticism is warranted in evaluating any estimate of income from organized criminal activities, an often-cited figure is that organized crime in Japan is a ¥7 trillion ($70 billion) industry.[37] This equates to gross revenues of approximately $750,000 per member. We are not aware of any scientific basis for this figure, but it is widely cited and loosely correlates to data on specific crimes as well as legitimate activity, and it is useful in drawing general comparisons.[38] A 1993 survey of 1,440 organized criminal firm made-member arrested suspects (959 responding!) shows that the income distribution is skewed to the top. Over 40 percent of the respondents reported annual income of $37,500–60,000. About 23 percent of the respondents reported less; 37 percent reported more, including 5.9 percent reporting income in excess of $120,000.[39] The same survey found part of the reason for the income disparity: A progressive tribute system, much like that found in other tournament systems, through which members pay increasingly larger taxes to higher-ranked personnel.[40]

The employment packages offered by organized criminal firms in Japan have lured large numbers of recruits. In 1963, membership of organized criminal firms stood at a peak of 184,091. By 1997, the number had fallen to 80,100, still a very large number. For the period 1957–97, the historical annual average is more than one firm member for every 1,000 of population. In the United States, a 1986 study estimated 50,229 members and associates of La Cosa Nostra (though not by any means the only organized crime organization in the United States, arguably the closest analog to Japanese organized criminal firms in scope and function), while FBI figures place that number at only 18,700.[41] Even taking the higher figure, members of La Cosa Nostra account for only about one of every 5,000 persons.

Just as organized criminal firms hire members and affiliates in good times, so do they fire them in bad times. If a member is discharged from the firm, postcards are sent to other firms announcing the member's departure. Only through formal reinstatement may the member rejoin the firm. Until then, he is banned from joining another firm, is "warned against roaming the streets aimlessly, and must refrain from the use of mannerisms and styles of the gangster"[42]—a sensible policy given firms' profitability. Members also quit. Although statistics on exactly how many and how often are unavailable, police figures show that in 2001, 1,474 members quit when their firms folded. If conditions are bad enough, organized crime firms, like more conventional firms, merge, reorganize, or dissolve.

2. Trademarks and visibility Identifying members of Japanese organized criminal firms is not difficult. Members and firms are well versed in the display of what one commentator calls "trademarks."[43] They are easily identified on the streets of Tokyo by their dark glasses, flashy suits, and punch-perm hair. Whenever possible, they scorn Toyotas and Hondas for Mercedes-Benzes and Lincoln Continentals. As if this were not enough, members are often marked by missing fingers (the result of rituals and punishment) and colorful, often full-body, tattoos.

In the United States, though members may be recognizable, most firms are not. As Joseph Castellano (the son of reputed mob boss Paul Castellano) put it, "What is a Gambino crime family? . . . Does this Gambino crime family have an office? Does the office have a plaque on the door that says, 'Gambino crime family'?"[44] In Japan, the answers would be, in reverse order, "yes," "yes," and "read our rules and creed." Firms have offices that are indeed adorned with gang emblems and signs. Like employees of traditional firms, members proudly distribute business cards displaying the firm logo. Larger firms have their own banners, publications, songs, and other promotional goods, including New Year's greeting cards and lapel pins. As one academic observer vividly described a local firm's offices:

Then there are the yakuza haunts themselves, the most prominent being that of Kanamachi Ikka . . ., located in a swanky, three-story brick and stucco structure . . .. It is hard to miss. The organization's name is prominently lettered in silver, alongside its gold coat of arms, over the entranceway. This publicity is not at all atypical . . .. The middle floor has a nondescript appearance, at least from the outside; but the top floor is done in the penthouse style with a bubble roof. The windows on the first two floors are glazed and barred.[45]

If the firm emblem, distinctive employees, and golden gates do not reveal identity, actions often will. Like John Gotti's famous Brooklyn fireworks displays, Japanese criminal firms are often engaged in public relations gestures to foster goodwill in the community. When the deadly 1995 earthquake struck Kobe, it was a branch of the Yamaguchi-gumi crime firm, not the government, that was first to bring relief to devastated neighborhoods. Within hours of the quake, the firm reportedly was handing out 8,000 meals a day from the parking lot next to its headquarters, and was distributing uncontaminated mineral water from its private well.[46] These activities, along with the easily recognized trademarks, help to identify firms and firm members both as providers of services and as issuers of credible threats.

3. Structure   Firm organization in Japan, as elsewhere, is complex and hierarchical. Typical is the Yamaguchi-gumi, with approximately 15,000 members, the largest of the Japanese firms. The Yamaguchi-gumi has three groups and five hierarchical levels, all overseen by the boss (*oyabun*). The president presides over underbosses, who preside over lieutenants, member–soldiers, and staff organizations.

4. Activities   Organized criminal firms in Japan focus much of their attention on the traditional underworld trades of gambling, pornography, prostitution, and drugs. Legitimate businesses run by firm members have an underworld aroma as well; one survey finds that the top businesses in which made-members engage are street stalls (managed by 5,552 surveyed members), lending agencies (3,239), bars (3,129), strip clubs and spas (2,692), restaurants (2,596), and construction firms (2,171).[47] But they do more. They also head informal creditors' committees, settle civil disputes, and finance everything from golf courses to resort hotels. In Japan, as in other systems, "boundaries between legitimate and illegitimate activities begin to blur."[48] Police estimate that roughly half of organized criminal firm income comes from such gray-area activity.[49]

Crucially, many of the activities of Japanese organized criminal firms track the institutional problems we identified in Section II.A. The influence of organized crime is readily apparent in bankruptcy and debt collection, property development, dispute settlement, shareholders' rights, and finance. Thus, in many ways, organized criminal firms are the missing transaction cost engineers in the Japanese system. This makes the line between legitimate and illegitimate conduct all the more opaque. As discussed below, so pervasive is the influence of organized crime in these gray areas that special terms have been coined in Japanese to describe the underworld entrepreneurs who exploit each of these opportunities.

Organized criminal firms in Japan, for example, play a pervasive role in the resolution of financial distress. Beginning in 1953, a class of professionals called *seiriya* ("fixers") emerged to assist in the reorganization and liquidation processes. These professionals operate outside the legal system and are closely tied to organized crime. The Japanese Federation of Bar Associations in 1995 estimated that 100 *seiriya*, not including assistants and staff, offered general bankruptcy services.[50] Fixers can profit from distressed firms in various ways. They might offer protection services to the debtor or insert themselves into a leadership role on the creditors' committee by demonstrating expertise in corporate reorganizations. Another favored tactic is to obstruct the foreclosure and auction process by leasing space in a building serving as collateral. Because Japanese law heavily favors tenants, this simple act can virtually paralyze foreclosures. For creditors, fixers might extract concessions from debtors, increase the size of the debtor's estate by engaging in debt collection activities, or provide prompt disposition of assets held as collateral. The only English-language study of the fixers to date concludes that these professionals, with their intimate knowledge of the reorganization and liquidation processes, serve as substitutes for bankruptcy lawyers and for the formal bankruptcy regime in general.[51]

These fixers are often preceded or accompanied by *toritateya*, or debt collectors. Debt collectors raise the penalties for nonpayment through the typical tactics of such professionals throughout the world, but they are also known to publicly denounce debtors in their residential neighborhoods from high-decibel sound trucks. Fearful of threats and intimidation, and unwilling to face complicated bankruptcy laws, some debtors turn for help to the *toritateya*'s white knight counterpart—the *yonigeya*. *Yonigeya* literally means "one who helps another flee in the night." Such operators—sometimes from organized criminal firms, sometimes not—assist debtors in relocating and establishing new identities.

Closely related to fixers and debt collectors in some of their activities are the *jiageya* ("land fixers"). Real estate developers retain these specialists to convince reluctant landowners or tenants to part with their property interests. Recall that Japanese law makes it virtually impossible to evict tenants, creating major holdout problems. As one leading crime figure puts it (no doubt with some hyperbole), "without [*jiageya*], cities wouldn't be able to develop."[52] Sometimes the *jiageya*'s tactics are subtle: A phone call, for example, suggesting that a holdout would be well advised to move, can be a powerful incentive to vacate the premises. Occasionally they are creative: For example, they may organize a loud motorcycle conference in front of the coveted property. At other times, they are ruthless: Smashing windows, dumping garbage, and beating up the truly recalcitrant. For these services, anecdotal evidence indicates that they charge nearly 10 percent of the parcel's sales price.[53]

Like fixers and land specialists, *jiageya* have developed expertise on both sides of a transaction. Some operate as *apaatoya* ("apartment fixers"), taking the tenant's side in landlord–tenant disputes. As with the *seiriya* fixers, years of exploiting the legal system to their own advantage have resulted in levels of expertise among the *jiageya* that surpass that of many lawyers.

While the relative scarcity of lawyers in Japan has been much celebrated in the United States, the situation just described suggests that low lawyer populations can create serious problems. In fact, parties to civil disputes of all types in Japan sometimes turn to organized crime-linked *jidanya* ("settlement specialists") to help resolve their problems. Traffic accident victims, for example, may hire a gang member to convince the other driver to provide compensation. Once again, these professionals epitomize entrepreneurialism at the boundary between the legitimate and the illicit. Accounts of *jidanya* by Japanese commentators routinely allude both to the beneficial aspects of their settlement services in the absence of other trained professionals, and to the illegal and even violent nature of their work.[54] Not surprisingly, some members of organized criminal firms view themselves as "lawyers for the dark side of society" [*urashakai no bengoshi*].[55]

The costs of using *jidanya* appear to compare favorably with those of the formal legal system. Although lawyers' fees vary, most are reasonably close to the fee schedule published by the Japanese Federation of Bar Associations that we reprinted in Chapter 2.[56] Using this official fee schedule as a base, for a traffic accident in which a plaintiff requests ¥20 million ($200,000) in damages and receives 15 million, a plaintiff would pay the attorney a retainer of slightly over ¥1 million and a "success fee" of about 1.68 million, for a total fee of about ¥2.75 million ($27,500). By comparison, a *jidanya*'s usual fee is said to be 15 percent of the award received—in this case ¥3 million ($30,000)—minus actual medical damages.[57] Although in this case a *jidanya* might cost as much as $2,500 more than a lawyer, a plaintiff who hires a *jidanya* avoids paying a lawyer's upfront nonrefundable retainer and initial consultation fee, eliminates court costs, and in most cases receives damages much more quickly than formal procedures would allow. These figures are estimates at best; if the estimates approximate actual costs, however, it is not difficult to imagine situations in which a plaintiff would turn rationally to such specialists, particularly in rural areas where licensed attorneys are scarce.

While *jidanya* usually target individuals and small businesses, even large, prestigious Japanese companies sometimes deal with criminal firms. As we saw in the previous chapter, corporate extortion by *sokaiya* gangster–racketeers historically has been widespread in Japan, where institutions foster low levels of corporate disclosure. Currently some 430 *sokaiya* are working in Japan, down from 6,000 in the early 1980s before increased enforcement and disclosure policies took effect. Whether the *sokaiya* actually monitor management on behalf of shareholders is, of course, open to question. The point is that a problematic institutional environment for the exercise of shareholders' rights in Japan gives rise to this distinctive class of underworld professional.

Finally, Japan's heavily regulated financial markets traditionally left a large unsatisfied demand for capital. As elsewhere, some frustrated entrepreneurs and consumers turn to lenders offering funds at usurious rates. In Japan, the unsatisfied demand for funds has long been partially satisfied by *sarakin* loan sharks (legitimate *sarakin*, short for "salaryman finance," also exist). More recently, organized crime affiliates have moved into mainstream areas of finance.

Table 6.1. *Institutional gaps and illicit private ordering entrepreneurs*

Service area	Organized crime service provider	English translation
Bankruptcy	*Seiriya*	Fixer
Debt collection	*Toritateya/Yonigeya*	Debt collector/One who helps another flee in the night
Landlord–tenant issues	*Jiageya/Apaatoya*	Land fixer/Apartment fixer
Dispute settlement	*Jidanya*	Settlement specialist
Shareholders' rights	*Sōkaiya*	General meeting operator
Financial services	*Sarakin*	Loan shark

Table 6.1 summarizes the institutional problems and corresponding organized crime entrepreneurs in Japan.

Perhaps a 1993 government survey best sums up the relationship between the legal regime and the activities of organized crime in Japan: It found that 12 percent of the Japanese public believes that Japanese organized criminals are a necessary evil. Respondents based their acceptance of organized crime in large part on the slowness of the legal system in resolving civil conflicts and the efficiency of the mob.[58]

5. Enforcement and the Anti-Organized Crime Act   Organized criminal firms in Japan are aided in these activities by a cozy relationship with police. But the police-organized crime relationship in Japan is not corruption strictly defined-illegal payments to a public agent to obtain benefits. Stories of corrupt Japanese police officers—and indeed even bare allegations of Japanese police corruption—are relatively rare. Instead, the relationship is better described as symbiotic. Again Ramseyer and Nakazato are instructive:

> Ironically, the lower rates of violent crime in Japan may also result from the way the police have generally failed to imprison the leaders of the organized crime syndicates . . .. For in failing to do so, they have brought an organizational stability to the underworld. That stability, in turn, has kept turf battles far more modest than among the urban street gangs in the United States.[59]

The symbiosis sometimes extends beyond the police into political relations, a realm in which it does give rise to corruption. In the construction industry, Japan appears to be what Brian Woodall aptly terms a "clientelist state" that encourages collusion among politicians, bureaucrats, and influential actors in the private sector—including members of organized criminal firms.[60] Several major scandals, including one in which the then-presiding vice-president of the ruling Liberal Democratic Party issued special favors to a package delivery company in exchange for access to organized criminal firms, exemplify this relationship.

Such scandals led the National Police Agency (NPA) in 1991 to sponsor the Anti-Organized Crime Act, a measure designed to get tough on organized criminal firms.[61] Pursuant to the Act, prefectural public safety commissions, in consultation with the National Public Safety Commission that is effectively controlled by the police, have the power to name organized criminal groups as "designated firms." Members of "designated firms" are prohibited from using the name or insignia of the firm while conducting fourteen types of extortionist acts such as demanding donations, subcontracts, payment for product liability complaints, or loss compensation for securities transactions, each of which previously fell into a liminal region between legality and criminal extortion. In 2001, firms that were so designated numbered twenty-four, a figure that rarely changes. If a member of a designated firm conducts such an act, the prefectural public safety commission or chief of police can issue an injunction, the violation of which can result in one year's imprisonment or a fine of up to ¥1 million ($10,000). An average of 1,597 injunctions were issued in the period 1992–2001, including 2,238 in 2001.

III. EMPIRICAL ANALYSIS

This section analyzes empirical data from Japan to examine the relationship between the formal institutions for enforcing rights discussed in Section II and the success of organized criminal firms. Ideally, we would like to examine data on such factors as annual income of firms and members, and the number of civil mediations, private bankruptcy foreclosures, and other activities that are conducted by members. Only with such data could we test with complete confidence the accuracy of our hypothesis that organized crime is an entrepreneurial response to institutional shortcomings. Unfortunately, such data are unavailable. Nonetheless, Japan provides a wealth of unexamined data dwarfing that available for other countries with prominent organized crime networks, including the United States, permitting extensive investigation into the origins and role of organized crime in that country.

We divide organized crime activity into two categories for clear analysis. First, we analyze unarguably criminal activity. We then turn to regression analysis to analyze gray zone activities that are not necessarily criminal, but that compete with state-provided enforcement services and other public goods. We estimate a model that is consistent with our hypothesis about the origin and role of organized criminal firms in the civil realm.

A. Crime Data

Whatever else they may do, members of Japanese organized criminal firms commit crimes. Table 6.2 sets forth the number of persons arrested annually in Japan for various violations, with a breakdown of firm members to non-firm members. Firm members constitute 9 percent of all arrested persons—a strikingly high number considering that members account for only 0.06 percent of the total population.

An examination of individual crimes yields equally interesting results. If arrest rates properly reflect incidence of crime, members are disproportionately involved

Table 6.2. *Percentage of arrested persons affiliated with organized criminal firms, 2001*

Crime	Number of persons arrested	Number of members of organized criminal firms arrested	Ratio of organized crime members arrested to total number of persons arrested
General crimes as defined by Penal Code:			
Murder	1,416	305	0.22
Robbery	3,797	596	0.16
Rape	1,486	201	0.14
Violence	8,119	1,165	0.15
Bodily injury	29,359	5,021	0.17
Intimidation	1,458	591	0.41
Extortion	11,261	3,290	0.29
Larceny fraud	162,610	2,623	0.02
Gambling	1,905	1,164	0.61
Total (including others)	309,649	19,668	0.06
Other crimes:			
Stimulants	18,903	7,720	0.41
Narcotics	217	26	0.12
Prostitution	1,225	253	0.21
Weapons	3,055	711	0.23
Gambling on bicycle races	357	338	0.95
Gambing on horses	360	270	0.75

Source: Data from selected issues of Hanzai Hakusho [White Paper on Crime] (2001).

in prostitution, gambling, extortion, and intimidation,[62] and in illegal purchase and sales of stimulant drugs. By contrast, members are much less likely than non-members to be arrested for larceny or other forms of theft, which are normally against the internal rules of organized criminal firms, and perhaps do not require the same degree of expertise and organization as more "complex" crimes.

When a member is arrested, a prosecutor may either prosecute, not prosecute, or suspend prosecution. For selected offenses, we calculated the percentage of members prosecuted and compared it with the percentage of non-member suspects prosecuted. We found that members of firms are, on average, much more likely than non-members to be prosecuted for penal code offenses (71.6 percent compared to 61.7 percent) and certain specific offenses such as murder, various forms of gambling, and prostitution. They are, however, slightly less likely than non-members to be prosecuted for certain specific crimes such as violence, extortion, and sales and purchases of stimulant drugs. This evidence, combined with the arrest evidence, tends to show a lack of bias in favor of members for at least some crimes (perhaps due in part to high recidivism among firm members). Although police may turn a blind eye to certain types of offenses, members are more likely than non-members to be arrested and prosecuted for crime, implying, at least, that criminal firm success cannot be attributed solely to non-enforcement of criminal laws.

B. Regression Analysis

The data presented above confirm that the business of organized criminal firms is—in part at least—crime. Our claim, however, is that there is much more to understanding the origins and role of organized crime than this tautology. We turn now to regression analysis to explore our hypothesis.

1. Variables   In this section, we make use of existing data to construct variables for regression analysis. For each variable, we collected data covering the thirty-year period ending in 2001.[63] We make no claim that each variable is perfect; in each case, the variable represents the best available proxy for the concepts discussed earlier in this chapter.

The dependent variable, MEMBERS, is the annual total number of "made" and affiliated members of organized criminal firms, divided by the total annual population of Japanese males ages 20–49. We estimated males in this age group to comprise the approximate relevant supply of MEMBERS, and formulated the variable in this way to account for population variation.[64] Although membership is a less satisfying proxy for success than more direct measures like income, the focus on membership rates is particularly appropriate given our interest in why organized crime emerges and flourishes. In any event, we find it highly unlikely that membership in any organization is impervious to exogenous factors affecting its overall success. Figure 6.1 shows the data graphically for MEMBERS.

The validity of our results depends, of course, on the accuracy of the MEMBERS data. These data are calculated by the NPA, an organization of the central government directed by a "highly educated administrative elite."[65] Each year, the NPA collects data from the police forces of each of the forty-seven

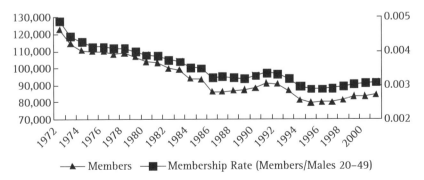

Figure 6.1. *Members of organized crime firms and membership rates, 1972–2001*

prefectures, the smallest administrative unit in Japan's police system. As discussed above, the existence and location of organized criminal firms are discernable to any moderately informed observer. The location of a given firm is thus readily known to the prefectural police, who usually assign several officers to monitor its operations. These officers, some of whom work out of offices, some on the street, and some out of Japan's famed *koban* ("police boxes"), report to their superiors in the prefectural offices on the number of members and affiliates of each firm. Police stationed in *koban* collect a variety of important data, including "persons owning weapons, rented houses and apartments that might serve as hideaways for fugitives, people with criminal records, and the organizational structure and membership of local gangs."[66] Rarely, if ever, is the membership of any firm a secret, and police duly record it with the other information. These membership data are reported by prefectural police to the NPA.[67]

Five factors further bolster our confidence in the accuracy of membership data. First, because the methodology for determining membership has not changed over time, any existing bias will be present for each year and will not affect trend data. Second, the police are arguably in an excellent position to make these calculations, given the close relationship between police and organized criminal firms in Japan. Third, the police data are generally consistent with other measures of membership and are considered to be accurate. Fourth, our on-site investigation of firm records in three separate police stations in Tokyo and neighboring Saitama prefecture, in which we found organized and extremely detailed data (including member photos, license plate numbers, family records (including girlfriends and children born out of wedlock), cellular phone numbers, and in some cases, preferred bars, restaurants, drinks, and barbers), leads us to believe that record-keeping procedures are accurate. Finally, the findings of an in-depth ethnographic survey of Japanese organized crime, the author of which met regularly with members of the firm under study, conform to the national statistics on organized crime, providing independent support for the validity of police data.[68]

Our decision to quantify success as MEMBERS is further supported by data on the number of organized criminal firms.[69] As Figure 6.2 shows, the number of organized criminal firms was highest in Japan's postwar growth period and during the bubble economy—further indication that the number of members is a good proxy for firm success.

The independent variables, described in Table 6.4 along with our results, are of three types: (*a*) major avenues of state-sanctioned rights enforcement (such as bankruptcy proceedings or civil litigation); (*b*) a central mechanism of organized crime enforcement (extortion); and (*c*) general indicators of macroeconomic health having a possible bearing on membership in illicit organizations.

1. Hypotheses   Recall our central claim: Organized crime is a substitute for state enforcement institutions. We accordingly advance the following hypotheses regarding our data. First, we predict that MEMBERS will be positively correlated to the number of profitable transactions such as extortion. Second and more

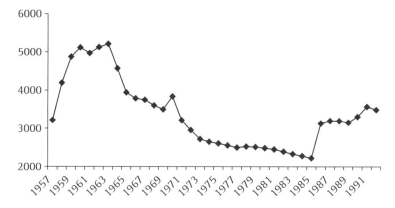

Figure 6.2. *Numbers of firms, 1957–92*

importantly, we postulate that the demand for organized criminal firm services, as evidenced by an increase in firm membership, is negatively correlated to the demand for such services from the state. Four such negative correlations are relatively intuitive: as persons turn to the state or to state-sanctioned intermediaries for services such as dispute settlement, bankruptcy, real estate foreclosures, and financing,[70] we expect MEMBERS to decline. We find no *a priori* reason to hypothesize the nature of the relationship of the four other variables (gross domestic product per capita, reported crimes, land prices, and the unemployment rate) included in our regression.

The institutional analysis of Section II gives us some confidence in our hypotheses. A breakdown of organized crime services by service area indicates at least anecdotally that long-term decreases in membership and number of firms (see Figures 6.1 and 6.2) may be the result of increases in institutional efficacy and in the number of state-sanctioned rights-enforcement agents. The relationship can be seen in the shareholders' rights service area, the province of *sokaiya*. As corporate disclosure institutions have improved, and derivative litigation rules have eased to encourage a rise in suits to approximately 300 in 2000 (up from about twenty *total* suits for the preceding forty years; see Chapter 2), *sokaiya* numbers, as we saw in Chapter 5, have fallen dramatically. By contrast, in the bankruptcy service area, which was subject to relatively little institutional change in the period covered by our analysis, the number of *seiriya* fixers varied little or perhaps even increased. Our regression analysis attempts to quantify these relationships more precisely.

2. Methodology We constructed a model to examine correlations between the variables selected. Because of the time-series nature of our data, we transformed our variables to mitigate common statistical problems. Although the transformations were necessary to specify the model properly, one consequence is that we place high demands on the MEMBERS variable. The data transformation requires correlation of the *rate* of change of the variables, while our claim relates to changes in the numeric values of the variables. Still, such methodology greatly reduces many of the problems of time-series data, and statistically significant results using our strict methodology represent a very robust test of our theory.

3. Results   The results of the multivariate regression analysis appear in Table 6.3. For each entry, we show the coefficients, then the absolute value of the *t*-statistics (conventional two-sided). Statistical significance is further indicated by the asterisks.

Table 6.3. *Correlates of MEMBERS of organized criminal firms*[a]

Variable (Δ logs)	Coefficient	*t*-stat	Predicted sign
BANKRUPT	−0.011	−0.067	−
CIVIL	−0.422	−2.001**	−
CRIME	0.468	2.330**	?
EXTORT	0.320	1.527	+
GDPCAP	0.179	0.828	?
LAND	0.113	0.477	?
LOANS	−0.569	−2.251**	−
PROPAUCT	0.685	2.284**	−
UNEMPLOY	−0.189	−0.966	?
Intercept	−0.006	−1.185	
Adjusted R^2	0.372		
Observations	30		

** Indicates significance at 95% level.

[a] Our model successfully mitigated the potential problems of heteroskedasticity, serial correlation, and multicollinearity. We also ran a model that included the year as a trend variable (DATE) to control for spurious correlation. The results differed only slightly. Because no analysis of any two independent variables yielded statistically significant correlations, we conclude that our methodology also was successful in mitigating multicollinearity. We also experimented with several more complex models, including 2SLS and OLS models using lagged variables, but again did not obtain significantly different results.

Note: The table is based on the standard regression model $Y_t = \alpha + \beta X_t + \epsilon_t$. To mitigate heteroskedasticity and serial correlation, we then take the first differences and log the variables, transforming using the equation $\log y_t - \log y_{t-1} = \log(y_t/y_{t-1})$. The dependent variable MEMBERS is the annual total number of "made" and affiliated members of organized crime firms, divided by the total annual population of Japanese males ages 20–49. The independent variables are as follows: BANKRUPT is the total annual yen amount of bankruptcies. CIVIL is the total number of new civil cases filed in district court. With this variable we attempt to capture a host of institutional constraints, including litigation filing fees, attorney availability, and attorneys' fees. CRIME is the number of crimes reported to the police. EXTORT is the total number of extortion cases reported to the police. GDPCAP is the GDP per capita. LAND is the average price of land in Japan's six largest cities: Tokyo, Yokohama, Nagoya, Osaka, Kyoto, and Kobe. LOANS is the value, in 100 millions of yen, of loans and discounts of major banking accounts outstanding at the end of each year. PROPAUCT is the number of suits brought in district court to force the auction of real estate posted as collateral. UNEMPLOY is the unemployment rate.

As predicted, the model indeed found negative correlations for the civil cases, loans, and bankruptcy variables, although the bankruptcy variable was insignificant. The statistically significant negative correlation between MEMBERS and the civil cases variable is strong support for the theory that organized criminal firms substitute for state-sponsored dispute mediation mechanisms. Similarly, the significant negative correlation between loans issued and MEMBERS indicates that firms' loan sharking business competes directly with loans issued by governmentally licensed and regulated banks. The data clearly suggest a trade-off between resort to state institutions and the success of organized criminal firms, as measured by membership.[71]

The property auction variable, which we predicted would be negatively correlated to MEMBERS, was in fact positively correlated. We interpret this unexpected result as an indication that auctions of property are different from ordinary civil suits. Unlike ordinary civil suits (which are significantly negatively correlated to MEMBERS), if a lender chooses to utilize state-provided services, an organized criminal firm can *still* profit by rigging auctions and purchasing foreclosed properties at discounts, or by otherwise disrupting the auction.[72] Simply put, the more property auctions, the more opportunity that exists for organized criminal firms to extort money from the participants. We also note that the property auction variable is not merely a proxy for economic downturn or increased bankruptcies, as the inclusion of the GDP per capita and bankruptcy variables in our regression holds such effects constant.

The crime variable, about which we were unable to form an *a priori* hypothesis, was significantly positive: More crime correlates with more members. The direction of correlation might be an artifact of a recent increase in crime. The number of reported crimes in 2001 was more than double the number of crimes twenty years earlier, represents a 50 percent increase over 1997, and the rates of increase reached double digits only in the last four years of the sample. When we ran the regressions with a model that ends in 1997 data, the crime variable was significantly *negative* (this discrepancy is the only substantial difference that arises in a comparison of the two models). While this negative relation might be indicative of reporting trends (victims may be less likely to report crime committed by organized criminal firms), given the relative stability of organized crime statistics, we are inclined to attribute the correlation to the symbiotic relationship between organized crime and the police in Japan.[73] The difference in sign that we see in the two models might be a result of changed enforcement strategies or a shift in firm resources and strategies.

The correlation of MEMBERS to our three supply-side variables, the unemployment rate, GDP per capita, and land prices, was statistically insignificant, indicating that firm membership is not influenced as much by the supply of personnel or macroeconomic conditions as by the demand-side factors discussed above.[74] Members do not appear to join organized criminal firms simply because there are no other "legitimate" employment options. Nor does firm membership increase solely as a result of macroeconomic growth.

Finally, to test whether our results might simply be a reflection of factors that affect all firms in the Japanese economy, we constructed a new model in which we regressed a new dependent variable, the annual number of employees of Japan's six largest trading houses, on the same independent variables. Trading houses, which have no equivalent in the United States, provide a rough legal counterpart to organized criminal firms in the sense that they are largely involved in the service industry and specialize as intermediaries between commercial parties. The total number of employees of these organizations— 40,000–50,000 for each year—is also directly comparable with MEMBERS. The new regression model had low explanatory power, and not one of the independent variables was statistically significant. While the comparison is not perfect, the results suggest that our primary model captures factors that are specific to the success of *organized criminal* firms, and not firms as a whole.

Regression analysis, of course, indicates correlations but cannot prove causation. It is, thus, possible (though the data suggest otherwise) that causation is reversed: Instead of crime, litigation, and lending affecting membership rates, it could be that membership rates are actually driving the rates of crime, litigation, and lending. While the first such causal link is plausible, we actually find it unlikely that organized criminal firm membership drives crime levels, because almost 90 percent of Japanese crime is larceny, a crime that members rarely commit, and because the inclusion of the extortion variable holds constant one major type of firm-dominated crime. We find the reverse causal relationship of membership on litigation and lending to be even more implausible, as modest changes in membership are unlikely to change overall litigation and bank lending patterns. Still, even assuming that our model reverses some of the actual causal linkages at work, the findings of negative *correlations*, nevertheless, support our hypothesis that state enforcement and enforcement by organized crime are substitutes.

C. Additional Regression Analysis of Law Enforcement Measures

The above analysis does not include one final element that may affect firm success: Enforcement of anti-firm measures by the police. We did not include this factor because for each of the variables serving as a proxy for law enforcement efforts, we did not have a complete time-series database, or the variable violated the assumptions of the multiple regression model. We separately analyze those variables here; Table 6.4 displays the results of the separate bivariate regressions.

1. Arrest rates Surprisingly, MEMBERS is positively and marginally significantly correlated to the total arrest rate (the total number of organized criminal firm arrestees divided by MEMBERS) and highly significantly correlated to the made member arrest rate (the total number of made member arrestees divided by the total number of made members). Several explanations are possible. The correlations might be the result of community crackdown (police arrest a greater

Table 6.4. *Bivariate linear regressions of MEMBERS on law enforcement variables*

Independent variable	r	t-stat	p-value
Total arrest rate (1972–2000)	0.345	1.907	0.067
Arrest rate of made members (1983–2000)	0.731	4.291	0.001
Anti-Organized Crime Act injunctions (1992–2001)	−0.614	2.056	0.079

percentage of members as organizations grow larger and more visible), a replacement phenomenon (perhaps more than one new member is needed to replace each jailed experienced member), or even a data-gathering quirk, as new members might replace members who are in prison, while prisoner–members remain on the firms' membership lists.

We also found a significantly positive correlation using a lagged MEMBERS variable to both the total arrest rate ($r = 0.573$, $t = 3.56$, $p = 0.001$) and the made member arrest rate ($r = 0.792$, $t = 5.183$, $p = 0.000$). We attribute these correlations to a form of iatrogenic effects: Arrests in one year lead to an increase in organized crime members in the subsequent year due to the signaling effect that arrests have on risk and status-seeking potential members.[75]

2. Anti-Organized Crime Act enforcement   Pursuant to the Anti-Organized Crime Act, police may issue injunctions to firms that are designated under that law. We have such data only for the ten-year period beginning with the Act's 1992 effective date. For that limited period, we found a negative and marginally significant correlation between such orders and membership in organized criminal firms. We also found a stronger negative correlation using a lagged MEMBERS variable ($r = -0.819$, $t = 3.778$, $p = 0.007$). We guardedly conclude from these data that enforcement of the Act has negatively affected the success of organized criminal firms.

IV. IMPLICATIONS

Our theory on the entrepreneurial origins of organized crime, supported by the empirical evidence from Japan, has two closely related implications. First, treating organized crime as *crime* may be a relatively ineffective approach to the problem. Second, state ordering is fundamentally important to private ordering; organized crime flourishes where property rights and enforcement institutions are misaligned.

A. Law Enforcement Efforts

Our data suggest that targeting members of organized criminal firms for traditional law enforcement efforts may be ineffective and possibly even counterproductive.

At least in Japan, the cohesion and appeal of gang life appears to be *enhanced*, rather than diminished, by criminal prosecution. The approach taken under the Japanese Anti-Organized Crime Act is to address organized crime in quasi-regulatory rather than traditional law enforcement terms. The Act, which authorizes the issuance of injunctions against specific entrepreneurial activities central to the success of Japanese organized criminal firms, appears promising on some levels and merits further study by other countries.

B. Reducing Organized Crime through Institutional Engineering

More important than the enforcement data is the conclusion drawn from our inquiry into the origins and role of organized crime. This chapter has provided theoretical and empirical support for the claim that private ordering by organized criminal firms is a substitute for state-provided and state-sanctioned enforcement mechanisms. As the Japanese experience illustrates, many private ordering schemes may be beneficial to social cohesion and economic growth. Private ordering in the face of misaligned state structures or inadequate numbers of rights-enforcement and information agents can, however, have a dark side where the state's traditional functions are privatized by groups that are not tethered to the legal norms and political consensus on which state authority is based. While possibly efficient on a transaction-by-transaction basis, dark-side private ordering is harmful because it helps advance undeniably criminal activities such as drugs and prostitution, while corroding the framework for legitimate rights enforcement. We believe one key to reducing organized crime, therefore, is institutional re-engineering to reduce incentives for the formation of rights-enforcement agents operating outside of state and social sanction. To understand this conclusion more concretely, it is instructive to analyze the Japanese situation in greater detail.

The dark side of private ordering emerges in Japan from three closely related factors. First, as shown in Section II, in several key areas of Japanese economic activity, the government, acting through the legislature and the courts, has failed to get the institutions "right," resulting in major transaction costs for private parties seeking to play by the state's rules. We have surveyed obstacles to the smooth enforcement of contracts, resolution of disputes, and financing of firms in Japan. Some of the obstacles, such as those found in the financial markets, are the result of conscious policy decisions. Others, such as the problematic formal bankruptcy regime, appear to be largely the result of happenstance. Whatever the cause, in a number of key areas of economic and social governance, playing by the rules of the game as set by the Japanese state is a costly endeavor.

Costly institutional environments may be overcome by Coasean bargaining. Efficient private ordering, of course, is often possible through the spontaneous interactions of community members. This phenomenon is well documented in the literature, and several important examples from Japan were presented above. Indeed, Japan's economic success and social stability are virtually inexplicable without reference to bright-side private ordering. Sometimes, however, costly institutional environments cannot be overcome without the intervention of transaction cost engineers.

Second, the next step in understanding the dark side of private ordering in Japan, therefore, is the recognition that enforcing private bargains as well as state rules often requires coordination, economies of scale or scope, or large investments in human capital and information. Where the state blocks or fails to encourage the development of rights-enforcement agents to navigate complex transactional environments, organized groups operating beyond state and social norms may emerge to satisfy the unmet demand for transaction cost engineering. Thus, in Japan, inefficiencies in the background rules of the game are exacerbated by the shortage of attorneys, accountants, investment bankers, credit-rating agencies, and other professional producers and analysts of information crucial to rights enforcement. (Our analysis of recent changes in the Japanese legal profession in chapter 8 provides grounds for optimism that this problem is being partially addressed).

In various complex areas of Japanese economic and social governance, organized criminal firms are the only enterprises with the human and monetary capital required to provide alternatives to inefficient state mechanisms. Legitimate firms do not emerge to fill the institutional gaps for several reasons. Precisely because some of the activity is prohibited by the state, legitimate firms rarely enter the market.[76] More importantly, in the absence of workable legal mechanisms, enforcement requires credible threats of physical violence: State coercion must be privatized. Finally, a variety of barriers to entry, including economies of scope, relations with police, and outright intimidation of competition help organized criminal firms maintain increasing returns and thwart competition from legitimate sources. These same factors help to explain the persistence of extensive organized criminal activity in an otherwise stable, democratic, and economically advanced society such as Japan. Thus, the stimulation of state-sanctioned rights-enforcement and information agents is a crucial aspect of organized crime eradication.

It is instructive to note that the leaders of the campaign to increase the number of attorneys and judges, reduce the scope of the monopoly of Japanese attorneys, and adopt other reforms designed to increase the availability of legal procedures and the professionals that we describe in detail in Chapter 8 were Japanese business groups and conservative politicians. These conservative groups, which are not a natural lobby for law reform of this type, appear to have coalesced around the issue for precisely the reason indicated by our theory: A shortage of state-sanctioned rights-enforcement and information agents seriously compromises the ability to engage in bright-side private ordering, reinforcing reliance on either the state's informal authority (bureaucratic guidance) or illicit entrepreneurs (organized criminal firms).

Third, the prevalence of private ordering of all kinds dampens demand for greater state and state-sanctioned enforcement activity, resulting in fewer incentives to rectify the first two problems. Stated differently, Japan illustrates that states can miss out on enforcement network and learning externalities. Laws and enforcement institutions exhibit increasing returns characteristics. Widely used laws are likely to be well serviced by lawyers and judges. The more laws are used, the more they will lead to the development of precedents and the sophistication of legal professionals. The growth of experienced, state-sanctioned rights-enforcement and information agents, in turn, is likely to foster demand for law reform generally.

Conversely, the histories of regions as diverse as Sicily, Russia, and Japan demonstrate that when a state begins institution-building with a significant gap between formal legal rights and enforcement mechanisms, it risks missing out on valuable network and learning externalities, creating ample demand for both bright-side private enforcement and dark-side gang enforcement. As one commentator puts it, "when the law has no way of enforcing contract, the underworld provides it: a man submits to the prospect of personal violence as the last resort in contract enforcement . . . Evidently there is some part of this racket that thrives on a void in our legal and financial institutions."[77]

Although our general prescription is one of institution-building, some studies have found that parties may turn to privately ordered alternatives *despite* the existence of well-functioning institutions. But these findings appear to be limited to communities that encourage reliance on group-specific, reputation-based internal rules and norms—a relational structure not likely to dominate transactions between organized criminal firms and consumers of dispute resolution and debt collection services. Accordingly, we suspect that dark-side private ordering cannot effectively compete with efficient state institutions in most service areas. Nevertheless, there is no guarantee that efficient public ordering will supplant highly engrained dark-side private ordering. The point, then, is not to convert private ordering into public ordering, but to set state incentives so that entrepeneuralism is channeled into outlets that reinforce rather than erode legal and social norms.

Institution-building, of course, is much easier to prescribe than to accomplish. Despite a state's best efforts at institutional re-engineering, a residual of organized crime may exist in most societies. This is due in large measure to the impossibility of creating frictionless enforcement mechanisms. Some organized crime may even be socially and economically desirable, if the alternative is disorganized crime and dysfunctional state ordering. Indeed, in societies like post-communist Russia, organized crime may be one of the few alternatives to chaos. Thus, the complete eradication of organized crime, at least in the short term, is not a realistic goal for transitional states. Rather, our analysis of the Japanese case suggests that transitional states should concentrate their efforts on creating viable financial intermediaries, workable structures for dispute resolution and debt collection, and an adequate supply of state-sanctioned rights-enforcement agents, including, most importantly, a highly trained legal profession. In so doing, they will encourage enforcement network and learning externalities and reduce incentives for the organization of criminal firms.

CONCLUSION

In this chapter, we have established theoretically and empirically a linkage between state institutions and organized crime. Inefficiencies in state property rights structures and a shortage of state-sanctioned rights-enforcement agents have been a recipe for illicit entrepreneurialism in Japan.

To understand organized crime in Japan and elsewhere, scholars should shift their attention from defining the phenomenon to distinguishing between its prosaic criminal components and its entrepreneurial enforcement characteristics. To combat organized crime, governments might be well advised to direct their resources not at crime control *per se*, but at creating, or facilitating, proper property rights-enforcement institutions. Such a strategy may not completely eliminate organized crime. In the absence of such an approach, however, organized crime will continue to flourish.

NOTES

1. See, for example, Howard Abadinsky, Organized Crime 7 (2nd edn 1985); Denny F. Pace and Jimmie C. Styles, Organized Crime: Concepts and Control 21 (2nd edn 1983); Richard A. Posner, Economic Analysis of Law 242 (4th edn 1992); Diego Gambetta, The Sicilian Mafia: The Business of Private Protection 155 (1993).

2. See, for example, Robert C. Ellickson, Order Without Law: How Neighbors Settle Disputes (1994); Mark D. West, Legal Rules and Social Norms in Japan's Secret World of Sumo, 26 J. Legal Stud. 165, 187 (1997); Lisa Bernstein, Opting Out of the Legal System: Extralegal Contractual Relations in the Diamond Industry, 21 J. Legal Stud. 115, 157 (1992).

3. See Robert D. Cooter, Decentralized Law for a Complex Economy: The Structural Approach to Adjudicating the New Law Merchant, 144 U. Pa. L. Rev. 1643, 1678–94 (1996) ("community failures").

4. See Ronald J. Gilson, Value Creation by Business Lawyers: Legal Skills and Asset Pricing, 94 Yale L. J. 239, 255 (1984).

5. See, for example, John Owen Haley, The Spirit of Japanese Law 38, 79, 134–9, 199 (1998).

6. Peter Reuter, Research on American Organized Crime, in (Robert J. Kelly, Ko-Lin Chin and Rufus Schatzberg, eds., Handbook of Organized Crime in the United States 91 110 Greenwood 1994).

7. Thomas C. Schelling, Choice and Consequence 160–2 (1984).

8. Gambetta, The Sicilian Mafia, *supra* note 1, at 17, 7. See also Donald Black, Crime as Social Control, 48 Am. Soc. Rev. 34 (1983); Diego Gambetta, Mafia: The Price of Distrust, in Diego Gambetta, ed., Trust: Making and Breaking Cooperative Relations 158, 158, 1988.

9. See, for example, Federico Varese, Is Sicily the Future of Russia? Private Protection and the Rise of the Russian Mafia, 35 Archives Européennes de Sociologie 224, 225–6, 257–8 (1994).

10. Francis Fukuyama, Trust: The Social Virtues and the Creation of Prosperity 26–8 (Free Press 1995).

11. See, for example, World Values Study Group, World Values Survey, 1981–84 and 1990–93 (ICPSR 6160) (1994), available online at http://www.icpsr.umich.edu/cgi-bin/archive.prl?path = ICPSR&num = 6160. Cf. Toshio Yamagishi, Shinrai no Kōzō [The Anatomy of Trust] (1988) (noting differences between natural trust and strategic trust to reduce transaction costs).
12. See Gambetta, *supra* note 1, at 16–19, 80; see also Barbara Alexander, The Rational Racketeer: Pasta Protection in Depression Era Chicago, 40 J. L. & Econ. 175, 184–5, 198 (1997).
13. In two influential articles, Thomas Schelling proposed that market structures and economic principles generally applicable to all forms of organization apply to illegal markets controlled by organized criminal firms. Thomas C. Schelling, What is the Business of Organized Crime?, 20 J. Pub. L. 71 (1971), reprinted in Schelling, *supra* note 7, at 179, 182–3; Thomas C. Schelling, Economics and Criminal Enterprise, 7 Public Interest 61 (1967), reprinted in Schelling, *supra* note 7, at 158, 162–4.
14. See Gambetta, *supra* note 1, at 77–81, 252.
15. Thráinn Eggertsson, Economic Behavior and Institutions 36 (Cambridge 1990); Kai Konard and Stergios Skaperdas, The Market for Protection and the Origin of the State, Centre for Economic Policy Research Discussion Paper No 2173 (June 1999).
16. See, for example, Edwin O. Reischauer, Japan: The Story of a Nation 123 (3rd edn 1981) (describing foreclosure of mortgages); R. P. Dore, Land Reform in Japan 14–17 (Oxford 1959) (describing the "recurrent pattern" of "[i]ndebtedness, the mortgaging of land, and eventually the transfer of ownership"); Takeo Ono, Nōson Shi [History of Farm Villages], in Tokyo Keizai Shinbunsha, ed, 9 Gendai Nihon Bunmei Shi [History of Modern Japanese Civilization] 47, 48 (1941) (stating that in some areas of Japan landowners were forced into debt by a new tax system).
17. See Section of Special Records, Foreign Office, Japanese Government, Compiler, IV Documents Concerning the Allied Occupation and Control of Japan: Commercial and Industrial 109 (1949).
18. See John O. Haley, Administrative Guidance Versus Formal Regulation: Resolving the Paradox of Industrial Policy, in (Gary R. Saxonhouse and Kozo Yamamura, eds., 1986) Law and Trade Issues of the Japanese Economy: American and Japanese Perspectives 107, 122.
19. Patrick Shea and Kaori Miyake, Insolvency-Related Reorganization Procedures in Japan: The Four Cornerstones, 14 UCLA Pac. Basin L. J. 243, 245 (1996) (describing reorganization laws adopted from Germany, England, and the United States and noting the resulting overlap).
20. Frank Packer and Marc Ryser, The Governance of Failure: An Anatomy of Corporate Bankruptcy in Japan 11, Working Paper No 62, Center on Japanese Economy and Business, Columbia University (1992).
21. Theodore Eisenberg and Shoichi Tagashira, Should We Abolish Chapter 11? The Evidence from Japan, 23 J. Legal Stud. 111, 116 (1994).
22. Shea and Miyake, *supra* note 19, at 246.
23. Paul Sheard, The Main Bank System and Corporate Monitoring and Control in Japan, 11 J. Econ. Behav. & Org. 399, 411–12 (1989).
24. Bengoshi hō [Attorneys Law], Law No 205 of 1949, arts. 72–73 (1998). Only licensed attorneys may participate in court proceedings through which monetary obligations are enforced.

25. Saiken kanri kaishūgyō ni kansuru tokubetsu sechihō [Servicer Law], Law No 126 of 1998, art. 5(4) (1998).

26. J. Mark Ramseyer and Minoru Nakazato, Japanese Law: An Economic Approach 38 (1999).

27. See Gilson, *supra* note 4, at 255.

28. See Ronald J. Gilson and Robert H. Mnookin, Disputing Through Agents: Cooperation and Conflict Between Lawyers in Litigation, 94 Colum. L. Rev. 509, 512, 564 (1994).

29. Japanese law has historically required that all corporate bonds be collateralized, with major banks serving as trustees. Banks encouraged the adoption of collateral requirements in the 1930s and blocked the rise of credit-rating agencies that could have diminished the importance of secured bond issues. Kazumasa Niimi, An Analysis of Bond Rating in Japan: Its History, Status, and Future, Japan Research Q 35, 73, 85 (Autumn 1992).

30. See Frank G. Bennett, Jr., Civil Execution in Japan, 177 Nagoya Univ. J. L. & Pol. 1, 1–2 (1999).

31. Takatoshi Ito and Kazuo Ueda, Tests of the Equilibrium Hypothesis in Disequilibrium Econometrics: An International Comparison of Credit Rationing, 22 Intl. Econ. Rev. 691 (1981).

32. For example, until the mid 1990s, corporate bond issues were required to be collateralized regardless of the size or creditworthiness of the issuer. See Niimi, *supra* note 29, at 72–86.

33. Frank F. Y. Huang and Michael S. Vaughn, A Descriptive Analysis of Japanese Organized Crime: The Boryokudan from 1945 to 1988, 2 Intl. Crim. Just. Rev. 19, 42 (1992).

34. Id.

35. David E. Kaplan and Alec Dubro, Yakuza: The Explosive Account of Japan's Criminal Underworld 144 (1986).

36. Ikuya Sato, Kamikaze Biker: Parody and Anomy in Affluent Japan 169 (Chicago 1991).

37. See, for example, Atsushi Mizoguchi, Urashakai no Seiji Keizaigaku [The Political Economy of the Underworld], in Yakuza to iu Ikikata: Toshi no Sokoni Sumu Otokotachi no Monogatari [The Life of the Yakuza: Stories of Men Living at the Bottom of the City] 178, 182 (Shinji Ishii ed., 1986).

38. These data have been called "a colossal underestimate." Karel van Wolferen, The Enigma of Japanese Power: People and Politics in a Stateless Nation 101 (1990) (referring to an estimate of income from illegal activity of ¥1.5 trillion). A 1990 police survey of organized criminal firm members was used to estimate the total income of organized criminal firms at $10.42 billion, divided into $2 billion for legal activities and the remainder to illegal and "gray zone" activities. See Hisao Kato, Soshiki Hanzai no Kenkyū: Mafia, Ra Kōza Nosutora Bōryokudan no Hikaku Kenkyū [A Study of Organized Crime: A Comparative Study of the Mafia, La Cosa Nostra, and Japanese Gangs] 124 (1992); Kozo Tanaka, Minbō no Teguchi [Extortion Handbook] 171 (1992).

39. 1993 Keisatsu Hakusho [White Paper on Police] 32 (1994). For comparison, the average yearly contract earnings of all employees in 1993 was $33,504. The average dentist, for example, earned approximately $65,000; janitors earned about $30,000. Nihon Tōkei Nenkan [Japan Statistical Yearbook] (1996).

40. 1993 Keisatsu Hakusho [White Paper on Police], *supra* note 39, at 28.

41. President's Commission on Organized Crime, Report to the President and the Attorney General, The Impact: Organized Crime Today 476, 488 (GPO 1986).

42. David Harold Stark, The Yakuza: Japanese Crime Incorporated 109 (1981) (unpublished Ph.D. dissertation, University of Michigan).

43. Gambetta, *supra* note 1, at 127–55.

44. Jeffrey Goldberg, The Don is Done, New York Times Magazine 25, 26 (Jan. 31, 1999).

45. Edward Fowler, San'ya Blues: Laboring Life in Contemporary Tokyo 20–1 (1996).

46. James Sterngold, Gang in Kobe Organized Aid for People in Quake, New York Times 9 (Jan. 22, 1995); Where the Government Fails, the Yamaguchi-gumi Succeeds, Mainichi Daily News 9 (Feb. 5, 1995).

47. Norikiyo Hayashi, Sōshiki Bōryoku no Ichi Danmen: Aru Sōsakan no Kiseki [A Section of Organized Violence: A Track Traced by a Detective] 100 (1996).

48. John Owen Haley, Authority Without Power: Law and the Japanese Paradox 183–4 (1991).

49. Akira Mizoguchi, Yakuza to Kane [Yakuza and Money] 21 (1992). 34.8% of income is said to come from drugs, see id., which is said to yield profit margins of 15,000%. Akira Hinago, Urakeizai Pakuri no Teguchi 99 [Handbook of 99 Underground Economy Ripoff Artists] 120–1 (1995).

50. Nihon Bengoshi Rengokai [Japanese Bar Association], Minji Kainyū Bōryoku: Chinō Bōryoku to Tatakau Bengoshi [Violent Intervention in Civil Affairs: Attorneys Against "Intellectual" Violence] 14 (Shōji Hōmu Kenkyūkai revd. edn, 1995).

51. Packer and Ryser, *supra* note 20, at 27–9.

52. David Holley, Japan Mob Muddies Real Estate Loan Crisis: Banking Woes Underline the Key Role Gangsters Play in Land Development. Critics Say Yakuza Could Gain Foothold in Economy if Bailout is Mishandled, LA Times A1 (Feb. 24, 1996). See also Seiji Iishiba, Nihon Shakai no Kōzō Henka to Bōryokudan [The Changing Structure of Japanese Society and Organized Criminal Firms], 985 Jurisuto 58, 63 (1991) (noting that "it does not make economic sense to develop a golf course following legal procedures. A demand for the back-door shortcut of the underworld results.").

53. Mizoguchi, *supra* note 37, at 187. A typical charge for land transaction services by legitimate providers is 3%. Id. Of course, legitimate providers merely broker transactions and do not attempt to remove holdouts.

54. See, for example, Kazuhiro Yonemoto, The Shimane Bar Association: All Twenty-One Members Strong, 25 Law in Japan 115, 121 (Daniel H. Foote, trans., 1995); Takeyoshi Kawashima, Dispute Resolution in Contemporary Japan, in Law in Japan: The Legal Order in a Changing Society 41, 47–8 (Arthur von Mehren, ed., 1963).

55. See Kyōji Asakura, Danchi Ninkyōden [A Chivalrous Tale of Neighborhood Protection] in Yakuza to iu Ikikata, *supra* note 37, at 23, 28 (Shinji Ishii, ed. 1986).

56. Nichibenren [Japanese Bar Association], Hōshū Nado Kijun Kitei [Standard Rules Regarding Compensation], Oct. 1, 1995.

57. Tsubasa Aoki, Jidanya Shūdan [Settlement Specialist Groups] 15 (1988).

58. Twelve Percent of Japanese Consider Mobsters a "Necessary Evil", Agence France Presse (Apr. 19, 1993).

59. Ramseyer and Nakazato, *supra* note 26, at 182. See also Matoshi Kamata, Nihon no Chika Teikoku: Jimintō Kaisha Bōryokudan no Toraianguru [The Japanese Underground Empire: The Triangle among the Liberal Democratic Party, Corporations, and Gangs] (1993) (discussing firm political ties).

60. Brian Woodall, Japan Under Construction: Corruption, Politics, and Public Works 8–9 (1996).

61. Bōryokudan'in ni yoru futōna kōi no bōshi nado ni kansuru hōritsu [Anti-Organized Crime Act], Law No. 77 of 1991.

62. Intimidation occurs when one person threatens or attempts to threaten another with injury to his life, person, liberty, reputation, or property, or to the same of a relative, and carries a maximum penalty of two years imprisonment or a fine of less than ¥300,000. Keihō [Penal Code], Law No. 45 of 1907, art. 222 (1995). Extortion occurs when one person causes or attempts to cause another person to surrender property, or when a person gains unlawful profit, and carries a penalty of not more than ten years imprisonment. Id., at art. 249.

63. Unless otherwise indicated, data are from selected issues of four Japanese governmental publications, Hanzai Hakusho [White Paper on Crime], Keisatsu Hakusho [White Paper on Police], Shihō Tōkei Nenpō (Minji/Gyōsei hen) [Annual Report of Judicial Statistics (Civil and Administrative Cases)], and Nihon Tōkei Nenkan [Japan Statistical Yearbook].

64. Population data from selected issues of Kōseishō, Jinkō Dōtai Tōkei [Ministry of Health and Welfare, Vital Statistics].

65. Walter L. Ames, Police and Community in Japan 183 (1981).

66. Peter J. Katzenstein, Cultural Norms and National Security: Police and Military in Postwar Japan 64 (1996). Police are also aided by the fact that firms normally control a specific turf.

67. In a telephone interview with a senior NPA official, we suggested that the data might either be high because of firm boasts, or low because of local police desire to appear effective in controlling firms. The first concern was rebuffed with the same point raised by the local officers—the actual numbers are no real secret, and firm exaggerations would be easily falsified. The second concern, the official explained, was mitigated by (*a*) officer integrity, (*b*) additional auditing of local data directly by NPA officials and the National Public Safety Commission, and (*c*) the fact that the NPA asserts only indirect control over prefectural units, creating little incentive to distort data. West Telephone Interview with Section Vice-Chief of Organized Crime Countermeasures Section 1, Criminal Bureau, NPA (Dec. 15, 1998).

68. Stark, *supra* note 42, at 10–11.

69. Data on the number of firms are not available after 1992.

70. A positive correlation between MEMBERS and the financing variable might exist if a high percentage of bank loans went to criminal firms. Two official measures of such activity exist. First, the National Police Agency estimates that more than 10% of banks' bad loans are to organized criminal firms. See David Lister and Patrick Sawer, Gangster Link to £9 billion Japan Bank's Collapse, Evening Standard 4 (Sept. 28, 1998). Second, a March 1999 survey by the Housing Loan Administration Company found that organized criminal firms or self-proclaimed rightist groups were involved in 42% of the cases in which the collection of nonperforming loans left by defunct *jusen* housing loan companies was disrupted. Survey: Gangs Stalling Collection of Jusen Loans, Daily Yomiuri 1 (Mar. 31, 1999). Organized criminal firms' share of the 42% figure represents some combination of loans to gangs and the hiring of gangs to prevent collection of loans.

71. Had the relationship between loans issued and MEMBERS been positive, it might have indicated that loans went to organized criminal firms. That it was not is an

indication that although some loans might, as the anecdotes and estimates suggest, be going to organized criminal firms, those loans in fact are going to a small subset of the largest, most sophisticated criminal firms. To test for this, we checked the correlation between the membership rates (members divided by the number of 20- to 49-year-old males) of the three biggest firms—the Yamaguchi-gumi, Inagawa-kai, and the Sumiyoshi-kai—and the loans variable. In fact, the relationship with the loans variable was significantly positive, an indication that although the issuance of loans by banks may, on average, negatively affect firms by competing with them for loan-sharking business, the largest firms may profit from loans quite directly if they are borrowers and not lenders.

72. See Hinago, *supra* note 49, at 30–31.
73. Low levels of crime may be attributable to enforcement by organized criminal firms. For example, organized criminal firms "actively cooperate[ ] with the police to keep foreign drugs out, thus protecting [their] own business and keeping Japan's drug problem manageable." Katzenstein, *supra* note 67, at 67.
74. The specification of MEMBERS as membership rates creates a fourth supply-side variable: Population of males ages 20–49. Results did not differ significantly when we substituted MEMBERS with the raw membership data, not accounting for population shifts. As Figure 6.1 suggests, the number of members tracks membership rates.
75. See Jeffrey Fagan, Juvenile Justice Policy and Law: Applying Recent Social Science Findings to Policy and Legislative Advocacy, 183 PLI/Crim 395 n 31 (1999).
76. The most obvious historical example in the United States is the domination by organized crime of alcohol markets during Prohibition that had formerly been, and subsequently became again, the province of legitimate firms.
77. Schelling, *supra* note 7, at 168.

7

Mergers and Acquisitions

INTRODUCTION

We now turn from the Japanese underworld to the world of legitimate Japanese firms, specifically, the market for mergers and acquisitions (M&A). As many readers are aware, historically Japan has had little takeover activity. But ending the inquiry there overlooks a multitude of unexplored issues. In this chapter, we show that an institutional environment much more highly textured than the conventional focus on cross-shareholding would suggest contributed to a homogenous approach to corporate governance in Japan. For a time, this governance system matched the production technology and competitive needs of Japanese firms extremely well. But as the political economy, technology, and competitive environment changed, the lack of M&A left Japanese firms without a crucial adaptation mechanism, reinforcing continued adherence to practices designed to complement a system that no longer functioned effectively.

Through institutional reform, Japan has in recent years taken steps to stimulate the market for corporate control. The preliminary results suggest that corporate actors have responded to the new institutional set, and that a more flexible formal environment for corporate decisionmaking—one in which mergers and hostile takeovers are both possible and valued as a strategic option—has spawned innovation and variation in governance practices ranging from board composition to transaction structure and the use of the courts.

To this Japanese corporate governance setting we apply two related and underappreciated insights from other fields. Economic theory holds that there is no universally efficient corporate organizational model; rather, different firms in different industries require diverse organizational forms.[1] Organizational behavior and corporate demography literature provide evidence that heterogeneous populations—groups, industries, and countries—outperform homogeneous ones.[2] Combining these insights, we argue that corporate governance systems that promote, or at least do not impede, organizational diversity are more likely to produce firms that are adaptable, receptive to new governance technologies, make effective decisions, and avoid shackling by inefficient norms. Thus, our first claim is straightforward: Diversity within a corporate governance system is a virtue.[3]

The second step of our argument is that a specific corporate governance tool—an active market for corporate control—is an effective way to promote these beneficial forms of diversity. To date, commentators have viewed M&A almost exclusively as a disciplining mechanism. Largely overlooked, however, is the potential for takeovers to broaden managerial outlook, expand strategic option sets, match governance technology with production processes, and contribute to a more robust market for legal innovation. The Japanese case illuminates this potential.

We hasten to add several caveats. Our claim is not that takeovers are universally beneficial; clearly some deals—maybe a few, maybe many–destroy value. Nor do we claim that takeovers are the sole, or necessarily the primary, mechanism through which firms achieve diversity in corporate governance. Even in Japan during the time period we examine, takeovers are by no means the only factor at work. Finally, our claim that intra-firm diversity is beneficial is not an implicit endorsement of statutes mandating the use of outside directors. By definition, firms need flexibility from the legal system to attain the governance structures that best suit their needs. Our claims are simply that an active market for corporate control is beneficial in ways that have not previously been recognized, and that this insight has important consequences both for institutional design issues and the convergence debate.

The chapter proceeds as follows. Section I discusses the theoretical foundations of the gains from organizational diversity, and describes how institutions conducive to an active market for corporate control improve the prospects of reaping those gains. Section II examines the historical (absence of a) market for corporate control in Japan. We present the most complete domestic and comparative data available on Japanese takeover activity. The data belie the claim that while hostile deals are rare, friendly deals are plentiful. In Section III, we link the historically low level of M&A activity to low quality financial disclosure as well as overly protective corporate law and tender offer regulations. We then show how these same features correlate to the lack of diversity in Japanese corporate practices, as an inflexible and high-cost environment led firms to adopt uniform governance techniques. Section IV first discusses recent institutional changes in the Japanese market for corporate control and the ensuing increases in M&A activity. Next, preliminary evidence is presented indicating that a deal-friendly environment correlates with increased governance innovations, a proliferation of non-standard corporate practices, and increased legal development. Section V discusses implications of our findings.

I. GAINS FROM DIVERSITY AND THE MARKET FOR CORPORATE CONTROL

Commentators engaged in the convergence debate have thus far ignored some important questions. For example, what are the central characteristics that any corporate governance system should contain? By what mechanism(s) might those features be transmitted from system to system?

A starting point for analyzing these questions is the work of economists Harold Demsetz and Kenneth Lehn. Demsetz and Lehn argue in essence that there are no central corporate governance characteristics. Because "the structure of corporate ownership varies systematically in ways that are consistent with value maximization," the management structure that works in one firm may not work best everywhere.[4]

Extending this insight, economist Masahiko Aoki has contributed important ideas that have yet to be utilized by participants in the convergence debate. Aoki theorizes that organizational diversity is a virtuous characteristic for economic systems. In a series of articles, Aoki argues that "maximum economic gains may be realized by implementing different organizational forms that correspond to the specific nature of each industry."[5] Diversity can be achieved by accommodating these forms.

The claim that diversity is a key feature of successful systems draws support from several sources. Organizational behavior scholars who study corporate demography, for example, note that two very successful U.S. industries, high tech in Silicon Valley and entertainment in Hollywood, are characterized by diverse organizational forms and high rates of demographic turnover. Increased organizational diversity in the beer and wine industry may explain increased consumption in the United States. The United States "stands out as extremely diverse," in organizational forms, while "the Soviet Union, before the collapse of state socialism, stood at the other pole." Thus, "the more diverse the population, the more likely that organizational structures exist that can deal effectively with the unexpected environmental events."[6]

Other studies provide more theoretical support for these claims. Economists Lu Hong and Scott Page have produced a model demonstrating that diversity among problem solvers increases the ability to solve difficult problems. "Being boundedly rational," they note, "only stifles good decisions if we are boundedly rational in the same way."[7] In biology, variation is a prerequisite for evolution.[8] Oliver Williamson, drawing on the work of Hayek and Barnard, claims "adaptability is the central problem of economic organization."[9] If so, then plasticity and variation are desirable—even essential—traits of a successful economic environment.

In perfectly competitive markets, diversity might be achieved naturally. As Demsetz theorizes, firms that survive in the long run will be those that have picked appropriate management structures.[10] But even Demsetz recognizes—and offers quantitative evidence in support of the claim—that "systematic regulation reduces the options available to owners."[11] By limiting managerial options, regulation and other factors diminish a system's ability to attain diversity. Again, Aoki elaborates and extends Demsetz's point: "The combined effect of such factors as the bounded rationality of individuals, evolutionary pressures, and institutional complementarity is a tendency for a more or less homogeneous organizational convention to be adopted throughout a particular economy. However, different organizational conventions will evolve in different nations."[12] Numerous recent studies highlight the tendency toward national convergence of organizational forms and corporate governance practices.[13]

Accordingly, a central question is how to prevent homogenizing institutional and evolutionary pressures from discouraging the optimal corporate governance diversity within national systems and within individual firms—diversity that might arise naturally in a perfectly competitive environment. One promising path toward organizational diversity is provided by the market for corporate control. Literature on the market for corporate control is vast, but most commentators make the same point: Takeovers mitigate agency problems. The threat of job loss for inefficient managers posed by a market for corporate control provides powerful incentives to advance shareholder interests.[14]

The literature discussed above, however, suggests a powerful alternative rationale for merger activity in general, and cross-border mergers in particular: promotion of organizational diversity both within and across firms. We hypothesize that increased merger activity correlates with heightened managerial, transactional, and legal innovation, as new perspectives are introduced into firm governance by the clash of perspectives between bidders and incumbents, and those clashes themselves spawn an expanded set of approved transactional and legal responses. Some of the gains may come from the enhanced discipline that exposure to global "best practices" brings. The motivation for our study, however, is the point that the best practice is one that properly aligns governance institutions with the needs of specific firms, not the adoption of a one-size-fits-all model.

To be sure, an active market for corporate control is not the only way of achieving diversity in a system.[15] We simply argue that international convergence toward an active market for corporate control may be one powerful way to endogenize a healthy level of diversity within economic systems.

To explore this new perspective, we now turn specifically to Japan. Aoki, along with many others, saw the main bank and stable shareholdings—institutions deeply rooted in the old political economy of Japan—as an alternative to the market for corporate control. One key—but overlooked—consequence of this prevailing organizational mode was relative homogeneity in governance structures. For a time, it did not matter, because this system of corporate governance matched the production needs and technology of Japanese firms extremely well. But those needs have changed and the main bank system has largely ceased to function, giving rise to an important natural experiment: How will the old system adapt, what institutions will grow up in its place, and what are the implications for corporate governance?

II. JAPANESE M&A IN HISTORICAL AND COMPARATIVE PERSPECTIVE

It will come as no surprise to most readers that Japan has not experienced much merger activity in the postwar period. So low is the level of activity in the world's second largest economy, however, that it demands deeper exploration than has been provided to date. Using a variety of official and unofficial sources of data, in this section we examine merger activity in Japan.

A. Merger Data

1. Official data Until January 1999, the Anti-monopoly Act required that every merger and asset sale be reported to the Japan Fair Trade Commission (JFTC).

Figure 7.1. *Mergers and asset sales reported, 1968–89*

Figure 7.1 shows the number of notifications received by the JFTC from 1969 to 1989.

These data, which show only about 1,000 mergers per year, may significantly overstate the level of merger activity in Japan. The JFTC data include mergers of tiny firms (including limited liability companies and limited partnerships) and intra-group mergers.[16] In the 1980s, for example, nearly two-thirds of all merger notifications were for mergers between firms with assets of less than ¥1 billion (U.S.$10 million at current exchange rates). About ninety-five percent of all mergers were for firms with assets of less than ¥50 billion ($500 million), and ¥100 billion ($1 billion) mergers averaged in the single digits.[17] The figure also shows that Japan has not experienced significant merger "waves" as in the United States. Although asset sales increased over the twenty-year period, mergers, at least by this measure, have remained at a relatively constant level.

2. Private data   Several unofficial sources of merger data are more instructive. Recof LLC, a Japanese M&A boutique, maintains merger data that exclude both intra-group mergers and transactions that involve changes only in preexisting equity positions, such as from majority to minority. Although these data are less comprehensive than the JFTC figures, they are likely to be a better indication of significant merger activity. These data show a gradual increase from 182 transactions in 1985 and 256 in 1989.

Thomson Financial maintains data on the number of merger announcements in Japan. From 1990 to 1994, purely domestic ("in-in") M&A averaged fewer than 100 transactions per year, with a gross average value of about ¥800 billion ($8 billion). During the same period, foreign acquisitions of Japanese firms ("out-in") averaged only about fifty transactions per year, with a total average value of only ¥50 billion ($500 million).

These data indicate that Japanese M&A activity is minuscule in comparison to U.S. levels. According to Mergerstat, the average number of U.S. merger announcements from 1990 to 1994 was 2,437, with a total average annual value of $135 billion. Even the U.S. data from as far back as 1963, the earliest on record in Mergerstat, are approximately 900 percent higher than the highest figures recorded for Japan at the peak of the economic bubble. In 1990, Japanese merger activity was approximately 0.4 percent of its GDP[18] in comparison to the U.S. figure of 1.8 percent.[19]

B. Tender Offers

Although the disparity between total merger activity in the United States and Japan is large, a comparison of tender offers in the two countries is even more striking. From 1971 to 1990, a total of three tender offers were made in Japan. By contrast, Mergerstat, defining tender offers as those seeking more than 10 percent of a target's shares and excluding self-tenders, recorded 218 tender offers in the United States for 1988 alone.

C. International Comparisons

Lest one conclude that these disparities simply reflect the oversized U.S. market for corporate control, data indicate that Japan's M&A activity is extremely low by any international measure. In a ranking of targets by nation, Japan had a 0.6 percent market share in 1997 (behind South Africa, Malaysia, and Bermuda).[20] In 1998, on the basis of M&A transaction value as a percentage of GDP, China's market for corporate control was three times larger than that of Japan; Australia's was twenty times larger; and the U.S. market was forty-six times larger.[21]

III. INSTITUTIONAL FOUNDATION FOR TAKEOVERS AND CORPORATE GOVERNANCE

Existing literature has provided incomplete answers to two basic questions on takeovers in Japan. First, why is merger activity so low? Academic explanations to date have focused almost exclusively on cross-shareholding. Second, what are the consequences of the absence of a market for corporate control? Only the agency cost issue has been discussed, followed by the ubiquitous reference to main bank monitoring. In this section, we uncover underlying reasons why deals are difficult, and expose the relationship between internal monitoring and homogeneous corporate governance practices in Japan.

A. Obstacles to a Market for Corporate Control

A recent report on corporate governance in leading economies assigns to Japan its second lowest rating on takeover barriers (meaning that they are among the most formidable in the world, behind only the Netherlands).[22] The report notes "visible, formal takeover defenses are not always as potent as those present by custom and practice that are invisible and informal. Japan, for instance, has the fewest variations in defenses against takeovers, but those it does feature are strong enough—thanks to unwritten rules of the market—to stop nearly all unwelcome bids."[23] The report identifies three almost universal and nearly insurmountable barriers in Japan: Core shareholders, cross-shareholding, and targeted stock placements to white knight investors.

In our view, these "barriers" are not root causes of low M&A activity, but instead are symptomatic of more fundamental, and less well understood, obstacles to the efficient transfer of corporate assets in Japan. Our task here is to explain the institutional factors that underlie these anti-takeover practices and to deepen understanding of the often-discussed barriers.

We begin with a startling fact: The average premium paid for shares in a tender offer in Japan is negative. We arrive at this conclusion by analyzing all fifty-nine tender offers made between 1990 and 2000 for which complete data are available. Building on a data set and methodology used by Merrill Lynch, we compared the offer price to the target's stock price on the day preceding the offer. So calculated, the average premium is −4.72 percent. Perhaps more important than the average is the distribution of premiums, which reveals a stark division between deals with positive premiums and deals with negative or zero premiums. Twenty-nine deals had negative or zero premiums, while thirty had positive premiums. The average positive premium was 24.5 percent, while the average negative premium was −37.4 percent.

Compare these figures with those of other large economies for the same period. Average premiums (by month) for European targets in 1999 ranged from 4 to 25 percent over the market price the day before the offer was announced. For U.S. targets in the three months ending in January of 2000, the average premium over the price one week before announcement of the offer was 35 percent.[24]

Setting aside the possibility of leaked information that drives up market price vis-à-vis bid price, at least two interrelated explanations for the prevalence of below-market tender offers in Japan are likely. First, as we saw in Chapter 5, the quality of financial information appears to be low. In such an environment, it may be rational for a bidder to pay a negative control premium to compensate for uncertainty. Second, the takeover procedures codified in the Securities Exchange Act, ostensibly designed to protect investors, may create incentives that actually work to the disadvantage of minority shareholders. We take up these explanations in turn.

The limited financial disclosure that Chapter 5 linked to sokaiya activity has historically also played a large role in dampening the market for corporate control in Japan, particularly by limiting foreign acquisitions of Japanese firms. Historically, public financial disclosure of useful information has been very limited. For example, consolidated financial statements were not mandatory until very recently, so liabilities and under-performing assets could be taken off a firm's balance sheet by moving them into subsidiaries. Curiously, many Japanese financial analysts only focused on parent companies, so stock prices did not necessarily reflect the corporate group's complete financial situation. Financial assets were recorded at cost. Pension liabilities were not required to be disclosed. Cash flow data were limited, and there was general unfamiliarity with discounted cash flow analysis. Moreover, both internal and external auditing practices tended to be minimalist and forgiving.

Limited information obviously raises the cost (reduces the number) of takeovers. Valuation is difficult, and concerns over undisclosed liabilities are hard to quell. The efficient transmission of information is all the more problematic because Japan has traditionally had few professional advisors specialized in M&A. Due diligence, thus, simultaneously becomes absolutely crucial and exceedingly difficult and time-consuming.

Tender offer procedures have served as a second structural impediment to takeovers. Tender offers were technically unregulated prior to the enactment of legislation in 1971, but no offers were made, at least in part because the lack of a legal framework caused many legal advisors to question their legality.[25] From 1971 until 1990, a ten-day waiting period and prior review of all offers by the Ministry of Finance were required, on the theory that Japanese courts would be reluctant to enjoin legally defective offers due to unfamiliarity with the new procedure.[26] As a prominent Japanese commentator has noted, this rationale reveals distrust of the judiciary and overconfidence in administrative agencies.[27] Not surprisingly, as noted above, only three tender offers were made during this period.

In 1991, Japan instituted a mandatory bid rule patterned after (but more stringent than) London's City Code. This rule (Securities Exchange Act § 27-2(1)(4)) requires that any off-exchange offer, the acceptance of which would result in the acquisition of more than 33.3 percent of the target's shares, be made through a tender offer to all shareholders. The rule is designed to protect minority shareholders by ensuring that they receive a pro rata share of any control premium, and to ensure disclosure of even a "private" purchase where a major shareholder would emerge.[28]

In fact, even Japanese policymakers acknowledge that the supposedly shareholder-protective mandatory bid rule has had adverse consequences.[29] In particular, while the mandatory bid rule may deter some inefficient bids, it has two unintended consequences that may work to the disadvantage of minority shareholders. First, the rule may dampen beneficial tender offer activity by increasing uncertainty and cost for erstwhile acquirers, who must incur the expense and unpredictability of a tender offer even to pass a relatively low shareholding threshold. This is particularly problematic because a tender offer cannot be used as the first of a two-step acquisition process to acquire 100 percent control of the target, since under Japanese law minority shareholders cannot be squeezed out for cash. Thus, often there may be little advantage to obtaining more shares than necessary to surpass the critical 33.3 percent level at which major corporate transactions can be vetoed pursuant to the Commercial Code.

Second, because once the mandatory bid rule is triggered the tender offer must be made to all shareholders, it may be difficult for large blockholders to achieve liquidity. The probability that the blockholder will be able to cash out completely declines as the premium increases, since the premium will encourage other shareholders to tender, and shares must be accepted on a pro rata basis. Accordingly, both acquirers and blockholders seeking liquidity have incentives to make "pre-arranged" tender offers at prices below prevailing market prices to ensure that other shareholders do not tender into the offering. We found that all twenty-one cases in which the negative premium exceeded 10 percent were pre-arranged by the bidder and a blockholder, usually founding shareholders, share-holding executives, or stable shareholding group companies. While we lack specific evidence, we assume these shareholders were willing to accept lower prices because of inside information, various forms of side payments, or an inability to demand prevailing market prices for large blocks in low-float Japanese markets.

An additional and related obstacle to M&A similarly grows out of the shareholder-protective stance of the Commercial Code. Several attributes of the Code make takeovers relatively unattractive. As noted above, there is no legal authority for cash-out or short-form mergers, so it is not possible to eliminate minority holdouts in the back end of a two-step acquisition. Perhaps more importantly, the Code has historically not provided managers with the flexibility to craft U.S.-style defensive mechanisms such as the poison pill. (As a technical matter, it appears that the recent code amendment could now facilitate issurance of a poison pill-like defensive mechanism). If a poison pill were put in place, presumably those measures would be reviewable by the courts and would have to be removed if found to be inconsistent with directors' duties to the corporation and its share-holders.[30] The lack of such litigation, however, has left the scope of directors' duties in Japan ambiguous. Ironically, the historical absence of law-based takeover mechanisms left risk-averse Japanese managers few alternatives but to resort to the draconian, relationship-based defense of cross-shareholding, which is gener-ally unreviewable by the courts. Quite plausibly, firms would have avoided or unwound unprofitable cross-shareholding investments if managers had been more secure in their ability to respond to unsolicited bids through legal devices.

One further potential obstacle to M&A remains to be addressed. It is often said that social and cultural distaste for the sale of corporate control, based on shame or corporate paternalism toward employees, is a major impediment to M&A in Japan. The social norm denigrating takeovers as unethical may have emerged as a substitute for a more fully developed and efficient set of ground rules for M&A activity. Here, the parallels with the United States are instructive. Prior to 1968, takeover activity in the United States was essentially unregulated. A social norm against hostile bids developed. Statutory and common law regulation of takeovers eventually proliferated, but in ways that did not completely shut down takeover activity. Deals were done, law was made. The ground rules for takeovers became clearer, and the norm virtually vanished.[31]

Japan's historical path differs. As in the United States, the legal vacuum sur-rounding takeovers led to a social norm against hostile bids. In Japan, however, specific anti-takeover regulation did not appear. Instead, the social norm was buttressed by relationship-based takeover defenses. Unlike U.S. regulation, the Japanese response virtually eliminated takeover activity. In the absence of takeovers, corporate legal development was slow, and the underlying norm denigrating the market for corporate control was reinforced.

B. Governance Traits

In this section, we show how this same institutional setting that constrains takeovers also contributes to a one-size-fits-all approach to corporate governance in Japan. A range of evidence indicates that many large Japanese firms have adopted strikingly similar—indeed one might say highly stylized—approaches to corporate governance. The point is not that the precise approach to these practices matters a great deal to corporate success. Rather, it is that Japanese firms appear to have adopted uniform practices without a compelling economic rationale for doing so. If the diversity theory outlined above has merit, this is not an optimal approach to corporate governance.

1. Low disclosure   Low quality disclosure in Japan, as discussed above, contributed to the lack of takeovers. It also led to widespread adoption of several corporate practices:

a. *Shareholders' meeting.* In 1997, 95 percent of first-section Tokyo Stock Exchange firms held their shareholder's meeting on the same Thursday in June. In 1990, 83.6 percent of all firms ended their meetings in less than 30 minutes.[32] As we noted in chapter 5, both are measures to prevent heckling activity by sokaiya.

b. *Fiscal year.* The Tokyo Stock Exchange reports that in 1996, 85 percent of first-section firms ended their fiscal year in March. All ten major national banks issued their annual reports on May 24.[33]

2. Commercial Code rules   The traditionally inflexible character of the Commercial Code, which virtually eliminated the possibility of takeover defenses beyond relationship-based shareholding, also encouraged conformity in other corporate governance practices:

a. *Auditors.* Until 2003, all large firms had statutory auditors designed to monitor management's compliance with law, regardless of their efficacy or the availability of substitutes, because they were mandated by the Commercial Code. (An important recent amendments to the code allow "large" firms to abandon the statutory auditor in favor of U.S.-style board committees).

b. *Board committees.* Again, until 2003, virtually no firms had formal committees of the board for significant matters such as executive compensation and audits, because they were not recognized by the Code. Indeed, the Code (Section 260(2)) prohibited the delegation of "important" board functions.

c. *Share transactions.* Share repurchases and stock splits are heavily regulated by the Commercial Code and historically have not been viable options for pursuing corporate strategy.

d. *Organizational concerns.* Until December 1997, holding companies were pro-hibited by the Antimonopoly Act, and similar structures were heavily regu-lated by intra-group cross-shareholding limits under the Commercial Code (sections 211-2, 241(3)). Although some companies found ways to avoid the ban, it rendered impermissible many corporate structures that are common elsewhere.

e. *Executive compensation.* Cash compensation is relatively low by international standards, leaving less room for variation.[34] Intra-industry executive com-pensation is virtually identical among leading firms, at least in part because large compensation packages and performance-based pay, which could create variation, remain rare.[35]

3. Other homogeneous practices

a. *Dividends.* Japanese dividends typically have no correlation to earnings, and are instead based on a fixed percentage of par value. In 1990, 24.7 percent of Tokyo Stock Exchange companies issued dividends of exactly ¥5 per share (equal to 10 percent of the standard ¥50 par value). Another 19.1 percent issued dividends of exactly ¥10 per share. Over 90 percent of all TSE firms paid dividends ranging from ¥5–10.[36]

b. *Boards of directors.* Postwar Japanese boards of directors have followed a well-established convention of large size, internal promotion, and lack of independent members. This convention is likely the result of widely held beliefs about the board's proper structure and role as employee representatives. These beliefs, in turn, are reinforced by an environment devoid of takeovers.

c. *Advisors.* Independent professional advice on corporate transactions is in short supply, raising problems both of access and uniformity of opinion. Severe state-set limitations on the number of licensed attorneys and the his-torical shortage of transactional work contribute to a dearth of attorneys with expertise in corporate matters. As a result, a short list of prominent attorneys and law firms handle virtually all sophisticated transactional work in Japan. Accounting advice is also limited, a phenomenon that may correlate with low quality information disclosure.[37]

d. *Share ownership patterns.* Stephen Prowse compared the ownership concen-tration of non-financial firms in Germany, Japan, the United States, and the United Kingdom. The mean percentage of shares held by the five largest share-holders in Japan is 33.1 percent, more than in the United States (24.4 percent) or the United Kingdom (20.9 percent), but far less than in Germany (79.2 percent). The interesting difference from our perspective, however, lies in the range of shareholding patterns in the various countries. Prowse reports that while Germany has a range of 5–100 percent, with a standard deviation from the mean of 31.7, Japan's range is 10.9–85 percent, with a standard deviation of only 13.8, the smallest in the sample.[38] In short, Japanese firms have less variation in ownership structure than firms in other leading economies.

C. Consequences

One consequence of the rules and practices discussed above can be seen in Figure 7.2, which illustrates the ratio of bust-up value to market capitalization for 779 non-financial Tokyo Stock Exchange firms. As the figure indicates, approximately 13 percent of these firms are trading below their bust-up value.[39] In other words, more than one of every eight public firms in Japan is worth more in liquidation than under current management. In the 1980s, there were U.S. firms trading below bust-up value. In contrast to the U.S. situation, however, there is no market action in Japan to dismantle these firms. Despite the obvious potential to profit by acquiring and then selling off the assets of these firms, bids are rare, suggesting that the transaction costs involved are prohibitive.

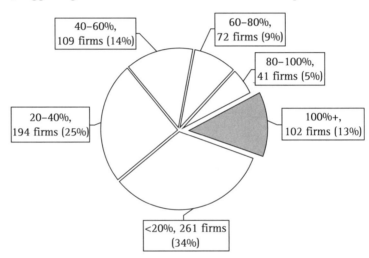

Figure 7.2. *Ratio of bust-up value to market capitalization, 2000*

Indeed, this intuition is reinforced by evidence from firms that do merge. Table 7.1 shows the time required from announcement date to closing for six recent, well-publicized Japanese and U.S. financial firm mergers. As Table 7.1

Table 7.1. *Time from announcement to closing, U.S. and Japan*

Country	Firm	Time required (in months)
Japan	Mizuho Financial Services (DKB/Fuji/IBJ)	31
Japan	Mitsui Sumitomo Bank	19
Japan	Sumitomo Fire & Marine/Mitsui Fire & Marine	20
U.S.	Chase/JP Morgan	4
U.S.	Travelers Group/Solomon Smith Barney	2
U.S.	Morgan Stanley/Dean Witter	3

Source: Goldman Sachs data, in Nobumithi Hattori, Tayōka suru Nichon Kigyō no Saihen Sukiimu [How Ever-Diversifying Japanese Firms can Restructure] 1599 Shōji Hamu 11, 23 (2001).

shows, time to closing for major deals is five to ten times longer in Japan than in the United States. At least in the case of Mizuho, commentators have pointed directly to institutional barriers, such as the Commercial Code requirement of approval of two-thirds of shareholders, as the cause of the delay.[40]

These data indirectly suggest an important relation between the lack of mergers and the lack of diversity in Japanese corporate governance. Because strategic differences among competitors in Japan are minimal, firms compete primarily on the basis of operational efficiency, leading to severe profit pressures.[41] An active market for corporate control could serve as a natural corrective to this problem both by weeding out unprofitable firms and by providing managers with strategic options to distinguish their firms from rivals. But transaction costs prevent many inefficient firms from being acquired, while the lack of differentiation among competitors reduces the potential for synergistic gains from mergers. In this manner, the lack of M&A in Japan, a product of institutional constraints, is inextricably linked with homogeneity in the corporate governance environment.

Within this linkage, however, lies potential. As the next section shows, primarily through deregulation and liberalization, institutions can be manipulated to invigorate the market for corporate control, which in turn can increase diversity among stakeholders, and create new options for strategic competition and firm governance.

IV. NEW INSTITUTIONS, MORE DEALS, NEW GOVERNANCE

We begin this section by surveying some key legal and accounting changes brought about in Japan's changing political economy. We then examine the impact of the new institutions on M&A activity, and reassess Japanese governance practices. We conclude by explaining why the pessimistic response of observers to the recent reforms is unwarranted.

A. New Institutions

1. Legal/Regulatory reforms   Japan's Commercial Code was amended more extensively in the 1990s than in any other period since the Occupation. Many of the significant reforms were designed to improve corporate governance.

Holding companies. In 1997, the Occupation-imposed ban on "pure" holding companies was eliminated. This change should have several important benefits for Japanese firms. Most basically, it will promote management reorganization through spinoffs, mergers, and corporate reorganizations. But it will also provide useful legal separation between strategic and operating units of the firm, and allow firms to differentiate personnel management systems. Firms may retain conventional "Japanese" employment patterns where useful, while introducing more diverse arrangements in other subsidiaries. Removal of the ban on financial holding companies will also facilitate reorganization of the financial industry into functionally diverse groups offering banking, securities, and insurance products and services.

Share-for-share exchanges. The Commercial Code was revised in 1999 to introduce share-for-share exchanges. This reform produces several benefits. Share exchanges can be used to create wholly owned subsidiaries. Capital gains taxes are not owed at the time of the share exchange. Time-consuming and expensive valuation procedures to protect creditors mandated by the Commercial Code for ordinary mergers are not required. Minority shareholders can be forcibly excluded from the subsidiary (although they become shareholders of the parent).

Spinoffs and splitoffs. A new statutory scheme provides a flexible framework for separating business units from parent companies. Among other benefits, court-appointed auditors are no longer required to value assets before transfers can be effected.

Corporate reorganizations. The Civil Rehabilitation Act, enacted in 2000, may promote acquisitions of financially troubled firms by providing more flexible and efficient reorganization procedures than its predecessor statute. It is now possible to do a pre-packaged bankruptcy, with the reorganized firm emerging under new ownership.

Stock options. Beginning in 1997, the Commercial Code formally authorized the issuance of stock options to certain firm employees. According to a Nikko Securities/Towers Perrin survey, the number of listed companies issuing stock options has nearly quadrupled from 121 in 1998 to 463 in 2001, up from zero in 1997 and representative of about one-sixth of listed companies.[42] As forms of executive compensation change, managers may increasingly discover incentives to "sell out" and encourage fellow shareholders to transfer control to a bidder. This process may alter the social cost/benefit calculus for managers, which traditionally has weighed heavily against the sale of corporate control.

Shareholder monitoring. We have seen in Chapter 2 how a seemingly technical change in procedural law in 1993 that lowered the cost of filing derivative suits led to a major increase in this form of shareholder monitoring. While we have also seen that the Japanese derivative suit mechanism suffers from the same attorney's fee-based incentive distortions that plague such suits in the United States, this shift toward heightened shareholder monitoring may place greater pressure on managers to explain their actions—such as declining to pursue a strategic alternative presented by a suitor—to their shareholders. Moreover, institutional investors, whose managers must answer to their own shareholders and beneficiaries, will likely face increased pressure to sell into an attractive offer, regardless of long-term relationships with the target firm.

2. Accounting reforms Japanese accounting standards have been revised significantly in the past several years to bring them substantially into conformity with International Accounting Standards. Stricter standards for consolidated accounting was introduced in fiscal year 1999. Mark-to-market accounting for financial assets was introduced in fiscal year 2001. Pension liabilities were required to be reflected on balance sheets beginning in fiscal year 2001. Cash flow statements were introduced in fiscal year 1999.

Assuming audit practices improve as well, these reforms can be expected to have a significant impact on corporate governance. The new rules enhance management transparency and provide powerful new incentives for restructuring or divesting under-performing assets. Perhaps most significantly, these reforms enable cross-country comparisons of financial statements between foreign and Japanese companies, which assists due diligence and valuation efforts. In the past, lack of international accounting comparability was a major obstacle to cross-border M&A in Japan.

B. More deals

Merger activity in Japan has increased significantly in recent years. Our sense, confirmed in discussions with practitioners, is that institutional reforms are a significant cause of the increase. Although still small in comparison to deal activity in the United States, the increase in the number, size, and structure of transactions in recent years is striking.

1. Merger data   As in Section II, we examined data from two private sources: Recof LLC and Thomson Financial. Both measures show marked increases in the 1990s, as shown in Figure 7.3. The Recof data, which showed approximately 250 M&A of Japanese firms in 1989, surpassed 300 in 1991, 400 in 1997, and 500 in 1997. The trend continues: Recof reports 847 transactions in 1999, 1,241 in 2000, and 1,348 in 2001.

The Thomson Financial data show a significant increase in domestic M&A. "In-in" M&A, which averaged fewer than 100 transactions per year during 1990–94, with a gross average value of about ¥800 billion ($8 billion), reached over 1,300 transactions in 1999, with a gross transaction value of ¥13 trillion ($130 billion). The number of "out-in" transactions, which averaged only about fifty per year during 1990–94, with a total average value of only ¥50 billion ($500 million),

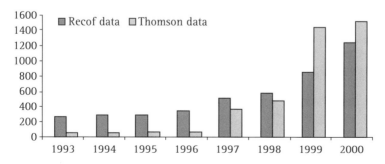

Figure 7.3. *Number of deals involving Japanese targets, 1993–2000*

increased to 227 transactions with a value of ¥3 trillion ($30 billion) in 1999. Japanese M&A has fared comparatively well even in global recession; while the worldwide M&A market fell by 45 percent from the first quarter of 2001 to the first quarter of 2002, the Japanese market fell by only about 2.5 percent.

There are no data available on the specific legal mechanics of each deal. But some mergers, such as the giant Mizuho Financial Group alliance that combined Dai-Ichi Kangyo Bank, Fuji Bank, and the Industrial Bank of Japan, have used the holding company structure. The newly established share exchange system also appears popular; one source lists seventeen such transactions in 1999 and another twenty-five in the first six months of 2000, involving such firms as Sony, Matsushita, Isuzu, and Toyota.[43] In the first fiscal year that spinoffs were legal, more than 200 such transactions occurred, including several combinations that would have not been undertaken absent the change.[44]

Although Mergerstat data for the United States remain considerably higher than the Japanese data, the gap shows signs of narrowing. Mergerstat shows a huge increase in U.S. M&A activity, from 2,997 transactions in 1994 to 9,278 in 1999, with a corresponding increase in transaction value from $226 billion in 1994 to $1.42 trillion in 1999. The U.S. market, in other words, was three to five times larger in 1999 than in 1994. The Japanese market, by contrast, grew by more than ten times during the same period. The increase may also be seen relative to gross domestic product. As noted above, in 1990 Japanese merger activity was approximately 0.4 percent of GDP. In 1999, Japanese merger activity was approximately 3.3 percent of GDP. In the Thomson Financial ranking of targets by nation, Japan moved from a 0.6 percent market share in 1997 to a fifth-place 4.5 percent market share in 1999, and to 5.5 percent in the first quarter of 2002.

2. Tender offer data   Tender offers likewise surged in the 1990s. Although only three tender offers were consummated in the 1970s and 1980s, by our count, sixty-four tender offers were made in the 1990s. The average annual transaction value rose from approximately ¥30 billion ($300 million) in 1994 to nearly ¥250 billion ($2.5 billion) in 1999.[45] Although these measures continue to pale in comparison to the U.S. figure of 799 completed tender offers for the same period,[46] it is apparent that significant increases in tender offer activity have recently occurred in Japan.

C. New Forms of Governance?

It is too early to document fundamental changes in organizational heterogeneity among Japanese firms, and we acknowledge the imprecision of the data available at this stage. Still, incremental changes in at least five areas are preliminary indications of potentially more fundamental future trends toward diversity. Although many factors contributed to the changes detailed below, their form and timing suggest interrelations both with institutional changes and with the increased merger activity that those changes engendered.

1. Boards of directors In the mid-1990s, many companies began to consider altering the composition of their boards through a reduction in size and the inclusion of outside directors. Survey data show an increase in firms displaying particular interest in reducing the number of directors from 28.6 percent to 46.2 percent from 1998 to 2000.[47] Of the firms reducing their boards, 79.9 percent scaled back to fewer than ten directors. By May 2001, 38.8 percent of first-section Tokyo Stock Exchange firms had added outside directors to their boards.[48] Moreover, diversity among board members is beginning to draw attention as a desirable distinguishing characteristic for Japanese firms.[49]

2. Officers Beginning in 1997, many corporations, in concert with reductions in board size, added a new corporate governance organ: the executive officer. Executive officers, an organ not formally authorized by the Commercial Code until 2002, have decisionmaking power but were not subject to derivative suit liability in the same manner as directors. Executive officers went from being a Sony innovation in 1997 to a fixture at over 200 firms by 1999. Survey data confirm that 71.4 percent of responding firms had adopted such a mechanism.[50]

Additional changes may soon be seen at the CEO level. Due in part to the success of Brazilian-born auto executive Carlos Ghosn of Renault in reviving Nissan Motor Company, other firms have appointed foreigners to top positions. Many Japanese companies have begun the "search for the perfect Ghosn clone."[51]

3. Cross-shareholding Cross-shareholding ratios, which began to decline in the early 1990s, reached an all-time low in 2000,[52] down from 18.39 percent by value (14.52 percent by number of shares) in 1987 to 10.64 percent (10.10 percent) in 2000. The long-term holding ratio, which includes not only confirmed cross-holdings but also one-sided stable shareholdings involving financial institutions, also reached new lows in 2000, falling from 45.77 percent by value (43.36 percent by number of shares) to 33.0 percent (31.34 percent) in 2000.

The decline in cross-shareholding reflects the erosion of one important practice that bred conformity in several areas of corporate conduct. More significantly, it may lead to further innovations in corporate governance as individual firms respond to a variety of new stakeholders, some of which will emerge as acquisitions become possible. In light of these changes, the managing director of the Federation of Economic Organizations (Keidanren) has called for further corporate and securities law revisions to reflect the "diversification of financial supply," characterized by such newly invigorated sources as venture capital.[53]

4. Employment relations Intriguing evidence on increased diversity in employment relations is provided by researchers Christina L. Ahmadjian and Gregory Robbins.[54] Ahmadjian and Robbins found statistically significant correlations between levels of foreign ownership and changes in downsizing, asset divestiture, and gross executive bonuses during the periods 1975–81 and 1991–97. Although the primary independent variable in their study was foreign ownership and not merger activity per se, these findings tentatively suggest that an active market for corporate control that includes cross-border acquisitions would further increase the type and range of corporate practices in Japan. The findings on downsizing and divestiture are particularly interesting because corporate norms are said to constrain such actions by Japanese managers.

5. Corporate practices As the work of Ahmadjian and Robbins suggests, firms with substantial foreign investment are more likely to deviate from conventional Japanese governance practices. As a crude test of this hypothesis, we compared the corporate governance characteristics of two sets of firms: (*a*) The eleven Tokyo Stock Exchange first-section firms listed by NLI Research Institute as having a shareholding ratio of foreigners by net investment in excess of 33 percent, and (*b*) the twenty-five public Japanese firms identified by Daiwa Research Institute as the top candidates for takeover.[55]

We examined four corporate governance measures: Number of directors, number of outside directors, number of executive officers, and the filing of a derivative suit against directors.[56] The results are provided in Table 7.2.

Although caution is obviously required in interpreting data from such a small sample, as Table 7.2 shows, firms with substantial foreign ownership are much more likely to have outside directors, to separate monitoring and decisionmaking functions through use of the executive officer system, and to be free of shareholder derivative litigation. Recent case studies also suggest that Japanese firms are becoming more responsive to foreign investors, even if takeovers remain difficult.[57]

Other evidence also suggests a proliferation of approaches to corporate governance:

Outside advisers. By the late 1990s, not only had firms begun to actively seek outside consulting advice, that advice came from more varied sources. In 2001, foreign investment banks such as Goldman Sachs dominated the Thomson Financial league tables, comprising six of the top ten financial advisers of announced deals involving Japanese targets, and eight of the top ten advisers in

Table 7.2. *Corporate governance characteristics*

Measure	>33% Foreign firms	Takeover-likely firms
Average number of directors	14.9	13.5
Percentage of firms with fewer than 15 directors	73	76
Average number of outside directors	0.9	0.56
Percentage of firms with outside directors	45	28
Average number of executive officers	4.8	0
Percentage of firms with executive officers	18	0
Percentage of firms with directors as derivative suit defendants	0	16

deals with Japanese targets, acquirers, or ultimate parents. While Japanese players like Nomura continue to be strong, foreign advice is significant because foreign investment banks currently appear to be a principal device by which new governance technology is transmitted in Japan.

Dividends. Although most companies continue to base dividends on share par value, considerable variation has arisen. In 1990, 24.7 percent of Tokyo Stock Exchange companies issued dividends of ¥5 per share. In 1999, that figure had fallen to 16.3 percent. The percentage of companies issuing dividends between ¥5 and ¥10 per share fell from 90 percent to 63.7 percent. The change in distribution cannot be attributed entirely to economic downturn; although the percentage of companies issuing no dividends rose from 7.7 percent to 20.5 percent, the percentage of companies issuing dividends of more than ¥10 per share rose from 23.7 percent to 30 percent for the same period.[58] More companies are also issuing dividends on a consolidated basis.[59]

Share repurchases. In 1995, a total of five companies implemented share repurchases. In 1998, following Commercial Code revisions, 1,179 companies announced buybacks, and 186 implemented them in that year.[60] Buybacks by listed companies in fiscal 2001 exceeded ¥2.3 trillion (about $20 billion) for over two billion shares, an increase of nearly 100 percent over fiscal 2000.[61]

Shareholders' meetings. Although most firms continue to hold their meetings on the same Thursday in June, some limited variation has begun to occur. As we saw in our discussion of sokaiya, the percentage of Tokyo Stock Exchange firms holding their meetings on that date fell to 68 in 2003. In part because of increased shareholder activism, and in part because of increased pressure from the courts,[62] the length and conduct of meetings have begun to vary. While 83.6 percent of firms in 1990 ended their meetings in less than 30 minutes, only 57.8 percent of firms did so in 2000.[63] Although not tremendous changes, these data at least tentatively suggest erosion of previously homogeneous practices.

Case studies. Anecdotally, there is also growing evidence that foreign acquisitions are inspiring innovations in many areas of corporate practice in Japan. Consider two brief examples among many:

1. Mazda, under Ford control, modified the widely used "*ringi*" corporate decisionmaking approach, in which proposals proceed up a long, formal ladder of managerial approvals. The number of approvals was reduced to three from more than twenty, and the entire process was transferred to the Internet.[64]
2. AXA, the French insurance group, "totally transformed" failing Japanese life insurer Nippon Dantai by eschewing the asset stripping approach followed by U.S. rivals in Japan and reorganizing the firm from within. It hired a new team of managers who had been successful in a wide array of industries including commercial banking, automotives, and Silicon Valley high tech. Within one year of the acquisition, new clients were up 28 percent, premiums were up 5 percent, and AXA's name recognition in Japan increased from 9 percent to 50 percent.[65]

These examples are particularly interesting because the acquirer's success appears to derive from the application of fresh ideas to existing Japanese practices, rather than wholesale adoption of foreign management concepts.

D. The Reality of Reform

Many academic and other observers doubt the effectiveness of legal reforms in altering Japanese corporate behavior.[66] More generally, commentators, asserting cultural or other reasons, voice skepticism that legal change is effective in Japan and doubt the utility of the government's recent reform efforts.[67]

The evidence presented here, however, suggests that such pervasive skepticism may be unwarranted. We have shown that in M&A, as in other areas of corporate governance, actors in Japan respond voraciously to changes in their legal and transaction cost environments. Some of the increase in M&A activity is plainly attributable to macroeconomic factors, as distressed firms are sold at bargain prices. This type of activity presumably will decline once the most troubled companies have been restructured. But evidence suggesting a broader opening of the market for corporate control does exist. While distress was present in one-third of the largest Japanese deals in the first half of 2001, the other two-thirds were motivated by globalization and consolidation trends.[68]

Four informal indications of a broader development of the market can also be found. First, hostile takeover attempts for firms that could not be characterized as financially troubled have been made in the 2000s, including one purely domestic bid. Second, many investment banks are no longer discouraging foreign clients from hostile bids. Third, large numbers of Japanese managers are seeking professional advice on defensive measures. Finally, in a move that some analysts expect to have lasting impact, New York-based Ripplewood Holdings LLC, the first non-Japanese investor to buy a Japanese bank, successfully pried open Japan's historically tight M&A finance market in 2003, securing a record ¥260 billion ($2.6 billion) for the takeover of Japan Telecom.[69] Anecdotal though it may be, this evidence suggests a potential social norm shift, as Japanese corporate actors begin to view takeovers as a viable and enduring part of the landscape. These developments, taken together with the formulation of major reforms to the Commercial Code, including provisions allowing the adoption of "U.S. style" board structures featuring independent committees in lieu of the traditional statutory auditor, indicate that the corporate governance environment in Japan, and the social norms than underlie it, have been altered to a degree that would have been unimaginable just five years ago.

The implications of these developments extend beyond corporate governance. The nascent market for corporate control also portends changes in traditional patterns of lawmaking and enforcement, buttressing our claim that deal structure and legal development are intimately linked. Commercial Code amendment and interpretation have long been the province of a small group of legal scholars and Ministry of Justice officials, who convened advisory committees to study—often for years—the propriety of potential amendments. Under this process, the law changed, but at a snail's pace and seldom in response to the exigencies of market transactions—"theory pushed," rather than "demand pulled" reform.[70] Directorial duties to investors, particularly in respect to contests for control, remain largely untested and unclear. But as commentators have remarked, "[i]f hostile M&A is coming to Japan, it is only [a matter of] time before its courts will answer such questions."[71] There is already substantial debate among legal scholars and practitioners over the permissible scope of defensive measures, including the new poison pill mentioned above. As these issues are eventually addressed through litigation and legal innovation, it seems inevitable that the Japanese courts will assume a more prominent role in corporate law development.

V. IMPLICATIONS

In this section, we briefly examine the implications of our findings for two prevalent perspectives on comparative corporate governance: "Law and finance" theory and the "functional substitutes" theory.

A. Takeovers and Investor Protections

The "law and finance" theory advanced in a series of empirical works by Rafael La Porta, Florencio Lopez-de-Silanes, Andrei Shleifer, and Robert Vishny ("LLSV"), predicts that the quality of legal protections for minority shareholders is an important determinant of share ownership patterns and capital market size.[72] Because takeovers are more likely to occur in countries where shares are widely dispersed and capital markets are large, all else being equal, the "law and finance" logic appears to dictate that countries with good legal protections for investors would have more takeover activity.[73] But we argued above that economic success depends in part on matching governance technologies to firms, not on abiding by one-size-fits-all rules. We also argued that corporate law that is too protective of minority shareholders (or at least law that favors formal procedural protections over disclosure and self-help) could stifle the market for corporate control and limit the gains from diversity in corporate governance. Because both claims are in tension with the imputed predictions of the LLSV model, we move beyond Japan to explore the correlation between legal regimes and M&A activity in the global context.

Following the LLSV methodology, we constructed a series of regressions of corporate control market measures on estimates of the quality of investor protection and several control variables. LLSV used such factors as ownership concentration and stock market capitalization as dependent variables. In our regressions, we used as dependent variables two separate measures of the corporate control market: The value of mergers in dollars and the number of merger deals. Our independent variables were identical to the ones used by LLSV in their

1997 regressions: Origin, anti-director rights, and one share equals one vote, GDP growth, the logarithm of real GNP, and the rule of law.

We found a marginally significant positive correlation for anti-director rights to merger value, and a significantly positive correlation to merger deals. To determine what was driving this correlation, we then disaggregated "anti-director rights" into its five subsidiary components: One share equals one vote, proxy-by-mail, shares blocked before meeting, cumulative voting, oppressed minorities mechanism, and percentage of share capital to call an extraordinary shareholders' meeting. We found that the positive correlation for anti-director rights appears to be driven almost exclusively by the cumulative voting variable, which is positive and significant. All other correlations were insignificant, and several were negative–including oppressed minorities mechanisms.

We have no definitive explanation for the correlation between cumulative voting and merger activity. We can theorize some possible reasons,[74] but the fundamental point of this exercise is not determining causation, it is that the relation between corporate activity and law is not easily expressed. LLSV and the genre of literature they inspired link the quality of law to relatively static phenomena–shareholding patterns and the size of a country's capital markets. But when M&A, a fundamental corporate transaction and a more fluid phenomenon, is examined, the relationship between the legal environment and corporate outcomes becomes much more complex. In the rest of the world as in Japan, a "high quality" institutional environment for the efficient transfer of corporate assets cannot be equated simply with statutory protections for minority investors.

B. Functional Substitutes in Comparative Corporate Governance Theory

The "functional substitutes" theory holds that all national corporate governance systems must basically solve the same set of problems, and functional substitutes exist across systems as means to solve this problem set. Accordingly, for over a decade, the conventional wisdom has held that "bank oversight replaces the market for corporate control in Japan."[75]

Our analysis, however, has suggested a serious problem with the conventional wisdom. The data show that many Japanese firms ripe for takeover, in fact, do not attract the attention of main banks. Thus, main bank-led restructurings are not a perfect substitute for an efficient market for corporate control. More centrally for our purposes, we have presented evidence suggesting that the market for corporate control is not simply a monitoring device; it is also a port of entry for outsiders with new perspectives on the firm, and an engine for legal innovation that displaces inefficient norms. Main banks, with their deep ties to conventional corporate and regulatory practices, simply cannot provide these benefits.

Just as bank monitoring cannot fully substitute for the market for corporate control, cross-shareholding is an imperfect substitute for takeover defenses formally based on a country's corporate law. By definition, informal, relationship-based defenses such as cross-shareholding are impervious to legal challenge.

As a result, they persist in isolation from judicial review, no matter how damaging to shareholders or other stakeholder interests, even if their sole purpose is management entrenchment. Law does not readily adapt to market imperatives, and the transaction costs of doing deals remain high.

CONCLUSION

In this chapter, we have posited that diversity in corporate governance is a virtue, and that the market for corporate control, far from being exclusively a monitoring mechanism, is useful in increasing diversity within economic systems and within firms. We have explored this new perspective through a detailed examination of new data on Japanese markets and institutions. We find that historically, the institutionally determined lack of M&A in Japan is integrally linked to a homogeneous corporate governance environment.

Notwithstanding the predictions of skeptics who doubt the efficacy of Japanese legal change, reform of "institutions for deals" in Japan is helping to transform the corporate landscape. These developments may lead to more effective monitoring of Japanese management. Perhaps even more importantly, M&A may spawn managerial and legal innovations incubated in the clash of perspectives between bidder and incumbent that motivates the takeover attempt. Although far from conclusive, the recent evidence suggests that increased organizational diversity may indeed be on Japan's horizon.

NOTES

1. Masahiko Aoki, Keizai Shisutemu no Shinka to Tagensei [Evolution and Diversity of Economic Systems] 30 (1995); Harold Demsetz and Kenneth Lehn, The Structure of Corporate Ownership: Causes and Consequences, 93 J. Pol. Econ. 1155 (1985). See also Masahiko Aoki, Information, Corporate Governance, and Institutional Diversity: Competitiveness in Japan, the USA, and the Transitional Economies 18 (2000) (translated by Stacey Jehlik); id., An Evolving Diversity of Organizational Mode and Its Implications for Transitional Economies, 9 J. Japn. & Int'l Econ. 330 (1995).

2. Glenn R. Carroll and Michael T. Hannan, The Demography of Corporations and Industries xx–xxii, 2, 8 (2000); Lu Hong and Scott E. Page, Problem Solving by Heterogeneous Agents, 97 J. Econ. Theory 123 (2001).

3. We are using the term "corporate governance" to mean the range of formal and informal mechanisms by which corporate decisions are made, monitored, and effected. It is the structural environment for corporate decisionmaking. "Diversity" for our purposes means "differences in problem solvers' perspectives and heuristics—variations in how people encode and search for solutions to problems." Lu Hong and Scott E. Page, Diversity and Optimality 2 (unpublished working paper, 1998). The literature suggests that two types of corporate governance diversity are beneficial: Inter-firm diversity, as firms or industries select the governance tools most appropriate to their competitive environment, and intra-firm diversity, as boards and other key decisionmaking units draw upon a range of problem solvers. Corporate governance diversity, then, cannot be confined to a single metric, but instead refers to variation not only in

structural features such as board size and composition, but also in such areas as methods of finance, stakeholder relations, and decisionmaking processes.

4. Demsetz and Lehn, *supra* note 1.

5. Aoki, Information, *supra* note 1.

6. Carroll and Hannan, *supra* note 2, at xx–xxii, 2, 8.

7. Hong and Page, *supra* note 3; id., *supra* note 2, at 17.

8. Stuart A. Kauffman, The Origins of Order: Self-organization and Selection in Evolution (1993).

9. Oliver E. Williamson, The Mechanisms of Governance 102 (1996).

10. Harold Demsetz, The Structure of Ownership and the Theory of the Firm, 26 J. L. & Econ. 375 (1983).

11. Demsetz and Lehn, *supra* note 1, at 161. Though not addressed by Demsetz and Lehn, achieving intra-firm diversity is likely hobbled by collective action problems among shareholders. While a diverse board may be efficient, shareholders might lack the information needed accurately to match board composition with the firm's decision-making needs. See Lucian Ayre Bebchuk and Mark J. Roe, A Theory of Path Dependence in Corporate Ownership and Governance, 52 Stan. L. Rev. 127, 167 (1999).

12. Aoki, Information, *supra* note 1, at 131.

13. Gerald F. Davis, Agents without Principles? The Spread of the Poison Pill through the Intercorporate Network, 36 Admin. Sci. Q. 583 (1991); Neil Filgstein, The Spread of the Multidivisional Form among Large Firms, 1919–79, 50 Am. Soc. Rev. 377 (1985); Bruce H. Kobayashi and Larry E. Ribstein, Evolution and Spontaneous Uniformity: Evidence from the Evolution of the Limited Liability Company, 34 Econ. Inquiry 464 (1996); Mark S. Mizruchi, Similarity of Political Behavior among Large American Corporations, 95 Am. J. Soc. 401 (1989).

14. Frank H. Easterbrook and Daniel R. Fischel, The Economic Structure of Corporate Law (1991); Micheal C. Jensen and Richard S. Ruback, The Market for Corporate Control: The Scientific Evidence, 11 J. Fin. Econ. 5 (1983); Henry G. Manne, Mergers and the Market for Corporate Control, 73 J. Pol. Econ. 110 (1965). Several non-agency cost explanations have also been offered, but these focus on synergy gains (see Bernard Black and Joseph Grundfest, Shareholder Gains from Takeovers and Restructuring Between 1981 and 1986, 1 J. App. Corp. Fin. 5 (1988); Roberta Romano, A Guide to Takeovers: Theory, Evidence and Regulation, 9 Yale J. Regulation 119 (1992)) or market failures (see Easterbrook and Fischel, *supra*, at 1751–85). Perhaps the closest analog to our diversity perspective is the view of takeovers as an "equilibrating" or "adaptive" mechanism that is engaged when technological change alters the efficient boundaries of the firm, making a reshuffling of assets economically desirable. Ronald Gilson, The Political Ecology of Takeovers: Thoughts on Harmonizing the European Corporate Governance Environment, 61 Ford. L. Rev. 161 (1992).

15. We do not argue that diversity always leads to optimal, or even necessarily efficient, results. As Hong and Page, *supra* note 3, note, diversity of problem solvers may be problematic if people disagree on outcomes, miscommunicate, or have differing incentive structures. Moreover, while diversity may contribute to success, it may also be the cause of failed mergers in specific cases.

16. Of 126 Tokyo Stock Exchange firm M&A between 1992 and 1995, seventy-seven, or 61.1%, were combinations of a parent and a subsidiary (see Katsuya Yamazaki, Jōjō Kaisha no Saikin no Gappei, Eigyō Jōto tō ni kansuru Jittai Chōsa [Survey of Recent

Corporate Mergers and Acquisitions], 1405 Shōji Hōmu 25, 30 (1995). By our count, fifty-three of the 126 combinations were between firms with elements of the same name. Unlike the German situation (see Julian Franks and Colin Mayer, Ownership and Control of German Corporations, available at www.ssrn.com (2002)), we find no evidence in Japan of large block trades substituting for the market for corporate control.

17. Yamazaki, *supra* note 16.
18. Calculated using Thomson Financial data and GDP measures from the Japanese Economic Planning Agency.
19. Calculated using Mergerstat data and GDP measures from the US Bureau of Economic Analysis.
20. Thomson Financial, Merger Yearbook.
21. Jorg Raupach-Sumiya, Growing M&A Activities and their Impact on Japan's Corporate System (slides from presentation of the German Institute for Japanese Studies at the University of Tokyo, June 5, 2000).
22. Davis Global Advisors, Leading Corporate Governance Indicators 2000, 67–9 (2001).
23. Id., *supra* note 22, at 64.
24. Christian Kirchner and Richard W. Painter, Towards a European Modified Business Judgment Rule for Takeover Law, 2 Eur. Bus. Org. L. Rev. 353 (2000).
25. See Hideki Kanda, Developments in Japanese Securities Regulation: An Overview, 29 Int'l Law 599 (1995).
26. Misao Tatsuta, Proxy Regulation, Tender Offers, and Insider Trading, in Louis Loss et al., eds., (1983) Japanese Securities Regulation 178–9.
27. Id.
28. Hideki Kanda, Comparative Corporate Governance Country Report: Japan, in Comparative Corporate Governance: The State of the Art and Emerging Research 921 (Klaus J. Hopt et al., eds., 1998).
29. Japan External Trade Organization (JETRO), Trends in Japan's M&A Market 84–5 (2000).
30. See, for example, *Shūwa K. K. v. K. K. Chūjitsuya*, Tokyo District Court, 1317 Hanrei Jihō 28 (July 25, 1989) (voiding target management's white knight stock placement as unfair where "primary purpose" of issuance was to dilute holdings of bidder and to maintain control over the company).
31. Martin Lipton and Paul K. Rowe, Pills, Polls and Professors: A Reply to Professor Gilson, 27 Del. J. Corp L. 1 (2002).
32. Shōji Hōmu Kenkyūkai, Shikkō Yakuin Seido ni Kansuru Ankeeto Shūkei Kekka [Summary of Results of Survey Regarding Executive Officers], 182 Shiryōban Shōji Hōmu 79 (1990).
33. Jon Choy, Japanese Executives Still Not Sharing with Shareholders, JEI Report, July 12, 1996.
34. See John M. Abowd and David S. Kaplan, Executive Compensation: Six Questions that Need Answering, 13 Journal of Economic Perspectives 145, 146 (1999).
35. Yoshio Nakamoto, Shōhō Zenmen Kaisei e no Kihontekina Shiten [Basic Views on Commercial Code Revision], 1574 Shōji Hōmu 17 (1998).
36. Zenkoku Shōken Torihikijo Kyōgikai, Kigyō Gyōseki oyobi Haitō no Jōkyō [The Status of Corporate Performance and Dividends] (2000).
37. In 1988, Japan had only 8,000 CPAs, compared to approximately 250,000 in the United States and 65,000 in the United Kingdom (see Robert J. Ballon and Iwao

204 Economic Organizations and Corporate Governance in Japan

Tomita, The Financial Behavior of Japanese Corporations 170 (1988). In the same year, all major Japanese banks and securities houses combined had a total of only 338 M&A staff (see Carl W. Kester, Japanese Takeovers: The Global Contest for Corporate Control 9 (1991)).

38. Stephen Prowse, Corporate Governance: Emerging Issues and Lessons from East Asia. World Bank Group Paper (2000).
39. *Source*: Nomura Research Institute. Bust-up value is defined as cash and cash equivalents + investment securities − short and long-term debt. Calculated for 779 non-financial Tokyo Stock Exchange Firms as of November 2000.
40. Charles Smith, In Japan, M&A accelerates, but hurdles remain, The Daily Deal, Jan. 3, 2002, available in LEXIS.
41. Michael E. Porter et al., Can Japan Compete? 78–91 (2000).
42. Record 463 Firms Offer Stock Options, Daily Yomiuri, June 19, 2001, at 14.
43. Masatoshi Kikuchi, TOB, Kaisha Bunkatsu ni yoru M&A Senryaku [M&A Strategy: Takeovers and Spin-offs] 118–19 (2000).
44. Kaisha Bunkatsu: 1 nen de 200 ken [200 Spin-Offs in One Year], Nihon Keizai Shinbun, Mar. 31, 2002; Kaisha ha Kōshite Henshin Saseru [This is How Corporations Will be Changed], Shūkan Tōyō Keizai, Apr. 6, 2002, at 42, 43–5.
45. Kikuchi, *supra* note 43, at 36.
46. Mergerstat, Mergerstat Review 39 (2000).
47. Tokyo Shōken Torihikijo, Kooporeeto Gabanansu ni Kansuru Ankeeto no Chōsa Kekka ni Tsuite [Results of Corporate Governance Survey] (Nov. 30, 2000).
48. Shagai Torishimariyaku 38% ga Sennin [38% Choose Outside Directors], Nihon Keizai Shinbun, June 16, 2001, at 1.
49. Diversity Distinguishes IY Bank, Nikkei Weekly, June 11, 2001, at 13.
50. Shōji Hōmu Kenkyūkai, Shikkō Yakuin Seido ni Kansuru Ankeeto Shūkei Kekka [Summary of Results of Survey Regarding Executive Officers], 182 Shiryōban Shōji Hōmu 26 (1999).
51. Miki Tanakawa, Imitating Mr. Ghosn in Japan, New York Times, May 20, 2001, at Section 3, page 2.
52. Nissei Kiso Kenkyūjo, Kabushiki Mochiai Jōkyō Chōsa 2000 nendo Ban [2000 Cross-Shareholding Survey] (2001).
53. Yoshio Nakamura, Shōhō Zenmen Kaisei e no Kihontekina Shiten [Basic Views on Commercial Code Revision], 1574 Shōji Hōmu 17, 20 (2000).
54. Christina L. Ahmadjian and Gregory Robbins, A Convergence of Capitalism? Foreign Shareholders and the Spread of Investor Capitalism to Japan, unpublished working paper (2000).
55. Masatoshi Kikuchi, TOB Sareyasui Kigyō 25sha [25 Easily Taken-over Companies], Ekonomisuto, Mar. 14, 2000, at 60–2. The Daiwa rankings are determined strictly by an accounting formula that does not take into account corporate governance factors: (cash − long term securities − sales × 5% + investment securities (not including those of affiliates) + unrealized capital gains on stock × 60% + land × 50% + unrealized capital gains on land × 30% − interest-bearing debt)/price.
56. The first three factors are from Nihon Keizai Shinbunsha, Kaisha Nenkan [Corporate Yearbook] (2000). Derivative suit information is from lists in 202 Shiryōban Shōji Hōmu 178 (2001).
57. See Jason Singer, Bridgestone Provides Case Study in Japan's Liberalization, Wall Street Journal, May 30, 2001, at A19.

58. Zenkoku Shōken Torihikijo Kyōgikai, *supra* note 36.
59. See Kigyō no Haitō Renketsu Be-su ni Henshin, Keiei to Shōhō no Mujun Kaishō [Companies Changing to Consolidated Dividends, Eliminating Contradiction Between Management and Commercial Code], Nihon Keizai Shinbun, June 12, 2001, at 17.
60. Takahiro Yasui, Corporate Governance in Japan, OECD Paper, Mar. 3, 1999, at 26; Hua Zhang, Share Repurchases in Japan: Market Reaction and Actual Implementation, unpublished working paper, available at www.efmaefm.org/hzhang.pdf.
61. Jisha Kabu Kai Baizō, 2 Chō Enchō [Share Repurchases Double to Exceed 2 trillion], Nihon Keizai Shinbun, April 28, 2002, at 1.
62. See *Takashi* v. *Shikoku Denryoku*, 1440 Shōji Hōmu 39, Supreme Court, Nov. 12, 1996 (finding practice of seating employees in front to regulate meeting times to be unlawful).
63. Shōji Hōmu Kenkyūkai, Kabunushi Sōkai Hakusho [White Paper on Shareholders' Meetings] 1234 Shōji Hōmu 3 (1990);. Shōji Hōmu Kenkyūkai, Kabunushi Sōkai Hakusho [White Paper on Shareholders' Meetings], 1579 Shōji Hōmu 3 (2000).
64. Mark Fields, Remarks of President of Mazda Motor Corporation, at Columbia University, Mar. 23, 2001.
65. Regis Arnaud, Nothing Axa-dental about Success, Far Eastern Economic Review, Mar. 22, 2001, at 48; Francoise Kadri, AXA Builds Up Strength in Japan Despite a Harsh Climate for Insurers, Agence France-Presse, May 28, 2001, available at WL 2415657.
66. Columbia Conference, The New Rhetoric and Realities of Corporate Governance, panel discussion at Corporate Japan: The Beginning of a New Era?, held Mar. 23, 2001; Hilton L. Root. Asia's Bad Old Ways, 80(2) Foreign Affairs 9 (2001).
67. Philip Lochner, Corporate Japan: Beginning of a New Era?, Conference held at Columbia University, Mar. 23, 2001.
68. Gary Stead, Remarks at ACCJ, Tokyo, June 18, 2001.
69. Ripplewood hired seven investment banks as advisors and convinced normally reluctant lenders to finance the LBO with a strategy mastered in the United States by Kohlberg Kravis Roberts: The payment of "near-record" fees. Jason Singer, Buyout May Boost Market for Financing Deals in Japan, Wall Street Journal, Aug. 18, 2003, at C1, C9.
70. Zenichi Shishido, Reform in Japanese Corporate Law and Corporate Governance: Current Changes in Historical Perspective, unpublished working paper (1999).
71. Anthony E. Zaloom and Kanako Muraoka, Judgment Call Asian M&A: Go With What Works, The Daily Deal, May 15, 2000, at 15.
72. Rafael La Porta et al., Legal Determinants of External Finance, 52 J. Fin. 1131 (1997); id., Law and Finance, NBER Working Paper 5661 (1996); id., Law and Finance, 106 J. Pol. Econ. 1113 (1998); id., Corporate Ownership Around the World, 54 J. Fin. 471 (1999).
73. This interpretation of LLSV is consistent with Mario Pagano and Paolo Volpin, The Political Economy of Corporate Governance. CSEF Working Paper No. 29 (2000). We find the opposite implication from the LLSV research—that takeovers would be rare where legal protections are good because they force managers to operate firms in an efficient and shareholder-regarding manner—far less plausible.
74. Cumulative voting enables minority shareholders to elect their own representatives, and those representatives are more likely than other board members to seek or respond to takeover bids. Another possible explanation is that firms with cumulative

voting have relatively weak boards. Weak boards could conceivably lead to more merger activity, either because the market for corporate control tends to replace weak managers, or because those managers lack shareholder backing to maintain effective defensive devices. Alternatively, the correlation may be affected by some lurking or confounding variable not included in our regressions, or it may even be spurious. Empirical evidence that could lead to a firmer conclusion is lacking.

75. Jonathan R. Macey and Geoffrey P. Miller, Corporate Governance and Commercial Banking: A Comparative Analysis of Germany, Japan, and the United States, 48 Stan. L. Rev. 73, 81 (1995). A significant exception was Gilson and Roe, who qualified the conventional wisdom by pointing out that main banks may not constrain the waste of free cash flow as well as hostile takeovers. Ronald J. Gilson and Mark J. Roe, Understanding the Japanese Keiretsu: Overlaps Between Corporate Governance and Industrial Organization, 102 Yale L. J. 871 (1993).

8

Lawyers and Bureaucrats

INTRODUCTION

Many scholars and journalists who cover Japan have long claimed that the bureaucracy rules the Japanese economy. The most famous expression of this claim is Chalmers Johnson's depiction of Japan as a "plan rational state" led by capable bureaucrats, as opposed to a "regulatory, or market rational state" such as the United States. Consider Johnson's distinction:

In Japan the [elite economic] . . . agencies attract the most talented graduates of the best universities in the country, and the positions of higher-level officials in these ministries have been and still are the most prestigious in the society . . . [T]he elite bureaucracy of Japan makes most major decisions, drafts virtually all legislation, controls the national budget, and is the source of all major policy innovations in the system. Equally important, upon retirement, . . . these bureaucrats move from government to powerful positions in private enterprise . . .

In market rational systems such as the United States, public service does not normally attract the most capable talent, and national decision-making is dominated by elected members of the professional class, who are usually lawyers, rather than by the bureaucracy.[1]

The supposed prominence of bureaucrats during Japan's economic heyday implicates a broader question, one to which a large literature is devoted: The relationship between lawyers and economic growth. A decade ago, economists produced a spate of statistical research indicating that lawyers (and implicitly law) are a drag on the economy, and bad for society to boot. For example, Stephen Magee, William Brock, and Leslie Young (Magee et al.) asked whether "redistributive lawyering reduces GNP growth rates."[2] They found a negative correlation between the ratio of lawyers per doctor (used to normalize countries at different stages of development) and the growth of GNP per capita for a sample of thirty-five countries for the period 1969–80, and conclude that the answer is a resounding yes. Economists Kevin Murphy, Andrei Shleifer, and Robert Vishny (Murphy et al.) sought to test the talent-diversion theory more directly by examining the ratios of law students and engineering students to total college population across a large sample of countries.[3] They found that economic growth was negatively correlated to the law student ratio and positively correlated to the engineering student ratio. They conclude "lawyers are indeed bad, and engineers good, for growth" because "if law is an attractive major, the quality of rent seekers is higher, and hence, indirectly, the quality of entrepreneurs is lower, and technological progress and income growth are smaller."[4] Even some of America's most prominent academic lawyers publicly supported this view.[5]

This research and commentary suggested that societies the world over have a choice: they can nurture engineers and other innovators who produce wealth, or they can churn out lawyers and other rent seekers, who will redistribute wealth and contribute to the complexity and adversarial nature of human interaction. Legal scholars retorted that lawyers, far from functioning as an albatross around the economy's neck, are "transaction cost engineers" who add value to deals by reducing the uncertainties inherent in imperfect market exchanges.[6]

Common to many entries in this debate was reference to Japan. Coincidentally or otherwise, at the height of the academic controversy Japan had few lawyers—fewer than 13,000 in 1985—and a booming economy. For law skeptics, Japan was "Exhibit A, displaying the inverse relation of lawyers to economic vigor."[7] Law agnostics criticized the "armchair comparativists" for drawing simplistic conclusions from the Japanese data.[8] Today, the contours of the lawyer debate have shifted. Over the past several years, a formidable literature has developed around the central idea that the quality of law and its enforcement (which presumably implicates lawyer access and quality) have major effects on such economically central areas as corporate structure, capital formation, and the ability of a system to rebound from exogenous shocks.[9] To date, however, insights from this paradigm shift in economics have not been reflected in the literature on lawyers and economic growth.

As the debate on law has shifted, so too has "Exhibit A" changed—changes that we have tried to illuminate in the preceding chapters of this book. The Japanese economy has suffered an entire decade of low or negative growth, asset deflation, financial crises, and rising unemployment. Financial and other markets have been deregulated, the bureaucracy has suffered considerable setbacks in policy and public opinion, and demand for legal services is growing as the number of corporate transactions and the legal risks of those involved escalate.

In this chapter, we explore the changing roles of law and bureaucratic regulation in Japan during a time of dramatic economic and institutional transformation, by examining changes in the market for legal elites. We define Japanese "legal elites" as the top 200–300 law graduates in a given year who could successfully pursue highly compensated careers in either the upper echelons of the most prestigious ministries (such as the Ministry of Finance, MOF) or in Japan's largest and most prestigious law firms. They are, in short, fast-track career bureaucrats and transactional lawyers. These legal elites, many of whom would have in the past opted for a bureaucratic career, have begun to join the bar in ever-increasing numbers.

Our central claim is that the shift in employment patterns of legal elites is primarily caused by changes to the legal institutions and political economy of Japan, reflecting a conscious move toward more transparent, "law-based" mechanisms of governance. To be sure, the underlying institutional setup in society is not the only factor that affects individual career decisions; idiosyncratic considerations such as the guidance of a mentor, the choices of one's peers, or the desire to follow in (or avoid) a parent's professional footsteps may also be critical in individual cases. Nonetheless, we find considerable evidence that the relative attractiveness of careers in government and law has been affected by new legal rules designed to strengthen market discipline over Japanese firms and to reduce bureaucratic discretion—whether the original source of that discretion was a dominant bureaucracy (as Chalmers Johnson claimed) or in political slack creating room for bureaucratic agents to serve the wishes of their politician principals (as other observers have argued more recently).

In making this claim, we deepen the exploration of two themes that run throughout the book. First, we have argued that institutional design in the form of both formal laws and informal norms and practices provides powerful incentives for human endeavor. In Chapter 6, for example, we showed how various rights-enforcement gaps resulting from Japanese institutional design are filled by the entrepreneurial impulses of organized crime syndicates, in a phenomenon we called "the dark side of private ordering." Here, we show that in analogous fashion, the governance void created by the decline of the Japanese bureaucracy has opened avenues of opportunity for elite lawyers. Although hardened law skeptics may disagree, we view this as a decidedly "bright side" development for private ordering.

Second, throughout the book we have argued that Japan is becoming a more "law-oriented" society. Here, by examining previously unexplored career data on law graduates, we are able to test the validity of this assertion systematically and in a novel fashion. In the process, we also shed new light on the age-old question—Japan: Who Governs?[10]

The chapter proceeds as follows. Section I presents empirics on the career choices of Japanese legal elites. We show that legal elites are forsaking the bureaucracy for law. In Section II, we explain how institutional change underlies this reallocation of talent. Section III analyzes implications from our findings for the debates over Japanese governance and the impact of talent allocation on economic growth.

I. CAREER CHOICES OF LEGAL ELITES

Elite law students in Japan have two basic, and until very recently, mutually exclusive career options: The bureaucracy or the legal profession. Each involves very specific and patterned career paths, marked by admission to law departments of elite public and private universities, cram school preparation, and passage of difficult state-sponsored standardized tests. After briefly describing each stage, we show changing career patterns over time. We present several measures of these changes, and while no single measure alone necessarily captures the phenomenon adequately, the entirety of the data strongly suggest a shift in social stature, authority, and income from the bureaucracy to the bar.

A. The Path of Legal Elites

University students who excel as academics become elite bureaucrats and lawyers by passing through a similar gatekeeper—the standardized test. In this section, we describe the two tests: For lawyers, the bar exam (*shihō shiken*), and for bureaucrats, the civil service exam (*kokka kōmuin isshū shiken*).

1. Lawyers: shihō shiken   With a handful of statutory exceptions, all legal professionals in Japan (i.e. lawyers, judges, and prosecutors) must take and pass the bar examination, which consists of three parts. Part I is a multiple-choice test composed of sixty questions, equally divided among constitutional law, civil law, and criminal law. In 2003, 6,986 of 50,166 candidates (14 percent) passed this 3½-hour test, and thus earned the right to sit for Part II in that year. Part II is the most difficult part of the bar exam, consisting of essays in the fields of constitutional law, civil law, criminal law, commercial law, and civil and criminal procedure. In 2003, 1,201 candidates (2 percent) passed this test, earning the right to sit for Part III that year or the following year. Part III is a four-day oral test of knowledge of constitutional law, civil law, criminal law, and civil and criminal procedure. Candidates spend 15–20 minutes each day fielding questions from two examiners. In 2003, 1,170 candidates (2 percent, about one-fourth of whom are women) passed this portion of the test, making it one of the easier hurdles as a percentage matter (97 percent of Part II passers).[11] Candidates who pass this exam are admitted to the Legal Training and Research Institute (LTRI), where they receive eighteen months of formal legal training before being admitted to the legal profession. Because they are technically classified as civil servants during that period, they are paid a monthly base salary of ¥208,300, or about $30,000 annually including bonuses, by the state.[12]

We have discussed the scarcity of lawyers in Japan and its *negative* consequences in Chapter 6. Suffice it to say that Japan has few lawyers. At the end of 2003 Japan had slightly more than 20,000 lawyers, up from 14,000 in 1990, 11,600 in 1980, and 9,000 in 1970. Even with recent expansion in the ranks of the bar, as of April 2000, of the 253 court districts in Japan, seventy-one were "zero-one districts," with no lawyers or only one, as 75 percent of the bar is concentrated in Tokyo and Osaka.[13] The number of transactional lawyers in large firms remains quite small, perhaps 600–800.[14]

2. Bureaucrats: kokuichi   By definition, all fast-track elite bureaucrats have taken and passed the First-Tier Civil Service Examination. Although the exam is issued in several fields, including such law-related fields as administration and economics, "law dominates. For first-class bureaucrats who expect to rise to the top of the most prestigious agencies, with virtually no exception, the field is law (*hōritsu-shoku*)."[15] The national civil service exam has three tiers, with each tier reflecting a different level of the bureaucracy. For potential elites, however, the first tier is all that matters.

The First-Tier Civil Service Examination, which is divided into two parts, is heavily geared toward testing legal knowledge. Part I is a 3-hour, fifty-five-question multiple-choice test of general knowledge. Twenty-five of the questions test reading comprehension and logic and thirty questions, from which the candidate must choose twenty, test science, literature, and social sciences. Part II is a 3½-hour essay test of legal knowledge, followed by a 2-hour essay test of general knowledge in which the candidate answers one of two questions.[16] After passing the civil service exam, elite ministries make employment decisions based on candidates' national ranking. Unlike bar examinations in the United States, where all that matters is obtaining a score above a predetermined passing threshold, Japanese civil service exam takers compete for the highest scores, for only the best will actually be hired. Hiring is determined by the personnel departments of individual agencies and ministries. In 2000, of 38,841 total candidates for all First-Tier positions, 7,937 candidates took the exam in law, 255 passed, and only 149 eventually were offered and accepted positions (leaving 110 passers without positions). Of these 149, eight went to the MOF, nine to the Ministry of Justice, twenty-six to the Ministry of Public Management, Home Affairs, Posts and Telecommunications, fourteen to the Ministry of Economy, Trade and Industry (METI, formerly known as MITI), and thirteen to the Ministry of Education. We examine hiring trends in the next section.[17]

Passing the exam qualifies a passer for employment at twenty-eight ministries and agencies, but legal elites are primarily only concerned with the most prestigious ministries. The top choices among elite University of Tokyo students are the MOF, METI (the former MITI), the former Ministry of Home Affairs, and the National Police Agency, the so-called "four dynasties." Hiring by these ministries, however, does not necessarily lead to a law-related career. Although legal recruits are trained in and tested on the law, upon arrival at the ministry, they are in fact rotated among departments and not assigned distinctly legal tasks. As Japanese legal scholar Setsuo Miyazawa puts it, "Law graduates are hired essentially because they are considered to be smarter than others."[18]

B. Test Data

In this section, we analyze long-term and recent trends in examination-taking, examination-passing, and employment decisions of young legal elites. We begin by looking at national statistics. To get a more precise understanding of developing phenomena, we then look at data from elite universities. We examine the phenomenon of double-passers before turning to data on quasi-lawyers.

1. National data The nationwide data on the civil service exam and the bar exam show a marked shift. We begin with the data on the bar exam. Figure 8.1 shows the number of individuals who took the bar exam from 1960 to 2002.[19] As the figure shows, with the exception of a slight decrease in takers in the 1980s (when Japan's private sector boomed in the bubble economy), both the

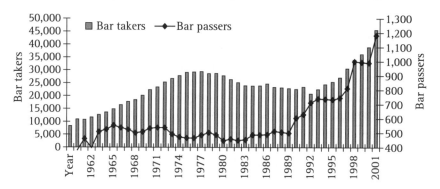

Figure 8.1. *Bar exam takers and passers, 1960–2002*

number of those who took the bar exam and failed and those who took the bar exam and passed have risen significantly over time. The rise in the past decade is particularly significant. In 1991, 22,596 candidates sat for the bar exam. By 1998, that number topped 30,000, and in 2002, the number was 45,622.

The number of passers is determined by a predetermined formula. Prior to 1991, the LTRI admitted approximately 500 students each year. Although the number was firmly grounded in the bar's desire to limit competition, it also reflected the physical constraints of the LTRI, which was said to be capable of housing only 500 students. After 1991, the LTRI gradually raised the number of passers to the approximately 1,000 students that are now admitted. Still, the test remains statistically difficult to pass; because of the increase in takers, the pass rate remains at about 2.5 percent. The average age of passers has fallen from nearly 29 to just over 27 from 1990 to 2002, but even in 2002, 38.5 percent of passers needed more than five years of study to pass.[20] Of 2001 passers, only fifty-three, or 5.4 percent, passed on their first try.[21] Future changes to the system, including a tripling of the annual 1,000 figure and an introduction of U.S.-style graduate law schools, are discussed in Section III.

As the number of bar takers and bar passers has increased, the number of students who sit for and pass the elite civil service exam has fallen.[22] Figure 8.2 shows the number of takers and passers for the twenty-five-year period from 1978 to 2002. As Figure 8.2 shows, the number of exam takers has declined twice in the period. The first decline comes in the late 1980s, as the Japanese bubble economy boomed. This decline roughly tracks the decline in the number of bar takers in the same period (see Figure 8.1), a correlation that strongly suggests that potential test takers of both types chose other profitable careers, at least for the years in question. After the bubble burst, the number of civil service exam takers increased, but not to the level of the early 1980s. The number of takers then declined in 1997, falling to a twenty-five-year low in 1998. Although the number has risen incrementally in the last three years, the average number of takers in 1998–2002 remains much lower than the same figure for the

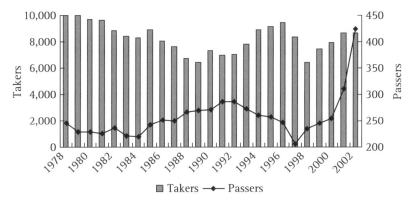

Figure 8.2. *Law civil service exam takers and passers, 1978–2002*

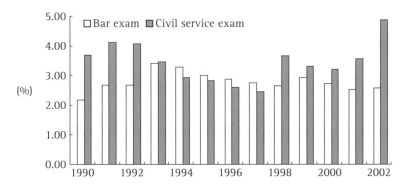

Figure 8.3. *Comparative exam pass rates, 1990–2002*

previous five years. Since the decline comes in the absence of either unusual economic prosperity or a similar downward trend in the bar exam, more complex, and perhaps less transient, forces may be at work. Still, the absence of a definitive long-term trend over the period suggests that additional data examination is necessary, and we do so in the next subsection with university-specific data.

Assuming arguendo that the number of civil service exam takers is decreasing in the long term, fewer persons might opt to take the civil service exam if the pass rate were lower. But the data in Figure 8.3 on civil service exam *passers* suggests that the drop in exam *takers* is not a response to grading, as the number of passers has actually increased steadily, if slightly, since 1997. The post-1997 pass rate is significantly higher than the pass rate for the early 1980s, when the sit rate was high. In fact, as Figure 8.3 shows, in percentage terms, it has become easier to pass the civil service exam than the bar exam. Yet, applicants for the civil service exam do not show the same long-term increase as bar exam applicants.

Table 8.1. *Law hires by elite bureaucracy by exam year*

Exam year	(a) Passers	(b) Hires by spring, 2 years later	(b)/(a)
2000	255	149	58.4
1999	246	145	58.9
1998	235	135	57.4
1997	206	121	58.7
1996	247	158	64.0
1995	258	158	61.2
1994	261	174	66.7
1993	272	164	60.3
1992	286	181	63.3
1991	287	180	62.7
1990	271	176	64.9

The recent and apparent long-term decrease (or at least lack of a long-term increase) in civil service exam takers is also interesting in light of relatively constant employment data. Our interviews with those in hiring suggest that the number of persons that elite ministries wish to hire has remained relatively constant over time. While data on this point are not publicly available, we do have data on actual hires. Table 8.1 shows the number of law-educated persons hired by the elite bureaucracy within the twenty-month period following the exam for each exam year (e.g. data for the 1999 exam year are for hires through March 31, 2000).[23]

As Table 8.1 shows, both the raw number of hires and the number of hires as a percentage of exam passers has fallen in the last decade. But the decrease has been minimal; the raw number hired by 2002 from the 2000 test was only sixteen persons fewer than the figure from the 1990 test. The number of persons eventually hired as a percentage of exam takers remains at about 2 percent. This is only slightly lower than the rate at which candidates pass the bar exam, which virtually guarantees employment.

It is plausible that the small decline in hiring might affect the number of candidates for the exam. Candidates have access to information, as the number of anticipated hires in each category is announced before each year's test. But current university students preparing for the exam told us that they were either unaware of the historical decline or that they considered it unimportant, and in fact the recent slight increase in takers is consistent with that explanation.

Recent developments suggest that the bureaucracy itself views these trends as indicating a decline in popularity of the profession and not a transient phenomenon. Specifically, the bureaucracy has adopted two institutional strategies, and is considering a third, in response to competition from the bar for legal elites. First, until 2000, the Lawyers' Law (art. 30) prohibited attorneys from serving as government employees; the only exceptions were certain enumerated high-level positions such as prime minister. But in response both to increased competition from the bar for high-quality candidates and to the shift to a more law-oriented society, the Diet passed a special law in late 2000 that, among other things, amended the Lawyers' Law to allow lawyers to serve in certain short-term positions of less than five years in the bureaucracy.[24] A handful of lawyers (in 2002, one such lawyer told us that he estimated the number to be five) now work in the elite bureaucracy, primarily in finance-related positions, and the number is expected to increase.

Second, in 2001, in direct response to competition for candidates from the expanding bar, the government introduced a plan to double the number of civil service exam passers.[25] Finally, in spring 2002, the National Personnel Agency and other related entities began to debate a new policy by which a graduate of one of Japan's graduate law schools (which opened in April 2004, see infra) would be given identical standing for hiring purposes as a law civil service exam passer.[26] While it remains unclear how these current and proposed changes might affect career decisions of candidates or hiring decisions of individual ministries and agencies, the direct threat posed by the bar for bureaucratic jobs is apparent.

2. Data from elite institutions   To further investigate the phenomena suggested by the national data, we obtained data from specific elite universities. Over 100 schools offer undergraduate degrees in law. But as suggested above, bar exam takers and passers are dominated by a handful of schools. In 2001, of the 38,930 students sitting for the bar, 19,726, or about half, were from seven schools: Waseda, Chuo, Tokyo, Keio, Meiji, Kyoto, and Doshisha universities.[27] Many law departments have never graduated a single bar-passer, and even prestigious schools might only have a handful of passers. Table 8.2 lists the ten schools with the most bar exam passers in each of 2001, 2000, and 1999.[28]

As Table 8.2 shows, the top ten schools in 2001 accounted for 792 of the 990 passers, or 80 percent, and while the rankings may change, the schools included in the list are unchanged from year to year.

Table 8.2. *Bar exam passers, by university*

School	2001 Passers	2000 Passers	1999 Passers
University of Tokyo (national)	206	198	229
Waseda University (private)	187	140	139
Keio University (private)	100	116	95
Kyoto University (national)	90	108	112
Chuo University (private)	76	102	92
Hitotsubashi University (national)	36	41	46
Osaka University (national)	34	29	28
Meiji University (private)	27	17	21
Jochi University (private)	19	17	28
Doshisha University (private)	17	31	25

Table 8.3. *Law civil service exam passers, by university*

School	2001 Passers	2000 Passers	1999 Passers
University of Tokyo (national)	136	113	106
Waseda University (private)	31	32	26
Kyoto University (national)	28	22	30
Keio University (private)	30	22	16
Hitotsubashi University (national)	11	6	13
Chuo University (private)	9	7	8
Tohoku University (national)	2	7	6
Osaka University (national)	5	6	3
Doshisha University (private)	7	2	5
Ritsumeikan University (private)	8	4	2

As Table 8.3 shows, the civil service exam data show a remarkably similar hierarchy. In 2001, the University of Tokyo accounted for 44 percent of passers, the top four schools accounted for 73 percent, only eighteen schools had more than one passer, and only thirty had *any* passers. These patterns allow us to examine data on two specific schools with a high degree of confidence that they accurately represent a very large percentage of the population of legal elites.

First, we examine the data from the University of Tokyo (commonly referred to as Todai). Todai is widely viewed as the breeding ground for the elite of the elite, and with good reason. Historically, elites have come overwhelmingly from Todai, and admission to Todai, especially its law department, is a virtual guarantee of career success.[29] Because Todai comprises such a large portion of the sample, we asked administrators in the Todai law department to provide us with a list of the number of Todai law students in every year for the past ten years who (*a*) passed the bar exam whether as a student or a graduate, (*b*) passed the bar exam while still a student (possible after two years of university), (*c*) matriculated to the LTRI upon graduation, (*d*) passed the law civil service exam while still a student, or (*e*) entered the bureaucracy upon graduation. The results, from an average graduating class of about 600 to 700, are in Table 8.4.

The data in Table 8.4 are consistent with the nationwide data. Although the trend is perhaps not as readily observable as in the national data, the number of bar exam passers who are Todai graduates has increased over time. The number of Todai students who pass the bar while still enrolled at the university has remained relatively steady over time, a reflection, perhaps, of the difficulty of that feat, or perhaps of recent changes in the grading system.[30] As the LTRI number shows, with some allowance for yearly overlap, almost all passers attend the LTRI upon graduation. One recent survey taken by the Todai campus newspaper shows that the LTRI is now the number one destination of Todai graduates;[31] another shows that more than two-thirds of Todai law students take the exam or plan to do so.[32]

Table 8.4. *Career choices of Todai legal elites, 1991–2000*

Year	Bar examination passers			Law civil service examination passers	
	(a) U of Tokyo	(b) Current U of Tokyo	(c) To LTRI	(d) Current U of Tokyo	(e) To bureaucracy
2000	198	62	60	84	70
1999	229	61	46	97	80
1998	213	79	55	87	72
1997	188	77	62	71	74
1996	181	84	84	126	99
1995	166	52	48	109	99
1994	161	61	56	130	107
1993	137	54	48	149	120
1992	126	53	59	164	133
1991	133	57	50	178	133

If the decline in the popularity of a bureaucratic career were not clear from the national data, the Todai data offer more convincing evidence. Both the number of Todai students passing the civil service exam and the number of students choosing to join the bureaucracy upon graduation have significantly declined over time, and by a magnitude that greatly surpasses the overall national decline shown in Table 8.1. Combining data from Tables 8.1 and 8.4 shows that while 62 percent of passers in 1991 were Todai undergrads, in 1998 the figure was 34 percent, 37 percent in 1999, and 39 percent in 2000. Complementary data from various issues of *Gakunai Kōhō*, Todai's internal weekly newsletter, show a marked decline in the number of law students who upon graduation became "civil servants," including those who take local bureaucratic posts: In 1990, 176 of 619 students, in 1995, 182 of 705, and in 2001, 82 of 601. If, as is often said, Todai law students are the elite of the elite, the bureaucracy is no longer getting the most elite students in anywhere near the numbers it once did.

If hiring practices change over time to favor or disfavor a particular school such as Todai, the above data might be driven not by student choice but by hiring practices. Because there in fact is evidence of political pressure to decrease the number of Todai hires, we gathered additional hiring data. We were able to obtain passing and hiring data from the National Personnel Agency for the 1999, 2000, and 2001 tests on Todai and the second highest-passing school, Waseda University (a private institution). Those data are in Table 8.5.

As Table 8.5 shows, pass rates remained relatively constant for both schools. The percentage of Todai passers (including current students and graduates) hired decreased slightly in the three-year period; but so did the percentage of Waseda passers hired. While again our sample is small and far from definitive, the limited available evidence suggests that occasional political pressures to decrease the number of Todai hires have had little effect, and that the decrease in interest in the bureaucracy that we see at Todai is likely supply-driven, and not demand-driven.

A similar story is seen at Kyoto University (Kyodai). Kyodai is another large national university, second only to Todai in prestige, and the first choice of many students from western and southern Japan. An organization called *Hōyūkai*, analogous to a PTA and affiliated with the Kyoto University Law Department, publishes an annual bulletin in which it notes the employment plans of the previous spring's graduates. Data are compiled by the law department's administration. Table 8.6 lists the career choices for Kyodai legal elites for the period 1992–2002.

Again, Table 8.6 shows results similar to the national and Todai numbers. Those headed toward legal careers comprised only 13 percent of the class in 1992, but 42 percent of the class in 2002. The bureaucrat data are especially striking. In the past, as many as twenty-seven students headed to elite bureaucrat positions. But in 2002, only eleven did, and in 2001, only nine. While caution is, of course, warranted when dealing with such a small number of observations, our discussions with Kyodai faculty lead us to suspect that it is not merely a fluke that recent measures are the lowest in the decade.

Table 8.5. *Law civil service hiring from Todai and Waseda*

Year	Todai			Waseda		
	Takers	Passers (as a % of takers)	Hires (as a % of passers)	Takers	Passers (as a % of takers)	Hires (as a % of passers)
2001	478	136 (28.5)	92 (67.6)	442	31 (7)	13 (41.9)
2000	421	118 (28.0)	85 (72)	388	32 (8.2)	20 (62.5)
1999	388	196 (27.3)	77 (72.6)	409	26 (6.4)	14 (53.8)

Table 8.6. *Career choices of graduating Kyoto University legal elites*

Year	Total graduating	(a) To LTRI	(b) Bar exam study	(a) + (b) (% of total)	To elite bureaucracy (% of total)
2002	413	39	135	174 (42)	11 (3)
2001	435	64	92	156 (36)	9 (2)
2000	418	59	96	155 (37)	21 (5)
1999	385	46	73	117 (28)	16 (4)
1998	384	35	56	91 (26)	25 (7)
1997	428	48	65	113 (24)	23 (5)
1996	424	42	55	97 (23)	23 (5)
1995	417	37	51	88 (21)	27 (6)
1994	392	25	46	71 (18)	22 (6)
1993	421	26	24	50 (12)	27 (6)
1992	408	31	21	62 (13)	24 (6)

3. Double-passers Each year, a handful of overachievers, perhaps about twenty, pass both the civil service test and the bar exam. Taking both tests involves risks. Although one can pass the bar examination with a "low" score with relatively little consequence, passing the civil service exam without a high ranking limits one's employment chances. Taking both exams in the same year is an especially risky strategy, as it lessens the time one can devote to each. A common strategy, comparatively less risky but still quite difficult, is to pass one test in one's third year of university, and the other in the fourth year.

Some double-passers pursue only one career option. For these persons, having "been taught to define their lives according to such crucial tests," the test score is a sign of worth that "looks good on resumes."[33] But because of the time, energy, and money involved, many double-passers pursue the two careers consecutively. We are told in interviews that after taking two tests, the idea of throwing one option away simply seems wasteful.

Double-passers, thus, have two primary options for pursuing both careers. First, they can receive legal training and enter the bureaucracy later. Although technically possible, this is actually rather difficult, as ministries historically have been reluctant to accept older candidates for new positions. Alternatively, an easier option is to join the bureaucracy and quit after two or three years to become a lawyer.

We failed to find substantial data on these so-called "double-passers," as such data are simply not collected systematically by any organization. Bureaucrats keep no formal count of employees who have passed the bar, and legal organizations keep no formal count of legal professionals who have passed the civil service exam. However, we did obtain some information on double passers from law firms.

With almost 200 lawyers, Nagashima, Ohno & Tsunematsu is one of Japan's largest and most prestigious law firms. According to its 2004 Martindale-Hubbell directory entry, six of its lawyers, one partner and five associates (up form three in 2003), are former elite bureaucrats as we have defined the term. The partner, a 1986 University of Tokyo graduate, joined the Ministry of Foreign Affairs in 1986, left in 1990 to become a lawyer, and was admitted to the bar in 1993. The five associates, two from Waseda and three from the University of Tokyo, joined the firm after stints at the MOF and MITI.

Importantly, each of these lawyers, like their counterparts at other large Japanese firms, is relatively young. The partner, born in 1963, was admitted in 1993. The associates were born in 1967, 1970, 1971, and 1972(2) and were admitted to the bar in 1995(2), 1998, 1999, and 2000. The youth of these lawyers reflects the newness of the trend among double-passers. According to our interview sources, double-passers ten years ago would have remained career bureaucrats, or would have left the bureaucracy to become a lawyer only in unusual circumstances. Now, though small in number thus far, young double-passers are comparatively more likely to choose law as their lifelong profession. They seem to join only the largest and most elite firms (which is reflected in our lack of more widespread data), but they do become lawyers. Both senior attorneys and young double-passers to whom we spoke expect the trend to continue.

4. Quasi-lawyers Finally, we obtained data on quasi-legal professionals. In Japan, because of the small number of lawyers, a variety of other professionals with training in law fill the gaps. Although these quasi-lawyers are not legal elites by our definition, their employment trends may shed light on changes in the market for legal elites.

We have data on two groups of quasi-lawyers. First, "judicial scriveners" (*shihō shoshi*) are licensed specialists in real estate and corporate registration and documents submitted to courts. Scriveners are required to take a difficult government-issued test to be licensed; pass rates hover around 3–4 percent. Although scriveners come from a very different pool than elite lawyers, some potential candidates may be affected by similar labor market factors. In fact, we find that the number of scrivener test takers has increased dramatically, from about 16,000 takers in the 1980s to 21,475 in 1998, 21,839 in 1999, in 2000, 23,190 in 2001, and 28,454 in 2003, while the pass rate remains below 3 percent.[34]

A second group of quasi-lawyers on which we have data are employees of legal departments (*hōmubu*) of large corporations. While we lack definitive data on the supply of legal elites into these jobs, we have some data on industry demand. Candidates for these positions are primarily hired directly out of college through interviews and not standardized tests (although some students take the multiple choice portion of the bar exam as an additional credential with which to impress recruiters). The *most* elite students generally do not take corporate jobs; our interviews strongly suggest that they choose between the bar and the bureaucracy. But at least in the case of prestigious multinational corporations, some candidates come from the same pool of students as lawyers and bureaucrats.

Recent survey data show that the average number of employees in the legal department per corporation is increasing, from 5.2 in 1990, to 6.1 in 1995, to 6.4 in 2000.[35] The same survey shows that the total number of legal employees hired by firms mid-career is increasing, from 181 persons at 115 of 888 surveyed firms in 1995 to 491 persons at 290 of 1,008 firms in 2000. Another survey showed that in the next five years, 47 percent of firms planned to increase the size of their legal staff, while only 4.2 percent planned to shrink it.[36]

While not definitive, the evidence on these two groups of quasi-lawyers shows remarkable consistency with the evidence on lawyers, and contrasts with the evidence on elite bureaucrats. This combination of trends suggests that the career decisions of legal elites are not idiosyncratic, but instead are made at least partially in response to more fundamental changes in the Japanese economy and society.

C. Salary and Employment Data

In this section, we analyze salary and employment data for the two professions. We find that, in general, compensation for elite lawyers has increased, while lifetime compensation packages for elite bureaucrats are declining. Competition for elite lawyer jobs is increasing, while competition for elite bureaucrat jobs is decreasing.

1. Elite lawyers Very little information is publicly available on elite lawyer salaries. At least in part because of the relatively small size of the organized bar, there is no Japanese equivalent of the *American Lawyer* magazine to publish salaries.[37] The closest substitute is the decennial survey of attorneys, recently named the *Bengoshi [Attorney] Census*, conducted by the Japan Federation of Bar Associations. The most recent, conducted in 2000, was sent to all 17,416 then-members of the bar. Only 5,560 responded, yielding a response rate of about 33 percent. The survey found an average annual income of ¥15,031,233, or about $150,000. Seventy-seven attorneys, or 1.4 percent, reported income in excess of ¥70 million ($700,000). These, of course, are the partners at the largest law firms; in fact, only 124 responding attorneys were in firms of more than twenty lawyers, and only sixty-four in firms of more than fifty lawyers. Overwhelmingly (88 percent), respondents were from offices of five or fewer attorneys.[38]

To better explore compensation arrangements, we attempted to collect additional data directly from elite attorneys. Because lawyers are reluctant to discuss salary data publicly, we obtained most of our salary data through sources who asked that the identity of his or her firm remain confidential.

According to the hiring partner at one large, elite Tokyo firm (firm L), the salary range for first-year associates at major law firms is ¥10–16 million, or about $100,000–160,000. Some firms adopt fixed salaries for junior associates, while others adopt an hourly salary system that reflects that associate's billable hours. Other firms, including firm L, adopt a fixed salary for junior associates and an hourly bonus system for mid-level and senior associates. Some firms also include a bonus component based on performance.

At a smaller elite Tokyo firm (firm S), we were told that first-year associates receive a flat ¥10 million ($100,000) salary. Second-year associates receive a base salary of less than 10 million, but they receive extra payments based on billable hours and performance. Because first-year associates are required to handle many tasks that do not result in billable hours, such as recruiting and organization of parties, the flat rate is more attractive to them.

We received additional information from a Tokyo legal recruiting service that recruits Japanese lawyers for joint ventures with U.S. firms. Recommended salary packages for partner-level lawyers with ten years of experience are ¥60–80 million ($600,000–800,000), ¥20–35 million ($200,000–350,000) for associates with six years of experience and an overseas post, ¥10–16 million ($100,000–160,000) for associates with 2–4 years of experience and an overseas post, and ¥7–10 million ($70,000–100,000) for new associates with less than two years of experience. For all packages, bonuses are negotiable.

Tokyo salaries have increased slightly in the last decade despite the dramatic increase in supply of young attorneys. A former associate of firm L tells us that starting salaries in 1990 were ¥8 million ($80,000). One relatively large firm that specializes in securities work offered ¥10.5 million ($105,000) to new associates in 1998, a sum that was seen as above-market at the time but now is the norm. We are informed that until 2000, firm S, which now pays ¥10 million to first-year associates, paid first-years ¥8 million, with the possibility of bonuses up to a total of ¥9 million.

We have limited additional data on elite lawyers outside of Tokyo. There are very few, and virtually all of them are located in Osaka. These Osaka elite lawyers work on a combination of international and domestic deals. Starting salaries for elite Osaka associates in 2002, we are told, began at ¥7.75 million for first-year associates, and were expected to increase to ¥10.5 million by the fourth year. While these figures represent slight increases over salaries of the 1990s, they apparently are not representative of Osaka lawyers who do purely domestic work. For this group, the increased number of new lawyers recently has caused some firms to lower starting salaries after several increases in the 1990s. But elite Osaka salaries remain high, we are told, in order to compete with Tokyo firms.

At the large firms in both Osaka and Tokyo, competition for elite jobs is increasing. Hiring partners whom we interviewed told us that they are seeing "larger pools of better and better candidates each year." Although some opponents of bar expansion had voiced concerns that expansion might lower quality, according to Tokyo hiring partners, the number of qualified attorneys is actually increasing, at least in part because would-be bureaucrats are becoming lawyers.

2. Elite bureaucrat salaries   Unlike lawyer salaries, bureaucrat salary data are publicly available. But a large portion of an elite bureaucrat's compensation comes not directly as a government salary, but in a post-retirement private post. We, thus, present data on both elements of bureaucratic compensation.

In 2000, the base starting salary for an entry-level bureaucrat in Tokyo was ¥206,304 per month for an administrative position, and ¥221,648 for a research position. Each works out to an annual salary of approximately $20,000, or approximately one-third to one-eighth of a junior associate's compensation. Extra payments are possible; those employees with spouses, for instance, are given an additional ¥16,000 per month. Employees are given up to ¥27,000 for rent per month, up to ¥50,000 per month for public transportation, and a bonus equal to 4.75 times the monthly salary. If a young bureaucrat received all of these bonuses, his or her annual salary would still be less than $40,000 annually, or no more than half of what the bureaucrat could earn as an elite lawyer.[39]

Salary increases with seniority. A vice-minister (of which there are now 36) of a Ministry, an "11th rank" officer, earns a monthly salary of ¥1,346,000, or an annual salary of about $135,000. Below vice-minister are ten ranks of officers, the largest class of which, with 581 bureaucrats, is the "6th rank." These officials, who include division and department heads, earn a monthly salary of ¥937,000, or about $100,000 annually. The retirement bonus for career bureaucrats is approximately thirty-five times monthly salary. This works out to approximately $800,000 in the case of a senior vice-minister and for a section chief, approximately $300,000.[40]

These figures still pale in comparison to the compensation of elite lawyers. For a career bureaucrat, however, the lifetime compensation scheme is nevertheless attractive, even in comparison to lawyers' income, because of *amakudari* ("descending from heaven"), the practice by which senior ministers "retire" to high-paying jobs at other firms. The additional income from *amakudari* can be large: Sources suggest $200,000–300,000 annually, not including the additional rewards of office space, company cars, boondoggle trips, and multiple retirement bonuses.[41]

This is nice work if you can get it, but anecdotal evidence suggests that the practice of *amakudari* has declined significantly in recent years:

Even officials at the powerful Ministry of Finance have virtually no chance of securing an important executive position at such prestigious banks as Mitsubishi, Sumitomo, Dai-Ichi Kangyo, or the Industrial Bank of Japan. . . . *Amakudari* prospects for MITI bureaucrats are becoming increasingly limited to electric power companies, steel manufacturers, and consumer electronics companies, all of which are under MITI's strong control.[42]

We examined several quantitative data sources to attempt to determine the validity of the anecdotal data. The official source is a report of the National Personnel Authority, known colloquially as the White Paper on Amakudari.[43] Article 103 of the Civil Servant Law[44] stipulates that a public official may not accept a high-level private post for two years after retirement with any firm with which he has been connected in the past five years. Any official who wishes to accept such a post can only do so with the permission of the National Personnel Authority in the form of a waiver. Figure 8.4 represents the number of waivers given by the Authority from 1988 to 2001.[45]

The data show a distinct and substantial decrease over time, but their significance is open to a variety of interpretations. Officials might be increasingly

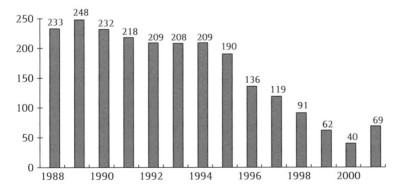

Figure 8.4. *Amakudari waivers by NPA, 1988–2001*

retiring to positions that do not require a waiver, or waiting more than two years to avoid requesting the waiver. The slight increase from forty in 2000 to sixty-nine in 2001 is said to be the result of (a) government reorganization and (b) decisions by Ministry of Finance and other officials to postpone their waiver requests while in the midst of a spate of scandals in 2000.[46]

Fortunately, three other sources of data are available. First, Teikoku Databank conducts an annual survey of *amakudari* by public officials to banks, particularly by Bank of Japan and Ministry of Finance officials. According to their September 2001 report, 127 bank officers and directors are the result of *amakudari*, a figure down 7.3 percent from the previous year. They also report a steep decline in the number of *amakudari* officials serving as "representative director" (essentially the CEO) of their private sector employees, declining by 38.6 percent to forty-nine officials.[47]

Second, in a 1995 article on *amakudari*,[48] Ulrike Schaede attempted to measure the proliferation of *amakudari* by counting the number of directors at Japan's 100 largest companies who had previously held high public posts. She found that as late as 1991, 177 of 3,605 directors, or 4.9 percent of all directors at the 100 largest firms, were former public officials. Two-thirds, or sixty-seven of the 100 firms, employed such directors.

To compare 2001 data with Schaede's results, we conducted a similar test. We chose the 100 largest companies from the Financial Times 500 and again gathered data from the latest (2001) edition of *Kaisha Nenkan*. We found, first, that the number of board members has drastically decreased in the last decade, from 3,605 in Schaede's study to 1,111 in ours. Next, we found that only *six* of the 100 firms had directors who were former bureaucrats, and those six firms had only one such director each. Tellingly, one of those directors was a former public prosecutor from the Ministry of Justice, presumably appointed for compliance and control reasons.

While these data strongly suggest a decline in *amakudari*, they are by no means conclusive, as bureaucrats might be retiring to firms with which they did not work directly as bureaucrats (thereby eliminating the waiver requirement), non-banks, or smaller firms. To explore these issues further, we hand-collected data from *Kigyō Keiretsu Sōran* (Data book on Corporate Cross Shareholding and Affiliations), published by Tōyō Keizai. This exhaustive publication lists the number and background of all directors and officers for all listed companies, 1,985 in 1990 (data as of August 1, 1989), and 2,430 in 2000 (data as of October 1, 1999). We found that from 1990 to 2000, the number of such directors and officers fell nearly 20 percent, from 761 to 615. The decline is apparent in both the number of companies that have such directors and officers (397 in 1999 to 366 in 2000) and the average number of such positions at companies that hire ex-bureaucrats (1.92 in 1990 to 1.68 in 2000). Interestingly, the decrease came despite a 22 percent increase in the total number of companies and a 13 percent increase in gross domestic product, either of which might have been expected to increase the potential for *amakudari*. It, thus, appears that private *amakudari* has declined significantly in the last decade, with negative consequences for elite bureaucrat incomes.

Still, this evidence pertains to *amakudari* practices in private firms. A large number of *amakudari* officials retire to *public* corporations known as *tokushu hōjin*, or "special corporations." As of December 2001, seventy-seven such corporations existed.[49] Officials have historically been free to accept such positions because the Civil Servant Law regulates only *amakudari* employment by private corporations. The available evidence suggests that *amakudari* to these special corporations occurs regularly. A 1992 study found that 60 percent of the 784 managing directors of the ninety-two public corporations then in existence achieved their positions by *amakudari*.[50] In 2000, in response to public criticism, the government began releasing the names and positions of senior retirees. In that year, 78 of 538 retirees joined special corporations, a number comparable to the number of private *amakudari* waivers.[51]

While the practice of *amakudari* to special corporations continues, the Japanese government has adopted a policy of reducing the practice in recent years. In 1996, guidelines were passed to limit the percentage of *amakudari* board members at such corporations to fewer than one-third.[52] In 2001, under the leadership of a newly formed bureaucratic reform agency, the Diet passed a law specifically designed to reform and limit special corporations.[53] In addition, formal plans to eliminate seventeen special and approved corporations and to privatize forty-five more were announced.[54] The negative attitudes toward special corporations accompanied by these concrete policy changes make reliance on *amakudari* to complete one's lifetime compensation package increasingly risky.

Such factors, we are told by personnel department officials at elite ministries, have caused a decrease in the quality of the pool of applicants for elite positions. We are told by these officers that the very best and brightest, perhaps the top ten candidates in a given year, continue to join the bureaucracy in relatively high numbers, and in so doing seek "prestige and affirmation of their intelligence." But the same officials lament that a decade ago, the top 100 would likely have been "sure hires." Beyond the top ten, quality declines. This phenomenon, officials tell us with no small measure of concern, is the result of a loss of candidates to the bar.

D. Summary

The data presented above suggest a pattern. The number of persons who take the bar, pass it, and become lawyers is increasing, while the average number of persons who sit for the civil service exam has fallen in the last five-year period in spite of increasing pass rates and relatively constant hire rates. At elite schools, the same trends apply; an increasing number of legal elites are choosing the bar over the bureaucracy. Quasi-lawyer numbers are also increasing. We have less evidence on double-passers, but at least some appear to be choosing the bar in cases in which they would not in the past. Bar compensation has increased; lifetime bureaucrat compensation is declining with the demise of *amakudari* practices. Though difficult to measure precisely, the mean quality of entry-level candidates to the bureaucracy appears to be declining, while the bar is admitting expanding numbers of highly talented youth.

From this evidence, we conclude that the bar is receiving an increasingly large share of legal elites, and increasingly higher compensation, to the detriment of the bureaucracy. We have considerable confidence in this assessment, given the quantitative data, our interviews, reforms enacted both to increase the number of elite bureaucrats and to allow the bureaucracy to hire lawyers, and anxious public statements by those in charge of bureaucratic reform that the bar is taking the "best candidates." But at least two other explanations might be possible.

First, perhaps the pool of candidates for the bar differs from the pool of candidates for the bureaucracy in some meaningful way. If so, the increase in the bar and the decrease in the bureaucracy might not be related. But this is simply not the case. It is common knowledge that a small group of the top undergraduate law students spend considerable time and energy determining which of these two career paths to take, and some, content on keeping all options open, take the tests for both professions. Our interviews with those in charge of hiring reinforce the conclusion that elite bureaucrats and lawyers are drawn from the same talent pool.

Second, perhaps test numbers are not an accurate reflection of career decisions. True, some legal elites take tests for resume value, or simply to prove their intellectual acumen. But our data reflect post-testing employment decisions as well. Interviews with those in charge of hiring at large firms and elite bureaucracies confirm these patterns. Law firms (and U.S. law schools with graduate degree programs that accept Japanese students) are deluged with young attorney resumes that improve each year, while ministry officials tell us that the number and quality of entry-level candidates continues to decline.

II. INSTITUTIONAL CHANGE AND THE RE-ALLOCATION OF TALENT

What accounts for these developments? Professional career decisions are complex,[55] but the changes in employment decisions of Japanese legal elites just documented correlate temporally with significant structural changes in Japan, many of which were explicitly designed to move the locus of governance from the bureaucracy to the legal system.[56]

A. Institutional Change

The change in employment patterns among Japanese legal elites reflects a basic change in the rules governing the Japanese economy.[57] Of course, law is often responsive to, as well as the vanguard of, social and economic change. These new rules were prompted by a tangible shift in public attitudes regarding the place of law and bureaucratic oversight in the Japanese economy. This shift, which may be largely attributable to the economic debacle of the 1990s (especially to the Ministry of Finance's inability to handle Japan's bad-loan problems), was expressed in a variety of ways, including election outcomes and the media. Yet, a simple shift in attitudes without accompanying changes in incentive structures would not likely lead to the phenomena described above.

While we have separated several strands of institutional change for purposes of analysis and clarity of exposition, we do not claim to have a complete understanding of how these changes rank in terms of importance, or the exact chain of causation through which the labor market is evolving. Nor is our claim that every young legal elite in Japan explicitly considers these developments when deciding whether to become a lawyer or bureaucrat.[58] Some might, but most simply react to their environment, acting, like Friedman's billiards player, "as-if" they had formally calculated their responses.[59] Our aim here is simply to describe several salient changes in that environment.

Over the past decade and at an accelerating pace, the rules of the game for economic lawmaking and enforcement have undergone a palpable change, corresponding to social and political sentiment that Japan needs to move from a system of bureaucrat-orchestrated economic management to a more market-oriented system based on principles of transparency and individual responsibility. Concrete manifestations of the shift are apparent in numerous areas.

One development is widespread deregulation in fields such as finance and telecommunications, designed to reduce government intervention in the economy and society.[60] The most prominent examples are in the areas most relevant to business lawyers, including mergers and acquisitions (discussed in Chapter 7) and financial products.[61] In addition, code or statutory reforms have increased organizational flexibility for corporations and banks, while expanding the menu of transactional options. Simultaneously, these new business opportunities and structures are generating novel legal risks, such as shareholder litigation and internal compliance issues. Thus, deregulation gives elite lawyers a role in transactional and advisory work they lacked under a regime replete with mandatory rules and advance governmental approvals. For example, as a prominent business lawyer notes, while banks once turned to informal regulatory guidance for "insurance," they now seek legal opinions.[62]

Fortifying the deregulation movement is a series of new statutes designed to circumscribe bureaucratic discretion and increase monitoring of agency action. For example, an Administrative Procedure Act formalizes rulemaking procedures and restricts the use of informal "administrative guidance,"[63] a Freedom of Information Act compels disclosure of certain information held by national agencies upon request,[64] and new ethics rules regulate the use of nonpublic information, the receipt of gifts, and *ex parte* contacts by public officials.[65] In addition to these measures, some ministries are seeking to enhance self-monitoring by adopting a system in which subordinates evaluate their superiors.[66] Even if, as is highly likely, each of these legal measures imperfectly accomplishes its objectives, the plain purpose and plausible cumulative effect of these new rules is to reduce bureaucratic autonomy, enhance political and private sector monitoring of agency action, and limit the informal perks of government service. It would not be surprising if this new legal environment diminished the attractiveness of a bureaucratic career.

At the same time the bureaucracy has been publicly criticized and subjected to enhanced monitoring, the legal system and its practitioners have received favorable attention as a vital outlet for the protection of citizens' and business interests and a critical counterweight to the declining role of agency oversight. In 1997, an administrative reform council whose report led to the restructuring of the Japanese central government ministries, stated that the "'rule of law' constitutes an essential base for promoting deregulation, aiming at abolishing unclear advance administrative control and converting to an after-the-fact review/remedy type society."[67]

Even some of the most conservative sectors of Japanese society have become law optimists—indeed, they have been in the vanguard of the law expansion movement. Not coincidentally, both the *Keidanren*, a powerful big business lobbying group, and the ruling Liberal Democratic Party (LDP) issued reports in the late 1990s strongly advocating the strengthening and expansion of the legal system.[68] Of course, the change in heart did not occur in a political vacuum; shifts in public opinion prompted elected politicians to respond by reducing the scope of bureaucratic discretion. As one knowledgeable commentator notes, "it is clear that business groups and, to a lesser extent, LDP politicians, are indicating that people need more access to the law. It appears that they are trying to create a new orthodoxy in Japanese society."[69]

These proposals led to the appointment by the Prime Minister of a Judicial System Reform Council, which spent two years formulating its recommendations. The Council's final report in 2001, "For a Justice System to Support Japan in the 21st Century," states that the objective of the Council was to "define clearly 'what we must do to transform both the spirit of the law and the rule of law into the flesh and blood of this country . . .'"[70] The Council's recommendations are sweeping. A partial list includes taking measures to make trials more efficient and to make better use of expert testimony, expanding access to the courts by lowering filing fees and reinforcing the legal aid system, increasing the size of the legal profession and reforming legal education through the introduction of US-style graduate law schools, and diversifying the judiciary. Concrete steps have already been taken to implement some of the Council's recommendations, particularly as they relate to reform of the legal profession and legal education.[71]

Developments in the courts further reflect and reinforce the movement from bureaucratic discretion to law. The best example is a recent shareholder derivative suit known as the Daiwa case.[72] As discussed in chapter 2, in 2000, the Osaka District Court rendered a $775 million judgment against the directors of Daiwa Bank for breach of duty under the Commercial Code. The directors were found liable for failing to institute a compliance system to detect unauthorized trades in the bank's New York branch, and for failing to make timely disclosure of the trading losses to US banking authorities, even though the directors were operating at the suggestion or acquiescence of the Ministry of Finance in delaying disclosure. It is hard to overstate the significance of this case, which, in substantive legal terms and shock value to the business community, has the combined impact of two well-known Delaware cases, *Caremark* and *Van Gorkom*, which played a major role in delineating the contours of directors' duties in the United States. Though ultimately settled during the appeal process for a fraction of the initial award, the District Court's theory of liability was preserved and entered as a final judgment against the directors.

Most striking about the case is the potential shift in the balance of corporate lawmaking and enforcement power it represents. The court's finding of enormous personal liability against the directors and the state-of-the-art theory on which that finding is based—a decision consistent with, if broader in some respects than current US corporate fiduciary duty law—both heightens the need for sophisticated preventive law advice in the Japanese corporate setting and belies the long-standing view of the Japanese judiciary as too cautious and detached from commercial affairs to play a useful role in the resolution of complex business disputes. Finally, the court's summary rejection of a key strand of the defendants' defense—that the board was acting at the behest of a powerful ministry—is striking in its implicit declaration that the *courts*, not the bureaucracy, are the final arbiters of the law in Japan. In this last respect, the case has parallels in existing Japanese case law.[73] The specter of losing the shield of bureaucratic protection and being exposed to massive personal liability for corporate governance shortcomings, however, had a novel impact on the business and legal communities.

III. INTERPRETATION OF FINDINGS

Together, these developments provide a compelling explanation for the new employment trends among legal elites. Quite simply, elite legal talent is migrating to its highest-valued-added uses. In what may be the beginning of broad, long-term structural transformation, the highest-value-added uses are shifting from the generalist bureaucracy to an expert-oriented legal system.

This phenomenon has two important implications for academic literature: First, theories about how Japan is governed need revision and updating. The view of Japan as a "plan rational" state orchestrated by bureaucrats may always have been exaggerated in reality, if not perception. Whatever its past validity, our data cast considerable doubt on its existence today. Even theorists who have long posited the existence of a more pluralist and accountable Japanese polity will now have to account for law, courts, and lawyers as more central and vibrant forces in the Japanese political economy.

Second, analyzing the role of lawyers in promoting or hindering economic growth is far more complex than the most prominent of the previous studies suggest. Numerous commentators, with a supportive nod to Japan, have suggested that societies encourage their most talented youth either to pursue innovation in "productive careers" (and reap economic gains) or rent seeking in law (and invite stagnation). But simple measures of the population of legal professionals, without an analysis of the institutional context in which they function and the alternative occupations available to talented youth, may be highly misleading. Nothing in Japan's experience suggests that the allocation of talent into the bureaucracy or law independently determines economic performance; rather, the experience indicates that talent follows power and profit, which are determined by a complex amalgam of institutional factors and social sentiment.

Since we anticipate several specific objections to these conclusions, we respond to them in some detail here. In the process, we elaborate upon and confirm several strands of our argument.

1. Scandal   In recent years, the Japanese bureaucracy, and particularly the super-elite Ministry of Finance, has been plagued by scandal. It might be argued that the observed employment shift results from a temporary public reaction, as legal elites avoid employment in a tainted sector, and not a long-term shift in power.

Scandal, however, is rarely exogenous to prevailing power structures. Inappropriate or unlawful conduct is often revealed only after the collapse of the regime in which it occurred without detection or punishment, as a new regime pursues a new agenda. Many of the corrupt practices in the Japanese bureaucracy were unearthed over the past five years by public prosecutors, at the same time as the institutional changes described above took root. From this perspective, heightened public perception of scandal is not simply noise in the data, but another sign of increased reliance on the rule of law in Japan.

2. Other incentives to choose law   Perhaps some other factor besides institutional change is motivating the move of high-level legal elites to law. We see at least three possibilities: Salary increases, job security, and internationalization of the economy.

It may well be that legal elites are moving from the bureaucracy to law because of the increased lifetime compensation differential; elite lawyers now get paid more relative to bureaucrats than they did a decade ago, and they are less likely to be plagued by scandal or downsizing that could threaten job security. But as with scandal, compensation is not exogenous to institutions. While it may be that legal elites are responding most directly to changes in relative compensation levels, those changes are a reflection of deeper structural shifts, several of which we have discussed above.

In a related manner, perhaps legal elites are joining the large, international Japanese law firms (as opposed to smaller, primarily domestic ones) not because of institutions, but because of internationalization. Due to foreign pressure, economic distress, and other factors, foreign investment in Japan has increased, raising the market for international legal services. Again, however, these developments did not occur in a vacuum. While "globalization" has undoubtedly played some role in the shift, underlying this abstract phenomenon are specific legal changes making international transactions such as cross-border mergers and acquisitions more feasible, which in turn increase the compensation of lawyers who handle such transactions. Our interviews, as well as those of long-time Tokyo practitioners Yasuharu Nagashima (the founder of one of Japan's four largest and most elite firms) and Anthony Zaloom (of counsel at another), show that the fastest-growing source of revenue at the elite firms is domestic work, which now accounts for as much as two-thirds of all revenues.[74] Nor can "globalization" explain the apparent decline in attractiveness of careers at internationally oriented ministries such as METI and the Ministry of Foreign Affairs.

3. Decline in court budgets Contrary to our claim that the role of law is expanding, the percentage of the annual budget allotted to the court system has declined over time. The court system has never received more than one percent of the national budget. In 1955, its share was 0.91 percent. It has fallen ever since, to an all-time low of 0.36 percent in 1999.[75] A skeptic might take this as a sign of legal system decline.

Investing this data with great significance, however, would be a mistake. First, Japanese judges are compensated as well or better than their U.S. federal counterparts, suggesting that the profession is held in high regard.[76] Second, the decrease is explained in part by the substantial increase in the economy and annual budget over the past half-century.[77] Finally, the judiciary historically has been very weak in promoting its own case for additional expenditures. While the modest budgetary allocation to the courts may suggest a lack of political sway in fiscal affairs, it is hardly the most reliable indicator of the courts' role in society.

4. Dual rent-seeking If *both* lawyers *and* bureaucrats are principally engaged in rent seeking or rent extraction, the change in employment patterns we have documented is insignificant, since the aggregate amount of talent diverted from productive uses in Japan remains relatively constant.

This might be a plausible interpretation of our findings, but it is hard to reconcile with certain facts. For example, most Japanese bureaucrats, while trained in law, actually do not perform legal work; lawyers obviously do. Therefore, the movement toward the bar reflects a major shift in the substantive work performed by one of the most elite and highly talented segments of the Japanese work force. It seems unlikely that this change is insignificant. It also suggests that if both lawyers and bureaucrats are engaged in rent seeking or rent extracting, they go about this task in very different ways.

Moreover, treating both professions as rent seeking is inconsistent with the premise underlying the talent diversion theory itself, since in Japan and other high-growth economies in Asia that figured so heavily in the empirical confirmation of this theory, rapid growth coincided with extensive bureaucratic involvement in the economy.[78]

5. Inverse relation   Some might claim that our findings support the work of
the law skeptics by showing a continuing inverse relation between lawyer population and economic growth in Japan. When lawyer population was low in the
1980s, the economy boomed. As the number of legal professionals increased
throughout the 1990s, the economy stagnated—because, a skeptic might argue,
lawyers' redistributive activities inhibited growth.

This interpretation of the data, however, is highly implausible. Lawyer population in Japan has been low on an international comparative scale since the
formal establishment of the profession in the nineteenth century.[79] Yet, Japan's
most dramatic economic growth did not occur until after the Second World War.
Moreover, lawyer population increased significantly in percentage terms from
1940 to 1985, coinciding with a remarkable period of economic growth in Japan.
Similarly, it is implausible that the incremental increases of about 200 members
per year to the Japanese bar that occurred in the 1990s "caused" the negative
economic growth in that period.

In fact, the Japanese data suggest no relation between lawyer population and
economic growth. Figure 8.5 shows the number of lawyers, number of bar takers,
and real GDP growth from 1960 to 2000.[80] As Figure 8.5 shows, the number of
bar takers increases at a much higher rate than the number of lawyers, a result
of the artificial numerical controls on the size of the bar. The figure also shows
high growth in the 1960s and contemporaneous low numbers of lawyers and bar
takers. But over the sustained period neither measure has any obvious relation
with economic performance.

We found similarly ambiguous results when we used units of analysis (similar
to those of Murphy et al.) that attempt to measure talent allocation among a
broader population at an earlier stage in career development. We found that the
percentage of Japanese university students majoring in law has declined over
time, from 9.99 percent in 1960 to 8.18 percent in 1999, and that the ratio of law
majors to engineering majors also fell, from about 0.65 in 1960 to about 0.42 in
1999. Neither trend has any clear relation to macroeconomic indices.

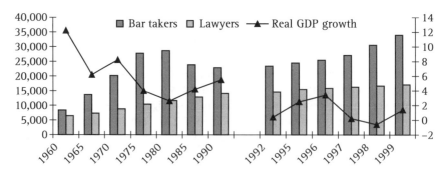

Figure 8.5. *Lawyers, bar takers, and GDP growth, 1960–2000*

Our detailed examination of "Exhibit A" suggests that no simple relation exists between the allocation of talent and economic growth. Recent calls from the Japanese business sector for more law and legal professionals (not more engineers) belie the notion that lawyers are destructive to economic growth. Moreover, the Japanese experience suggests that the alternative occupations available to erstwhile attorneys may not be the entrepreneurs and engineers that economists contemplate in their studies. Ultimately, the Japanese experience suggests that the allocation of talent in society follows from, rather than determines, the rules of the game for economic and social activity.

CONCLUSION

"It is really upsetting," one law professor at a prestigious Japanese university told us, "how our graduates are not going to the bureaucracy anymore. They simply are not interested in the positions of power." We appreciate the sentiment, but in this chapter, we have argued from the data that legal elites are still pursuing positions of power—it is simply that the nature of those positions has changed. A transformation in economic and political institutions is bestowing upon the bar some of the authority that once resided in the bureaucracy. Japan's experience over the past decade, while only representing a single country, provides strong support for the view that a lawyer's value added is heavily dependent upon the structure of the economy and politics as a whole. As Japan moved from an informal, *ex ante* model of bureaucratic management toward a more flexible, *ex post* and law-based model of governance, power, prestige, and profit have shifted from the top-tier civil service to elite legal practitioners.

Given the unique position of Japan in the debate over lawyers and economic growth, commentators would do well to understand the implications for growth and governance of that country's allocation of talent. Close analysis of Japan's experience over the past several decades suggests that the engagement of legal and bureaucratic actors in the economy was in considerable tension, though neither regime is necessarily inconsistent with economic growth. Rather, the allocation of talent in Japanese society appears to follow from, rather than determine, institutional design and performance. It seems unremarkable that in seeking to improve the quality of its legal institutions to enhance economic performance, Japan would simultaneously increase the population and stature of its legal professionals. Acknowledging that fact, however, requires revising the conventional wisdom both about who governs Japan and the role of lawyers in the economy.

NOTES

1. Chalmers Johnson, MITI and the Japanese Miracle 20–1 (1982).
2. Stephen P. Magee et al., Black Hole Tariffs and Endogenous Policy Theory (1989).

3. Kevin M. Murphy et al., The Allocation of Talent: Implications for Growth, 106 Q. J. Econ. 503 (1991).
4. Id., at 526.
5. See, for example, Derek C. Bok, A Flawed System of Law Practice and Training, 33 J. Legal Ed. 570 (1983); Lawrence H. Tribe, Too Much Law, Too Little Justice: An Argument for Delegalizing America, Atlantic Monthly, July 1979, at 25.
6. Ronald J. Gilson, How Many Lawyers Does it Take to Change an Economy?, 17 Law & Soc. Inq. 635 (1993); Ronald J. Gilson, Value Creation by Business Lawyers: Legal Skills and Asset Pricing, 94 Yale L.J. 239 (1984).
7. Marc Galanter, Predators and Parasites: Lawyer Bashing and Civil Justice, 28 Ga. L. Rev. 633, 671 (1994).
8. See, for example, Robert C. Clark, Why So Many Lawyers: Are they Good or Bad?, 61 Fordham L. Rev. 275, 279; see also Gilson, Value Creation, *supra* note 6, at 312.
9. See, for example, Rafael La Porta et al., Legal Determinants of External Finance, 52 J. Fin. 1131 (1997); id., Law and Finance, 106 J. Pol. Econ. 1113 (1998); id., Corporate Ownership Around the World, 54 J. Fin. 474 (1999).
10. Chalmers Johnson, Japan: Who Governs: The Rise of the Developmental State 18–19 (1995).
11. Ministry of Justice of Japan, Shihō shaken dainiji shaken shutsuganshasū/gōkaku shasū nado no suii [Changes in Bar Application and Pass Rates], at www.moj.go.jp/PRESS/021113/14syutu-gou.html (last visited Feb. 7, 2003) [hereinafter Changes in Bar Application and Pass Rates].
12. See Kōmuin Kyūyō Benran [Civil Servant Salary Manual] 212 (ōkurazaimukyōkai ed., 2001) [hereinafter Civil Servant Salary Manual].
13. Nihon Keizai Shinbunsha, Shihō Keizai ha Tō [Justice: The Call from the Economy] 100 (2000); Shinjin Bengoshi Tōkyō to Ōsaka ni Shūchū [New Lawyers Concentrate in Tokyo and Osaka], Yomiuri Shinbun, Dec. 4, 2001, at 15.
14. Hideaki Kubori, Hōka Shakai e Nihon ga Kawaru [Toward a Legalized Japanese Society] 189 (1997).
15. See, for example, Takashi Tachibana, Tōdaisei ha Baka ni Nattaka [Have Tokyo University Students Become Stupid?] 191 (2001). In some ministries such as the Ministry of Health, top positions are often filled by gikan (technical specialists).
16. See National Personnel Authority of Japan, Kokka Kōmuin Saiyō Isshū Shiken [First-Tier Civil Service Examination], at www.jinji.go.jp/saiyo/shiken01.htm.
17. National Personnel Authority of Japan, Isshū Shiken Kubunbetsu Isshi Kekka [First-Tier Exam Results], at clearing.jinji.go.jp.8080/hakusyo/image/jine200202/tbl.2.1.25.gif.
18. Setsuo Miyazawa, Legal Education and the Reproduction of the Elite in Japan, 1 Asian-Pacific L. & Pol'y J. 2, 18 (2000), at www.hawaii.edu/aplpj/pdfs/02-miyazawa.pdf (last visited Nov. 21, 2002).
19. Shiryō 3 [Document 3], 1084 Jurisuto 70, 70 (1996); see Ministry of Justice of Japan, Shihō shiken dainiji shiken shutsuganshasu/gōkaku shasū nado no suii [Changes in Bar Application and Pass Rates], at www.moj.go.jp/PRESS/021113/14syutu-gou.html (last visited Feb. 7, 2003).
20. See Ministry of Justice of Japan, Heisei 14 Nendo Shihō Shiken Niji Shiken Kekka Ni Tsuite [Regarding the 2002 Bar Examination Results], at www.moj.go.jp/PRESS/021113-1.html.
21. Chart, 256 Hōgaku Kyōshitsu 146 (2002).

22. National Personnel Authority of Japan, Jinjiin, Kōmuin Hakusho [White Paper on Civil Servants] 326 (2000); National Personnel Authority of Japan, Isshū Shiken Kubunbetsu Jisshi Kekka [Results of First-Tier Examination by Category], at www.jinji.go.jp/saiyo/fsaiyo03.htm (last visited Feb. 7, 2003).

23. See generally Jinjiin, Nenji Hōkukusho [Annual Report], 1991–2003.

24. Ippanshoku no Ninkitsuki Shokuin no Saiyō oyobi Kyūyo no Tokurei ni Kansuru Hōritsu [Law Related to Special Provisions for the Employment and Compensation of Regular Term Employees], Law No. 125 of 2000, art. 7.

25. See, for example, Michio Muramatsu, Kōmuin Seido Kaikaku Keikakutekini, Shiken Seido kara Chakushu [Reforming the Civil Service System: Starting with the Examination System], Nihon Keizai Shinbun, Oct. 8, 2001, at 18.

26. Kyakufusho no Wakate Shokuin ni Taisuru Saiyō Shiken Hiaringu no Gaiyō [Outline of Hearings on Hiring Tests for Young Employees at Various Agencies and Ministries], Mar. 5, 2002.

27. Ministry of Justice of Japan, Heisei 13 Nendo Shihō Shiken Dai Niji Shiken Daigaku Betsu Gōkakusha [2001 Bar-Passers by University], at www.moj.go.jp/PRESS/011109/13-2univ.html.

28. Id.

29. See generally Makaoto Aso, Nihon no Gakureki Eriito [Japanese Academic Elites] (1991); Ryūkichi Kitagawa and Jun Kainuma, Nihon no Eriito [Japanese Elites] (1985); Miyazawa, *supra* note 18, at 24–6.

30. Candidates who pass the bar examination at their first, second, or third attempts receive priority over candidates with more attempts. This system, begun for takers of the 1996 essay test (for candidates who had first taken the multiple-choice test after 1993), dictates that 2/11 of candidates before 2002, and 2/9 after 2002, must come from this pool of early takers. Shihō Shiken Hō [Bar Examination Law], Law No. 140 of 1949, art. 8; Shihō Shiken Kanri Iinkai Kisoku [Bar Examination Committee Rules], art. 1; Ministry of Justice of Japan, Shihō Shiken Juken Annai, [Bar Exam Information], at www.moj.go.jp/KANBOU/jinji01.html#04 (last visited Nov. 15, 2002). Candidates may thus gain strategic advantage by waiting until they are most prepared to take the examination.

31. See Shinji Miyada, Ankeeto Chōsa ni Miru Sekirara Tōdaisei [The Plain Truth about University of Tokyo Students as Seen in Survey Results], in Ronsō/Tōdai Hōkai [Debate: The Collapse of the University of Tokyo] 152, 191 (Yō Takeuchi ed., 2001).

32. Tōkyō Daigaku Hōgakubu, Hōgakubu no Kyōiku oyobi Gakusei Seikatsu ni kansuru Jittai Chōsa Hōkokusho, reprinted in Shihō Seido Kaikaku Shingikai, Session 14 (Mar. 2, 2000), exhibit 9, in Shihō Seido Kaikaku Shingikai Zenkiroku CD-ROM supplement to 1208 Jurisuto (2001).

33. Tadahide Ikuta, Kanryo: Japan's Hidden Government 47 (Hideo Yanai trans., 2000).

34. Nihon Shihō Shoshikai Rengōkai, Shihō Shoshi Seido no Gaiyō to Shokumu no Jittai [Current Status and Outline of the Judicial Scrivener System] 23 (2001), updated by authors with figures from Ministry of Justice of Japan, Heisei 14 Nendo Shihō Shoshi Shiken no Shutsugan Jōkyō ni Tsuite [2002 Judicial Scrivener Test Data], at http://www.moj.go.jp/SHIKEN/SHOSHI/h14shutsugan.html.

35. Kaisha Hōmubu [Corporate Legal Departments], Bessatsu NBL 63, at 56 (2001). We find no significant increase in the total number of law graduates from elite universities who

choose to work in private industry; we only find this modest change in the role that elite law graduates fill within those companies.

36. Nihon Keizai Shinbunsha, *supra* note 13, at 228.
37. The average profit per equity partner among the 100 highest grossing American firms in 2000 was $801,350. At the highest firm, Wachtell, the average profit per partner was $3.2 million. The Am Law 100, Am. Law, July 2001, at 131, 173–4.
38. The complete survey remains unpublished. Survey data are listed at Bengoshi Sensasu [Lawyer Census], at www.nichibenren.or.jp/shinki2.htm, and a summary is published in 319 Nichibenren News 3, 3 (Aug. 1, 2000).
39. See National Personnel Authority of Japan, Kokka Kōmuin Saiyō Isshū Shiken [First-Tier Civil Servant Test], at www.jinji.go.jp/saiyo/shiken01.htm (last visited Nov. 22, 2002); Civil Servant Salary Manual, *supra* note 12, at 36–40.
40. Civil Servant Salary Manual, *supra* note 12, at 567–79; Kazuma Tsutsumi, Kyōdaishōchō Amakudari Fuhaihakusho [White Paper on Amakudari from Large Ministries and Agencies] 57 (2000).
41. See, for example, Ken'ichi Ohme, Heisei Kanryōron [Heisei-Era Bureaucratology]; Kazumi Tsutsumi, Kanryō Amakudari Hakusho [White Paper on Bureaucratic Amakudari] 43–4 (1997).
42. Ikuta, *supra* note 33, at 15.
43. Eiri Kigyō e no Shūshoku no Ninchi ni kansuru Nenji Hōkokusho [Annual Report on Approval of Employment in Private Industry], unpublished paper circulated annually by National Personnel Authority.
44. Kokka Kōmuinhō [Civil Servant Law], Law No. 120 of 1947, art. 103.
45. Jinjiin, Nenji Hōkukusho [Annual Report], 1989–2002.
46. Amakudari 7nen buri Zō [Amakudari Up for First Time in 7 Years], Asahi Shinbun, Mar. 28, 2002, at 3. The same article notes that 827 persons in 2001 accepted positions at ranks below section chief, which do not require waivers. These data, obtained for the first time by the Asahi Shinbun through a FOIA request in 2002, include not only elite bureaucrats, but also mid-level employees who have taken only the Second- or Third-Tier Exam. Id.; see Amakudari Zōka, Kachō Hōsakkyū Ikamo Hatsu Kōhyō [Amakudari Increases, First Public Disclosure of Below-Section-Chief Data], at http://www.asahi.com/politics/update/0327/010.html.
47. Teikoku Databank, Ltd., Dai 7kai Ginko e no Amakudari Jittai Chōsa [Empirical Study of Amakudari to Banks] (2001).
48. Ulrike Schaede, The "Old Boy" Network and Government–Business Relationships in Japan, 21 J. Japan. Stud. 293 (1995).
49. Tokushu Hōjin Nado Kaikaku Suishin Honbu, Tokushu Hōjin Nado Seiri Gōrika Keikaku [Plan to Manage and Normalize Special Corporations], at www.gyokaku.go.jp/jimukyoku/tokusyu/gourika/mokiji.pdf.
50. Takenori Inoki, Japanese Bureaucrats at Retirement: The Mobility of Human Resources from Central Government to Public Corporations, in The Japanese Civil Service and Economic Development, at 213, 217 (Hyung Ki Kim et al. eds., 1995).
51. Controversial Job-Landing Prevalent in Japan, Jiji Press Ticker Service, Dec. 21, 2000, available at LEXIS, News, Japan.
52. Government to Restrict Bureaucrats on Taking Jobs at Nonprofit Public Firms, Nikkei Weekly, Aug. 26, 1996, at 4.
53. Tokushu Hōjin Tō Kaikaku Kihonhō [Basic Law to Reform Special Corporations], Law No. 58 of 2001.

54. Haishi 17, Min'eika 45 Tokushu Hōjin Kaikaku Kettei [Decision in Plan to Reform Special Corporations: Eliminate 17, Privatize 45], Asahi Shinbun, Dec. 18, 2001, at 14.

55. For a sample of the relevant labor market literature, see, for example, David N. Laband and Bernard F. Lentz, Self-Recruitment in the Legal Profession, 10 J. Labor Econ. 182 (1992) (presenting data indicating that legal knowledge is transmitted from parent to child and is a significant factor in a child's decision to follow in a parent's legal footsteps); Robert M. Sauer, Job Mobility and the Market for Lawyers, 106 J. Pol. Econ. 147 (1998) (modeling career choices of US law school graduates as a self-selection mechanism based on unobserved heterogeneity in abilities and expected future returns).

56. The employment shift may not necessarily represent a preference shift. As legal scholar Shozo Ota pointed out to us, some candidates (not the most elite) may have always "preferred" the bar to the bureaucracy, but only through institutional changes such as the expansion of the bar were they able to achieve their goals.

57. Cf. Douglass C. North, Institutions, Institutional Change, and Economic Performance (1990). One reader of the article suggested a more prosaic reason for the shift: The rise of a huge cram school industry to prepare students for the bar exam. However, we view this phenomenon as a symptom rather than a cause of the shift in job market preferences. Cram schools also exist to prepare students for the civil service exam, and bar cram schools have been in existence for a long time. It seems unlikely that the growth of the cram school industry is causing more students to seek careers in law. More likely, the industry is growing in response to consumer demand.

58. When journalist Tadahide Ikuta interviewed bureaucratic "escapees" who left their posts to pursue other careers, he received a mix of personal and instrumental explanations. One ex-bureaucrat stated that he left because "passing the bar exam was what I was really after," while another lawyer and ex-bureaucrat stated that "a lawyer would be rewarded by his clients for working hard to represent their interests, but an official gets no such feedback." Ikuta, *supra* note 42, at 62. Relying on extensive interview evidence, researchers find that Japanese lawyers, not unlike their US counterparts, often drift into legal careers in order to "keep their options open." See Carl Schneider and Atsushi Kinami, Becoming a Lawyer, paper delivered at Change, Continuity, and Context: Japanese Law in the Twenty-First Century, University of Michigan Law School, Apr. 6, 2001.

59. See, for example, Milton Friedman, Essays in Positive Economics 21 (1953).

60. See generally Jurō Hashimoto and Junji Nakagawa eds., Kisei Kanwa no Seijikeizaigaku [The Political Economy of Deregulation] (2000).

61. While an increase in salaries for business lawyers at large international firms may be caused in part by increased international trade, institutional changes in domestic economics such as the ones we have described for Japan that are facilitating that trend. See Chapter 7.

62. Nihon Keizai Shinbunsha ed., *supra* note 36, at 72 (quoting Hideki Matsui of Mori Sogo).

63. For analysis of the law, see Tom Ginsburg, System Change? A New Perspective on Japan's Administrative Procedure Law, in The Multiple Worlds of Japanese Law: Disjunctions and Conjunctions (Tom Ginsburg et al eds., 2001).

64. Gyōsei kikan no hōyu suru jōhō no kokai ni kansuru hōritsu, [Freedom of Information Act], Law No. 42 of 1999.

65. Kokka kōmuin no rinri hō [Ethics Law for National Civil Servants], Law. No. 125 of 1999.
66. Buka ga Jōshi no Kinmu Hyōka [Subordinartes to Evaluate Superiors], Kyoto Shinbun, Nov. 25, 2001, at 1.
67. Cited in Judicial Reform Council, Recommendations of the Judicial System Reform Council—For a Justice System to Support Japan in the 21st Century, available at www.kantei.go.jp/foreign/judiciary/2001/0612report.html.
68. See Setsuo Miyazawa, The Politics of Judicial Reform in Japan: Judiciary, Legal Education, and Legal Aid, reprinted in Curtis J. Milhaupt et al., Japanese Law in Context: Readings in Society, the Economy, and Politics 103, 105 (2001). Lobbying by business groups—lawyers' clients—was a primary factor in the Japan Federation of Bar Associations' decision to pass a resolution supporting an increase in the size of the bar. West Interview with Masakazu Kuboi, President, Japan Federation of Bar Associations, Tokyo, Japan, Feb. 26, 2002.
69. Miyazawa, in Milhaupt et al., *supra* note 68, at 103, 105.
70. Judicial Reform Council, Recommendations of the Judicial System Reform Council— For a Justice System to Support Japan in the 21st Century, available at www. kantei.go.jp/foreign/judiciary/2001/0612report.html.
71. For example, it has already been decided that new entrants to the legal profession should be increased to 3,000 annually. The Japan Federation of Bar Associations has calculated that with an annual increase of 3,000 lawyers, prosecutors, and judges, the number of persons in these three categories will total 82,380 in 2025, an increase of over 400 percent from the current level. The predicted decline in the Japanese population will bring the number of persons per lawyer to 1,468. Document 22, Hōsō Jinkō ni Tsuite [Regarding Legal Population], Shihō Seido Kaikaku Shingikai Zenkiroku CD-Rom, *supra* note 32. Reform of Japanese legal education roughly along U.S. lines is also proceeding. Sixty eight organizations, including prestigious universities, the Tokyo Bar Association, and some tiny "no name" schools received approval to establish American-style law schools. The schools opened in 2004.
72. *Nishimura* v. *Abekawa*, 199 Shirōban shōji hōmu 284 (Osaka D. Ct. Sept. 20, 2000).
73. See *Japan* v. *Sekiyu Renmei*, 983 Hanrei Jihō 22 (Tokyo High Court, Sept. 26, 1980); *Japan* v. *Idemitsu Kōsan K. K.*, 985 Hanrei Jihō 3 (Tokyo High Court, Sept. 26, 1980), both in Milhaupt et al., *supra* note 68, at 553–63 (J. Mark Ramseyer trans) 2001.
74. Interview with Anthony Zaloom, July 5, 2002; see also Yasuharu Nagashima and E. Anthony Zaloom, paper presented at Law in Japan: A Turning Point, Conference at Asian Law Center, University of Washington, August 23, 2002.
75. De-ta Mukku Minji Soshō [Data on Civil Matters], Jurisuto Zōkan 179 (2000).
76. A Supreme Court Justice earns a monthly base salary of ¥1,682,000, or about $190,000 annually; a High Court Judge earns ¥1,492,000, or about $150,000 annually, subject to rank, and to increases of up to 12% depending on the region of one's employment. ōkurazaimukyōkai ed., *supra* note 12, at 214.
77. Indeed, Japanese military spending, which has been less than 1% of GDP for most of the postwar period and currently hovers around 1%, is still sizeable enough in absolute terms to rank Japan second or third in the world in annual military expenditures.
78. To determine whether legal elites choose between the bar and the bureaucracy based on comparative opportunities to redistribute wealth as opposed to broader institutional factors, we examined the relation of government expenditures as a percentage

of GDP to both elite legal careers. If large numbers of legal elites select the bureaucracy for its redistributive potential, we might expect to observe a correlation between trends in the civil service exam and changes in government spending. We observed no such relation.

79. There were 1,345 lawyers in Japan in 1890, 5,498 in 1940, 7,343 in 1965, and 12,830 in 1985. De-ta Mukku *supra* note 75, at 82.

80. 1991 data are unavailable due to a change in methodology.

9

Looking Ahead

We have tried to deliver three basic messages in this book. First, both formal law and informal rules such as business practices and social norms matter a great deal to the structure of the Japanese economy. Second, these institutions—again, both the formal and informal rules—are changing, despite outward appearances of a decade of stagnation. Third, actors are responding to these changes, which alter incentives and constraints at work in the economy. Basic though these points may be, we think no one has delivered these messages in the depth and with the supporting evidence presented in this book.

Most importantly perhaps, the evidence suggests that in the mix of formal and informal rules that govern Japanese firms and set the incentive structure for other economic actors, formal rules are gaining in importance. Indeed, we saw evidence of this shift in every area we examined—corporate governance, deal making, banking, entrepreneurial finance, and the suppression of organized crime. Concomitantly, professional facilitators and enforcers of formal rules are becoming increasingly important. This was most apparent in our examination of the allocation of legal talent, but it can also be seen in the increased demand for plaintiffs' lawyers in derivative litigation, and the demand for corporate professionals to handle merger and acquisition transactions. In the past, bureaucrats, generalist salarymen, and gangsters were the economy's fixers. But the increasing importance of formal rules empowers a group of actors that did not play a central role in the postwar Japanese economy in its heyday—lawyers. The role of lawyers in the Japanese economy, and in society generally, will continue to increase at the expense of informal institutional entrepreneurs.

Existing scholarship provides at least a partial theoretical framework in which to understand this phenomenon. Informal rules (what we have referred to as "norms" throughout the book) tend to have greater force in close-knit communities in which long-term repeat play is anticipated, and credible, if informal, sanctions can be applied to deviants. In broad terms, these factors characterize postwar Japanese financial markets, corporate networks, and many other aspects of the economy. The changes we have chronicled in the book—increased foreign investment, the emergence of serious divisions among interest groups over the allocation of financial losses, declining authority and prestige of the bureaucracy in its role as "regulatory cartel cop," and improved information about markets and the regulatory process itself—portend a more diverse, divisive, open, and transient society. These developments do not portend the end of social norms, of course. Nor do they necessarily mean that Japan is rushing toward convergence with US institutions. Rather, they suggest that norms will continue to evolve—leading, reinforcing, and coevolving with the incentive and penalty structures provided by the increasingly prominent formal legal system.

On balance, we think the expansion of law is a positive development for Japan, but we cannot reach a firm conclusion on this point today. Lest readers accuse us of engaging in a lawyerly dodge, we will explain why it is too early to be definitive about the long-term consequences of the institutional shifts currently underway. First, as we have emphasized throughout, it seems virtually impossible—at least in a single study—to identify precisely and measure the causal factors that are driving all of these institutional changes. How much is attributable to "globalization"? How much is attributable to the economy? To demographic changes? To shifts in preferences or political alignments? We did our best to lend some analytical coherence to the task of sorting out causation, but we do not pretend to know exactly why all of these changes are happening. Without knowing causation, we must be cautious about reaching firm conclusions on underlying phenomena. To take only the most obvious example of uncertainties about causation, are changes in norms driving—or following— reforms in laws and regulations?

Second, the snapshot of Japan that we have provided in this book is almost certainly of a transitional moment, not of institutional equilibrium. Of course, all economies are constantly changing. But we trust readers will agree that an unusual number of complementary economic systems and subsystems are currently being transformed in Japan. Indeed, the very existence of so much institutional flux made the subject matter attractive to us. Thus far, the pattern of mutually reinforcing institutional feedback is moving the rules of the game in a discernable direction—toward a more formal, *ex post*, law and market-oriented system. But more changes are certainly coming, and the path of reform could be altered by as yet unforeseen events or unanticipated consequences. Again, to proffer only the most basic example, if by some small miracle the Japanese economy were to turn around quickly and sustainably, how many of the reforms we have discussed would be abandoned or slowed? We do not know, but we expect the number is nontrivial. Thus, before one passes final judgment, it seems prudent to first determine whether these trends constitute a fundamental shift. Our strong sense at this writing is that they do. But we will have to wait and see.

Finally and most importantly, one could find theory and historical experience suggesting that a "move to law" is positive or negative for a given country. Current World Bank reform initiatives place heavy emphasis on "rule of law" concerns such as minority shareholder protections, transparent and formal government procedures, advance notice and comment for regulatory actions, judicial resolution of disputes, and so on—precisely the reforms Japan is now emphasizing. Yet, the rapid postwar economic growth of the East Asian economies, particularly Japan's, has always presented a serious problem for theorists who draw a tight link between economic success and the rule of law in the World Bank sense. (Some argue that China's rapid growth poses a similar problem for rule of law theorists today.) In the high growth era, Japan, Korea, and Taiwan may have done decent jobs of ensuring minimum levels of property rights protections, holding corruption down to workable levels, and so on, but they were hardly model "rule of law" states as that term is commonly used. In fact, there is tremendous institutional variety among economically successful states. *A priori*, not much can be said about the appropriate mix of formal and informal rules in an economy. "Getting the institutions right" is crucial for economic growth, but different systems have "gotten them right" in different ways, at different stages of development.

Good or bad, there are limits to increased legalization, and we see little danger that Japan is heading toward a train wreck of litigation and lawyers. Limits will be imposed and enforced through social, economic, legal, and other forces. Although Japanese litigation rates have risen significantly, we do not expect Japan's social fabric to stretch so thin as to move Japan near the top in world litigation rates, or to make litigation the first response to disputes in Japan. We do not expect Japanese lawyers to overtake their US counterparts either in population or in power any time in the foreseeable future.

While it is too early to pass final judgment on the evolving institutional setup in Japan, we find grounds for considerable optimism in the events of the past decade. One thing is clear: Policymakers should pay careful attention to the rules of the game, not only to address Japan's current economic problems but also to create a sound incentive roadmap for the long transition that lies ahead for that country, as it confronts enormous issues brought on by demographic changes, global competitive pressures, and shifting social attitudes. Indeed, in vital areas, this is exactly what policymakers have done, and the resulting changes seem both appropriate and to be leading to favorable results thus far (again, subject to the disclaimer about causation). As we tried to demonstrate throughout the book, whether formal or informal, rules generating perverse incentives lead (eventually) to bad outcomes. Rules that properly align incentives and give economic actors the freedom to fashion desired outcomes at low cost generally achieve good results. It is our hope that this book has helped to inform the debate as to which rules are which, at least for Japan at the beginning of the twenty-first century.

Index

abuse-of-rights doctrine 22
accounting data disclosure 116–17, 185–6,
    188
accounting profession 154
accounting reforms 192–3
adaptive efficiency 48
administrative guidance 16–17
Administrative Procedure Act 227
agricultural credit cooperative system
        84, 100, 101
    funding of *jusen* companies 84, 85,
        87–8
    negotiations with founding institutions
        90–3
    see also *jusen* problem
Ahmadjian, Christine L. 195–6
amakudari 17, 76, 82, 223–5
Anti-Monopoly Act 182, 189
Anti-Organized Crime Act 160–1, 170
    enforcement 169
Aoki, Masahiko 2–3, 181, 182
apaatoya (apartment fixers) 158
attorneys:
    career paths 210
        incentives to choose law 230–1;
            institutional change and 226–9
    debt collection 152
    economic growth relationships 207–8,
        229–30, 232–3
    examination data 211–20
    fees of 19–20, 29–33
        court-awarded derivative suit fees 30; elite
            attorneys 31; non-elite attorneys 32–3;
            settlement practice 30
    market for 28–30
    quasi-lawyers 220
    salary and employment data 221–2
    scarcity of 153, 158–9
    see also legal elites
auditors 188

Bank of Japan 99, 154
bank system 13–14, 151–2
    employment patterns 76
    see also financial industry
bankruptcy 151–2

bar examination 210
    see also examination data
bargaining norms 75, 77–8
    brokerage and facilitation 77
    channelled political intervention 77–8
    internal cooperation 77
    negotiated inter-jurisdictional resolution 77
Berle, Adolf 47
Black, Bernard 54–5, 64
blackmail 111, 112–13, 138
    filibuster blackmail 129–38
    see also corporate information, sokaiya and;
        sokaiya
board committees 188
boards of directors 17–18, 189, 195
Bradley, Michael 24–5
Brock, William 207
brokerage and facilitation 77
bubble economy 85, 136–7
    impact on *jusen* companies 85–6
bureaucracy 207, 228
    scandal 230
bureaucrats 207
    career paths 210–11
        incentives to choose law 230–1;
            institutional change and 226–9
    examination data 211–20
    salary data 222–5

cartel theory 74, 75, 79
    see also regulatory interaction in financial
        industry
Castellano, Joseph 156
Chisso corporation 112
Chubu Electric case 33
civil rehabilitation 151
Civil Rehabilitation Act 192
civil service examination 210–11
    see also examination data
Commercial Code 11–12, 114–15, 187
    reform 191–2, 198–9
    rules 188–9
composition 151
compulsory composition 151
convoy policy 79, 100
coordinated decisionmaking 75

corporate arrangement 151
corporate contract 13–18
  bank relations 13–14
  board structure and relations 17–18
  employment relations 15–16
  government-business relations 16–17
  inter-corporate relations 14–15
corporate control, market for 179–82
  obstacles to 184–8
  see also mergers and acquisitions
corporate culture 15–16
  risk tolerance 61–2
corporate governance 45, 179–82
  bank-centred, market-centred dichotomy
    47–8
  benefits of organizational diversity 180–2
  institutional foundation 184–91
    new institutions 191–3
  legal framework 11–13
  new forms of governance 194–8
  reality of reform 198–9
  stylized approaches 188–9
    consequences 190–1
  venture capital significance 46–8, 65–6
  see also corporate control, market for
corporate information, sokaiya and 116–29,
    138–9
  information acquisition 122–3
  information concealment 118–21
    deterring disclosure 120–1; enforcement of
      disclosure laws 119–20; maintaining
      secrecy 118–19; meeting length
      relationships 135
  regulation and 124
  reputation and 123–4
  types of information 116–18
    financial and accounting data 116–17;
      past bad acts 117–18; personal
      information 118
  uses for negative information 124–8
    financial instruments 125–7; lawsuits
      124–5; publication 127–8
corporate reorganization 151, 192
corruption 111
  see also sokaiya
court budgets 231
cross-shareholdings 14–15, 195
culture 5
  corporate culture 15–16
    risk tolerance 61–2

Dai-Ichi Kangyo Bank (DKB) 109
Daiwa Bank 9, 25, 89, 120, 228–9

debt collection:
  attorneys 152
  toritateya 158
Demsetz, Harold 180, 181
deposit insurance system 98
deregulation 227–8
derivative suits *see* shareholder derivative
    suits
designated firms 161
directors' and officers' (D.O) liability insurance
    22, 35–6
diversity benefits 180–2
dividends 189, 197
dual rent-seeking 231

economic growth related to lawyer ratio 207–8,
    229–30, 232–3
Eisenstein, Irving 12
employment relations 15–16, 195–6
enforcement 36–8
entrepreneurialism 46, 48, 52
  funding for 154–5
    see also venture capital
  organized crime as illicit entrepreneurialism
    146–7, 149
examination data 211–20
  bar examination 210
  civil service examination 210–11
  data from elite institutions 215–18
  double-passers 219–20
  national data 211–15
  quasi-lawyers 220
executive compensation 189
exit options, venture capital market 54–6, 62–3
extortion 111, 112–13
  see also corporate information, sokaiya and;
    sokaiya

financial data disclosure 116–17, 185–6, 188
financial industry:
  bank system 13–14
  bargaining norms 77–8
  employment patterns 76
  structure of 76
  substantive norms 79–80
  see also regulatory interaction in financial
    industry
financial reform 96–7, 98–9
financial repression 154–5
Financial Supervisory Agency (FSA) 98–9
Financial System Research Council 94–5
Financial System Stabilization Committee
    89, 90

Financial System Stabilization Fund 95
firm rescue 14
fiscal year 188
Fischel, Daniel 24–5
foreign securities firms 127–8
formal rules 1, 241
    changes 1
Freedom of Information Act 227
"functional substitutes" theory 199, 200–1
funding sources, venture capital markets
        53–4, 62

Gambetta, Diego 148
Ghosn, Carlos 195
Gilson, Ronald 54–5, 64, 153
government enforcement 36–8
government-business relations 16–17

Haley, John 3
Hazama 25
holding companies 191–2
home mortgage lending business 81–2, 83
    see also *jusen* problem
Hong, Lu 181

Iguchi, Toshihide 120
Iida, Hideto 32
illicit entrepreneurialism 146–7, 149
improper solicitation 114–15
    see also sokaiya
incentives, in venture capital markets 56–9
informal rules 1, 241
    changes 1
information *see* corporate information,
        sokaiya and
initial public offerings (IPOs) 55–6, 63, 64–5
innovation 45–6, 48
    incentives for 52
    merger activity relationships 182
    see also venture capital
institutional approach 1
institutional reform 4–5, 179
    deregulation 227–8
    employment patterns of legal elites and
        226–9
    legal institutions 208–9
    re-engineering for organized crime reduction
        170–2
institutions 1, 4
    legal institutions 3
inter-corporate relations 14–15
inter-jurisdictional negotiation 7
introduction finance 83

Investment Enterprise Limited Liability
        Association Law 63
Italian *disturbatori* 128–9

Janome Sewing Machine case 30
Japan Fair Trade Commission (JFTC) 182–3
Japan Premium 89
jiageya (land fixers) 158
jidanya (settlement specialists) 159
Johnson, Chalmers 207
judicial scriveners 220
Judicial System Reform Council 228
jusen problem 73–4, 81–97, 99–103
    agricultural credit cooperatives as sources of
        funding 84, 85, 87–8
    bubble economy impact on *jusen* companies
        85–6
    establishment and monitoring of *jusen*
        companies 81–3
    financial liberalization and *jusen* company
        business 83–4
    resolving the problem 86–97, 100–3
        Diet debate 96; financial reform legislation
        96–7; government's *jusen* resolution plan
        93–5; initial attempts to restructure *jusen*
        loans 86–9; loss allocation 92, 93–5;
        negotiations 90–3; secondary loss
        dispute 95; supplemental loss-coverage
        fund 97

Kabunushi Onbuzuman 31
keiretsu system 14–15
Koike, Ryuichi 109, 113, 131
Konō v. *Konō Chemical Co* 30
Kyoto University (Kyodai) 218

La Cosa Nostra 156
La Porta, Rafael 199
labor mobility 60, 63
landlord–tenant issues 152–3
law 3–4, 172
    see also legal reforms
law enforcement 168–70
    anti-Organized Crime Act enforcement 169
    arrest rates 168–9
'law and finance' theory 199–200
lawyers *see* attorneys
legal elites 208–26
    career paths of 210–11
        incentives to choose law 230–1;
            institutional change and 226–9
    dual rent-seeking 231
    examination data 211–19

legal elites (*cont.*)
  fees of 31
  salary and employment data 220–5, 229–30
  see also attorneys; bureaucrats
legal institutions 3
  changes 208–9
legal reforms 172, 191–2, 242
  reality of 198–9
Lehn, Kenneth 180
lifetime employment system 60
limited partnerships 56
liquidity, venture capital market 54–6, 62–3
litigation fees 20–1
Lopez-de-Silanes, Florencio 199

Magee, Stephen 207
mandatory bid rule 186–7
Market of the High Growth and Emerging Stocks
    (MOTHERS) 63
Matsuzakaya 131
Mazda 197
Means, Gardiner 47
  stock price relationships 132–8
    information disclosure and 135;
      meeting control and 136; planned
      disclosures and 137–8; signals
      to investors 135–6; sokaiya
      manipulation 137
  see also sokaiya
mergers and acquisitions (M&A) 179–80
  'functional substitutes' theory 199, 200–1
  innovation and 182
  institutional foundation 184–91
    new institutions 191–3
  international comparisons 184
  'law matters' theory 199–200
  merger data 182–4, 193–4
  tender offers 184
  see also corporate control, market for
Mergerstat 183–4, 194
Ministry of Economy, Trade, and Industry
    (METI) 63–4
Ministry of Finance (MOF) 98–9
  jusen problem resolution see *Jusen* problem
  non-disclosure of information 121
  regulation of financial markets 55, 75–6,
      80, 124
  scandal 230
Ministry of International Trade and Industry
    (MITI) 124
Mitsubishi Heavy Industries 112
Miyakawa, Koichi 121

Mizuho Financial Group 194
mortgage lending *see* home mortgage lending
    business
Murphy, Kevin 207

Nagashima, Ohno & Tsunematsu 219
Nakazato, Minoru 152, 160
NASDAQ Japan 63
nemawashi 78
new institutional economic (NIE) analysis 1
Nihon Keizai Shinbun (Nikkei) 137–8
Nihon Sunrise case 30
Nikkō Securities case 22
Nippon Dantai 197
Nishimura, Yoshimasa 92
Nissan Motor Company 195
Nomura Securities 113–14, 131
norms 4–5
  bargaining norms 75, 77–8
  social norms 4–5, 241–2
  substantive norms 75, 79–80
  takeovers and 187–8
North, Douglass 2, 48, 65

officers 195
organizational diversity benefits 180–2
organized crime 122–3, 145–73
  activities 157–60
  as illicit entrepreneurialism 146–7, 149
  crime data 161–3
  income 155–6
  law enforcement measures 168–70
  membership 155–6, 163–8
  organized crime theory 147–9
    regression analysis 163–9
  police–organized crime relationships 160–1,
      164
  private ordering and 145–6, 149, 170–2
  reduction through institutional engineering
      170–2
  rights-enforcement role 145–7, 171–2
  structure 157
  trademarks and visibility 156–7

Page, Scott 181
partnership for investment purposes 58
past bad acts, exploitation by sokaiya 117–18
pension system 60
  role in venture capital market 53, 63
personal information, exploitation by sokaiya
    117–18
plan rational state 207, 229

police-organized crime relationships 160–1, 164
Posner, Richard 112
posting of bond 21, 25
private ordering 16, 17, 150–1, 153
 organized crime and 145–6, 149, 170–2
property rights 148, 149–50
 mismatch with enforcement mechanisms 148–9, 172
 see also rights-enforcement
Prowse, Stephen 189

quasi-lawyers 220

Ramseyer, Mark 3, 152, 160
Recof LLC 183, 193
regulatory interaction in financial industry 73–81, 99–103
 bargaining norms 77–8
 dynamics of cartel-like cooperation 78–80
 effects of cartel-like cooperation 80–1, 102–3
 institutional reforms 98–9
 Japanese finance as a regulatory cartel 75–8
 substantive norms 79–80
 see also *jusen* problem; Ministry of Finance (MOF)
rent-seeking 231
rights-enforcement 145–6, 149–55
 agents and dispute intermediaries 153–4
 bankruptcy 151–2
 debt collection 152
 landlord–tenant issues 152–3
 mismatch with property rights 148–9, 172
 organized crime role 145–7, 171–2
 shareholders' rights 153
risk tolerance 61–2
Robbins, Gregory 195–6
Roesler, Hermann 11
Romano, Roberta 24
rules 3–4, 241–3
 formal 1, 241
 informal 1, 241

salary data 220–5
 elite bureaucrats 222–5
 elite lawyers 221–2
Salwin, Lester 12, 18
sarakin 159
Sato, Ikuya 155
SCAP (Supreme Commander for the Allied Powers) 11
Schaede, Ulrike 224

secrecy, maintenance of 118–19
Securities and Exchange Law (SEL) 12, 39
Securities and Exchange Surveillance Commission (SESC) 119
Securities Exchange Act 185
security for expenses 21
seiriya (fixers) 157–8
settlements 25–8
 attorneys' fees and 30
Shareholders' meeting day 130–1, 132
Shareholders' meeting length 110–11, 131–2
share ownership patterns 189
share transactions 188, 197
 see also stock price
share-for-share exchanges 192
shareholder derivative suits 9, 10–11, 18–38
 benefits to shareholders 23–8
 historical background 18
 mechanics 18–19
 post-1993 incentives 22–3
 pre-1993 price incentives/disincentives 19–22
  abuse-of-rights doctrine 22; access to information 21–2; attorney fees 19–20; litigation fees 20–1; security for expenses 21
 reasons to sue 28–38
  bar benefits 28–33; insurance 35–6; non-monetary motives 33–4; public and private enforcement 36–8; sokaiya 34–5
 settlements 25–8
shareholder monitoring 192
Shareholder Ombudsman 31
shareholders' meetings 188, 197
 meeting length 110–11, 131–2
  stock price relationships 132–8
 role of 130–2
shareholders' rights 153
shingikai 76–7, 78
Shiroyama, Saburō 130
Shiryōban Shōji Hōmu 132–3
Shleifer, Andrei 199, 207
short sales 125–7
Sicily 148
Smith v *Van Gorkom* 9
social norms 4–5, 241–2
 takeovers and 187–8
sokaiya 34–5, 111–13, 138–9, 159, 165
 companies' options 113–14
  payment 113–14; resistance 114
 filibuster blackmail 129–38

sokaiya (*cont.*)
  information use *see* corporate information, sokaiya and
  legal aspects 114–16, 139
  magazine subscriptions 113–14, 116
  payments to 113–14
  stock price manipulation 137
Sony 59, 131
South Korean *chongheoggun* 128
special liquidation 151
spinoffs 192, 194
splitoffs 192
statutory auditor 39
stock options 57, 59, 63, 125, 192
stock price:
  manipulation by sokaiya 137
  meeting length relationships 132–8
    information disclosure and 135; meeting control and 136; planned disclosures and 137–8; signals to investors 135–6
stock purchase agreements 57
substantive norms 75, 79–80
  implicit government insurance 80
  no exit (no failure) 79
  responsibility and equitable subordination 79–80
  survival of the weakest 79, 100
suspension of bank transaction procedure 152
Suzuki 34–5

Takemura, Masayoshi 92
takeovers *see* mergers and acquisitions
tender offers 184, 185, 186–7
  data 194
  mandatory bid rule 186–7

Thomson Financial 183, 193
Tokai Bank 34–5
Tokyo-Mitsubishi Bank 35
toritateya (debt collectors) 158
trust, organized crime and 147–8

University of Tokyo (Todai) 216–18

venture capital 45–6
  significance in corporate governance 46–8
venture capital markets 48–66
  creation of 64–5
  funding sources 53–4, 62
  incentives 56–9, 63
  institutional change and developments 62–4
  Japanese market 51–2
  labor mobility and 60, 63
  liquidity 54–6, 62–3
  risk tolerance 61–2
  size 49
  United States market 49–50
Vishny, Robert 199, 207

Williamson, Oliver 181

yakuza 122
  see also organized crime
Yamaguchi-gumi 157
Yamaichi Securities 117, 120
yonigeya 158
Young, Leslie 207

zoku legislators 77, 78, 84

DISCARDED
CONCORDIA UNIV. LIBRARY
[CONCORDIA UNIVERSITY LIBRARIES]
SIR GEORGE WILLIAMS CAMPUS
WEBSTER LIBRARY